ORGANIZATIONAL BEHAVIOR

A BOOK OF READINGS

McGRAW-HILL SERIES IN MANAGEMENT
Keith Davis and Fred Luthans, Consulting Editors

ORGANIZATIONAL BEHAVIOR

A BOOK OF READINGS

KEITH DAVIS, Ph.D.

Arizona State University

FIFTH EDITION

McGRAW-HILL BOOK COMPANY

New York   St. Louis   San Francisco   Auckland
Bogotá   Düsseldorf   Johannesburg   London   Madrid
Mexico   Montreal   New Delhi   Panama   Paris
São Paulo   Singapore   Sydney   Tokyo   Toronto

ORGANIZATIONAL BEHAVIOR: A BOOK OF READINGS

3 4 5 6 7 8 9 0 DODO 7 8 3 2 1 0 9 8

This book was set in Helvetica by Rocappi, Inc.
The editors were William J. Kane and Annette Hall;
the cover was designed by Nicholas Krenitsky;
the production supervisor was Robert C. Pedersen.
New drawings were done by Scalor Publications, Inc.
R. R. Donnelley & Sons Company was printer and binder.

Library of Congress Cataloging in Publication Data
Davis, Keith, date   ed.
    Organizational behavior.

    (McGraw-Hill series in management)
    First (1959)—2d (1964) ed. published under title:
Readings in human relations; 3d (1969) ed.:   Human
relations and organizational behavior.
    Includes bibliographical references and index.
    1.   Organizational behavior—Addresses, essays,
lectures.   2.   Personnel management—Addresses, essays,
lectures.   3.   Industrial sociology—Addresses, essays,
lectures.   I.   Title.
HD58.7.D38   1977   658.3′008   76–51802
ISBN 0–07–015499–6

CONTENTS

PREFACE

Organizational effectiveness in work groups is a basic social need in order to prevent waste of human and economic resources. This book attempts to serve that need. It is designed to broaden and supplement case and regular text courses in organizational behavior, behavior in organizations, human relations, industrial psychology, behavioral science, and related courses. It also may be used for management seminars and discussion groups and for personal reading by managers.

The objective of this book is to present an integrated social science approach which recognizes that organizational behavior uses ideas from many disciplines. In the selection of articles, both conceptual frameworks and organizational practice are provided. Frameworks are necessary to analyze organizational behavior, but application of frameworks also is essential because it is the final test of effective organizational behavior.

The readings are organized into chapters that parallel subjects covered in current textbooks on organizational behavior, especially Keith Davis, *Human Behavior at Work: Organizational Behavior,* 5th ed., New York: McGraw-Hill Book Company, 1977.

The editor is especially grateful for the cooperation of authors and publishers who granted permission to use their materials.

Keith Davis

ORGANIZATIONAL BEHAVIOR
A BOOK OF READINGS

CHAPTER 1

ORGANIZATIONAL BEHAVIOR FRAMEWORKS

READING   1

THE HUMAN SIDE OF ENTERPRISE

Douglas McGregor*

It has become trite to say that the most significant developments of the next quarter century will take place not in the physical but in the social sciences, that industry—the economic organ of society—has the fundamental know-how to utilize physical science and technology for the material benefit of mankind, and that we must now learn how to utilize the social sciences to make our human organizations truly effective.

Many people agree in principle with such statements; but so far they represent a pious hope—and little else. Consider with me, if you will, something of what may be involved when we attempt to transform the hope into reality.

I

Let me begin with an analogy. A quarter century ago basic conceptions of the nature of matter and energy had changed profoundly from what they had been since Newton's time. The physical scientists were persuaded that under proper conditions new and hitherto unimagined sources of energy could be made available to mankind.

We know what has happened since then. First came the bomb. Then during the past decade, have come many other attempts to exploit these scientific discoveries—some successful, some not.

The point of my analogy, however, is that the application of theory in this field is a slow and costly matter. We expect it always to be thus. No one is impatient with the scientist because he cannot tell industry how to build a simple, cheap, all-purpose source of atomic energy today. That it will take at least another decade and the investment of billions of dollars to achieve results which are economically competitive with present sources of power is understood and accepted.

It is transparently pretentious to suggest any *similarity* between the developments in the physical sciences leading to the harnessing of atomic energy and potential developments in the social sciences. Nevertheless, the analogy is not as absurd as it might appear to be at first glance.

*From *Proceedings of the Fifth Anniversary Convocation of the School of Industrial Management, Massachusetts Institute of Technology,* Cambridge, Apr. 9, 1957. Reprinted with permission.

To a lesser degree, and in a much more tentative fashion, we are in a position in the social sciences today like that of the physical sciences with respect to atomic energy in the thirties. We know that past conceptions of the nature of man are inadequate and in many ways incorrect. We are becoming quite certain that, under proper conditions, unimagined resources of creative human energy could become available within the organizational setting.

We cannot tell industrial management how to apply this new knowledge in simple, economic ways. We know it will require years of exploration, much costly development research, and a substantial amount of creative imagination on the part of management to discover how to apply this growing knowledge to the organization of human effort in industry.

May I ask that you keep this analogy in mind—overdrawn and pretentious though it may be—as a framework for what I have to say this morning.

Management's Task: Conventional View

The conventional conception of management's task in harnessing human energy to organizational requirements can be stated broadly in terms of three propositions. In order to avoid the complications introduced by a label, I shall call this set of propositions "Theory X":

1 Management is responsible for organizing the elements of productive enterprise—money, materials, equipment, people—in the interest of economic ends.

2 With respect to people, this is a process of directing their efforts, motivating them, controlling their actions, modifying their behavior to fit the needs of the organization.

3 Without this active intervention by management, people would be passive—even resistant—to organizational needs. They must therefore be persuaded, rewarded, punished, controlled—their activities must be directed. This is management's task—in managing subordinate managers or workers. We often sum it up by saying that management consists of getting things done through other people.

Behind this conventional theory there are several additional beliefs—less explicit, but widespread:

4 The average man is by nature indolent—he works as little as possible.

5 He lacks ambition, dislikes responsibility, prefers to be led.

6 He is inherently self-centered, indifferent to organizational needs.

7 He is by nature resistant to change.

8 He is gullible, not very bright, the ready dupe of the charlatan and the demagogue.

The human side of economic enterprise today is fashioned from propositions and beliefs such as these. Conventional organization structures, managerial policies, practices, and programs reflect these assumptions.

In accomplishing its task—with these assumptions as guides—management has conceived of a range of possibilities between two extremes.

The Hard or the Soft Approach?

At one extreme, management can be "hard" or "strong." The methods for directing behavior involve coercion and threat (usually disguised), close supervision, tight controls over behavior. At the other extreme, management can be "soft" or "weak." The methods for directing behavior involve being permissive, satisfying people's demands, achieving harmony. Then they will be tractable, accept direction.

This range has been fairly completely explored during the past half century, and management has learned some things from the exploration. There are difficulties in the "hard" approach. Force breeds counterforces: restriction of output, antagonism, militant unionism, subtle but effective sabotage of management objectives. This approach is especially difficult during times of full employment.

There are also difficulties in the "soft" approach. It leads frequently to the abdication of management—to harmony, perhaps, but to indifferent performance. People take advantage of the soft approach. They continually expect more, but they give less and less.

Currently, the popular theme is "firm but fair." This is an attempt to gain the advantages of both the hard and the soft approaches. It is reminiscent of Teddy Roosevelt's "speak softly and carry a big stick."

Is the Conventional View Correct?

The findings which are beginning to emerge from the social sciences challenge this whole set of beliefs about man and human nature and about the task of management. The evidence is far from conclusive, certainly, but it is suggestive. It comes from the laboratory, the clinic, the schoolroom, the home, and even to a limited extent from industry itself.

The social scientist does not deny that human behavior in industrial organization today is approximately what management perceives it to be. He has, in fact, observed it and studied it fairly extensively. But he is pretty sure that this behavior is *not* a consequence of man's inherent nature. It is a consequence rather of the nature of industrial organizations, of management philosophy, policy, and practice. The conventional approach of Theory X is based on mistaken notions of what is cause and what is effect.

"Well," you ask, "what then is the *true* nature of man? What evidence leads the social scientist to deny what is obvious?" And, if I am not mistaken, you are also thinking, "Tell me—simply, and without a lot of scientific verbiage—what you think you know that is so unusual. Give me—

without a lot of intellectual claptrap and theoretical nonsense—some practical ideas which will enable me to improve the situation in my organization. And remember, I'm faced with increasing costs and narrowing profit margins. I want proof that such ideas won't result simply in new and costly human relations frills. I want practical results, and I want them now."

If these are your wishes, you are going to be disappointed. Such requests can no more be met by the social scientist today than could comparable ones with respect to atomic energy be met by the physicist fifteen years ago. I can, however, indicate a few of the reasons for asserting that conventional assumptions about the human side of enterprise are inadequate. And I can suggest—tentatively—some of the propositions that will comprise a more adequate theory of the management of people. The magnitude of the task that confronts us will then, I think, be apparent.

II

Perhaps the best way to indicate why the conventional approach of management is inadequate is to consider the subject of motivation. In discussing this subject I will draw heavily on the work of my colleague, Abraham Maslow of Brandeis University. His is the most fruitful approach I know. Naturally, what I have to say will be overgeneralized and will ignore important qualifications. In the time at our disposal, this is inevitable.

Physiological and Safety Needs

Man is a wanting animal—as soon as one of his needs is satisfied, another appears in its place. This process is unending. It continues from birth to death.

Man's needs are organized in a series of levels—a hierarchy of importance. At the lowest level, but preeminent in importance when they are thwarted, are his physiological needs. Man lives by bread alone, when there is no bread. Unless the circumstances are unusual, his needs for love, for status, for recognition are inoperative when his stomach has been empty for a while. But when he eats regularly and adequately, hunger ceases to be an important need. The sated man has hunger only in the sense that a full bottle has emptiness. The same is true of the other physiological needs of man—for rest, exercise, shelter, protection from the elements.

A satisfied need is not a motivator of behavior! This is a fact of profound significance. It is a fact which is regularly ignored in the conventional approach to the management of people. I shall return to it later. For the moment, one example will make my point. Consider your own need for air. Except as you are deprived of it, it has no appreciable motivating effect upon your behavior.

When the physiological needs are reasonably satisfied, needs at the next higher level begin to dominate man's behavior—to motivate him. These are called safety needs. They are needs for protection against danger, threat, deprivation. Some people mistakenly refer to these as needs for security. However, unless man is in a dependent relationship where he fears arbitrary deprivation, he does not demand security. The need is for the "fairest possible break." When he is confident of this, he is more than willing to take risks. But when he feels threatened or dependent, his greatest need is for guarantees, for protection, for security.

The fact needs little emphasis that since every industrial employee is in a dependent relationship, safety needs may assume considerable importance. Arbitrary management actions, behavior which arouses uncertainty with respect to continued employment or which reflects favoritism or discrimination, unpredictable administration of policy—these can be powerful motivators of the safety needs in the employment relationship *at every level* from worker to vice president.

Social Needs

When man's physiological needs are satisfied and he is no longer fearful about his physical welfare, his social needs become important motivators of his behavior—for belonging, for association, for acceptance by his fellows, for giving and receiving friendship and love.

Management knows today of the existence of these needs, but it often assumes quite wrongly that they represent a threat to the organization. Many studies have demonstrated that the tightly knit, cohesive work group may, under proper conditions, be far more effective than an equal number of separate individuals in achieving organizational goals.

Yet management, fearing group hostility to its own objectives, often goes to considerable lengths to control and direct human efforts in ways that are inimical to the natural "groupiness" of human beings. When man's social needs—and perhaps his safety needs, too—are thus thwarted, he behaves in ways which tend to defeat organizational objectives. He becomes resistant, antagonistic, uncooperative. But this behavior is a consequence, not a cause.

Ego Needs

Above the social needs—in the sense that they do not become motivators until lower needs are reasonably satisfied—are the needs of greatest significance to management and to man himself. They are the egoistic needs, and they are of two kinds:

1 Those needs that relate to one's self-esteem—needs for self-confidence, for independence, for achievement, for competence, for knowledge.

2 Those needs that relate to one's reputation—needs for status, for recognition, for appreciation, for the deserved respect of one's fellows.

Unlike the lower needs, these are rarely satisfied; man seeks indefinitely for more satisfaction of these needs once they have become important to him. But they do not appear in any significant way until physiological, safety, and social needs are all reasonably satisfied.

The typical industrial organization offers few opportunities for the satisfaction of these egoistic needs to people at lower levels in the hierarchy. The conventional methods of organizing work, particularly in mass production industries, give little heed to these aspects of human motivation. If the practices of scientific management were deliberately calculated to thwart these needs—which, of course, they are not—they could hardly accomplish this purpose better than they do.

Self-fulfillment Needs

Finally—a capstone, as it were, on the hierarchy of man's needs—there are what we may call the needs for self-fulfillment. These are the needs for realizing one's own potentialities, for continued self-development, for being creative in the broadest sense of that term.

It is clear that the conditions of modern life give only limited opportunity for these relatively weak needs to obtain expression. The deprivation most people experience with respect to other lower-level needs diverts their energies into the struggle to satisfy *those* needs, and the needs for self-fulfillment remain dormant.

III

Now, briefly, a few general comments about motivation:

We recognize readily enough that a man suffering from a severe dietary deficiency is sick. The deprivation of physiological needs has behavioral consequences. The same is true—although less well recognized—of deprivation of higher-level needs. The man whose needs for safety, association, independence, or status are thwarted is sick just as surely as is he who has rickets. And his sickness will have behavioral consequences. We will be mistaken if we attribute his resultant passivity, his hostility, his refusal to accept responsibility to his inherent "human nature." These forms of behavior are *symptoms* of illness—of deprivation of his social and egoistic needs.

The man whose lower-level needs are satisfied is not motivated to satisfy those needs any longer. For practical purposes they exist no longer. (Remember my point about your need for air.) Management often asks, "Why aren't people more productive? We pay good wages, provide good working conditions, have excellent fringe benefits and steady employment.

Yet people do not seem to be willing to put forth more than minimum effort."

The fact that management has provided for these physiological and safety needs has shifted the motivational emphasis to the social and perhaps to the egoistic needs. Unless there are opportunities *at work* to satisfy these higher-level needs, people will be deprived; and their behavior will reflect this deprivation. Under such conditions, if management continues to focus its attention on physiological needs, its efforts are bound to be ineffective.

People *will* make insistent demands for more money under these conditions. It becomes more important than ever to buy the material goods and services which can provide limited satisfaction of the thwarted needs. Although money has only limited value in satisfying many higher-level needs, it can become the focus of interest if it is the *only* means available.

The Carrot and Stick Approach

The carrot and stick theory of motivation (like Newtonian physical theory) works reasonably well under certain circumstances. The *means* for satisfying man's physiological and (within limits) his safety needs can be provided or withheld by management. Employment itself is such a means, and so are wages, working conditions, and benefits. By these means the individual can be controlled so long as he is struggling for subsistence. Man lives for bread alone when there is no bread.

But the carrot and stick theory does not work at all once man has reached an adequate subsistence level and is motivated primarily by higher needs. Management cannot provide a man with self-respect, or with the respect of his fellows, or with the satisfaction of needs for self-fulfillment. It can create conditions such that he is encouraged and enabled to seek such satisfactions *for himself,* or it can thwart him by failing to create those conditions.

But this creation of conditions is not "control." It is not a good device for directing behavior. And so management finds itself in an old position. The high standard of living created by our modern technological know-how provides quite adequately for the satisfaction of physiological and safety needs. The only significant exception is where management practices have not created confidence in a "fair break"—and thus where safety needs are thwarted. But by making possible the satisfaction of low-level needs, management has deprived itself of the ability to use as motivators the devices on which conventional theory has taught it to rely—rewards, promises, incentives, or threats and other coercive devices.

Neither Hard nor Soft

The philosophy of management by direction and control—*regardless of whether it is hard or soft*—is inadequate to motivate because the human needs on which this approach relies are today unimportant motivators of behavior. Direction and control are essentially useless in motivating people whose important needs are social and egoistic. Both the hard and the soft approach fail today because they are simply irrelevant to the situation.

People, deprived of opportunities to satisfy at work the needs which are now important to them, behave exactly as we might predict—with indolence, passivity, resistance to change, lack of responsibility, willingness to follow the demagogue, unreasonable demands for economic benefits. It would seem that we are caught in a web of our own weaving.

In summary, then, of these comments about motivation:

Management by direction and control—whether implemented with the hard, the soft, or the firm but fair approach—fails under today's conditions to provide effective motivation of human effort toward organizational objectives. It fails because direction and control are useless methods of motivating people whose physiological and safety needs are reasonably satisfied and whose social, egoistic, and self-fulfillment needs are predominant.

IV

For these and many other reasons, we require a different theory of the task of managing people based on more adequate assumptions about human nature and human motivation. I am going to be so bold as to suggest the broad dimensions of such a theory. Call it "Theory Y," if you will.

1   Management is responsible for organizing the elements of productive enterprise—money, materials, equipment, people—in the interest of economic ends.

2   People are not by nature passive or resistant to organizational needs. They have become so as a result of experience in organizations.

3   The motivation, the potential for development, the capacity for assuming responsibility, the readiness to direct behavior toward organizational goals are all present in people. Management does not put them there. It is a responsibility of management to make it possible for people to recognize and develop these human characteristics for themselves.

4   The essential task of management is to arrange organizational conditions and methods of operation so that people can achieve their own goals *best* by directing *their own* efforts toward organizational objectives.

This is a process primarily of creating opportunities, releasing potential, removing obstacles, encouraging growth, providing guidance. It is what Peter Drucker has called "management by objectives" in contrast to "management by control."

And I hasten to add that it does *not* involve the abdication of management, the absence of leadership, the lowering of standards, or the other characteristics usually associated with the "soft" approach under Theory

X. Much on the contrary. It is no more possible to create an organization today which will be a fully effective application of this theory than it was to build an atomic power plant in 1945. There are many formidable obstacles to overcome.

Some Difficulties

The conditions imposed by conventional organization theory and by the approach of scientific management for the past half century have tied men to limited jobs which do not utilize their capabilities, have discouraged the acceptance of responsibility, have encouraged passivity, have eliminated meaning from work. Man's habits, attitudes, expectations—his whole conception of membership in an industrial organization—have been conditioned by his experience under these circumstances. Change in the direction of Theory Y will be slow, and it will require extensive modification of the attitudes of management and workers alike.

People today are accustomed to being directed, manipulated, controlled in industrial organizations and to finding satisfaction for their social, egoistic, and self-fulfillment needs away from the job. This is true of much of management as well as of workers. Genuine "industrial citizenship"—to borrow again a term from Drucker—is a remote and unrealistic idea, the meaning of which has not even been considered by most members of industrial organizations.

Another way of saying this is that Theory X places exclusive reliance upon external control of human behavior, while Theory Y relies heavily on self-control and self-direction. It is worth noting that this difference is the difference between treating people as children and treating them as mature adults. After generations of the former, we cannot expect to shift to the latter overnight.

V

Before we are overwhelmed by the obstacles, let us remember that the application of theory is always slow. Progress is usually achieved in small steps.

Consider with me a few innovative ideas which are entirely consistent with Theory Y and which are today being applied with some success:

Decentralization and Delegation

These are ways of freeing people from the too-close control of conventional organization, giving them a degree of freedom to direct their own activities, to assume responsibility, and importantly, to satisfy their egoistic needs. In this connection, the flat organization of Sears, Roebuck and Company provides an interesting example. It forces "management by objectives'' since it enlarges the number of people reporting to a manager until he cannot direct and control them in the conventional manner.

Job Enlargement

This concept, pioneered by I.B.M. and Detroit Edison, is quite consistent with Theory Y. It encourages the acceptance of responsibility at the bottom of the organization; it provides opportunities for satisfying social and egoistic needs. In fact, the reorganization of work at the factory level offers one of the more challenging opportunities for innovation consistent with Theory Y. The studies by A. T. M. Wilson and his associates of British coal mining and Indian textile manufacture have added appreciably to our understanding of work organization. Moreover, the economic and psychological results achieved by this work have been substantial.

Participation and Consultative Management

Under proper conditions these results provide encouragement to people to direct their creative energies toward organizational objectives, give them some voice in decisions that affect them, provide significant opportunities for the satisfaction of social and egoistic needs. I need only mention the Scanlon Plan as the outstanding embodiment of these ideas in practice.

The not infrequent failure of such ideas as these to work as well as expected is often attributable to the fact that a management has "bought the idea" but applied it within the framework of Theory X and its assumptions.

Delegation is not an effective way of exercising management by control. Participation becomes a farce when it is applied as a sales gimmick or a device for kidding people into thinking they are important. Only the management that has confidence in human capacities and is itself directed toward organizational objectives rather than toward the preservation of personal power can grasp the implications of this emerging theory. Such management will find and apply successfully other innovative ideas as we move slowly toward the full implementation of a theory like Y.

Performance Appraisal

Before I stop, let me mention one other practical application of Theory Y which—while still highly tentative—may well have important consequences. This has to do with performance appraisal within the ranks of management. Even a cursory examination of conventional programs of performance appraisal will reveal how completely consistent they are with Theory X. In fact, most such programs tend to treat the individual as though he were a product under inspection on the assembly line.

Take the typical plan: substitute "product" for "subordinate being appraised," substitute "inspector" for "superior making the appraisal," substitute "rework" for "training or development," and, except for the attributes being judged, the human appraisal process will be virtually indistinguishable from the product inspection process.

A few companies—among them General Mills, Ansul Chemical, and General Electric—have been experimenting with approaches which involve the individual in setting "targets" or objectives *for himself* and in a *self*-evaluation of performance semi-annually or annually. Of course, the superior plays an important leadership role in this process—one, in fact, which demands substantially more competence than the conventional approach. The role is, however, considerably more congenial to many managers than the role of "judge" or "inspector" which is forced upon them by conventional performance. Above all, the individual is encouraged to take a greater responsibility for planning and appraising his own contribution to organizational objectives; and the accompanying effects on egoistic and self-fulfillment needs are substantial. This approach to performance appraisal represents one more innovative idea being explored by a few managements who are moving toward the implementation of Theory Y.

VI

And now I am back where I began. I share the belief that we could realize substantial improvements in the effectiveness of industrial organizations during the next decade or two. Moreover, I believe the social sciences can contribute much to such developments. We are only beginning to grasp the implications of the growing body of knowledge in these fields. But if this conviction is to become a reality instead of a pious hope, we will need to view the process much as we view the process of releasing the energy of the atom for constructive human ends—as a slow, costly, sometimes discouraging approach toward a goal which would seem to many to be quite unrealistic.

The ingenuity and the perseverance of industrial management in the pursuit of economic ends have changed many scientific and technological dreams into commonplace realities. It is now becoming clear that the application of these same talents to the human side of enterprise will not only enhance substantially these materialistic achievements but will bring us one step closer to "the good society." Shall we get on with the job?

READING 2

EVOLVING MODELS OF ORGANIZATIONAL BEHAVIOR

Keith Davis*

The affluent society of which John Kenneth Galbraith wrote some years ago has become even more affluent.[1] There are many reasons for this sustained improvement in productivity, and some of them are advancing technology, available resources, improved education, and a favorable economic and social system. There is, however, another reason of key significance to all of us. That reason is management, specifically the capacity of managers to develop organizational systems which respond productively to the changing conditions of society. In recent years this has meant more complex administrative systems in order to challenge and motivate employees toward better teamwork. Improvement has been made by working smarter, not harder. An increasingly sophisticated knowledge of human behavior is required; consequently, theoretical models of organizational behavior have had to grow to absorb this new knowledge. It is these evolving models of organizational behavior which I wish to discuss; then I shall draw some conclusions about their use.

The significant point about models of organizational behavior is that the model which a manager holds normally determines his perception of the organizational world about him. It leads to certain assumptions about people and certain interpretations of events he encounters. The underlying model serves as an unconscious guide to each manager's behavior. He acts as he thinks. Since his acts do affect the quality of human relations and productivity in his department, he needs to be fully aware of the trends that are occurring. If he holds to an outmoded model, his success will be limited and his job will be harder, because he will not be able to work with his people as he should.

Similarly, the model of organizational behavior which predominates among the management of an organization will affect the success of that whole organization. And at a national level the model which prevails within a country will influence the productivity and economic development of that nation. Models of organizational behavior are a significant variable in the life of all groups.

---

*From *Academy of Management Journal,* March, 1968, pp. 27–38. Copyright 1967. Reprinted with permission.

[1] John Kenneth Galbraith, *The Affluent Society* (Boston, Mass.: Houghton Mifflin, 1958).

Many models of organizational behavior have appeared during the last 100 years, and four of them are significant and different enough to merit further discussion. These are the autocratic, custodial, supportive, and collegial models. In the order mentioned, the four models represent a historical evolution of management thought. The autocratic model predominated 75 years ago. In the 1920s and 1930s it yielded ground to the more successful custodial model. In this generation the supportive model is gaining approval. It predominates in many organizations, although the custodial model probably still prevails in the whole society. Meanwhile, a number of advanced organizations are experimenting with the collegial model.

The four models are not distinct in the sense that a manager or a firm uses one and only one of them. In a week—or even a day—a manager probably applies some of all four models. On the other hand, one model tends to predominate as his habitual way of working with his people, in such a way that it leads to a particular type of teamwork and behavioral climate among his group. Similarly, one model tends to dominate the life of a whole organization, but different parts therein may still be pursuing other models. The production department may take a custodial approach, while supportive ideas are being tried in the office, and collegial ideas are practiced in the research department. The point is that one model of organizational behavior is not an adequate label to describe all that happens in an organization, but it is a convenient way to distinguish one prevailing way of life from another. By comparing these four models, we can recognize certain important distinctions among them.

THE AUTOCRATIC MODEL

The autocratic model has its roots deep in history, and certainly it became the prevailing model early in the industrial revolution. As shown in Figure 1, this model depends on power. Those who are in command must have the power to demand, "You do this—or else," meaning that an employee will be penalized if he does not follow orders. This model takes a threatening approach, depending on negative motivation backed by power.

In an autocratic environment the managerial orientation is formal, official authority. Authority is the tool with which management works and the context in which it thinks, because it is the organizational means by which power is applied. This authority is delegated by right of command over the people to whom it applies. In this model, management implicitly assumes that it knows what is best and that it is the employee's obligation to follow orders without question or interpretation. Management assumes that employees are passive and even resistant to organizational needs. They have to be persuaded and pushed into performance, and this is management's task. Management does the thinking; the employees obey the orders. This is the "Theory X" popularized by Douglas McGregor as the conventional

Figure 1   Four Models of Organizational Behavior

	Autocratic	Custodial	Supportive	Collegial
Depends on:	Power	Economic re-sources	Leadership	Mutual contri-bution
Managerial orienta-tion:	Authority	Material re-wards	Support	Integration and teamwork
Employee orienta-tion:	Obedience	Security	Performance	Responsibility
Employee psycho-logical result:	Personal de-pendency	Organizational dependency	Participation	Self-discipline
Employee needs met:	Subsistence	Maintenance	Higher-order	Self-realization
Performance result:	Minimum	Passive coop-eration	Awakened drives	Enthusiasm
Morale measure:	Compliance	Satisfaction	Motivation	Commitment to task and team

Source: Adapted from Keith Davis, *Human Relations at Work: The Dynamics of Organizational Behavior* (3rd ed.; New York: McGraw-Hill, 1967), p. 480.

view of management.[2] It has its roots in history and was made explicit by Frederick W. Taylor's concepts of scientific management. Though Taylor's writings show that he had worker interests at heart, he saw those interests served best by a manager who scientifically determined what a worker should do and then saw that he did it. The worker's role was to perform as he was ordered.

Under autocratic conditions an employee's orientation is obedience. He bends to the authority of a boss—not a manager. This role causes a psychological result which in this case is employee personal dependency on his boss whose power to hire, fire, and "perspire" him is almost absolute. The boss pays relatively low wages because he gets relatively less performance from the employee. Each employee must provide subsistence needs for himself and his family; so he reluctantly gives minimum performance, but he is not motivated to give much more than that. A few men give higher performance because of internal achievement drives, because they personally like their boss, because the boss is a "natural-born leader," or because of some other fortuitous reason; but most men give only minimum performance.

When an autocratic model of organizational behavior exists, the measure of an employee's morale is usually his compliance with rules and orders. Compliance is unprotesting assent without enthusiasm. The compliant employee takes his orders and does not talk back.

[2] Douglas McGregor, "The Human Side of Enterprise," in *Proceedings of the Fifth Anniversary Convocation of the School of Industrial Management* (Cambridge, Mass.: Massachusetts Institute of Technology, April 9, 1957). Theory X and Theory Y were later popularized in Douglas McGregor, *The Human Side of Enterprise* (New York: McGraw-Hill, 1960).

Although modern observers have an inherent tendency to condemn the autocratic model of organizational behavior, it is a useful way to accomplish work. It has been successfully applied by the empire builders of the 1800s, efficiency engineers, scientific managers, factory foremen, and others. It helped to build great railroad systems, operate giant steel mills, and produce a dynamic industrial civilization in the early 1900s.

Actually the autocratic model exists in all shades of gray, rather than the extreme black usually presented. It has been a reasonably effective way of management when there is a "benevolent autocrat" who has a genuine interest in his employees and when the role expectation of employees is autocratic leadership.[3] But these results are usually only moderate ones lacking the full potential that is available, and they are reached at considerable human costs. In addition, as explained earlier, conditions change to require new behavioral models in order to remain effective.

As managers and academicians became familiar with limitations of the autocratic model, they began to ask, "Is there a better way? Now that we have brought organizational conditions this far along, can we build on what we have in order to move one step higher on the ladder of progress?" Note that their thought was not to throw out power as undesirable, because power is needed to maintain internal unity in organizations. Rather, their thought was to build upon the foundation which existed: "Is there a better way?"

THE CUSTODIAL MODEL

Managers soon recognized that although a compliant employee did not talk back to his boss, he certainly "thought back!" There were many things he wanted to say to his boss, and sometimes he did say them when he quit or lost his temper. The employee inside was a seething mass of insecurity, frustrations, and aggressions toward his boss. Since he could not vent these feelings directly, sometimes he went home and vented them on his wife, family, and neighbors; so the community did not gain much out of this relationship either.

It seemed rather obvious to progressive employers that there ought to be some way to develop employee satisfactions and adjustment during production—and in fact this approach just might cause more productivity! If the employee's insecurities, frustrations, and aggressions could be dispelled, he might feel more like working. At any rate the employer could sleep better, because his conscience would be clearer.

Development of the custodial model was aided by psychologists, industrial relations specialists, and economists. Psychologists were interested in employee satisfaction and adjustment. They felt that a satisfied

---

[3] This viewpoint is competently presented in R. N. McMurry, "The Case for Benevolent Autocracy," *Harvard Business Review* (Jan.–Feb., 1958), pp. 82–90.

employee would be a better employee, and the feeling was so strong that "a happy employee" became a mild obsession in some personnel offices. The industrial relations specialists and economists favored the custodial model as a means of building employee security and stability in employment. They gave strong support to a variety of fringe benefits and group plans for security.

The custodial model originally developed in the form of employee welfare programs offered by a few progressive employees, and in its worst form it became known as employer paternalism. During the depression of the 1930s emphasis changed to economic and social security and then shortly moved toward various labor plans for security and control. During and after World War II, the main focus was on specific fringe benefits. Employers, labor unions, and government developed elaborate programs for overseeing the needs of workers.

A successful custodial approach depends on economic resources, as shown in Figure 1. An organization must have economic wealth to provide economic security, pensions, and other fringe benefits. The resulting managerial orientation is toward economic or material rewards, which are designed to make employees respond as economic men. A reciprocal employee orientation tends to develop emphasizing security.

The custodial approach gradually leads to an organizational dependency by the employee. Rather than being dependent on his boss for his weekly bread, he now depends on larger organizations for his security and welfare. Perhaps more accurately stated, an organizational dependency is added atop a reduced personal dependency on his boss. This approach effectively serves an employee's maintenance needs, as presented in Herzberg's motivation-maintenance model, but it does not strongly motivate an employee.[4] The result is a passive cooperation by the employee. He is pleased to have his security; but as he grows psychologically, he also seeks more challenge and autonomy.

The natural measure of morale which developed from a custodial model was employee satisfaction. If the employee was happy, contented, and adjusted to the group, then all was well. The happiness-oriented morale survey became a popular measure of success in many organizations.

Limitations of the Custodial Model

Since the custodial model is the one which most employers are currently moving away from, its limitations will be further examined. As with the autocratic model, the custodial model exists in various shades of gray, which means that some practices are more successful than others. In most cases, however, it becomes obvious to all concerned that most employers under

---

[4] Frederick Herzberg, Bernard Mausner, and Barbara Synderman, *The Motivation to Work* (New York: John Wiley and Sons, 1959).

custodial conditions do not produce anywhere near their capacities, nor are they motivated to grow to the greater capacities of which they are capable. Though employees may be happy, most of them really do not feel fulfilled or self-actualized.

The custodial model emphasizes economic resources and the security those resources will buy, rather than emphasizing employee performance. The employee becomes psychologically preoccupied with maintaining his security and benefits, rather than with production. As a result, he does not produce much more vigorously than under the old autocratic approach. Security and contentment are necessary for a person, but they are not themselves very strong motivators.

In addition, the fringe benefits and other devices of the custodial model are mostly off-the-job. They are not directly connected with performance. The employee has to be too sick to work or too old to work in order to receive these benefits. The system becomes one of public and private paternalism in which an employee sees little connection between his rewards and his job performance and personal growth; hence he is not motivated toward performance and growth. In fact, an overzealous effort to make the worker secure and happy leads to a brand of psychological paternalism no better than earlier economic paternalism. With the psychological variety, employee needs are dispensed from the personnel department, union hall, and government bureau, rather than the company store. But in either case dependency remains, and as Ray E. Brown observes, "Men grow stronger on workouts than on handouts. It is in the nature of people to wrestle with a challenge and rest on a crutch. . . . The great desire of man is to stand on his own, and his life is one great fight against dependency. Making the individual a ward of the organization will likely make him bitter instead of better."[5]

As viewed by William H. Whyte, the employee working under custodialism becomes an "organization man" who belongs to the organization and who has "left home, spiritually as well as physically, to take the vows of organizational life."[6]

As knowledge of human behavior advanced, deficiencies in the custodial model became quite evident, and people again started to ask, "Is there a better way?" The search for a better way is not a condemnation of the custodial model as a whole; however, it is a condemnation of the assumption that custodialism is "the final answer"—the one best way to work with people in organizations. An error in reasoning occurs when a person perceives that the custodial model is so desirable that there is no need to move beyond it to something better.

[5] Ray E. Brown, *Judgment in Administration* (New York: McGraw-Hill, 1966), p. 75.
[6] William H. Whyte, Jr., *The Organization Man* (New York: Simon and Schuster, 1956), p. 3.

THE SUPPORTIVE MODEL

The supportive model of organizational behavior has gained currency during recent years as a result of a great deal of behavioral science research as well as favorable employer experience with it. The supportive model establishes a manager in the primary role of psychological support of his employees at work, rather than in a primary role of economic support (as in the custodial model) or "power over" (as in the autocratic model). A supportive approach was first suggested in the classical experiments of Mayo and Roethlisberger at Western Electric Company in the 1930s and 1940s. They showed that a small work group is more productive and satisfied when its members perceive that they are working in a supportive environment. This interpretation was expanded by the work of Edwin A. Fleishman with supervisory "consideration" in the 1940s[7] and that of Rensis Likert and his associates with the "employee-oriented supervisor" in the 1940s and 1950s.[8] In fact, the *coup de grace* to the custodial model's dominance was administered by Likert's research which showed that the happy employee is not necessarily the most productive employee.

Likert has expressed the supportive model as the "principle of supportive relationships" in the following words: *"The leadership and other processes of the organization must be such as to ensure a maximum probability that in all interactions and all relationships with the organization each member will, in the light of his background, values, and expectations, view the experience as supportive and one which builds and maintains his sense of personal worth and importance."*[9]

The supportive model, shown in Figure 1, depends on leadership instead of power or economic resources. Through leadership, management provides a behavioral climate to help each employee grow and accomplish in the interests of the organization the things of which he is capable. The leader assumes that workers are not by nature passive and resistant to organizational needs, but that they are made so by an inadequate supportive climate at work. They will take responsibility, develop a drive to contribute, and improve themselves, if management will give them half a chance. Management's orientation, therefore, is to support the employee's performance.

Since performance is supported, the employee's orientation is toward it instead of mere obedience and security. He is responding to intrinsic motivations in his job situation. His psychological result is a feeling of participation and task involvement in the organization. When referring to his

---

[7] An early report of this research is Edwin A. Fleishman, *"Leadership Climate" and Supervisory Behavior* (Columbus, Ohio: Personnel Research Board, Ohio State University, 1951).

[8] There have been many publications by the Likert group at the Survey Research Center, University of Michigan. An early basic one is Daniel Katz et al., *Productivity, Supervision and Morale in an Office Situation* (Ann Arbor, Mich.: The University of Michigan Press, 1950).

[9] Rensis Likert, *New Patterns of Management* (New York: McGraw-Hill, 1961), pp. 102–103. (Italics in original.)

organization, he may occasionally say "we," instead of always saying "they." Since his higher-order needs are better challenged, he works with more awakened drives than he did under earlier models.

The difference between custodial and supportive models is illustrated by the fact that the morale measure of supportive management is the employee's level of motivation. This measure is significantly different from the satisfaction and happiness emphasized by the custodial model. An employee who has a supportive leader is motivated to work toward organizational objectives as a means of achieving his own goals. This approach is similar to McGregor's popular "Theory Y."

The supportive model is just as applicable to the climate for managers as for operating employees. One study reports that supportive managers usually led to high motivation among their subordinate managers. Among those managers who were low in motivation, only 8 per cent had supportive managers. Their managers were mostly autocratic.[10]

It is not essential for managers to accept every assumption of the supportive model in order to move toward it, because as more is learned about it, views will change. What is essential is that modern managers in business, unions, and government do not become locked into the custodial model. They need to abandon any view that the custodial model is the final answer, so that they will be free to look ahead to improvements which are fitting to their organization in their environment.

The supportive model is only one step upward on the ladder of progress. Though it is just now coming into dominance, some firms which have the proper conditions and managerial competence are already using a collegial model of organizational behavior, which offers further opportunities for improvement.

THE COLLEGIAL MODEL

The collegial model is still evolving, but it is beginning to take shape. It has developed from recent behavioral science research, particularly that of Likert, Katz, Kahn, and others at the University of Michigan,[11] Herzberg with regard to maintenance and motivational factors,[12] and the work of a number of people in project management and matrix organization.[13] The collegial model readily adapts to the flexible, intellectual environment of scientific and professional organizations. Working in substantially unprogrammed activities which require effective teamwork, scientific and profes-

[10] M. Scott Myers, "Conditions for Manager Motivation," *Harvard Business Review* (Jan.-Feb., 1966), p. 61. This study covered 1,344 managers at Texas Instruments, Inc.

[11] Likert describes a similar model as System 4 in Rensis Likert, *The Human Organization: Its Management and Value* (New York: McGraw-Hill, 1967), pp. 3-11.

[12] Herzberg *et al., op. cit.*

[13] For example, see Keith Davis, "Mutuality in Understanding of the Program Manager's Management Role," *IEEE Transactions on Engineering Management* (Dec., 1965), pp. 117-122.

sional employees desire the autonomy which a collegial model permits, and they respond to it well.

The collegial model depends on management's building a feeling of mutual contribution among participants in the organization, as shown in Figure 1. Each employee feels that he is contributing something worthwhile and is needed and wanted. He feels that management and others are similarly contributing, so he accepts and respects their roles in the organization. Managers are seen as joint contributors rather than bosses.

The managerial orientation is toward teamwork which will provide an integration of all contributions. Management is more of an integrating power than a commanding power. The employee response to this situation is responsibility. He produces quality work not primarily because management tells him to do so or because the inspector will catch him if he does not, but because he feels inside himself the desire to do so for many reasons. The employee psychological result, therefore, is self-discipline. Feeling responsible, the employee disciplines himself for team performance in the same way that a football team member disciplines himself in training and in game performance.

In this kind of environment an employee normally should feel some degree of fulfillment and self-realization, although the amount will be modest in some situations. The result is job enthusiasm, because he finds in the job such Herzberg motivators as achievement, growth, intrinsic work fulfillment, and recognition. His morale will be measured by his commitment to his task and his team, because he will see these as instruments for his self-actualization.

SOME CONCLUSIONS ABOUT MODELS OF ORGANIZATIONAL BEHAVIOR

The evolving nature of models of organizational behavior makes it evident that change is the normal condition of these models. As our understanding of human behavior increases or as new social conditions develop, our organizational behavior models are also likely to change. It is a grave mistake to assume that one particular model is a "best" model which will endure for the long run. This mistake was made by some old-time managers about the autocratic model and by some humanists about the custodial model, with the result that they became psychologically locked into these models and had difficulty altering their practices when conditions demanded it. Eventually the supportive model may also fall to limited use; and as further progress is made, even the collegial model is likely to be surpassed. There is no permanently "one best model" of organizational behavior, because what is best depends upon what is known about human behavior in whatever environment and priority of objectives exist at a particular time.

A second conclusion is that the models of organizational behavior which have developed seem to be sequentially related to man's psychological hierarchy of needs. As society has climbed higher on the need hierarchy, new models of organizational behavior have been developed to serve the higher-order needs that became paramount at the time. If Maslow's need hierarchy is used for comparison, the custodial model of organizational behavior is seen as an effort to serve man's second-level security needs.[14] It moved one step above the autocratic model which was reasonably serving man's subsistence needs, but was not effectively meeting his needs for security. Similarly the supportive model is an effort to meet employees' higher-level needs, such as affiliation and esteem, which the custodial model was unable to serve. The collegial model moves even higher toward service of man's need for self-actualization.

A number of persons have assumed that emphasis on one model of organizational behavior was an automatic rejection of other models, but the comparison with man's need hierarchy *suggests that each model is built upon the accomplishments of the other.* For example, adoption of a supportive approach does not mean abandonment of custodial practices which serve necessary employee security needs. What is does mean is that custodial practices are relegated to secondary emphasis, because employees have progressed up their need structure to a condition in which higher needs predominate. In other words, the supportive model is the appropriate model to use *because* subsistence and security needs are already reasonably met by a suitable power structure and security system. If a misdirected modern manager should abandon these basic organizational needs, the system would quickly revert to a quest for a workable power structure and security system in order to provide subsistence-maintenance needs for its people.

Each model of organizational behavior in a sense outmodes its predominance by gradually satisfying certain needs, thus opening up other needs which can be better served by a more advanced model. Thus each new model is built upon the success of its predecessor. The new model simply represents a more sophisticated way of maintaining earlier need satisfactions, while opening up the probability of satisfying still higher needs.

A third conclusion suggests that the present tendency toward more democratic models of organizational behavior will continue for the longer run. This tendency seems to be required by both the nature of technology and the nature of the need structure. Harbison and Myers, in a classical study of management throughout the industrial world, conclude that advancing industrialization leads to more advanced models of organizational behavior. Specifically, authoritarian management gives way to more constitutional and democratic-participative models of management. These developments are inherent in the system; that is, the more democratic models

---

[14] A. H. Maslow, "A Theory of Human Motivation," *Psychological Review* (L, 1943), 370–396.

tend to be necessary in order to manage productively an advanced industrial system.[15] Slater and Bennis also conclude that more participative and democratic models of organizational behavior inherently develop with advancing industrialization. They believe that "democracy is inevitable," because it is the only system which can successfully cope with changing demands of contemporary civilization in both business and government.[16]

Both sets of authors accurately point out that in modern, complex organizations a top manager cannot be authoritarian in the traditional sense and remain efficient, because he cannot know all that is happening in his organization. He must depend on other centers of power nearer to operating problems. In addition, educated workers are not readily motivated toward creative and intellectual duties by traditional authoritarian orders. They require high-order need satisfactions which newer models of organizational behavior provide. Thus there does appear to be some inherent necessity for more democratic forms of organization in advanced industrial systems.

A fourth and final conclusion is that, though one model may predominate as most appropriate for general use at any point in industrial history, some appropriate uses will remain for other models. Knowledge of human behavior and skills in applying that knowledge will vary among managers. Role expectations of employees will differ depending upon cultural history. Policies and ways of life will vary among organizations. Perhaps more important, task conditions will vary. Some jobs may require routine, low-skilled, highly programmed work which will be mostly determined by higher authority and provide mostly material rewards and security (autocratic and custodial conditions). Other jobs will be unprogrammed and intellectual, requiring teamwork and self-motivation, and responding best to supportive and collegial conditions. This use of different management practices with people according to the task they are performing is called "management according to task" by Leavitt.[17]

In the final analysis, each manager's behavior will be determined by his underlying theory of organizational behavior, so it is essential for him to understand the different results achieved by different models of organizational behavior. The model used will vary with the total human and task conditions surrounding the work. The long-run tendency will be toward more supportive and collegial models because they better serve the higher-level needs of employees.

[15] Frederick Harbison and Charles A. Myers, Management in the Industrial World: An International Analysis (New York: McGraw-Hill, 1959), pp. 40–67. The authors also state on page 47, "The design of systems of authority is equally as important in the modern world as the development of technology."

[16] Philip E. Slater and Warren G. Bennis, "Democracy Is Inevitable," Harvard Business Review (March–April, 1964), pp. 51–59.

[17] Harold J. Leavitt, "Management According to Task: Organizational Differentiation," Management International (1962), No. 1, pp. 13–22.

READING   3

DEMOCRACY IS INEVITABLE

Philip E. Slater
Warren G. Bennis*

Cynical observers have always been fond of pointing out that business leaders who extol the virtues of democracy on ceremonial occasions would be the last to think of applying them to their own organizations. To the extent that this is true, however, it reflects a state of mind which by no means is peculiar to businessmen, but characterizes all Americans, if not perhaps all citizens of democracies.

This attitude, briefly, is that democracy is a nice way of life for nice people, despite its manifold inconveniences—a kind of expensive and inefficient luxury, like owning a large medieval castle. Feelings about it are for the most part affectionate, even respectful, but a little impatient. There are probably few men of affairs in America who have not at some time nourished in their hearts the blasphemous thought that life would go much more smoothly if democracy could be relegated to some kind of Sunday morning devotion.

The bluff practicality of the "nice-but-inefficient" stereotype masks a hidden idealism, however, for it implies that institutions can survive in a competitive environment through the sheer goodheartedness of those who maintain them. We would like to challenge this notion, and suggest that even if all of those benign sentiments were eradicated today, we would awaken tomorrow to find democracy still firmly entrenched, buttressed by a set of economic, social, and political forces as practical as they are uncontrollable.

We will argue that democracy has been so widely embraced, not because of some vague yearning for human rights, but because *under certain conditions* it is a more "efficient" form of social organization. (Our concept of efficiency includes the ability to survive and prosper.) We do not regard it as accidental that those nations of the world which have endured longest under conditions of relative wealth and stability are democratic, while authoritarian regimes have, with few exceptions, either crumbled or eked out a precarious and backward existence.

Despite this evidence, even so acute a statesman as Adlai Stevenson argued in a *New York Times* article on November 4, 1962, that the goals of

*From "Democracy Is Inevitable," *Harvard Business Review,* March–April, 1964, pp. 51–53. Copyright 1964. Reprinted with permission.

the Communists are different from ours. "They are interested in power," he said; "we in community. With such fundamentally different aims, how is it possible to compare communism and democracy in terms of efficiency? You might as well ask whether a locomotive is more efficient than a symphony orchestra."

Isn't this simply the speech of an articulate man who believes that democracy is inefficient and doesn't like to say so? Actually we are concerned with locomotives *and* symphony orchestras, with power *and* community. The challenge for communism and democracy is, in fact, identical: to compete successfully for the world's resources and imagination.

Our position is, in brief, that democracy (whether capitalistic or socialistic is not at issue here) is the only system which can successfully cope with the changing demands of contemporary civilization. We are not necessarily endorsing democracy as such; one might reasonably argue that industrial civilization is pernicious and should be abolished. We suggest merely that given a desire to survive in this civilization, democracy is the most effective means to achieve this end.

DEMOCRACY TAKES OVER

There are signs, in fact, that our business community is becoming aware of this law. Several of the newest and most rapidly blooming companies in the United States boast unusually democratic organizations. Even more surprising is the fact that some of the largest of the established corporations have been moving steadily, if accidentally, toward democratization. Frequently they began by feeling that administrative vitality and creativity were lacking in the older systems of organization. In increasing numbers, therefore, they enlisted the support of social scientists and of outside programs, the net *effect* of which has been to democratize their organization. Executives and even entire management staffs have been sent to participate in human relations and organizational laboratories to learn skills and attitudes which ten years ago would have been denounced as anarchic and revolutionary. At these meetings, status prerogatives and traditional concepts of authority are severely challenged.

Many social scientists have played an important role in this development toward humanizing and democratizing large-scale bureaucracies. The contemporary theories of McGregor, Likert, Argyris, and Blake have paved the way to a new social architecture. Research and training centers at the National Training Laboratories, Tavistock Institute, Massachusetts Institute of Technology, Harvard Business School, Boston University, University of California at Los Angeles, Case Institute of Technology, and others have pioneered in the application of social science knowledge to the improvement of organizational effectiveness. So far, the data are not all in; conclusive evidence is missing, but the forecast seems to hold genuine promise: that it is possible to bring about greater organizational effectiveness through the utilization of valid social knowledge.[1]

System of Values

What we have in mind when we use the term "democracy" is not "permissiveness" or "laissez faire," but a system of values—a "climate of beliefs" governing behavior—which people are internally compelled to affirm by deeds as well as words. These values include:

1 Full and free *communication,* regardless of rank and power.

2 A reliance on *consensus,* rather than the more customary forms of coercion or compromise to manage conflict.

3 The idea that *influence* is based on technical competence and knowledge rather than on the vagaries of personal whims or prerogatives of power.

4 An atmosphere that permits and even encourages emotional *expression* as well as task-oriented acts.

5 A basically *human* bias, one that accepts the inevitability of conflict between the organization and the individual, but which is willing to cope with and mediate this conflict on rational grounds.

Changes along these dimensions are being promoted widely in American industry. Most important, for our analysis, is what we believe to be the reason for these changes: *democracy becomes a functional necessity whenever a social system is competing for survival under conditions of chronic change.*

*   *   *

[1] For a complete review of this work, see W. G. Bennis, "Effecting Organizational Change: A New Role for the Behavioral Scientist," *Administrative Science Quarterly,* September 1963.

CHAPTER 2
HISTORICAL FOUNDATIONS

READING   4

THE OBJECTIVE OF SCIENTIFIC MANAGEMENT

Frederick W. Taylor*

"And I want to make it perfectly clear, because I do not think it *is* clear, that my interest, and I think the interest of any man who is in any way engaged in scientific management, in the introduction of the principles of scientific management must be first the welfare of the working men. That must be the object. It is inconceivable that a man should devote his time and his life to this sort of thing for the sake of making more money for a whole lot of manufacturers."

＊   ＊   ＊

*Testimony before Industrial Relations Commission, April, 1914, quoted in Horace B. Drury, *Scientific Management,* Columbia University Studies in History, Economics, and Public Law, vol. LXV, no. 2 (New York: Longmans, Green & Co., Inc., New York, 1915), p. 204.

READING 5

AN INDUSTRIAL ORGANIZATION AS A SOCIAL SYSTEM

F. J. Roethlisberger
William J. Dickson*

We shall now attempt to state more systematically than was possible in a chronological account the results of the research and some of their implications for practice. . . .The point of view which gradually emerged from these studies is one from which an industrial organization is regarded as a social system. . . .

The study of the bank wiremen showed that their behavior at work could not be understood without considering the informal organization of the group and the relation of this informal organization to the total social organization of the company. The work activities of this group, together with their satisfactions and dissatisfactions, had to be viewed as manifestations of a complex pattern of interrelations. In short, the work situation of the bank wiring group had to be treated as a social system; moreover, the industrial organization of which this group was a part also had to be treated as a social system.

By "system" is meant something which must be considered as a whole because each part bears a relation of interdependence to every other part.[1]

⁜   ⁜   ⁜

*From *Management and the Worker* (Cambridge, Mass.: Harvard University Press, 1949), p. 551. Copyright 1939, 1967 by the President and Fellows of Harvard College. Reprinted with permission.

[1] "The interdependence of the variables in a system is one of the widest inductions from experience that we possess; or we may alternatively regard it as the definition of a system." Henderson, L. J., *Pareto's General Sociology,* Harvard University Press, 1935, p. 86.

READING 6

THE HAWTHORNE STUDIES: A SYNOPSIS*

From 1924 to 1933, the Western Electric Company conducted at its Hawthorne Works a research program or series of experiments on the factors in the work situation which affect the morale and productive efficiency of workers. The first of these, the so-called "Illumination Experiments," was studied in cooperation with the National Research Council of the National Academy of Sciences. In the remainder of the studies, the company was aided and guided by the suggestions of Professor Elton Mayo and several of his associates from Harvard University. Because of the large part that Harvard played in the project, it is often referred to as the Hawthorne-Harvard experiments or studies.

ILLUMINATION EXPERIMENTS

The purpose of the Illumination Experiments (1924–27) was to determine the "relation of quality and quantity of illumination to efficiency in industry."

Three formal experiments were conducted with various groups of workers. The intensity of illumination was increased and decreased and the effect on output was observed. The effect was puzzling. Output bobbed up and down in some groups or increased continually in others, or increased and stayed level in still others. But in no case was the increase or decrease in proportion to the increase or decrease in illumination.

After many objective tests, it appeared to the Western Electric people involved that:

1 Light was only one factor (and apparently minor) among many which affect employees' output.

2 The attempt to measure the effect of the light factor had failed because the other factors had not been controlled, and studies in regular shop departments or large groups involved so many factors that it was hopeless to expect to isolate any one of them.

At this point, the National Research Council withdrew from the studies, but Western Electric continued them, and soon thereafter had the collaboration of people from Harvard University.

* From *Industrial Engineering,* November 1974, pp. 14–15. Copyright 1974. Reprinted with permission. This very brief summary was extracted from *The Hawthorne Studies 1924/ 1974: A Synopsis,* a booklet published by Western Electric Company in conjunction with the 50th anniversary of the beginning of the famous Hawthorne Studies.

RELAY ASSEMBLY TESTS

Inasmuch as it had appeared that some of the odd effects of the illuminating experiments resulted from the way workers felt about what they were doing (i.e., speeded up because they thought increased production was expected, or slowed down because they were suspicious of the investigator's motives), the investigators tried to set up a situation in which the employees' attitudes would remain constant and unaffected, and other variables might be eliminated.

Assembly of relays was selected for carefully structured tests of factors that might influence productivity. These tests were conducted over a five-year period, 1927–32. The operators were chosen selectively, and given periodic physical examinations as one means of eliminating variables. The experiments were precisely controlled; detailed results were recorded.

During this same period a second relay assembly group of five assemblers was formed. The objective was to test the possibility that change to a small wage incentive group was responsible for improved performance.

The Mica Splitting Test Room was selected for another experiment on the effect of wage incentives. Here, changes in working conditions were introduced without changing the wage incentive plan.

SOME CONCLUSIONS

The underlying premises of both the illumination and the test room experiments had been that a change in working conditions would result in a change in production. A "good" change produces a good result (i.e., an increase in production); a "bad" change produces a bad result (i.e., a decrease in production).

When the illumination failed to substantiate this premise, it was assumed that extraneous factors had interfered, primarily the feelings and attitudes of the operators. Therefore the test room setup was devised with the idea of keeping the operators' attitudes constant while making other changes; there, presumably, the only reactions would be automatic physical reactions—the operators would work faster or slower.

But in their attempts to keep constant the attitudes of the girls in the test room, the investigators made many changes in the treatment of the girls which made their situation very untypical of workers in general. In the very attempt to prevent change, they introduced change.

More and more the investigators came to realize that the significant information they were acquiring had to do with the way people thought and felt—their attitudes. That is, change does not lead to a direct, automatic result; change affects the employee's attitude, *which in turn* affects the result.

So the chief result of the first two years of the Relay Assembly Test Room demonstrated the importance of employee attitude and preoccupations. All attempts to eliminate such considerations had been unsuccessful.

What practical consequences did these results have?

Management regarded these experiments as an attempt to compile a sound body of knowledge upon which to base executive policy and action. And although it was recognized that such research is a long-term proposition, management was ready to make use of any findings which seemed to have been sufficiently tested.

What impressed management most were the stores of latent energy and productive cooperation which could be obtained from people working under the right conditions. Among the factors making for these conditions the attitudes of the employees stood out as being predominant.

The conclusions led to further studies. The Interviewing Program, 1928–30, covering 21,000 employees, provided data of immediate value in improving working conditions, supervisory training, and other employee relations activities conducted by management. Of even more historical significance, it developed insights into methods of listening to and understanding an employee's view of his own personal situation. In short, this part of the program perfected the interviewing technique itself.

Later, the Bank Wiring Observation Room (1931–32) was set up to observe the worker in his work environment. It developed a method of studying group behavior that supplemented interviewing with actual on-the-job data on behavior patterns in the working group. Out of this phase came the concept of the informal organization and its influence on productivity, as well as other new information demonstrating the impact of social factors in the industrial setting.

READING   7

THE HIERARCHY OF NEEDS

A. H. Maslow*

*   *   *

1   There are at least five sets of goals which we may call basic needs. These are briefly physiological, safety, love, esteem, and self-actualization. In addition, we are motivated by the desire to achieve or maintain the various conditions upon which these basic satisfactions rest and by certain more intellectual desires.

2   These basic goals are related to each other, being arranged in a hierarchy of prepotency. This means that the most prepotent goal will monopolize consciousness and will tend of itself to organize the recruitment of the various capacities of the organism. The less prepotent needs are minimized, even forgotten or denied. But when a need is fairly well satisfied, the next prepotent ("higher") need emerges, in turn to dominate the conscious life and to serve as the center of organization of behavior, since gratified needs are not active motivators.

Thus, man is a perpetually wanting animal. Ordinarily the satisfaction of these wants is not altogether mutually exclusive, but only tends to be. The average member of our society is most often partially satisfied and partially unsatisfied in all of his wants. The hierarchy principle is usually empirically observed in terms of increasing percentages of nonsatisfaction as we go up the hierarchy. Reversals of the average order of the hierarchy are sometimes observed. Also it has been observed that an individual may permanently lose the higher wants in the hierarchy under social conditions. There are not only ordinarily multiple motivations for usual behavior, but in addition many determinants other than motives.

3   Any thwarting or possibility of thwarting of these basic human goals, or danger to the defenses which protect them, or to the conditions upon which they rest, is considered to be a psychological threat. With a few exceptions, all psychopathology may be partially traced to such threats. A basically thwarted man may actually be defined as a "sick" man, if we wish.

*   *   *

*From A. H. Maslow, "A Theory of Human Motivation," *Psychological Review*, vol. 50, 1943, pp. 394–395. © 1943 by the American Psychological Association. Reprinted with permission.

READING   8

THE CONCEPTS OF VALENCE AND EXPECTANCY

Victor H. Vroom*

*   *   *

THE CONCEPT OF VALENCE

We shall begin with the simple assumption that, at any given point in time, a person has preferences among outcomes or states of nature. For any pair of outcomes, *x* and *y,* a person prefers *x* to *y,* prefers *y* to *x,* or is indifferent to whether he receives *x* or *y.* Preference, then, refers to a relationship between the strength of a person's desire for, or attraction toward, two outcomes.

Psychologists have used many different terms to refer to preferences. The terms, valence (Lewin, 1938; Tolman, 1959), incentive (Atkinson, 1958b), attitude (Peak, 1955), and expected utility (Edwards, 1954; Thrall, Coombs, and Davis, 1954; Davidson, Suppes and Siegel, 1957) all refer to affective orientations toward outcomes. Other concepts like need (Maslow, 1954), motive (Atkinson, 1958b), value (Allport, Vernon, and Lindzey, 1951), and interest (Strong, 1958) are broader in nature and refer to the strength of desires or aversions for large classes of outcomes.

For the sake of consistency, we use the term valence throughout this book in referring to affective orientations toward particular outcomes. In our system, an outcome is positively valent when the person prefers attaining it to not attaining it (i.e., he prefers *x* to not *x*). An outcome has a valence of zero when the person is indifferent to attaining or not attaining it (i.e., he is indifferent to *x* or not *x*), and it is negatively valent when he prefers not attaining it to attaining it (i.e., he prefers not *x* to *x*). It is assumed that valence can take a wide range of both positive and negative values.

*   *   *

THE CONCEPT OF EXPECTANCY

The specific outcomes attained by a person are dependent not only on the choices that he makes but also on events which are beyond his control. For example, a person who elects to buy a ticket in a lottery is not certain of winning the desired prize. Whether or not he does so is a function of many chance events. Similarly, the student who enrolls in medical school is seldom certain that he will successfully complete the program of study; the person who seeks political office is seldom certain that he will win the election; and the worker who strives for a promotion is seldom certain that he will triumph over other candidates. Most decision-making situations involve some element of risk, and theories of choice behavior must come to grips with the role of these risks in determining the choices that people do make.

Whenever an individual chooses between alternatives which involve uncertain outcomes, it seems clear that his behavior is affected not only by his preferences among these outcomes but also by the degree to which he believes these outcomes to be probable. Psychologists have referred to these beliefs as expectancies (Tolman, 1959; Rotter, 1955; Atkinson, 1958b) or subjective probabilities (Edwards, 1954; Davidson, Suppes, and Siegel, 1957). We use the former term throughout this book. An expectancy is defined as a momentary belief concerning the likelihood that a particular act will be followed by a particular outcome. Expectancies may be described in terms of their strength. Maximal strength is indicated by subjective certainty that the act *will* be followed by the outcome while minimal (or zero) strength is indicated by subjective certainty that the act *will not* be followed by the outcome.

*   *   *

READING 9

THE PRINCIPLE OF SUPPORTIVE RELATIONSHIPS

Rensis Likert*

The principle of supportive relationships is a general principle which the members of an organization can use to guide their relationships with one another. The more fully this principle is applied throughout the organization, the greater will be the extent to which (1) the motivational forces arising from the noneconomic motives of members and from their economic needs will be harmonious and compatible and (2) the motivational forces within each individual will result in cooperative behavior focused on achieving organizational goals. The principle is stated as follows:

> The leadership and other processes of the organization must be such as to ensure a maximum probability that in all interactions and in all relationships within the organization, each member, in the light of his background, values, desires, and expectations, will view the experience as supportive and one which builds and maintains his sense of personal worth and importance.[1]

In applying this principle, the relationship between the superior and subordinate is crucial. This relationship, as the principle specifies, should be one which is supportive and ego-building. The more often the superior's behavior is ego-building rather than ego-deflating, the better will be the effect of his behavior on organizational performance. In applying this principle, it is essential to keep in mind that the interactions between the leader and the subordinates must be viewed in the light of the subordinate's background, values, and expectations. The subordinate's perception of the situation, rather than the supervisor's, determines whether or not the experience is supportive. Both the behavior of the superior and the employee's perceptions of the situation must be such that the subordinate, in the light of his background, values, and expectations, sees the experience as one which contributes to his sense of personal worth and importance, one which increases and maintains his sense of significance and human dignity.

* * *

*From *The Human Organization: Its Management and Value* (New York: McGraw-Hill Book Company, 1967), p. 47–48. Copyright 1967. Reprinted with permission.

[1] R. Likert, *New Patterns of Management* (New York: McGraw-Hill Book Company, 1961), p. 103.

CHAPTER 3
UNDERSTANDING PEOPLE IN ORGANIZATIONS

READING 10

CHARACTERISTICS OF ACHIEVERS

David C. McClelland*

Considerations like these focus attention on what there is about the job of being a business entrepreneur or executive that should make such a job peculiarly appropriate for a man with a high concern for achievement. Or, to put it the other way around, a person with high *n* Achievement has certain characteristics which enable him to work best in certain types of situations that are to his liking. An entrepreneurial job simply provides him with more opportunities for making use of his talents than do other jobs. Through careful empirical research we know a great deal by now about the man with high *n* Achievement, and his characteristics do seem to fit him unusually well for being a business executive. Specifically:

1 *To begin with, he likes situations in which he takes personal responsibility for finding solutions to problems.* The reason is obvious. Otherwise, he could get little personal achievement satisfaction from the successful outcome. No gambler, he does not relish situations where the outcome depends not on his abilities and efforts but on chance or other factors beyond his control. For example:

> Some business school students in one study played a game in which they had to choose between two options, in each of which they had only one chance in three of succeeding. For one option they rolled a die and if it came up, say, a 1 or a 3 (out of six possibilities), they won. For the other option they had to work on a difficult business problem which they knew only one out of three people had been able to solve in the time allotted.
>
> Under these conditions, the men with high *n* Achievement regularly chose to work on the business problem, even though they knew the odds of success were statistically the same as for rolling the dice.

To men strong in achievement concern, the idea of winning by chance simply does not produce the same achievement satisfaction as winning by their own personal efforts. Obviously, such a concern for taking personal responsibility is useful in a business executive. He may not be faced very often with the alternative of rolling dice to determine the outcome of a decision, but there are many other ways open to avoid personal responsibility, such as passing the buck, or trying to get someone else (or a committee) to take the responsibility for getting something done.

---

*From "Business Drives and National Achievement," *Harvard Business Review,* July–August, 1962, pp. 103–105. Copyright 1962. Reprinted with permission.

The famed self-confidence of a good executive (which actually is related to high achievement motivation) is also involved here. He thinks it can be done if *he* takes responsibility, and very often he is right because he has spent so much time thinking about how to do it that he does it better.

2 *Another characteristic of a man with a strong achievement concern is his tendency to set moderate achievement goals and to take "calculated risks."* Again his strategy is well suited to his needs, for only by taking on moderately difficult tasks is he likely to get the achievement satisfaction he wants. If he takes on an easy or routine problem, he will succeed but get very little satisfaction out of his success. If he takes on an extremely difficult problem, he is unlikely to get any satisfaction because he will not succeed. In between these two extremes, he stands the best chance of maximizing his sense of personal achievement.

The point can be made with the children's game of ring toss, some variant of which we have tried out at all ages to see how a person with high *n* Achievement approaches it. To illustrate:

> The child is told that he scores when he succeeds in throwing a ring over a peg on the floor, but that he can stand anywhere he pleases. Obviously, if he stands next to the peg, he can score a ringer every time; but if he stands a long distance away, he will hardly ever get a ringer.
>
> The curious fact is that the children with high concern for achievement quite consistently stand at moderate distances from the peg where they are most apt to get achievement satisfaction (or, to be more precise, where the decreasing probability-of-success curve crosses the increasing satisfaction-from-success curve). The ones with low *n* Achievement, on the other hand, distribute their choices of where to stand quite randomly over the entire distance. In other words, people with high *n* Achievement prefer a situation where there is a challenge, where there is some real risk of not succeeding, but not so great a risk that they might not overcome it by their own efforts.

Again, such a characteristic would seem to suit men unusually well for the role of business entrepreneur. The businessman is always in a position of taking calculated risks, of deciding how difficult a given decision will be to carry out. If he is too safe and conservative, and refuses to innovate, to invest enough in research or product development or advertising, he is likely to lose out to a more aggressive competitor. On the other hand, if he invests too much or overextends himself, he is also likely to lose out. Clearly, then, the business executive should be a man with a high concern for achievement who is used to setting moderate goals for himself and calculating carefully how much he can do successfully.

Therefore, we waste our time feeling sorry for the entrepreneur whose constant complaints are that he is overworking, that he has more problems than he knows how to deal with, that he is doomed to ulcers because of overwork, and so on. The bald truth is that if he has high *n* Achievement, he loves all those challenges he complains about. In fact, a careful study might well show that he creates most of them for himself. He may talk about quitting business and living on his investments, but if he did, he might then *really* get ulcers. The state of mind of being a little overextended is precisely the one he seeks, since overcoming difficulties gives him achievement satisfaction. His real problem is that of keeping the difficulties from getting too big for him, which explains in part why he talks so much about them because it is a nagging problem for him to keep them at a level he can handle.

3 *The man who has a strong concern for achievement also wants concrete feedback as to how well he is doing.* Otherwise how could he get any satisfaction out of what he had done? And business is almost unique in the amount of feedback it provides in the form of sales, cost, production, and profit figures. It is really no accident that the symbol of the businessman in popular cartoons is a wall chart with a line on it going up or down. The businessman sooner or later knows how well he is doing; salesmen will often know their success from day to day. Furthermore, there is a concreteness in the knowledge of results which is missing from the kind of feedback professionals get.

Take, for example, the teacher as a representative professional. His job is to transmit certain attitudes and certain kinds of information to his students. He does get some degree of feedback as to how well he has done his job, but results are fairly imprecise and hardly concrete. His students, colleagues, and even his college's administration may indicate that they like his teaching, but he still has no real evidence that his students have *learned* anything from him. Many of his students do well on examinations, but he knows from past experience that they will forget most of that in a year or two. If he has high *n* Achievement and is really concerned about whether he has done his job well, he must be satisfied with sketchy, occasional evidence that his former pupils did absorb some of his ideas and attitudes. More likely, however, he is not a person with high *n* Achievement and is quite satisfied with the affection and recognition that he gets for his work which gratify other needs that he has.

The case of the true entrepreneur is different. Suppose he is a book publisher. He gets a manuscript and together with his editors decides that it is worth publication. At time of issuance, everyone is satisfied that he is launching a worthwhile product. But then something devastatingly concrete happens—something far more definite than ever happens to a teacher—namely, those monthly sales figures.

Obviously not everyone likes to work in situations where the feedback is so concrete. It can prove him right, but it also can prove him wrong. Oddly enough, the person with high *n* Achievement has a compelling interest to know whether he was right or wrong. He thrives and is happier in this type of situation than he is in the professional situation.

Two further examples from our research may make the point clearer. Boys with high *n* Achievement tend to be good with their hands, to like working in a shop or with mechanical or electrical gadgets. What characterizes such play again is the concrete feedback it provides as to how well a person is doing. If he wires up an electric circuit and then throws the switch, the light either goes on or it does not. Knowledge of results is direct, immediate, and concrete. Boys with high *n* Achievement like this kind of situation, and while some may go on to become engineers, others often go into business where they can continue getting this kind of concrete feedback.

* * *

READING 11

PERSONALITY VS. ORGANIZATION

Chris Argyris*

Approximately every seven years we develop the itch to review the relevant literature and research in personality and organization theory, to compare our own evolving theory and research with those of our peers—an exercise salutary, we trust, in confirmation and also confrontation. We're particularly concerned to measure our own explicit model of man with the complementary or conflicting models advanced by other thinkers. Without an explicit normative model, personality and organization theory (P. and O. theory) tends to settle for a generalized description of behavior as it is observed in existing institutions—at best, a process that embalms the status quo; at worst, a process that exalts it. Current behavior becomes the prescription for future actions.

By contrast, I contend that behavioral science research should be normative, that it is the mission of the behavioral scientist to intervene selectively in the organization whenever there seems a reasonable chance of improving the quality of life within the organization without imperiling its viability. Before surveying the P. and O. landscape, however, let's review the basic models of man and formal organization.

*Reprinted by permission from the publisher from *Organizational Dynamics,* Fall, 1974, pp. 3-6. © 1974, AMACOM, a division of American Management Associations.

FUNDAMENTALS OF MAN AND ORGANIZATION

The following steps indicate how the worlds of man and formal organization have developed:

1 Organizations emerge when the goals they seek to achieve are too complex for any one man. The actions necessary to achieve the goals are divided into units manageable by individuals—the more complex the goals, other things being equal, the more people are required to meet them.

2 Individuals themselves are complex organizations with diverse needs. They contribute constructively to the organization only *if on balance,* the organization fulfills these needs and their sense of what is just.

3 What are the needs that individuals seek to fulfill? Each expert has his own list and no two lists duplicate priorities. We have tried to bypass this intellectual morass by focussing on some relatively reliable predispositions that remain valid irrespective of the situation. Under any circumstances individuals seek to fulfill these predispositions; at the same time, their exact nature, potency, and the degree to which they must be fulfilled are influenced by the organizational context—for example, the nature of the job. In their attempt to live, to grow in competence, and to achieve self-acceptance, men and women tend to program themselves along the lines of the continua depicted in Figure 1.

Together, these continua represent a developmental logic that people ignore or suppress with difficulty, the degree of difficulty depending on the culture and the context, as well as the individual's interactions with the key figures in his or her life. The model assumes that the thrust of this developmental program is from left to right, but nothing is assumed about the location of any given individuals along these continua.

A central theme of P. and O. theory has been the range of differences between individuals and how it is both necessary and possible to arrange a match between the particular set of needs an individual brings to the job situation and the requirements—technical and psychological—of the job itself, as well as the overall organizational climate.

We have written four studies that highlighted an individual's interrelationship with the work context. In each study, a separate analysis was made

Figure 1 Developmental Continua

Infants begin as	Adults strive toward
1 being dependent and submissive to parents (or other significant adult)	**1** relative independence, autonomy, relative control over their immediate world
2 having few abilities	**2** developing many abilities
3 having skin-surfaced or shallow abilities	**3** developing a few abilities in depth
4 having a short time perspective	**4** developing a longer time perspective

of each participant that included (1) the predispositions that he or she desired to express, (2) the potency of each predisposition, (3) the inferred probability that each would be expressed, and (4) a final score that indicated the degree to which the individual was able to express his or her predispositions.

A personal expression score enabled us to make specific predictions as to how individuals would react to the organization. We had expected individuals with low scores, for example, to state that they were frustrated and to have poorer attendance records and a higher quit rate—expectations that also showed how individual differences in predispositions were differentially rewarded in different types of departments. Bank employees with a need to distrust and control others, for example, instinctively opted for positions in the internal audit department of the bank.

So much for the model of man. Now to organizations, which have a life of their own, in the sense that they have goals that unfortunately may be independent of or antagonistic to individual needs. The next step was to determine if there was a genetic logic according to which organizations were programmed.

Observation and reading combined to suggest that most organizations had pyramided structures of different sizes. The logic behind each of these pyramids—great or small—was first, to centralize information and power at the upper levels of the structure; second, to specialize work. According to this logic, enunciated most clearly by Frederick Winslow Taylor and Max Weber, management should be high on the six organizational activities summarized in Figure 2.

This model assumed that the closer an organization approached the right ends of the continua, the closer it approached the ideal of formal organization. The model assumed nothing, however, about where any given organization would be pinpointed along these continua.

PERSONALITY VS. ORGANIZATION

Given the dimensions of the two models, the possibilities of interaction are inevitable and varied; so is the likelihood of conflict between the needs of

Figure 2　Continua of Organizational Activities

low	Designing specialized and fractionalized work	high
low	Designing production rates and controlling speed of work	high
low	Giving orders	high
low	Evaluating performance	high
low	Rewarding and punishing	high
low	Perpetuating membership	high

individuals and the structured configuration of the formal organization. The nature of the interaction between the individual and the organization and the probability of conflict vary according to the conditions depicted in Figure 3.

From this model, we can hypothesize that the more the organization approaches the model of the formal organization, the more individuals will be forced to behave at the infant ends of the continua. What if—still operating at the level of an intellectual exercise—the individuals aspired toward the adult end of the continua? What would the consequences be? Wherever there is an incongruence between the needs of individuals and the requirements of a formal organization, individuals will tend to experience frustration, psychological failure, short-time perspective, and conflict.

What factors determine the extent of the incongruence? The chief factors are: first, the lower the employee is positioned in the hierarchy, the less control he has over his working conditions and the less he is able to employ his abilities; second, the more directive the leadership, the more dependent the employee; and last, the more unilateral the managerial controls, the more dependent the employee will feel.

We have said that individuals find these needs difficult to ignore or suppress, and if they are suppressed, frustration and conflict result. These feelings, in turn, are experienced in several ways:

- The employee fights the organization and tries to gain more control—for example, he may join a union.
- The employee leaves the organization, temporarily or permanently.
- The employee leaves it psychologically, becoming a half-worker, uninvolved, apathetic, indifferent.
- The employee downgrades the intrinsic importance of work and substitutes higher pay as the reward for meaningless work. Barnard observed almost 40 years ago that organizations emphasized financial satisfactions because they were the easiest to provide. He had a point—then and now.

We want to emphasize several aspects about these propositions. The personality model provides the base for predictions as to the impact of any

Figure 3   Conditions of Interaction

If the individual aspired toward	And the organization (through its jobs, technology, controls, leadership, and so forth) required that the individual aspire toward
1 adulthood dimensions	1 infancy dimensions
2 infancy dimensions	2 adulthood dimensions
3 adulthood dimensions	3 adulthood dimensions
4 infancy dimensions	4 infancy dimensions

organizational variable upon the individual, such as organizational structure, job content, leadership style, group norms, and so on. The literature
has concentrated on employee frustration expressed in fighting the organization, because it's the commonest form of response, but we shouldn't
ignore the other three responses.

In a study of two organizations in which technology, job content, leadership, and managerial controls confined lower-skilled employees to the
infancy end of the continua, their response was condition three—no union,
almost no turnover or absenteeism, but also apathy and indifference.

Last, we believe that the model holds regardless of differences in culture and political ideology. The fundamental relationships between individuals and organizations are the same in the United States, England, Sweden,
Yugoslavia, Russia, or Cuba, A drastic statement but, we think, a true one.

✳   ✳   ✳

READING 12

THE PSYCHOLOGICAL CONTRACT

Michael H. Dunahee
Lawrence A. Wrangler*

✳   ✳   ✳

THE THEORETICAL FRAMEWORK OF A PSYCHOLOGICAL CONTRACT

The concept of a contract between the employer and his employees usually brings to mind a situation involving a union. While the union contract is
a formal written document, it bears many similarities to the psychological
contract. The formalization of a union contract, at least initially, is intended
to legalize what the employees felt was fair in the first place. Usually, employees are dissatisfied with various aspects of the work relationship and
are "ripe" when the organizer appears. Their initial demands are usually
intended to bring the "pluses" and "minuses" back into balance, as they
perceive the discrepancy. Then, over the years a union contract becomes

*From "The Psychological Contract: A Conceptual Structure for Management/Employee
Relations," *Personnel Journal,* July 1974, pp. 519–520 and 525–526. Copyright July 1974 by
Personnel Journal, Inc. Reprinted with permission.

very specific and detailed as more and more facets of work relationships are spelled out in the legally binding agreement.

Where there is no union, no such legal document exists. Yet, organizations should realize that there is a contract of sorts that binds every employee and the employer together. Like the union contract, it becomes very specific and detailed over a period of time. However, unlike the union contract it is not written. Rather, it is a psychological agreement between two parties, and it is a much broader concept than the traditional use of the word "contract" in industrial relations. It is a reality that has a great many implications for productivity and individual satisfaction. This contract is concerned with the organization's expectations of the individual employee and the employee's attempts to meet those expectations. It also includes expectations of the employee, and the employer's continuing willingness to satisfy his needs.[1]

The dynamic quality of the psychological contract means that the individual and organization expectations and the individual and organization contributions mutually influence one another. In other words, the relationships between the manager and the managed is interactive, unfolding through mutual influence and mutual bargaining to establish and maintain a workable psychological contract.[2] This contract is not written into any identifiable formal agreement between employee and organization, yet it operates as powerfully as its legal counterpart. Furthermore, it is not static; it is an evolving set of mutual expectations. Thus, neither party to the transaction, since the transaction is such a continuing one, fully knows what he wants over the length of the psychological contract, although each acts as if there were a stable frame of reference which defines the relationship.[3]

*   *   *

CONCLUSIONS

The significance of the psychological contract is simply that it is the responsibility of each individual manager to maintain a workable psychological contract with each employee under his control. This becomes a simple process when the manager realizes that the concept of a "psychological contract" is *not* a new or another managerial style, but a base on which any "managerial style" can be built. Thus, whether the manager is a practitioner of Theory X, System 3, motivators and hygiene factors, or sensitivity training, he is working under a psychological contract with his employees. Any "managerial style" will work in practice as long as there is a workable and equitable (as perceived by each party) psychological contract in existence.

If this is so, then how is such a contract brought into existence? There are several key elements to a psychological contract. Briefly they are:

1 A well structured job with clear job responsibilities. This must be mutually understood at the beginning of employment and at successive stages during the employment relationship. The job responsibilities do not have to be written; what is vital is the understanding between the two parties to the contract.

2 Continuous feedback between the two parties to the contract. Again, whether this occurs in a written format (i.e.—performance appraisal) is immaterial. What is vital is a continuous dialogue between employer and employee concerning the conditions of the contract. This must occur in an open and free environment, with either party to the contract feeling free to approach the other with contract clarifications or modifications. This can only be accomplished through management awareness that each employee brings to the work situation certain expectations. It is these expectations which must be dealt with on a daily basis through effective two-way communications. The employee must be given the opportunity to communicate with his employer about his expectations and fears. There must be a constant interchange of thoughts and feelings to avoid misinterpretation of the contract, and ultimately dissatisfaction for one or both of the parties.

It is evident that the superior and subordinate must frequently negotiate and renegotiate the provisions of the psychological contract. This is basically the communication concept, but it is also something more, because it's possible for two people to communicate to a great extent, but not communicate about the right things. It is possible for superior/subordinate communication to degenerate into a discussion of minor points that really have no significant bearing on the total work relationship. The psychological contract is more. It gets right down to the nitty gritty of man/job relationship. It is the superior saying, "This is what I'm willing to give to you in exchange for your giving the following to me and to the job." It is the employee saying, "I will give to you what you ask if you will give to me the following things." Thus, the concept of the psychological contract limits the discussion to the key and most important factors.

3 There must be a continuing emphasis on the man and the job. Currently, popular thinking of emphasizing the man (i.e.—Hertzberg) or the job (i.e.—Taylor) must be modified and combined to include the man and the job as a total system. What should result is an integrated theory of job design[7] which meshes the beliefs and practices of the industrial engineering approach to job design with that of the more recent behavioral science theories.

4 The psychological contract must be relevant to the "bottom line." That is, the compensation received for a job must have a relationship to the psychological contract that is in existence.

If the negotiations of the psychological contract throughout the organization can be documented and tracked by the corporate personnel department, it is possible to find out what kinds of things employees are looking for as important provisions to their psychological contract, and thereby gear employee relations programs to those things most desired by employees. The individual supervisor can also provide valuable feedback to the organization if he find that he is unable to negotiate satisfactory workable psychological contracts with a significant number of his employees because of an identifiable deficiency on the part of the organization. Employee relations programs aimed at solving those deficiencies can be related to profitability. For example, a simple case would be where a supervisor would say, "I cannot fill this job with competent people if we are going to pay such a low salary and ask people to work in this kind of environment. I cannot negotiate that contract." Therefore, in order to fill that job we would have to either increase salaries and/or spend money to improve the environment, and this then could be related to the bottom line.

REFERENCES

1 David A. Kolb, Irwin M. Rubin, and James M. McIntyre, *Organizational Psychology: An Experiential Approach* (Englewood Cliffs, N.J.: Prentice-Hall, 1971), p. 7.
2 Harry Levinson, *Men, Management and Mental Health* (Cambridge, Mass.: Harvard University Press, 1963), p. 36.
3 *Ibid.,* p. 37.
＊　　＊　　＊
7 William N. Penzer, *Productivity and Motivation through Job Engineering* (AMACOM: American Management Association, 1973), p. 8

READING   13

SEEING EYE TO EYE: PRACTICAL PROBLEMS OF PERCEPTION

John Senger*

Byron Cartwright, Plant Superintendent, ran his fingers worriedly through his thick, greying hair. He had a tough decision on his hands. With Frank Bauer's retirement he was faced with the problem of selecting a new fore-man for the machine shop. But instead of the usual problem of a dearth of qualified people to promote, Byron felt that he had two equally well quali-fied men to take over. Pete Petroni and Sam Johansen were both highly skilled machinists, conscientious workers, liked and respected by the other men in the department.

To help make up his mind, Byron called Pete and Sam into his office separately to talk to them about how they thought the shop should be run. He didn't actually say to either of them that he was considering them for the foremanship, but they knew why they were there. In fact the other men in the shop had been talking for some time about which one of them would succeed "Mr. Bauer." Both Pete and Sam were aware of these discussions and their own obvious qualifications for the job.

Byron even felt that either man had so much potential talent that one of them could succeed him as superintendent some day. With the new equip-ment orders in, it looked like a bright future for the machine shop—a great opportunity for the man he selected. That's what was bothering him so much. Which man?

But this was Byron's perception of the matter: opportunity, advance-ment, achievement, getting-ahead. He didn't know what was going on in-side Pete's head. Pete, as a matter of fact, was very upset by the prospect. He recognized the "opportunity" and the extra hundred bucks every month. A chance to get his wife, Marge, a car of her own and additionally, put something away in the bank. But Pete just doesn't like to tell other people what to do; he doesn't want the responsibility for planning the shop's work and keeping everyone busy. He doesn't want to be involved in paperwork—he doesn't even do that at home. Marge pays all the bills and figures the taxes and does the family planning.

What Pete loves is being a machinist. He likes the odor of the hot metal as it curls, shining away from the cutting edge of the turning tool. He likes the "feel" of the calipers as he slips them over the surface of a finished part, checking dimensions. He likes the precision, the craftsmanship, the sense of productiveness of his occupation. Pete likes to use his long, strong fingers for something besides shuffling papers. He doesn't want to tell other guys what to do. He doesn't want the responsibility for somebody else's work.

Byron Cartwright finally does make the decision to promote Sam, and he feels guilty every time he passes Pete hunched over his lathe. But, boy, is Pete relieved! He tells Byron how pleased he is that Sam is going to be the new foreman. But Byron doesn't really believe him. Pete, however, could take a deep breath for the first time in weeks without the worried tightness across his chest. Marge, his wife, is a little disappointed. She thought he deserved the promotion—he'd been there longer than Sam. But she had also been aware of Pete's edginess the past several weeks, and his noticeable relief since the announcement.

People's actions, emotions, thoughts and feelings are triggered by their perceptions of their surrounding situations. In the instance above, Byron Cartwright perceived the shop foremanship situation in one way—as a reward, a chance to get ahead, an opportunity to exercise authority, an achievement. Pete Petroni perceived it in quite a different way—as a threat, taking responsibility for others' mistakes, forcing his will on others, being separated from his lathe. Pete, while friendly and well-liked, preferred doing his own thing—alone.

Pete's perception is somewhat unusual in our "achieving society," but by no means rare. Even at that, Pete would have probably accepted the promotion. He was expected to, and Pete is enough of a child of his culture not to question that it is important to accept promotions and "get ahead," much as he might dislike it. That, after all, was his conflict.

But the point here is not about attitudes toward achievement, but about kinds of perception. The same set of circumstances can result in widely divergent perceptions. And differences in perception between managers and their subordinates make managing a tougher job.

We sense that people do see things differently. But we are at times so much a captive of our own perceptual sets that it becomes virtually impossible to see things as others see them. Part of the difference in what people perceive can be explained by the fact that they do *see different* things. Some of what is there to be seen may be physically obscured or unavailable knowledge to one perceiver. After all, Pete had never supervised and couldn't really accurately assess the situation. It might not be as bad as he thinks. But the important thing is that this information was not available to him, and this affected his perception.

Even greater differences in perception are the result of selectivity. One's senses are so overwhelmed by the mass of stimuli vying for attention that in order to carry on any directed activity we must somehow decide what we want most to attend to and block out or sublimate perceptual inputs that aren't related to that activity. If we go too far with selectivity, however, we block out some useful information and make it much more difficult to understand, or even be aware of, another's perception. Cartwright is an achiever, and to be an achiever he has to block out and sublimate distracting non-achievement oriented stimuli. In the process, he blocks out a perception of how someone like Pete Petroni sees things.

ORGANIZATION OF PERCEPTION

Selectivity is an important means of handling the perceptual overload. We further attempt to handle the myriad of perceptual inputs by various manners of organizing perceptions. A group of German psychologists, identified with the organization of perceptions, called themselves Gestalt psychologists, and placed great emphasis upon the organization and interrelationship of perceptions. No, Virginia, there was no one named Wolfgang Gestalt. Gestalt is a German word essentially meaning to organize.

Common methods of organizing perceptions include grouping, figureground and closure. These techniques which we unconsciously utilize in an effort to cope with the mass of stimuli were first identified in connection with visual perception, but they help explain nearly as well much of social perception, as will be seen in the following illustrations.

FIGURE-GROUND

When Doris Graham started to work as secretary to Myron Green in the accounting department, the whole place and the people in it were a kind of amorphous blur in her mind. Slowly, it seemed, features of her new environment began to emerge. At first she was only really aware of chief accountant Myron Green's name and face, and employment manager Dave Brigg's name and face. As she began taking dictation and typing, she began to realize Mr. Portley was an important figure to Myron Green and, therefore, to her. Otto Kowalski seemed helpful and Bill Crandell nice, but she didn't really define them against the background of the rest of the accounting department at first. Then, after a couple weeks or so, they began to emerge as people as well as important contacts in her job as secretary.

Here we see the figure-ground phenomenon at work. Certain "figures," Myron Green, Dave Briggs, Mr. Portley, Otto Kowalski and Bill Crandell emerge from the "ground" represented by the people and things that make up the rest of the Accounting Department and the company. Then, slowly, the entire department begins to emerge as a "figure" against the "ground" of the entire company. Dave Briggs was the person to emerge as a "figure." (She had memorized his name from the slip of paper given her at White Collar Employment Agency before she ever got out to the company.) He had made her feel comfortable and a little as if she belonged. But now, only several weeks later, because of lack of contact, he was fading into the general company "ground" as the Accounting Department became a more distinct entity. Here we see the phenomenon of figure-ground reversal, not unlike the visual eye trick which occurs when silhouetted designs can be seen to reverse themselves, so that when, for example, the design is looked at one way, a white vase (the figure) appears against a dark background, and when the white portion of the design is perceived as the ground, the dark portions appear to represent a new figure, two faces.

This reversal was also seen by Doris, back when she was identified by the rest of the office as attached to Mr. Green, and she herself identified with Myron Green more than she did with the others. As time went on, she and the rest of the office got to know one another better. Sometimes when she knew Mr. Green and Mr. Portley were going to be away from the office for a certain period of time, she would pass the information along to the gang and they could all relax a little. A mutual trust developed and the office group began to emerge as the figure, while Myron Green and Mr. Portley tended to become a part of the general company background.

Figure-ground, a pheonmenon long known as a visual parlor stunt, is a useful means of organizing our perceptions. It is a helpful way to think about what we see and experience and why we happen to perceive some things the way we do.

GROUPING

Stan Menke eased the Mustang to a stop in one of the lines of traffic funneling out of the South Parking Lot, and half turned to address Allyn White in the back seat. "Whaddya think the raise is going to be this time, Allyn?" "Gee, I dunno," replied Allyn. But Allyn, by now, wasn't surprised that Stan should ask him about details of important company decisions. So did Pete Petroni and Juan Fernandez, the other guys in the pool. All were older and had been with the company much longer than Allyn. Stan was a foreman and Allyn just a clerk. Juan was active in the union and knew a lot about how the wage negotiations were going. But Stan asked Allyn. Why?

Because Allyn worked in the accounting department, and the accounting department was on the second floor with the executive offices. Allyn wore a coat and tie, as did Mr. Portley and the rest of the executives. So Allyn was being "grouped" with the seat of the power in the company and was thought to be privy to important information. The fact that this was not the case didn't prevent the grouping from taking place.

This tendency to group persons or things that appear to be similar in certain ways, but not in all, is a common means of organizing our perceptions. Because these persons and things are similar in certain ways, but not all, distortion of perception can take place, as was the case with Allyn.

Grouping helps us learn, it helps us remember, it is a valuable cognitive device, but it does carry with it the not infrequent cost of perceptual distortion.

A common example of grouping in the organization: The design engineers, the industrial engineers, the production engineers, the cost people, the production control group, who may be every bit as realistic and shop-problem oriented as the people on the shop floor, are viewed by the shop as "unrealistic," "too theoretical," "head-in-the-clouds," "ivory tower" and generally unconcerned with the shop. Why? Because they operate out of the second floor, don't wear blue collars (though some wear sport shirts and no ties) and are educated differently. They are up there with the sales people, the administrative people, the office girls and others less involved with production. They are *grouped* with those less involved with the factory floor. Proximity and similarity contribute strongly to grouping. Some lack of awareness of shop problems among the engineers, cost accountants and production control people is perhaps justified, but certainly not to the degree the grouping indicates.

It should be re-emphasized, on the other hand, that *grouping,* like *figure-ground,* helps us organize and cope with our environment. Without such aids we would be overwhelmed by detail, forced to make too many decisions. When the guys in the shop see somebody wandering around in a coat and tie and assume he's somebody pretty important, they are *usually* right. It's just that more than occasionally such generalizations can be misleading if followed blindly.

CLOSURE

Otto Kowalski is big and broad shouldered. He has a thick neck and a jutting jaw. He never wears a coat in the office, and works with his sleeves rolled up, his tie pulled down and his collar open. He walks like a bear with a slight charley horse. His voice is very deep and coarse. He looks tough, although he's not tough at all. Otto is not a stevedore, but an accountant. On Saturday afternoons he listens to the symphony on FM, not the excited voice of a television sports announcer. Or he tends his roses. People who know Otto only casually find this all very confusing. Why? Because Otto's appearance, voice and bearing send out certain perceptual signals from which the observer begins building a perceptual image of Otto. Big, loud guys with rolling gaits are "jocks," right? Tough, right? Aggressive, insensitive, kinda dumb, right? Wrong. Otto isn't any of these things. He is sensitive, intelligent, not particularly athletic, and gentle. Then why is almost everyone wrong about Otto on first impression?

Because of the perceptual phenomenon of "closure." Big, muscular guys are frequently stereotyped as athletic, aggressive, tough, insensitive, and, often, not too smart. It doesn't make any difference if this is the case or not. It's a common belief and when we meet someone who looks like Otto, we start with those parts of his apparent behavior we observe, and then fill in the gaps left by those parts we don't observe; that is, we "close." It is just like seeing a line that curves around until it almost meets itself. We see it as a circle with a gap in it, not a curved line. We meet someone and like several things about him. So we go right ahead and close and assume that we also like the many other characteristics of this person. The tendency to assume that because we like someone, almost everything about him is good, is referred to as a "halo effect," a special case of closure.

And then there's Myron Green. He has a sallow complexion, round shoulders, a bald head, wears rimless glasses, terribly conservative clothes and a perpetual scowl. Myron Green is, therefore, cold, aloof, over-meticulous, inhibited, unathletic, has a "Friden for a brain," and is kind of sneaky, right? Right! You see we don't miss them all. But it's seductively easy to fill in an image based upon incomplete evidence and come up with the *wrong* answer.

Organization of our perceptions helps us cope with an overabundance of perceptual information, but it also misleads us sometimes, and we should be aware of this possibility, both in ourselves and others. We don't react equally to all stimuli that bombard us, but select or attend to certain of them.

ATTENTION: EXTERNAL FACTORS

Industrial engineer Eldon Peavey's clothes are not conservative. Some people refer to them as "far out," some say "flashy," some say "too much." But no one can really ignore them—or Eldon. And that's Eldon's intent. He wants to attract attention to himself, and we do find ourselves attending to guys like Eldon. The biggest, brightest, loudest things clamor for our attention. Over in accounting, Otto Kowalski attracts our attention because he is so big. Like six feet four, and two hundred and thirty-five. We therefore will perceive Otto and Eldon before we perceive others less large or more mousey. If two objects are competing for our attention at the same time we shall perceive the more intense first. The Safety Department was thinking about this when they painted the exposed moving parts of machines red, in contrast to the drab grey of the rest of the machine. Size and intensity are important attention-getters.

Why did the Peabody Company finally close a deal with Harry Balou, even though Harry's price on the pumps was higher than that of the competition? Largely because Harry kept beating away at them about the superiority of "his" pumps. Monthly, sometimes weekly visits. Brochures. Telephone calls. Personal letters. He constantly reiterated the advantage of the pumps. Peabody finally had to pay attention. *Repetition* has been known for a long time by salesmen, and particularly advertisers, as an excellent means of attracting attention. When the company was big on the "Zero Defects" campaign in an attempt to cut down on scrap costs and improve quality, the term was seen everywhere. Taped to machines, on every bulletin board, in the company magazine, under windshield wipers in the parking lot, on the sign board in front of the factory, over the loud speaker system, in the cafeteria. Repeated and repeated and repeated. And it did appear to have an effect on quality and scrap. Certainly everyone was aware of the campaign.

The noticeability of coats and ties in the shop was previously mentioned. And the men who go up to the office from the shop are just as noticeable because of their clothes. Contrast also attracts attention. Byron Cartwright is usually pretty subdued and quiet-spoken at the weekly foreman's meetings, so when he's upset about something and raises his voice a little, everyone snaps to. If he shouted all the time, his change of tone wouldn't be as effective. Contrast again. And it works the other way. Myron Green keeps a very close eye on everything and everyone in the accounting office, and when he steps into Mr. Portley's office or is preoccupied with someone or something else, his subordinates immediately sense it. The termination of a stimulus can be nearly as attention-provoking as its onset.

ATTENTION: INTERNAL FACTORS

"Bleeding us! Taking what rightfully belongs to us workers. How can Portley have that big fat smile on his face with his right hand stuffed so deep into my wallet? Look at this picture in the paper. Look at him! Proud that he's taking 18% profit out of the company. Bragging about it. Look at my hands. Look at your own hands. That's what makes the pumps—and the money—for this company! Not Portley sitting around on his big fat chair in his big fancy office! Not the stockholders. What have they ever done to turn out one single pump? Little old ladies doing nothing but pampering their dogs are the ones who get all that profit. Doing nothing. And their dogs eat better than I do!"

Sean O'Flaretty, fiery old unreconstructed Trotskyite, was very upset by Mr. Portley's announcement in the company paper that profits were up for the year. Holding forth to the luncheon crowd lounging on the castings pile outside the foundry, as orange peels, egg shells and "baggies" were gathered up and stuffed back into lunch boxes, Sean continued, "I ask you guys, why is it we do all the work around here and Portley and the little old ladies take all the money out of the place? It's not fair, never been fair, and one of these days you guys will quit sitting around doing nothing and demand your rightful share."

Obviously Sean—and maybe several others—was upset by the increased profit announcement. Why? Because the word "profit" to Sean is like a red flag to a bull. The word to him is filtered through a set of values which perceive profits as money taken away from the workers. Mr. Portley doesn't see it that way at all. He has a different set of filters. And he sees profits as evidence of a healthy organization, a feedback as to how well he is running the company, a source of income to those persons who had risked their savings in his enterprise, the generation of new wealth which can cause the company to expand and flourish.

The values, interests, beliefs and motivations that people have, tend to distort their perceptions. It is little wonder people have difficulty understanding one another when the values they hold cause them to perceive the same word quite differently. To Mr. Portley, "profit" is a very satisfying term; to Sean O'Flaretty, a threat.

Postman, Bruner and McGinnies tested people to find what their major value orientations were. Then for a brief millisecond they flashed the words representing these values on a screen. The time the word remained on the screen was gradually increased until it was there long enough to be recognized by all the participants in the experiment. It was found, for example, that those persons with a strong religious value orientation were able to see the word "religion" when it was on the screen for a very brief instant. Others, less religiously oriented, required that the word be on the screen for a longer period before they recognized it. Things that are important to us, those which we value, are the ones we perceive.

SET

Sam Johansen looked up from the schedule board to see Pete Petroni bending over his lathe, while beside him the tote pan for finished parts contained only a dozen of the counter-shafts Pete was making up for a special order, No. 5008. Sam stood beside Pete and watched for a while. "Say, Pete," he asked, "what's wrong with this job that it's taking you so long to get it out?" "Long?" from Pete, "I only got started on this job just this morning." "Well, then you oughta be half done. I only see twelve in the tote pan. Are the rest of them someplace else?" Sam wanted to know. "Ye gods, no, Sam," replied Pete, "whaddaya mean? It takes a little while to make all these double-oh-one cuts." ".001? Are you holding those things to a .001 tolerance?" blurts Sam. "Lemme see the print. Yeah, see here, it says .01. Right there. See?" "Oh, my pet cow!" grumbled Pete, "you mean all these little deals are only supposed to be held to .01. How could I have done that? I'll tell you how I did it. I haven't done anything to that loose a tolerance in five years. I just simply read another 'oh' in there. Oh, my pet cow!" "Yeah, that's probably it, Pete," replied Sam. "The new guys who normally do this kind of work were tied up on long runs, so I simply scheduled it over here." "I sure didn't see there was just one 'oh' behind that point. Well, yah got a dozen nice expensive countershafts, Sam. I'm awful sorry," said Pete dejectedly. Pete had a *preparatory set*, an expectancy, to see what he saw: one more order for highly skilled, close tolerance work of the kind he was accustomed to doing. We go through life having our perceptions influenced by such preparatory sets. Our previous experience prepares us to see something such as we have seen before, and it's not just a matter of past experience, either. What we need and want to see also causes a perceptual set.

We all have sets, as the result of previous experiences and as the result of personal needs and interests. What might simply look like an old letter to you or me may be an object of intense interest to a stamp collector. An automobile enthusiast may pick out the exhaust tone of a Ferrari which is lost in the cacophony of traffic noises, to someone else. To see Juan Fernandez take a couple of quick steps from his turret lathe to deposit a finished part in a tote pan and then move briskly back to start work on the next piece appears to be efficient performance, to most people. But the fellows in industrial engineering immediately identify the action as evidence of an inefficient job layout. The way they see it, *no* steps should be taken, and better yet, the part should come out of the chuck and drop immediately into a tote pan untouched by Juan. The industrial engineers have a set to perceive wasted motion, which most of us miss. We are set to perceive what we value, what we're interested in, what we are trained to see, and what we've seen before.

PROJECTION

Allyn White turned into the accounting office and was just about to close the door behind him when the tail of his eye caught a glimpse of Eldon Peavey coming down the hall behind him. He didn't close the door all the way, but left it slightly ajar. Now Eldon was quite obviously not coming into the accounting department, but was headed for his desk in the industrial engineering department two doors down. But Allyn just couldn't shut the door in his face. Why? Because Allyn felt that Eldon would perceive the act as a personal rejection. Eldon probably wouldn't even have noticed, and had he noticed, he wouldn't look upon a closing door as an act of rejection. You had to get a lot more blunt than that before Eldon felt rejected. But Allyn, in the same situation, would have felt rejected. So what Allyn was doing was *projecting* his own feelings.

We can misinterpret others' actions and motives rather markedly, as a result of projection. Our perceptions are distorted in the direction of our own needs and attitudes, which we tend to assume are needs and attitudes shared by others. If one tends to be insincere, he perceives others as being insincere. Sears and Frenkel-Brunswick found that to be true in experimentation with both American and Austrian students.

Myron Green tends to be a sneaky sort and, sure enough, he distrusts everyone else a good deal. We saw Byron Cartwright assuming that because he liked achieving, directing and taking responsibility, Pete Petroni did, too. Otto Kowalski likes to help people, and so assumes that nearly everyone else does, also, to his frequent disillusionment. Projection is a very common, internalized perception distorter. An acute form of perceptual distortion, through over-simplification, is stereotyping.

STEREOTYPE

Dave Briggs, employment manager, was working his way down through the pile of recently received application letters, when he came to a resume that caused him to emit a low whistle and reach for the telephone. Dialing quickly, Dave got Ed Yamamoto, chief engineer, on the phone. "Ed," enthused Dave, "I think I have the group leader for the bi-valve pump section." The bi-valve pump design section had been getting along without a direct supervisor since last February, when Hal Coombs had left the company. Herb Borgfeldt, senior man in the section, had twice refused the job, saying he was a designer, not a straw boss, and no one among the rest of the men in the section was experienced enough to take over as supervisor. The job really needed an expert pump designer, preferably with some supervisory experience.

"Graduated from Cal Tech, honors, three years with Livermore Radiation Lab, seven years with Cleveland Pump, last two and a half as supervisor of the bi-valve section. Lessee, two patents in own name, paper in 'Hydraulic Occlusion' at last year's SME meeting—" "Wow!" from Ed. "—and her letter says she wants to relocate here to be close to her mother, and since we are the only pump manufacturer in town, I can't see why we can't get her."

"Wait one minute," Ed burst forth, "you said 'her'?" "Yeah," replied Dave, "Ann Farmer. She apparently grew up here. Lessee, went to Horace Mann High School, where she was salutatorian and editor of the year book." "A woman!" snorted Ed. "Look, I'm no male chauvinist, you understand, but this is no job for a girl! There's lots of pressure. She'll be too emotional to run things, too illogical to think through design problems, too absorbed with details to see the big picture, too—" "W-a-i-t," protested Dave. "I'm not insisting you hire this engineer, but you did sound enthusiastic when I read her qualifications." "Well, *sure,* who wouldn't be? Cal Tech, supervisory experience, patents, papers, honors. But you hadn't told me he's a her!"

Ed is going through a form of perceptual distortion known as *stereotyping,* a form of categorization. Categorization is, of course, an extremely useful cognitive device, permitting us to handle and understand large bodies of complex information. Used restrictively, however, it causes the observer to draw conclusions from too narrow a range of information, and to generalize too many other traits from this minimal data, usually relating to the categorization of people. The way it works is for the perceiver to have established several ready-made, oversimplified categories of people who he thinks possess a few distinctive characteristics. Then he classifies the people he meets into one of these categories. The classification is made on the basis of one or a very few characteristics. The person so classified is then assumed to have all the characteristics thought to represent the category. Ed classified Ann Farmer as a woman, not as an engineer. Under Ed's "woman" classification are the characteristics of emotionalism, illogic, detail-mindedness, etc. Ed's prejudiced, but then there are those who would stereotype Ed as an engineer, which to them would tend to mean that he is unemotional, socially inept and so on. Stereotypes are usually learned young and go unquestioned. The learning usually takes place out of intimate contact with those assigned to the stereotyped category; therefore, the resulting attributed characteristics cannot help but be distorted.

SELECTIVE PERCEPTION AND BEHAVIORAL REVERSAL

Mabel Lindsey, typing pool supervisor, is aware that the girls in the typing pool don't like the clatter and din of working together in one big, noisy room; she knows they prefer doing work for one or a few people rather than typing whatever is parceled out to them, that they dislike the lack of individuality being a member of the pool implies. She is aware that Charlotte Bettendorf's loudness and exhibitionism irritate the rest of the girls in the pool, and that her own perfectionism is often hard to live with. She is aware of all these irritants *at the subconscious level.* To protect her own sanity, she has sublimated her awareness of these irritants and does not really perceive them anymore at the conscious level. If she were to consciously perceive and be sensitive to all the needs of her girls, she wouldn't have time to do anything else. In order to get on with her work, she must selectively stifle those perceptions of disturbing stimuli which don't contribute to what she perceives as important to her job as typing pool supervisor. This phenomenon has been described by Harold Leavitt as a self-imposed psychological blindness which helps persons maintain their equilibrium as they pursue their goals.

    If, on the other hand, all in the same week, first Betty, and then Claudine and then Hope were to complain about the noise, the irritation might break through Mabel's selective defense. She might then immediately burst in upon office manager Clyde Ferguson and demand that the ceiling be insulated. Selective perception with its blackout of mild disturbances, can suddenly change to acute perception when the irritant exceeds a certain threshold. At this point, the individual shifts his attention sharply and fully to the irritant. As Leavitt puts it, "The distant irritation increases to a point at which it becomes so real, so imminent, and so threatening that we reverse our course, discard the blindfold and preoccupy ourselves completely with the thing we previously ignored." The phenomenon is a complex one, because if things are threatening, they must be fended off, but in order to fend them off they must first be seen. Therefore, in order for one to protect himself from threat, he must first perceive the threat and then manage to deny to himself that he has seen it. This combination of selective perception and defensive behavior helps explain some actions on the part of others that would otherwise be extremely puzzling.

SELF-PERCEPTION

Bill Crandell, senior accountant, doesn't really think much of Bill Crandell. The company's personnel records show Bill's intelligence to be in the upper 98th percentile of the general population. He has clear-eyed good looks, with an open, ingenuous expression appealing to everyone. He moves with an easy grace. No one else can put others at their ease as readily as Bill does. His MBA is from a prestigious business school. He is vice president of Midwestern division of the CPA Association. He has an adoring wife and two happy kids doing well in Lakeside Heights Elementary School. Everyone likes Bill. But Bill doesn't like himself very much.

He doesn't feel that he's doing nearly as well as he should, professionally. He doesn't feel that he is providing adequately for his family. He can't afford household help, nor the riding lessons his daughter wants so much, and he can only just manage to rent a place at the lake for the family during the summer.

If only he had the ability to concentrate like Otto Kowalski. If he only had Myron Green's coldly efficient approach. If he could only speak in public like Eldon Peavey. If he could acquire Mr. Portley's ability to see the big picture.

So, bright, charming Bill Crandell sees himself as plodding, ineffectual Bill Crandell. He has a self-percept that is not at all realistic, but realistic or not it's the one he has. It causes him to be depressed a lot of the time, and it seems to be developing into a self-fulfilling prophecy. Bill sees himself as pleasant but ineffectual, and as a result, he is becoming pleasant but ineffectual. He doesn't extend himself much anymore. He just takes orders from Myron Green. His intelligence and training permit him to do an adequate job, but he shows very little initiative. He loves being with people because it takes his mind off his own problems. But even this tends to be self-defeating. He spends more and more time talking, and less time working. A low self-percept is a difficult cross to bear.

Low self-percept? Not so with Gordon Green. Although no brighter than Bill Crandell and not nearly as charming, Gordon thinks of himself as a real winner. He chose industrial engineering in college because he figured this would be the place he could learn more about the operation of a company faster than from any other starting point. As he saw it, he could quickly move up to chief, then shift over into line management as superintendent, then VP of production and right on up. Gordon thinks he's good and he is, though probably not *that* good. But as a result, he probes every opportunity to see where he can make his impact. Gordon's self-percept is high, but not excessively high. He *may* accomplish many of his goals. In the case where one's perception is too high, the accompanying lack of realism can often cause a poor social adjustment. It can also result in a series of too-ambitious undertakings that can't end up anywhere but in failure. Still, society probably has more to gain from those with high self-percepts than from those with low ones. The high self-perceivers will at least *try* many things, and some are bound to be successful.

READING   14

ORGANIZATIONAL PROFILE OF THE DISSATISFIED MANAGER

Lyman W. Porter*

Managers as well as rank-and-file workers have needs which they attempt to satisfy through their jobs. And, just as the case is with the rank and file, in some circumstances these needs are relatively well satisfied and in other situations they are not. Recent studies (5, 6, 7, 8) that we have carried out at the University of California, Berkeley, have been aimed at uncovering the picture of managerial satisfactions as it is related to the structure of organizations. In other words, we have been interested in finding out the types of managerial positions and the types of organizations that seem to be providing relatively the most, or, conversely, the least, amounts of need satisfaction for the manager. Also, we have been concerned with the question of which particular types of needs seem to be best or least satisfied throughout management. The present paper, then, will summarize some of these findings and discuss their possible implications.

For many years social scientists interested in the work situation (mainly industrial psychologists and industrial sociologists) concentrated their efforts on studying the poor downtrodden factory worker. Numerous investigations were made of the causes and consequences of worker dissatisfaction. Curiously, almost none of these studies ever considered the question of possible job dissatisfaction among managers. The reasons are probably many, but at least two important ones were the greater availability of rank-

*Reprinted from *Personnel Administration,* May–June 1965, pp. 6–11. Copyright 1965 by Society for Personnel Administration, 1221 Connecticut Avenue, N.W., Washington, D.C. 20036.

and-file workers for attitude studies and the assumption that if dissatisfaction existed anywhere in an organization it existed only, or primarily, at the nonmanagement level. Managers and executives "obviously" had very little to be dissatisfied about, and therefore it wasn't worth the time and additional effort in trying to measure their attitudes.

In recent years, however, managers and the managerial echelons have begun to be put under the social science microscope for intensive study. As a result, we have begun to realize that perhaps our traditional industrial psychological or sociological way of thinking of employees as being just two types—workers and managers—is a somewhat oversimplified way of looking at the manpower complement of organizations. More and more this simple dichotomy between workers and managers seems outmoded. As social scientists we are much more likely these days to differentiate among managerial positions—e.g., line positions in contrast with staff positions, middle managers as compared to top managers, and so forth. Management, in a word, is not homogeneous; there are differences among managerial positions that have consistent relationships with the job attitudes expressed by managers.

To collect our data on the job satisfaction attitudes of managers we distributed a lengthy questionnaire to several thousand managers through the facilities of the American Management Association. More than 1,900 of these questionnaires were returned, giving us a sample that was composed of managers who occupied a variety of types of positions in organizations of different size and function. Through demographic-type questions at the end of the questionnaire we were able to break down the sample in such a way as to permit comparisons between and among different groups of managers occupying particular types of positions in specific kinds of organizations.

The part of the questionnaire that provided the data to be discussed in this article contained a list of characteristics of the job (e.g., the feeling of security, the opportunity for independent thought and action, etc.) which pertained to a system of classification of needs developed by Maslow (3). This theoretical grouping of needs is based on the notion of a "hierarchy of prepotency" of needs, in which certain needs, such as physiological and safety needs, are more basic and prepotent than other needs, such as esteem needs. In our questionnaire, items were developed to tap each of 5 areas of needs: security, social, esteem, autonomy, and self-realization needs.

For each item or job characteristic, 3 questions were asked in the following rating format:

The opportunity for independent thought and action in my management position:

a How much is there now? (min) 1 2 3 4 5 6 7 (max)
b How much should there be? (min) 1 2 3 4 5 6 7 (max)
c How important is this to me? (min) 1 2 3 4 5 6 7 (max)

To obtain a measure of *dis*satisfaction, the answer to part (a) "How much is there now?" was subtracted from the answer to part (b) "How much should there be?" for each item. The larger the difference between these two answers, the greater is the presumed dissatisfaction. To gauge the importance of different needs we used the answer to part (c) of each item.

Keeping in mind the nature of our measures of need dissatisfaction and need importance, we can now turn to the basic research question: Where do we find the most frequent indications of dissatisfaction within the management parts of organizations? To answer this question we analyzed our data along three major structural properties or dimensions of organizations: organizational levels, line-staff hierarchies, and total organization size. In other words, any particular respondent could be classified by (a) his organizational level (lower, lower-middle, upper-middle, vice-presidential, or presidential), (b) the type of hierarchy he was in (line or staff hierarchy), and (c) the size of the company for which he worked (small, medium, or large).

ORGANIZATIONAL LEVEL

Of these three structural variables, the one with the greatest impact on job attitudes was organizational level. For 3 of the 5 need areas—esteem, autonomy and self-realization needs—there was a consistent and statistically significant trend for dissatisfaction to increase the lower the level of management. At first glance one might be tempted to say "Well, this is obvious and perfectly predictable in advance." However, two aspects of the findings would suggest that this is not necessarily the case. First, not all of the 5 types of needs showed increasing dissatisfaction with decreasing managerial rank. The data indicated that needs for security and for worthwhile social relationships were just as well satisfied at middle and lower managerial levels as they were to the vice-presidential and presidential levels. It appears, therefore, that being at or near the bottom of the managerial ladder is relatively disadvantageous in some but not all aspects of the job situation. Second, the strong trends that were revealed for esteem, autonomy and self-realization needs must be evaluated in light of the fact that dissatisfaction was measured by the difference between obtained and expected fulfillment. Lower-level managers were not just reporting that they were "getting less" than higher-level managers; they were, in effect, saying that what they were getting was not meeting their expectations as much as was the case of managers at higher levels. In other words, the data showed that lower-echelon managers have lower expectations than do higher-level managers, but even with these lower expectations the gap between reality and a desired state of affairs is larger at each lower organizational level.

Incidentally, it should be pointed out that differences in average age between lower-level and upper-level managers did not account for the results across organizational levels. In studying the effects of organizational level, the sample was subdivided by four age categories as well as by five management level categories. In this way it was possible to determine whether certain trends existed in one or more age groups but not in other age categories. This type of analysis indicated that the same pattern of findings relating dissatisfaction to level of position within organizations did hold up from one age group to another, and that therefore, the fact that lower-level managers are on the average younger than higher-level managers does not explain the results.

As we previously mentioned, one of the questions asked in connection with each job characteristic or item was the importance of it to the individual. The results for these questions on importance, when levels of management are compared, showed that there was some tendency for higher-level managers to attach more importance than lower-level managers to self-realization and autonomy needs, but no such tendency for the other 3 types of needs. Even for the former two types of needs the trends were less consistent than similar trends for these needs in terms of dissatisfaction. That is to say, management level seems to be more closely associated with feelings of need dissatisfaction than with need importance.

LINE AND STAFF POSITIONS

Let us now turn to the second of our structural variables—the horizontal dimension of difference between line and staff types of positions. In the past few years several writers (1, 2, 4) have contended that the traditional distinction between line and staff positions that has existed in many organizations is or should be, decreasing. Our findings, of course, cannot measure changes over time. However, they can serve to tell us whether, at the present point in time, there are attitudinal differences between managers in the two types of positions. To help us answer this question, the respondents were asked to classify themselves as working in a line job, a staff job, or a job combining line and staff responsibilities.

The results for line-staff comparisons showed that staff managers were slightly but consistently more dissatisfied than line managers. And, furthermore, managers who reported working in combined line/staff jobs showed an intermediate level of dissatisfaction, being more satisfied than the pure staff managers but less so than the pure line managers. The two need areas that produced the biggest differences in satisfaction between line and staff respondents were esteem and self-realization needs. Interestingly enough, these two types of needs were both rated as about equal in importance by the two managerial groups. On the other hand, the autonomy need area was regarded as much more important by line than by staff managers, but it was a need equally well satisfied in both groups.

Over-all, our findings based on line-staff comparisons do not at the present time seem to lend support to McGregor's recent statement that

"indirectly, perhaps, but definitely and increasingly, the industrial organization is being run by the staff" (4, p. 156). If the picture painted by McGregor
were the case, one might expect to find staff managers indicating relatively
greater satisfaction than line managers, but our results go in the opposite
direction. At the very least, our findings point to the line-staff distinction as
being one of the factors influencing managerial job attitudes. It is, however,
a much less influential factor than organizational levels.

SIZE OF COMPANY

Our third major comparison involved differences in job satisfaction attitudes between managers working in small companies versus those working
in large companies. Size probably has been studied more frequently than
any other single structural variable pertaining to organizations. Invariably,
these studies have shown that small size is associated with more favorable
job attitudes in general, and greater job satisfaction in particular. Most of
the previous research, however, has compared different size units (i.e.,
work groups, departments, factories) operating within single total organizations. This is not the same thing as making comparisons among different
organizations which vary on total size. It is conceivable that the previous
results for intra-organization size comparisons might not hold for inter-or-
ganization comparisons. One other point worth noting about almost all previous research on size is the fact that the attitudes studied were those of
rank-and-file workers rather than managers. Again, it is conceivable that
these previous findings on size might not apply if managers rather than
workers are the objects of investigation.

    To study the impact of size, we classified each of our respondents into
one of three size-of-company categories (based on the total number of
employees in the organization for which the manager was working): small
(1–499), medium (500–4,999), and large (over 5,000). As was the case with
line-staff comparisons, management level was controlled when comparisons by size were carried out. (Since there was an insufficient number of
large company presidents in the sample, comparisons by size could only
be made with each of the other four levels of management.)

    Size of company did not seem to have a clear and unequivocal rela-
tionship to perceived job satisfaction. At the two lowest levels of management, respondents working in large companies were consistently more dissatisfied in almost all need areas than were those working in small
companies; however, at the upper-middle and vice-presidential levels, the
results were reversed with the small company managers reporting more
dissatisfaction than their counterparts in large companies. (Managers in
middle-size companies, by the way, tended to report intermediate degrees
of satisfaction between the other two groups at each managerial level.)
Thus, the results seemed to indicate that in order to determine the effects
of company size on managerial job satisfaction one must specify the man-

agement level being considered. Our findings suggest that there may be a point in the organizational hierarchy, apparently a point somewhere in middle management, at which the obvious disadvantages that are frequently associated with working for a large corporation are outweighed by advantages.

Although size, in conjunction with level, seems to have some definite relationships with feeling of job dissatisfaction within management, it has relatively little association with the amount of importance attached to various needs. Only the social need area produced differences in answers between small company and large company managers, with the latter group attaching greater importance to this area. This particular finding regarding the differential importance of social needs may indicate that either more socially-oriented individuals choose to join larger organizations, or the experiences of working in larger organizations force managers in those companies to pay more attention to these needs. Our data do not permit us to determine which of these is the more likely possibility.

So far, we have been considering differences between and among different groups of managers across one or more types of needs. To complete our picture, we must say a few words about the differences in satisfaction and importance among the five types of needs across all of management. That is, which needs are perceived by the manager to be the least satisfied and the most important, *regardless* of his organizational position? This question can be quickly answered. Of the five types we studied, self-realization and autonomy needs were the two kinds of needs that were both least satisfied and, at the same time, considered to be the most important needs. This finding was almost universally true throughout management. Whether the manager held an upper-level or lower-level position, was in a line or a staff position, or worked for a large or a small company seemed to have little effect on how the needs were ranked in terms of their *relative* dissatisfaction and importance. Self-realization and autonomy needs were almost always ranked first and second, respectively, for both dissatisfaction and importance, while the other three types of needs—security, social, and esteem needs—were more or less tied for the three remaining ranks.

THE PROFILE AND SOME IMPLICATIONS

We can now briefly sketch our completed profile of the dissatisfied manager: The manager who believes his present degree of need fulfillment does not live up to his expectations is more likely to be found in lower than in higher management, is somewhat more likely to be found in a staff than in a line job, is more likely to be found in a large company than a small company if he is at a lower managerial level but not if he is in upper management, and he definitely regards his self-realization and autonomy needs as his most important but least satisfied needs in his management job.

Having proceeded to outline this profile on the dissatisfied manager, we ought to go one step further and consider some of its possible implications. The potentially most important implications, of course, concern the possible relationships to managerial performance. In other words, does managerial dissatisfaction affect managerial performance? This question can be looked at in two ways: First, given two managers who occupy the same types of positions in the same type of organization, is the relatively more dissatisfied manager a poorer performer? Second, does the absolute level of dissatisfaction in different types of managerial positions have any overall effect on managerial performance? Neither of these questions can be answered conclusively, but we can offer some speculations.

Considering the first of the two questions we have just posed, we have some unpublished data on a different sample of some 400 managers from 5 organizations which indicate that the relatively more dissatisfied manager is rated by his superior as a relatively poorer performer. In other words, there is a small (but statistically significant) negative correlation between the amount of dissatisfaction and the degree of good job performance. Given this result one might be tempted to make the hasty conclusion that the dissatisfaction is "causing" the relatively poorer job performance. Our interpretation, however, is just the opposite: we believe that it is the quality of the manager's performance which is leading to his relative degree of dissatisfaction (compared to other managers holding the same types of positions). Without going into all of the arguments for this interpretation, which will be made in detail in a future publication, our hypothesis is that in most cases the manager's relative satisfaction is based upon the rewards and opportunities given to him by his superiors and that these (rewards and opportunities given by the superiors) are in turn based on the manager's performance. If the manager is a relatively poor performer he is given relatively fewer rewards and challenging opportunities and this leads to his relative dissatisfaction. It is, of course, possible that his dissatisfaction can then affect his future performance and make it of even poorer quality than it has been. Although this certainly must occur in some situations for some managers, we doubt whether it is a frequent state of affairs.

In the preceding paragraph we have been discussing the situation involving *relative* dissatisfaction for managers in the same type of organizational position. Let us turn to the second of our questions concerning possible relationships of dissatisfaction to performance, namely, does the absolute level of satisfaction or dissatisfaction have an overall effect on managerial performance? We would argue that it may, at least indirectly. Throughout all of management there seems to be dissatisfaction with the degree to which self-realization and autonomy needs are being fulfilled. Even in positions as high as ones in upper-middle management (e.g., division managers, plant managers, major department managers), 50 and 60% of our respondents expressed some degree of dissatisfaction with regard to such items as "the opportunity for personal growth and development," "the feeling of self-fulfillment," and "the opportunity for independent thought and action." At lower levels the percentage of managers dissatisfied in these need areas was even greater. What effects could this situation have on performance? Again, we doubt whether there is any direct effect on the manager's day-to-day performance in the tasks assigned to him. However, this may not be the most important consideration. What the overall level of dissatisfaction of autonomy and self-realization needs could indicate is that organizations are not making the most of their managerial resources. In other words, the typical manager, especially at lower levels, may be under-utilized by the organization. He may be carrying out his presently assigned tasks in a perfectly satisfactory manner, *but* his organization may not be providing him with the additional challenges he is capable of handling. We have no direct evidence to offer on this point, but our findings indicate that more managers probably could be given greater opportunities for satisfying needs for autonomy and self-realization which might result in more effective performance by the organization as a whole.

REFERENCES

1 Brown, A. Some Reflections on Organization: Truths, Half-Truths, and Delusions. *Personnel,* 1954, *31* (1), 31–42.
2 Fisch, G. G. Line-Staff Is Obsolete. *Harvard Business Review,* 1961, *39* (5), 67–79.
3 Maslow, A. H. *Motivation and Personality.* New York: Harper, 1954.
4 McGregor, D. *The Human Side of Enterprise.* New York: McGraw-Hill, 1960.
5 Porter, L. W. Job Attitudes in Management: I. Perceived Deficiencies in Need Fulfillment as a Function of Job Level. *Journal of Applied Psychology,* 1962, *46,* 375–384.
6 Porter, L. W. Job Attitudes in Management: II. Perceived Importance of Needs as a Function of Job Level. *Journal of Applied Psychology,* 1963, *47,* 141–148.
7 Porter, L. W. Job Attitudes in Management: III. Perceived Deficiencies in Need Fulfillment as a Function of Line versus Staff Type of Job. *Journal of Applied Psychology,* 1963, *47,* 267–275.
8 Porter, L. W. Job Attitudes in Management: IV. Perceived Deficiencies in Need Fulfillment as a Function of Size of Company. *Journal of Applied Psychology,* 1963, *47,* 386–397.

CHAPTER 4
MOTIVATION AND JOB SATISFACTION

READING 15

THE MEANING OF MOTIVATION: THE SELF-CONCEPT

Saul W. Gellerman*

Systematic research into the motivation of people at work has had a late start, partly because the sources of other people's behavior were thought to be so self-evident that research hardly seemed necessary. It is already clear, however, that we are not nearly as knowledgeable about the reasons why people behave as they do as we once thought we were. Research results indicate that many traditional ideas about motivation are too simple, or too pessimistic, or both.

Motivation, as we commonly use the term, is our speculation about someone else's purpose, and we usually expect to find that purpose in some immediate and obvious goal such as money or security or prestige. Yet the particular goals that people seem to be striving for often turn out, on analysis, to be the instruments for attaining another, more fundamental goal. Thus wealth, safety, status, and all the other kinds of goals that supposedly "cause" behavior are only paraphernalia for attaining the ultimate purpose of any individual, which is to be himself.

The ultimate motivation is to make the self-concept real: to live in a manner that is appropriate to one's preferred role, to be treated in a manner that corresponds to one's preferred rank, and to be rewarded in a manner that reflects one's estimate of his own abilities. Thus we are all in perpetual pursuit of whatever we regard as our deserved role, trying to make our subjective ideas about ourselves into objective truths. When our experiences seem to be confirming those ideas, we are likely to feel that life is good and the world itself is just, but when we are denied the kinds of experiences to which we feel entitled, we are likely to suspect that something is drastically wrong with the world.

*   *   *

*From *Motivation and Productivity* (New York: American Management Association, Inc., 1963), p. 290. Copyright 1963. Reprinted with permission.

READING 16

AN INTERVIEW WITH FREDERICK HERZBERG: MANAGERS OR ANIMAL TRAINERS?*

MR: Maybe the best place to start is with the title of one of your Harvard Business Review *articles, "One More Time: How Do You Motivate Employees?"*

Herzberg: Historically, we have to begin with a grant I received to investigate the whole area of job attitudes when I was at Psychological Services in Pittsburgh. This particular interest originated during my days in the Graduate School of Public Health. After I got my Ph.D., I went to Public Health School and received an M.P.H. in what's called Industrial Mental Health—it's never been properly defined. When I went to Psychological Services as research director, I was interested in aspects of mental health, which certainly included job attitudes. The first stage of this research program, obviously, was to review the literature in the field, and my staff and I did a very comprehensive review of that literature. We had a bibliography of 3,000 books and articles. The result was a book called *Job Attitudes: Review of Research and Opinion,* a scholarly review of what was known on attitudes from 1900 to 1955.

However, when we had finished *Job Attitudes: Review of Research and Opinion* we could make no sense out of it. It seemed that the human being was forever debarred from rational understanding as to why he worked.

We looked again at some of the data describing what people wanted from their jobs and noticed that there was a hint that the things people said positively about their job experiences were not the opposite of what they said negatively about their job experiences; the reverse of the factors that seemed to make people happy in jobs did not make them unhappy. So what happens in science, when your research leads to ambiguity? You begin to suspect your premises. In my Public Health School days I had conceived the concept that mental health was not the opposite of mental illness; that mentally healthy people were just not the obverse of mentally sick people.

So I took a stab on the basis of mental health not being the opposite of mental illness and came up with a new concept.

MR: That was your core insight?

Herzberg: That was the core insight. I said, perhaps we're talking about two different modalities. Job satisfaction, let's use that term, and job dissatisfaction are not opposites; they are completely separate continua, like hearing and vision. If this is true, if we recognize that they are separate continua, then they must be produced by different factors and have their own dynamics. That was the stab I made.

Then I said, O.K., let's test this idea. Obviously, what had to be done was to find out what made people happy separately from finding out what made people unhappy. And you couldn't just ask people, "What do you like about your job?" That's like asking, "How do you feel?"—a nonsensical question. In fact, two questions must be asked: What makes you happy on the job? And, equally important, What makes you unhappy on the job?

MR: Your methodology was different, too, as I recall.

Herzberg: Yes, people respond for the sake of responding. And they tend to give the answers that will win the approval of the people asking the questions. You ask people a lot of questions in a public opinion poll and you get a lot of answers without any real feelings about them. Instead of asking people what makes them happy or unhappy, I thought it would be better to get at the kinds of experiences that produced satisfaction or dissatisfaction with a job. By doing these two things—by asking two questions where one was usually asked and by obtaining my data from analysis of the kinds of experiences people had rather than what they say makes them happy and unhappy—I found that the two systems existed.

With the appearance of the two systems, my thinking that what makes people happy and what makes people unhappy were not the same things was verified. In analyzing the commonalities among the factors that make people definitely unhappy or definitely happy, I found that the factors which make people happy all are related to what people did: the job content. Contrariwise, I found that what made people unhappy was related to the situation in which they did their job: job environment, job context—what I called hygiene factors. So now you have a finding that makes much more sense. What makes people happy is what they do or the way they're utilized, and what makes people unhappy is the way they're treated. That pretty much summarizes my second book, *The Motivation to Work.*

MR: Then in your third book, Work and the Nature of Man, *you searched for the psychological underpinnings for your theory.*

Herzberg: Why does job content make people happy? Yes. I had to ask that question. Further research and experience suggested what makes people unhappy is pain from the environment. We have this in common with all animals. We're all trying to adjust to the environment—to avoid pain. On the other hand, man is also different from an animal and what makes him different is that he is a determiner, whereas the animal is always determined. What man does determines his human characteristics—I cannot become psychologically taller unless I do things.

So I developed the Adam and Abraham concept, the two natures of man. As Adam, he's an animal, and as an animal he tries to avoid pain from the environment as all animals do. As Abraham, he's a human being, and as a human being he's not the opposite of an animal, he's qualitatively different. His dynamic is to manifest his talents, and the only way he can manifest his talents is by doing things that allow him to develop his potential. In short, *Work and the Nature of Man* provided the rationale for the findings of what motivated men to work.

In summary, you had a three-step sequence. First, what we knew about job attitudes from the past made no sense, so we had to look at the problem differently. Second, when the problem was redefined, a very different research result was obtained. Third, I had to explain the research results. Now I have a theory, documented with research and supported by an understanding of why the theory worked. You ask, how do you apply it? Now we come to "One More Time."

MR: How do you apply the theory? That was also the subject of the last chapter in Work and the Nature of Man.

Herzberg: "One More Time" does two things. First, it suggests that you can get people to do things as Adam, and you can get people to do things as human beings—but the ways you get them to do things are very different. To get people to do things as animals, you move them. When I respond as an animal because I want to avoid being hurt, that's movement. I called it KITA, for "kick in the ass." When a human being does something, he's motivated. The initiative comes from within. Further, I showed how the various techniques of human relations are just different forms of positive and negative KITA.

Second, I went on to demonstrate the difference between management by movement and management by motivation or job enrichment. How, by changing what people do, you motivate them to do better work. I described how job enrichment paid off handsomely in one company—AT&T, although it wasn't identified as such in the article. Since then, many other companies have applied job enrichment with equal success. That's what happened in the past.

Most of my work now consists of looking at the total problem of mankind living in society through motivation-hygiene theory. Not only must we reorient our management thinking in terms of how you motivate people for better P&L statement, but how we apply the same theory to develop a sane society. AT&T faces not only problems with dial tones and profits, but the central and more crucial problem of whether or not it can survive as a social institution in our society. Of course, the problem is not unique to AT&T. It faces every institution.

That pretty much summarizes motivation-hygiene theory, what it is, how it came to be, and where it is going.

* * *

READING 17

HOW DO YOU MOTIVATE YOUR ENGINEERS AND SCIENTISTS?

Keith Davis*

It is an old story, retold in one company after another with little more than a change in the employee's name. Joe is a qualified and capable engineer. He has the right academic training, his mind is quick, and he knows how to solve problems. Joe has a great amount of potential for creative contributions to his organization. *But* Joe does not seem to be motivated. He comes to work on time and does whatever he is told to do, but he seldom does more than that. The work he does is standard and routine. You feel sure that he is not accomplishing more than one-half of his potential, but somehow that potential is locked within him. You have not been able to release it, although you have tried several "pep talks" with him to try to get him going. Sometimes he does improve for a week or a month after one of your pep talks, but then he drops back to his old habit patterns. You do not know what to do next.

Motivation is a complex and difficult subject in all organizations, and perfection with it is not a realistic hope today. You may never be able to get Joe to be more than an average engineer! However, every year we are learning more about motivation. If you can apply this new knowledge, your *probabilities* increase for getting above-average performance from Joe. This article focuses on one of these developments in motivation which appears to be essentially important for motivating engineers, scientists, and other intellectual employees. It is called the motivation-maintenance model. First, the model will be discussed in general. Then a small-scale study of engineers will be used to verify the usefulness of the motivation-maintenance model.

* Adapted from *Arizona Business Bulletin*, February 1969, pp. 27–32. Reprinted with permission.

Although this study concerned only engineers and a few scientists, the motivation-maintenance model applies to all types of intellectual and professional work, and even to less skilled office and factory jobs to some extent.

MOTIVATION-MAINTENANCE MODEL

Frequently in the past, management has used authority and threats to achieve employee performance. This is negative motivation. As management has become more sophisticated, it has applied positive motivation by offering various "goodies"—often in the form of fringe benefits—to the employee for better performance. Though the latter approach is usually superior to the former, neither has been notably successful in getting superior performance from most employees. A number of years ago a psychologist, Frederick Herzberg, and his associates began a long-run research project to determine why. Their research eventually led to the motivation-maintenance model for producing improved employee performance.

In a classical "dog story" Herzberg has explained why earlier approaches usually produced only moderate results.[1] He explains that when he had a young puppy and wanted it to move, he kicked it (negative motivation) and it moved. In this situation, Herzberg was motivated and the dog was not. It simply moved to avoid being kicked again. After the dog had completed its obedience training, when Herzberg wanted the dog to move, he held up a dog biscuit (positive motivation). Though some persons would see this as an ideal form of motivation, Herzberg says that it is not. Again, it is Herzberg who is motivated to have the dog move. The dog simply wants a dog biscuit! In the first instance Herzberg pushed the dog, and in the second instance he pulled it; but in each case it was *Herzberg's* motivation that caused the result.

The difficulty with both the push and the pull is that they are based on a simple stimulus-response psychology. They are *external* to the dog; hence, they depend on someone else's motivation. Though these forms of motivation are appropriate for a dog, a human being is a thinking, feeling creature; therefore, an ideal form of motivation for a person is an inner motivation. While it is recognized that external forms of motivation (preferably positive) must continue to be used with people because human relationships are not perfect, it is desirable to have as much inner motivation as possible.

Inner motivation is especially necessary for creative and intellectual persons, because external motivation is less effective in reaching these higher-order brain functions. You can, for example, threaten or persuade a person to do manual work of reasonable quality, but these approaches are of little help in causing a person to be creative. Creativity and intellectual work require inner motivation. Since more and more modern jobs require creative responses, management must develop more internal motivation in employees if it is to be effective. What is needed is a built-in generator in the employee, rather than an external push or pull.

In developing the motivation-maintenance model, Herzberg and his associates conducted depth interviews with approximately two-hundred engineers and accountants in the Pittsburgh area. In these interviews the employees explained in detail situations in which they felt especially motivated and satisfied in their jobs, and other situations when they were not motivated and were dissatisfied. The researchers found that employees named different types of conditions for (1) favorable, highly-motivated job feelings, and (2) unfavorable job feelings. For example, if a feeling of achievement led to favorable feelings, the lack of achievement was rarely given as a cause for unfavorable job feelings. The result was the motivation-maintenance model of job performance, also called a two-factor model of motivation.[2]

The two-factor model sees two essentially different types of job conditions affecting an employee in different ways. The maintenance factors are necessary to prepare or *maintain* an employee ready for motivation, somewhat in the way that a machine must be maintained for top-quality performance. When the maintenance factors are absent or poorly provided, an employee is dissatisfied. When they are reasonably present, an employee is brought up to a neutral state ready to be motivated; but they do not by themselves bring motivation. They primarily prevent dissatisfaction and prepare the employee to respond to motivation.

For many years managers have been wondering why their fancy personnel policies and elaborate fringe benefits did not increase employee motivation. The maintenance concept explains why. These benefits are needed to maintain the employee (prevent dissatisfaction), but they are not strong motivators. Maintenance factors include job security, company policies, normal salary, working conditions, and human relations with supervisors and peers.

Looking now at motivational factors, when they are present on the job, they strongly motivate the employee. They give the employee a built-in generator. When they are absent, the employee is unmotivated, but not necessarily dissatisfied. There is only a neutral state, provided that maintenance factors are still available. Motivational factors include achievement, recognition, advancement, the work itself (challenge, feeling of service to humanity, and so on), possibility of growth, and responsibility held.

In a nutshell, the maintenance factors explain why a worker quits (dissatisfaction), and the motivational factors explain why a worker who stays with an organization is—or is not—strongly motivated. It can also be observed that the maintenance factors are primarily external rewards provided by the employer or others. The motivational factors, on the other hand, are primarily internal rewards provided by the employee's job performance. They are something personally earned. They are a built-in generator.

The motivation-maintenance model has been criticized extensively.[3] For example, maintenance factors do sometimes motivate employees and motivational factors sometimes play a maintenance role;[4] but the key fact remains that each factor *predominantly* works in one direction only. The model is also less applicable to blue-collar work,[5] and there are some weaknesses in the research method. In spite of its limitations, however, the model has much reality in motivating engineers and scientists.[6]

THE PHOENIX STUDY

In order to test the applicability of the motivation-maintenance model, thirty-six engineers in one electronic firm were surveyed. Since only a few engineers in one firm were surveyed, one cannot generalize widely from the data; but the data do illustrate the usefulness of the motivation-maintenance model as a guide to management thinking. The Herzberg method was used, except that the engineers were surveyed by questionnaire rather than by interview. Questionnaires were distributed directly to the engineers rather than through their employer, and they were also returned directly. Through use of this method, it was hoped that there would be less hesitancy in reporting any dissatisfying job conditions.[7]

Each engineer was asked to report in detail a situation resulting in strongly favorable feelings toward the job and another situation resulting in strongly unfavorable feelings about the job. The replies were then factor-analyzed according to Herzberg's list of sixteen job factors in order to determine which factors were mentioned in each incident. Some incidents included more than one factor, in which case both factors were listed. For example, an engineer may have reported an unusual achievement and a special recognition for it. In this incident, the job factors of both *achievement* and *recognition* were recorded.

Results of the survey are reported in Table 1. The table shows the percentage of times that each job factor is reported in a job incident. If a factor is reported in favorable incidents more than in unfavorable incidents, then its *predominant* direction of force is as a motivator. An item is a maintenance factor when it is reported more in unfavorable incidents.

In general, the data support Herzberg's original study and other studies of this type. The same six factors which appear as motivators in earlier studies are reported as motivators in this study.[8] These factors are achievement, recognition, advancement, work itself, possibility of growth, and responsibility. The remaining factors are reported as maintenance factors with the exception of salary which is neutral (11 percent favorable and 11 percent unfavorable). Even this item does not differ greatly from other motivation-maintenance studies. In a composite of twelve studies covering 1,685 employees, salary as a maintenance factor is only 2 percent higher than as a motivator; so normal salary in general does not seem to be predominantly either a motivator or a maintenance factor.[9] In other words the

Table 1   Percentage of Job Factors Appearing in Favorable and Unfavorable Job Incidents Reported by Thirty-six Engineers

Job factor	Percent favorable*	Percent unfavorable*
Motivational Factors (ranked in order of favorable appearance)		
Achievement	55	8
Recognition	33	8
Advancement	22	3
Work itself	19	11
Possibility of growth	14	8
Responsibility	14	3
Maintenance Factors (ranked in order of unfavorable appearance)		
Company policy and administration	5	44
Supervision—technical	8	22
Interpersonal relations—supervisor	5	19
Salary	11	11
Interpersonal relations—peers	0	8
Job security	0	8
Personal life	0	5
Working conditions	0	5
Interpersonal relations—subordinates	0	0
Status	0	0

* The percentages for each column total more than 100 percent because more than one factor could appear in a single incident.

number of favorable feelings about salary is approximately offset by an equal number of unfavorable feelings about salary.

Motivators

With regard to motivators in Table 1, achievement is reported as a cause of favorable feelings by 55 percent of the engineers, which is approximately seven times as often as lack of achievement is a cause of unfavorable feelings. This means that achievement is a very important factor in the motivation of engineers. Most of the responses describing this factor reported the successful completion of a problem or assignment by the individual or by that person's group. It is evident that these engineers were motivated by problems to solve and by measurable milestones along the way which signified successful completion of an assignment. This interpretation is further confirmed by the fact that recognition for a job well done ranks second in number of items mentioned for favorable feelings. In summary, the engineers reported that they are motivated by opportunity for achievement; and, when they do achieve, they are further motivated by recognition accorded for their work.

With regard to advancement, it is mentioned as a cause of favorable feeling seven times as often as lack of advancement is a cause of unfavorable feelings. Moreover, only 3 percent mention lack of advancement as a cause of unfavorable feelings, compared with an average of 12 percent in the twelve similar studies mentioned earlier. This relationship reflects the fact that my study was made in a fast-growing company which had adequate opportunities for advancement and possibly also that the promotion policies of the firm were considered fair.

Advancement is especially important because of its long-lasting motivation effects. Research with more than seven hundred bank employees has shown that advancement ranks first among all motivators in causing favorable feelings which last over one year.[10]

With regard to intrinsic motivation from the work itself, 11 percent report dissatisfaction from the work itself. This percentage is much higher than the average of 4 percent reported in the twelve other surveys mentioned earlier. The relatively high dissatisfaction with this factor suggests that some engineers in this company feel they are loaded with unnecessary routine that could be performed by non-engineers.

Possibility of growth and responsibility also were primarily motivators with a small proportion (14 percent) of the group surveyed.

Maintenance Factors

As in other motivation-maintenance studies, company policy and administration ranked first as a cause of unfavorable feelings, being mentioned by 44 percent of the group.[11] Occasionally, when persons read data about the large number of unfavorable feelings concerning company policy and administration, they conclude that employees with these feelings are against company policy in general. However, extensive research with motivation-maintenance factors does not support this type of conclusion. With rare exceptions employees recognize the need for policies and procedures, and they do not object to most existing policies. What employees typically are saying is that policies and procedures often seem to stand in the way of better job performance, hence they frequently do generate unfavorable job feelings. Employees want to get the job done; so when a policy or procedure stands in their way, they resent it, even though they recognize the need for it. They also feel that policies are sometimes interpreted unfairly, or are not flexible enough to allow for their individual situation. In other instances they feel that reports and procedures uselessly consume valuable job time which could be better used.

Both job relations and interpersonal relations with supervisors rank next, as they do in the average of the twelve similar studies mentioned earlier. In my study, however, interpersonal relations with one's supervisor is given stronger emphasis as a unfavorable factor. This suggests that engineering supervisors in the firm studied perhaps need additional training in supervising people.

The remaining maintenance factors were given minimum emphasis, which suggests that there are two fundamental keys to maintaining employees ready for motivation. These keys are (1) sound company policy and (2) supervisors with both job and behavioral competence. As a matter of fact, these two keys will primarily produce the conditions for the six motivational factors; so in the final analysis the motivation-maintenance model could be substantially looking at two sides of the same coin.[12]

CONCLUSIONS

The motivation-maintenance model is a useful guide to improving the motivation of engineers and scientists, as well as other higher-level, white-collar employees. It improves our understanding of why some job factors primarily reduce job dissatisfaction, while other factors primarily increase motivation. It also helps us understand why large doses of fringe benefits and other "goodies" often do not motivate higher-level employees, though these benefits may keep the employees from quitting or prepare them to be motivated by capable leadership.

This small-scale study of engineers generally confirms the applicability of the motivation-maintenance model to engineering groups. Even though the sample is small, the distribution of job factors is quite similar to the average of twelve other studies covering 1,685 persons in various higher-level occupations. The study also indicates strong achievement motivation among the engineers; therefore, job conditions that can offer challenges and opportunities for achievement should be especially motivating.[13]

The model and the study together show that engineering managers should be able to improve retention and motivation of their people by providing a reasonable base of maintenance factors topped with motivational factors to the strongest extent possible.

REFERENCES

1 Frederick Herzberg, "One More Time: How Do You Motivate Employees?" *Harvard Business Review,* January–February, 1968, p. 54.
2 Frederick Herzberg, Bernard Mausner, and Barbara Synderman, *The Motivation to Work* (New York: John Wiley & Sons, Inc., 1959).
3 For example, see O. Behling, G. Labovitz, and R. Kosmo, "The Herzberg Controversy: A Critical Reappraisal," *Academy of Management Journal,* March, 1968, pp. 99–108.
4 For further details see Paul F. Wernimont, "Intrinsic and Extrinsic Factors in Job Satisfaction," *Journal of Applied Psychology,* February, 1966, pp. 41–50; and Ronald J. Burke, "Are Herzberg's Motivators and Hygienes Unidimensional," *Journal of Applied Psychology,* August, 1966, pp. 317–21.

5   Michael R. Malinovsky and John R. Barry, "Determinants of Work Attitudes," *Journal of Applied Psychology,* December, 1965, pp. 446–51.

6   For another study covering engineers see M. Scott Myers, "Who Are Your Motivated Workers?" *Harvard Business Review,* January–February, 1964, pp. 73–88. This study was made at Texas Instruments, Inc., an electronic firm. For a related study covering scientists and their managers see Albert B. Chalupsky, "Incentive Practices as Viewed by Scientists and Managers of Pharmaceutical Laboratories," *Personnel Psychology,* Winter, 1964, p. 392.

7   The survey was conducted by Donald A. Kunz, a graduate student, as part of a continuing study of the motivation-maintenance model.

8   Statistical tests for significance were not made because of the small number surveyed.

9   Herzberg, *op. cit.,* p. 57. These studies included many other occupations than engineering, such as lower-level supervisors, professional women, agricultural administrators, nurses, teachers, accountants, and Finnish foremen; consequently the data are comparable only as an indication of the general applicability of the motivation-maintenance model.

10 Keith Davis and George R. Allen, "Length of Time That Feelings Persist for Herzberg's Motivational and Maintenance Factors," *Personnel Psychology,* Spring, 1970 pp. 67–76.

11 The importance of this factor is confirmed in another type of study covering 3,691 scientists and research managers throughout the United States. Among their top three problems they listed both inappropriate management practices and too much time required for administrative trivia, although there was some variation according to type of industry in which they were employed. See Howard M. Vollmer, *Work Activities of Scientists and Research Managers: Data from a National Survey* (Menlo Park, Calif.: Stanford Research Institute, 1965), pp. 46 and 90.

12 Further discussion of the motivation-maintenance model is found in Keith Davis, *Human Relations at Work: The Dynamics of Organizational Behavior* (3rd edition; New York: McGraw-Hill Book Company, 1967) especially Chapters 3 and 17.

13 Achievement motivation is generally shown to be high among engineers. For a general discussion of achievement motivation see David C. McClelland, *The Achieving Society* (Princeton, N.J.: D. Van Nostrand Company, Inc., 1961).

READING   18

THE MANAGEMENT OF BEHAVIORAL CONTINGENCIES

Fred Luthans
Robert Kreitner*

It looks as if the path leading out of the jungle of management theory may
follow the guideposts of contingency theory—linking quantitative, behavioral, and systems concepts and techniques with economic, technical, environmental, and social variables affecting the organization and its people.

To date, there are only two well known contingency approaches to
management. The first, dealing with organizational design, resulted from
the work in the 1950s of Joan Woodward, who discovered the impact that
technology had on the British manufacturing firms she studied. Later, Paul
Lawrence and Jay Lorsch found an environmental impact on the internal
structures of the organizations they studied, and today, this contingency
approach to organization design is widely accepted in theory and practice.
Second, Fred Fiedler developed a contingency model of leadership effectiveness, which he found to be a function of the style—human relations-
oriented or task-directed—and the situation—favorable or unfavorable.
Fiedler objectively and systematically assessed the dimensions of particular situations according to position power, acceptance by subordinates,
and task definition and concluded that in very favorable and very unfavorable situations the task-directed leader was most effective, whereas in
moderately favorable and moderately unfavorable situations a human rela-
tions-oriented leader was most effective.

Here, we propose a third contingency approach, identified as organizational behavior modification, or O.B. Mod. Based on operant learning
theory and the principles of behavior modification, this approach assumes
that organizational behavior depends on its consequences, that organizational behavior with reinforcing consequences tends to increase in frequency, whereas organizational behavior with punishing consequences
tends to diminish in frequency. To be sustained, specific responses must
be reinforced or strengthened by immediate environmental contingencies.
The important point is that the relationship between behavioral responses
and their environmental consequences involves the concept of contingency, which this article discusses in terms of how it can be applied to the
management of human resources.

* Reprinted by permission of the publisher from *Personnel*, July–August 1974, pp. 7–16.
© 1974 AMACOM, a division of American Management Associations.

THE BEHAVIORAL CONTINGENCY CONCEPT

Contingency denotes a relationship in which something is dependent on chance or on the fulfillment of a condition. Behaviorists such as B. F. Skinner borrowed the word contingency for scientific behavioral analysis, and even in that context contingency denotes a dependent relationship, between observable behavioral events and certain environmental conditions. According to Skinner: "An adequate formulation of the interaction between an organism and its environment must always specify three things: (1) the occasion upon which a response occurs, (2) the response itself, and (3) the . . . consequences." The interrelationships among the three elements (occasion, response, and consequence) form a behavioral contingency. The process of breaking complex behavior down into the identifiable contingencies is called functional analysis.

The concept of behavioral contingency can be clarified by a simple example in a company. An employee's specific behavior of standing at the pay window will lead to the consequence of being paid only if it is payday. Hence, payday sets the occasion for the behavioral response of standing in front of the pay window and that, in turn, leads to the consequence of being paid. Tracing the dependent relationships backward, being paid is contingent (dependent) upon standing at the pay window, which is contingent upon its being payday. The three elements necessary for the existence of a behavioral contingency are present: occasion, response, and consequence. According to the premises of operant learning theory, behavior changes as a result of such a contingency. In other words, the employee learns to associate certain consequences with a specific behavioral response and a particular setting or occasion. He learns to stand in front of the pay window on payday, because that specific behavior in that particular setting consistently leads to the reinforcing consequence of being paid.

The three elements that collectively form a behavioral contingency and lead to its behavioral outcome are illustrated in Figure 1, in a schematic called the A→B→C functional analysis (antecedent—a, behavior—b, and consequence—c). It depicts the functional and empirically validated inter-

Figure 1   Behavioral Contingency
A ──→ B ──→ C   Functional Analysis

Antecedent ──→ A	Behavior ──→ B	Consequence C	Behavioral outcome
The previous occasion upon which a particular emitted behavior led to a specific type of consequence.	Specific and observable, quantifiable in terms of frequency of occurrence.	Reinforcing, punishing, or non-existent.	An increase or decrease in the frequency of the behavior or its extinction.

face between a specific behavior and its immediate antecedent and consequent environment. (In this context, environment includes the total human and nonhuman surroundings.)

Through past experience, organizational participants learn to associate specific consequences with various environmental settings. As a result, environmental cues are generated, which tell a person when certain behaviors have a good chance of leading to specific consequences. For example, the supervisor's office is often associated with punishing consequences. Thus, isolating the contingencies through functional analysis may help explain why otherwise creative, active, and outgoing work group members frequently become sullen upon entering their supervisor's office. The office cues, or signals, a high probability of forthcoming punishing consequences, because it has been the scene of punishing consequences in the past.

As has been shown, contingent consequences may be reinforcing, punishing, or nonexistent. Reinforcing consequences, as the term implies, strengthen replications of the preceding behaviors upon which they are contingent. Punishing and nonexistent consequences weaken preceding behaviors. (The word nonexistent may be misleading. What is meant is that, as a general rule, behavior with no contingent consequences tends to be repeated with decreasing frequency and eventually will disappear—that is, the nonreinforced behavior is extinguished.) In all cases, the consequence must be contingent upon a particular behavior if it is to alter the frequency of that behavior in the future.

The key to functionally defining the three general types of behavioral contingencies lies in measuring the frequency of the behavioral outcomes. For example, as a result of certain contingencies, does an employee punch in on time more or less often? If the frequency of the behavior increases, the contingency can be properly called reinforcing. A punishing or nonexistent contingency is responsible for a drop in frequency of behavior.

INDIVIDUALITY OF BEHAVIORAL CONTINGENCIES

Whether reinforcing or punishing, contingencies are idiosyncratic; one employee's reinforcer may be another's punisher. A manager who assumes that specific consequences will affect all employees' behavior in the same way falls into a commonly unheeded trap. A contingent manager must learn what turns individual subordinates on and what turns them off. Again, the common denominator in this determination is frequency of specific behavior outcomes, so a manager using the contingency approach must discerningly monitor the frequency of job-related behaviors that are to be changed.

There can be no rigid definitions of reinforcers and punishers. Only after observing behavior and charting its frequency can a contingency manager know whether a particular consequence was reinforcing or punishing. And managers cannot assume their subordinates will be reinforced or punished by the same consequences that they personally find reinforcing or punishing. To repeat, one employee's reinforcer may be another's punisher. The contingency manager must examine an employee's *reinforcement history*. What contingent consequences have reinforced or punished an employee's particular job-related behaviors in the past? If a particular behavior increased in frequency, then the contingent consequence was reinforcing. Conversely, if a specific behavior that led to a particular contingent consequence decreased in frequency, the consequence must have been punishing. Behavior that had no contingent consequence diminished in frequency from lack of reinforcement. By carefully examining reinforcement histories a contingency manager can use the past to predict the utility of future behavioral strategies.

Managers who absolutely accept or reject money as a motivator do not understand the contingency concept. Money *may* be reinforcing, but many modern compensation methods, especially those based on time, such as the hourly wage or fixed salary, are noncontingent. This means they do not tie specific pay to specific work.

If money is not seen as a motivator, careful functional analysis of present work behavior may turn up alternative reinforcers on the job. For example, if the task variables permit, contingent time off can be an excellent alternative reinforcer. A contingent time off plan makes early time off contingent upon satisfactory, stable performance. Task standardization is a necessary element of such a plan. In a routine task situation the employee seeks a direct connection between each piece or unit of work and getting off early.

There are many indicators on the current scene of the need for an alternative to more, more, and more money. For one, in the recent Chrysler settlement the major issue was mandatory overtime, not more money. While doing preliminary field research on contingent time off, the authors came across an interesting illustration of the desire for time off in lieu of more money. A manufacturing firm instituted a yearly plan whereby each of more than 85 production department employees doing routine tasks was given the option of taking 40 hours whenever he wished or selling back the unused time for money at the end of the year. (It should be noted that this plan supplemented a generous sick leave program.) To date, 73 percent of the maximum allowable time off has been taken; only three employees have not taken any of their 40-hour allotment. The contingency manager would take advantage of such a powerful reinforcer by making it contingent upon performance.

BEHAVIORAL CONTINGENCY MANAGEMENT BY O.B. MOD.

There are several steps in the process of becoming a contingent manager. The O.B. Mod. model shown in Figure 2 contains five essential steps: (1) identify, (2) measure, (3) analyze, (4) intervene, and (5) evaluate. The first step involves the identification of behavior problems. Inferred internal states and processes such as attitudes, needs, and drives have little utility in this approach. The behavior problems must be reduced to observable behavioral events that are measurable in terms of frequency. With behavior frequency as the basic datum, the contingency manager is prepared to measure the target behavior, shown in Step 2. The frequency of the problem behavior can be graphed as a function of occurrence and time; subse-

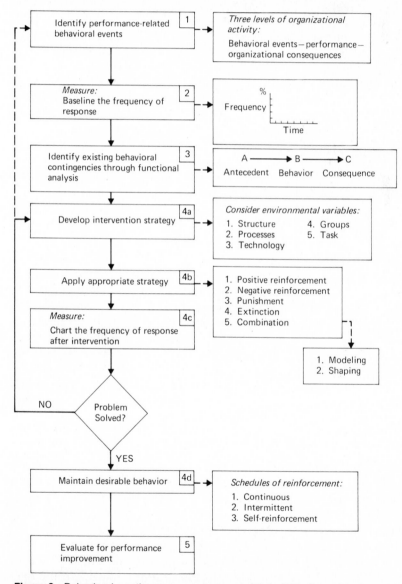

Figure 2 Behavioral contingency management. (*Note: This figure is adapted to agree with Fred Luthans and Robert Kreitner,* Organizational Behavior Modification, *Glenview, Ill.: Scott, Foresman and Company, 1975, p. 70. Copyright 1975. Reprinted with permission.*)

quent assessment of the effectiveness of various intervention strategies is possible only with an adequate baseline measure.

The functional analysis in Step 3 indicates what antecedent and consequent events are presently paired with the target behavior. Before any intervention is attempted, it must be ascertained what is maintaining the present behavior—a difficult but critical step. After consideration of relevant organizational environment variables, a contingency management intervention strategy is developed (Step 4a) and applied (Step 4b). When the intervention strategy is implemented, the frequency of the target behavior is again monitored by measuring (Step 4c). Random time samples may be utilized here to cut down the time-consuming work of charting relatively high-frequency behaviors.

Next, the question of whether or not the targeted behavioral problem has been solved is answered. If the problem behavior maintains its baseline frequency or even accelerates, then another strategy (recycle to Step 4a) must be developed or the entire process, starting with Step 1, must begin again. If the targeted behavior diminishes in frequency, then attention must be turned to maintaining its low frequency (Step 4d).

Often, especially when a combination of strategies (such as reinforcement plus extinction) is used, alternative desirable behaviors must be shaped and reinforced as the problem behavior diminishes. The maintenance of alternative desirable behavior starts on a continuous schedule and gradually moves to an intermittent schedule; self-reinforcement is the ultimate maintenance goal.

In the last step (5), an evaluation is made of the overall effectiveness of the particular contingency intervention strategy. Each contingency manager must build his own empirical data base to help determine the efficiency of various intervention strategies. What works for a manager in one situation may not work in another because of numerous complex human and organizational variables. And strategies that work for one manager may not work for another. As the manager's O.B. Mod. contingency skills develop, however, he will find that more and more behavioral performance problems are adaptable to the logic of the sequential steps shown in the model.

WHAT O.B. MOD. IS AND IS NOT

As the direct or indirect controller of much of a subordinate's work environment, the practicing manager is in a position to use O.B. Mod. in predicting and changing behavior by managing evironmental contingencies. It is important to note that the contingency manager manipulates the environment, not the person; the employee self-adjusts to his environment. Since a fundamental aspect of O.B. Mod. is the systematic management of contingencies, haphazard and intuitive managerial techniques not only are of little utility but actually may interfere with the process. Implicit in the systematic management of subordinates' work contingencies is self-control.

The manager himself is a significant part of an employee's immediate work environment, so in a sense environmental control by the manager is often tantamount to self-control. Noncontingent reinforcement and/or arbitrary and capricious reinforcement are the antithesis of sound contingency management.

It is very essential to distinguish systematically managed contingencies from accidental contingencies, which are a way of life in the typical work situation. Suppose a foreman in an exceptionally good mood bursts into the shop and socially reinforces several machine operators with solicitious conversation, jokes, and laughter. Suppose, too, that one of the operators was taking advantage of unsupervised time to work on a personal project and that in the past, the foreman has come down hard on those who used company time and tools for personal work. With the boss laughing and joking right in front of the illegal work, the worker might assume the foreman was aware of it but no longer cared. If the frequency of the operator's personal work on shop time increases, because the exuberant but thoughtless foreman had created an accidental reinforcing contingency, an already mistaken situation worsens a week or two later when the foreman severely reprimands the operator for misusing company time and property. The net result is a frustrated, confused employee who is completely out of tune with his work environment.

With systematically managed contingencies, on the other hand, the manager puts the worker in tune with his work environment. At the outset, care must be taken to structure the employee's expectations appropriately through relevant skill development, work environment orientation (an explanation of contingencies), and understandable instructions. Then the manager should systematically reinforce all desirable behavior and ignore or, as a last resort, systematically penalize undesirable behavior. As was said earlier, new behaviors have to be shaped by reinforcing successively closer approximations to the target behavior. Once the behavior is established, continuous reinforcement is called for and later, intermittent reinforcement at frequencies that will lead to improved performance and organizational goal achievement.

An O.B. Mod. approach is not the easy way to manage human resources—in fact, it may turn out to be the most difficult. However, preliminary research findings by the authors and their associates are very encouraging. A pilot program in a manufacturing firm was able to significantly increase the performance of every supervisor trained in O.B. Mod. Follow-up research in a number of organizations is currently in progress.

In contemporary management, human problems override technological ones. Chronic absenteeism, turnover, and quality control flaws on the operative level and diminished commitment, innovation, and leadership in the managerial ranks collectively constitute a major human resource challenge to management. For over two decades various behavioral approaches have been explored and used, with spotty results. Yet, realistic analysis shows that virtually all of today's human resource problems are behavior/performance problems. A systematic and reliable process that modifies behavior through control of environmental contingencies presents itself as a promising way to go.

With operant learning theory and the principles of behavior modification serving as the base, O.B. Mod. allows the practicing manager to get back to basics. Empirically validated and consistent man-environment contingencies enable this move to be disciplined, in contrast to the traditional bits-and-pieces approach. The impetus for O.B. Mod. contingency-based management of human resources must come from the practicing managers themselves, but the promise of potential payoffs in improved job performance should be a strong incentive for them to tackle it.

READING 19

OPERANT CONDITIONING IN ORGANIZATIONAL SETTINGS: OF MICE OR MEN?

Fred L. Fry*

The relatively old theoretical concept of operant conditioning has become a relatively new management technique. Operant conditioning, basically a product of Skinnerian psychology, suggests that individuals will emit responses that are rewarded, and will not emit responses that are either not rewarded or are punished. Recent authors have attempted to introduce— or re-introduce—the concept into the organizational setting. A current series of studies introduces the terminology organizational behavior modification, or O. B. MOD., and represents for the most part work by the authors who explain their theories in the preceding article.

It cannot be argued that operant conditioning is an invalid psychological concept. Work done over several years demonstrated that animals can be "taught" to respond in certain ways in order to obtain food or avoid shock. Similarly, work has been done in mental hospitals and with individ-

---

* Reprinted by permission of the publisher from *Personnel*, July–August 1974, pp. 17–24.
© 1974 AMACOM, a division of American Management Associations.

uals who cannot function normally. Research has shown that autistic and deaf children and certain others can benefit from operant conditioning methods. The recent work, however, has focused on operant conditioning as a viable technique for management of workers in an organizational setting. Although conceding that operant conditioning, in general, is indeed a viable concept and can influence behavior in certain cases, this author maintains that it is far overrated as a management technique. Operant conditioning in organizations, or O.B. Mod., can explain why many management problems exist; but it does not provide an acceptable alternative.

O.B. Mod. is criticized here on the following points: Organizations are more complex than Skinner Boxes; men are more intelligent than mice; O.B. Mod. is simply behavioral Taylorism; O.B. Mod. requires continuing reinforcement; and most of the effects supposedly the result of successful O.B. Mod. can be explained as a "Hawthorne effect."

ORGANIZATIONS VS. CONTROL BOXES

A classic statement is that "the biggest thing wrong with psychology is that experiments were made using either white rats or college sophomores. White rats aren't human and college sophomores are questionable." Control boxes are univariate tests of the stimulus/response relationships. Organizations are open systems with multivariate, multiple-cue, multiple-response situations. Expectancy theorists suggest that a single act may result in many different outcomes, each with its own valence. In operant conditioning terminology, this is saying that any response will elicit many rewards and punishments. We might consider, for example, the sources of rewards. The individual may be rewarded by the formal system, a variety of subgroups within the formal system, various informal groups in and out of the organization, and his own family. In essence, we can say that every social system to which an individual belongs is a potential provider of rewards. Thus, we can say that people will respond in ways that are rewarded, but management is only one of many sources of rewards. Stated formally, a persons' "reward set," the totality of all possible rewards for a given response, contains a large number of elements, many of which are beyond the control of the organization.

Somewhat separate from the multiple-reward problem is the complexity of the reward problem. A given reward may be highly valued by one individual but not valued at all by others. In fact, what is perceived as reward by one worker may be perceived as punishment by another. Suppose, for example, that two managers are "rewarded" for their favorable responses with a $1,000 bonus. One manager may consider this a significant reward and will continue his favorable responses. The second manager may see the bonus as punishment, rather than reward, perhaps because of perceived inequities or unfulfilled expectations of a larger bonus. The supervisor has a tough enough task to reward workers appropriately, but in addition, under O.B. Mod., he faces the problem of not knowing in advance how a given reward will be perceived. To complicate things, the consequence that the supervisor may see as punishment (or lack of reward) may be interpreted as a reward by the worker. (The authors of the preceding article assert that punishment is not punishment unless the act is extinguished. There is, in their view, no such thing as punishment that did not work. Although this may be a semantics problem, the concept is important. The question will be avoided here by using the phrase "perceived punishment.")

Coupled with the problem of the complex organization is the problem of lack of control over rewards by the organization. Luthans and Lyman suggest that "there are many reinforcers available to any supervisor," yet they themselves suggest that neither the pat on the back nor monetary rewards can be effectively used over time, and suggest that the supervisor should "make better use of the reinforcers that are already at hand on the job." But in considering this we are forced to ask just what reinforcers are "already at hand" for the supervisor. Certainly, one of the biggest problems in organizations is that pay, promotion, and fringe benefits are, in most cases, tied to seniority, not performance. They are almost totally beyond the control of the supervisor. When one ponders possible long-term reinforcers, he may discover that there really are very few reinforcers readily available to the supervisor. Only a small portion of an individual's reward set is controllable by the organization.

MEN MORE INTELLIGENT THAN MICE

In this writer's opinion, O.B. Mod. insults the intelligence of all but the most ignorant worker. Throughout the literature on O.B. Mod. the case is made that workers and supervisors should understand the importance of being contingent—the reinforcement should come as soon after the act as possible. Although this may be important for animals, man has developed an ability to remember the past and to expect from the future. The absurdity of this emphasis on immediacy to underscore contingency of rewards is illustrated by an example used by Luthans and Kreitner. To impress upon a worker the relationship between being late for work and docked pay, they suggest we "walk him to the pay section, where he observes the clerk calculate and subtract the pay adjustment." Presumably, the worker will better understand the relationship and therefore will repent.

If we consider the example, however, we see not only absurdity but a fallacy of O.B. Mod. First, we can assume that most workers are already aware of the relationship between lateness and docked pay. Thus, walking the individual to the pay section will do little if anything to increase the awareness of the relationship. The only punishment that might be derived from the exercise is the embarrassment of "being walked to the pay section," somewhat reminiscent of the gradeschooler being walked to the principal's office for a minor infraction. Second, many of us who underwent that "punishment" in our younger days will recall a certain amount of status associated with the act—enough in some cases to outweigh any punishment meted out. In the example given, rewards might include the chance to make acquaintance with the payroll clerk, not to mention the additional time off the job while making the trek. The example shows clearly, then, not how O.B. Mod. can be used effectively, but how it can backfire.

In the introductory sentences of this paper, I pointed out that operant conditioning has worked well with animals, mental patients, autistic children, and others. Here, I have said that the approach insults the intelligence of the average worker. The human subjects with whom it has worked well have had in common some impairment in their ability to fully utilize their intelligence. Even the literature dealing with the hard-core unemployables suggests that, because of environmental, cultural, or educational deficiencies, they cannot function properly. From these experiences I infer that operant conditioning may be a very valuable aid in working with those who either have a low intelligence or cannot properly use their intelligence. It is a logical extension of this observation to conclude that operant conditioning works best for those whose level of functional intelligence allows them to see only very short-run, lowest-order needs, as described by Maslow. These individuals may have the capability of perceiving only the close relationship between an act and an immediate reward. The general run of workers, we hope, are beyond that stage and, if so, O.B. Mod. cannot be expected to have the pervasive results claimed for it.

BEHAVIORAL TAYLORISM—AN OLD CONCEPT REVISITED?

Frederick Taylor is best remembered as the proponent of breaking jobs into minute parts, possibly recombining them into more efficient groupings of actions, and rewarding workers on the basis of their completion of these subparts. O.B. Mod. does essentially the same thing, if the theory is to be optimally effective. To an extent, then, it is nothing new, but simply an old concept revisited. Craig Schneier gives an example of O.B. Mod. in action (*Personnel,* May–June 1973). In this case, hard-core workers were originally given short on-the-job training in the overall procedures involved in packing a product. Turnover and dissatisfaction were severe. Then the jobs were studied and broken down, and training was given in each step of the process. Better results were achieved and credit was given to behavior modification, but couldn't credit have been given just as well to scientific management? Couldn't we say that the improved learning was the result of better, more efficient training and analysis of the tasks? I do not mean to disparage operant conditioning, but I do mean to suggest that the approach should not be considered a new and innovative management technique.

Since O.B. Mod. is very close to Taylorism, one of the criticisms of Taylorism also applies to it—that both are inherently autocratic methods of management. In both situations, the individual responds strictly because of the incentives (or avoidance of punishment). Responses are made without cognitive acceptance of the task. Most modern management theory, however, holds that higher levels of performance should be gained through rational acceptance of tasks, rather than through use of rewards and punishment.

THE PROBLEM OF CONTINUING REINFORCEMENT

If we accept the operant conditioning view that individuals will not emit responses unless rewarded, we then see the need for some type of continuing reinforcement. Psychologists tell us that intermittent reinforcement is preferable to fixed-interval reinforcement, but if we do not reward undesirable behavior and only intermittently reward desirable behavoir, the worker on the job may have a very low level of total reward, especially if the reward is monetary. Proponents of O.B. Mod. might suggest we make the reward larger, but that is not practicable in an organization that sets a fixed monetary total for workers. We have, then, not the ability to control total rewards, but only the ability to divide it up. Further, if the supervisor is to be able to administer these rewards appropriately, we must assume that he is closely monitoring performance in order to know how often to reinforce the response. Few supervisors have that much time available, and research has shown that, by and large, workers do not want close supervision anyway. If we don't monitor the operations closely, however, our intermittent reinforcing interval may become too spaced, and unintentionally the result will be extinction of the desired response. If we try to convince ourselves otherwise—that the worker will continue the response even if we forget or do not have time to adequately reinforce the behavior—we are violating the basic premise of operant conditioning, which is that only rewarded behavior will be emitted.

Related to the need for continuing reinforcement is the rewarding of approximations of the desired response. According to the theorists, we should reward responses that are successively closer to the desired response, yet, again, if we reward the approximations, it is those approximations that will be repeated, and the desired response will not be forthcoming. Nor do we have any real assurance that the next response will be closer to the desired response. Moreover, the intermittent reinforcement technique may complicate the problem. If, by chance, a response is exactly the desired but happens not to be reinforced, the subject should logically conclude that the response was *not* the desired one, and he will then focus more precisely on an earlier approximation. Thus, we have reinforced error.

DO EXTERNAL REWARDS EXTINGUISH INTRINSIC REWARDS?

A side effect of the problem associated with the need for continued reinforcement has recently been reported. O.B. Mod. theorists imply that, over time, the intrinsic rewards associated with work may surface and the need for externally provided rewards will be reduced. In effect, the job itself becomes a reinforcer. Edward Deci found, in an experimental situation, that utilizing external rewards actually *decreases,* not increases, the intrinsic motivation to do the task (*Human Resource Management,* Summer 1973). He suggests that relating tasks either to punishment or reward reduces the intrinsic pleasure of the task to such an extent that the task, rather than becoming a reinforcer per se, becomes dependent upon the reward.

For example, many professors do research in addition to teaching, and find it intrinsically rewarding. In many cases the external rewards are few, but through the research we feel we are "self-actualizing." In schools that typify the "publish or perish syndrome," however, teachers are under pressure to produce (or leave because of the pressure). Here we have people who no longer see research as intrinsically satisfying, because external rewards are explicitly tied to it. And to make matters worse, the university or department may find itself tied to the external rewards because it can no longer keep the active researcher *unless* he is paid for it. If the worker becomes dependent upon external reward, the organization is similarly dependent upon external rewards.

A last criticism of O.B. Mod. in the area of continuing reinforcement has to do with what can be called the diminishing marginal utility of rewards. As the total amount of rewards increases, the incremental utility of those rewards decreases. We see this in very well-paid workers who no longer value salary increases highly. We see it in the individual who continually receives the "pats on the back" for whom those pats on the back no longer mean much. We also see it in the worker who is frequently threatened with being fired, and for whom those threats are no longer threatening. People tend to become immune to the level of rewards or punishments they receive. If good performance is to be achieved, the reward set must take on successively higher values. If rewards are not increased, the propensity to perform well decreases.

HAWTHORNE EFFECTS MISINTERPRETED AS O.B. MOD. RESULTS

The Schneier example cited earlier suggested that hard-core workers improved performance when O.B. Mod. was used. This may have been the case; however, a more likely explanation, in addition to the one suggested earlier, is that performance improved because of the attention given to the workers. The process of breaking the tasks into subparts and rewarding completion of each forced the supervisors to give more attention to the workers. And since the work had to be checked to see if a reward was merited or not, the interaction by itself cannot be considered as a reward in the O.B. Mod. sense. Any theorists, and particularly the O.B. Mod. advocates, should be very careful about construing the Hawthorne effect as support for their theory.

To summarize, operant conditioning, or O.B. Mod., can be a useful tool, but it has been overrated as a management technique. The empirical evidence has shown primarily that operant conditioning can work with animals and those humans who, for one reason or another, cannot make full use of their intelligence. When it comes to management, operant conditioning is basically a univariate method applied to a multivariate organization and to individuals whose "reward set" contains elements not controlled by the formal organization. O.B. Mod. is in actuality a revival of Tayloristic management and has some of the same problems as scientific management. To be effective, O.B. Mod. requires continued reinforcement, a need that in turn causes other problems, including the possible reduction of intrinsic motivation. Last, many of the results attributed to O.B. Mod. could be the result of Hawthorne effects.

CHAPTER 5
INTERPERSONAL RELATIONS

READING 20

A STUDY OF THREE MANAGEMENT GROUPS

Chris Argyris*

1. The Supremacy of Pattern A

The three top-management groups manifested the same interpersonal relations, group dynamics, and organizational norms even though they represented (a) three different corporations with very different technologies, products, and external environments; (b) at three significantly different points in time; (c) with three significantly different histories and accomplishments in organizational development activities.

All the management systems were dominated by pattern A (see Figure 1).

These findings remained consistent almost regardless of the size of the group, the topic being discussed, the conditions of the external environment, the degree of organizational development that had occurred, and the attitudes people held toward individual and group development.

Figure 1   Behavior in Pattern A

Behavior tending to be more frequent	Behavior tending to be less frequent
Owning up to ideas	Owning up to feelings
Conforming to ideas	Individuality of ideas
Concern for ideas	
Openness to ideas	
Not helping others to express ideas and feelings	Helping others to express ideas
Inconsistent behavior	Consistent behavior

Rarely observed behavior
Experimenting with ideas or feelings
Concern for feelings
Trust of ideas or feelings
Helping others to express their feelings

*From *Management and Organizational Development: The Path from XA to YB,* (New York: McGraw-Hill Book Company, 1971), pp. 132–134. Copyright 1971. Reprinted with permission of McGraw-Hill Book Company.

The only major deviation from these findings was observed when a group was under stress. Under stress, groups seemed to magnify their pattern rather than change it. For example competitive, aggressive groups became even more competitive and aggressive.

For the reader interested in individual differences, we report that few seemed to be observed. Different executives tended to behave in the same manner when participating in the group meetings. It is as if the group settings attracted, coerced, or required certain kinds of behavior. The behavioral requirements tended to fit the expectations of the executives because our society programs people with "pyramidal values" which tend to result in pattern A. Executives are especially susceptible to these values.

This does not mean that individuals did not differ along characteristics such as openness, experimenting, etc. It is our hypothesis that they did differ, but one of the consequences of pattern A was to coerce them to suppress many of their differences. For example, many executives were interviewed who reported having strong feelings during the meetings, yet they did not express them because the expression of feelings was viewed as inappropriate. The few who reported they had expressed their feelings seemed, to the observers, to have done so in an intellectualized manner.

*   *   *

READING   21

SOME BENEFITS OF INTERPERSONAL CONFLICT

Richard E. Walton*

The premise of this volume is *not* that interpersonal conflict in organizations is necessarily bad or destructive, and that third parties must inevitably try to eliminate it or reduce it. In many instances, interpersonal differences, competition, rivalry, and other forms of conflict have a positive value for the participants and contribute to the effectiveness of the social system in which they occur. Thus, a moderate level of interpersonal conflict may have the following constructive consequences: First, it may increase the motivation and energy available to do tasks required by the social system. Second, conflict may increase the innovativeness of individuals and the system because of the greater diversity of the viewpoints and a heightened sense of necessity. Third, each person may develop increased understanding of his own position, because the conflict forces him to articulate his views and to bring forth all supporting arguments. Fourth, each party may achieve greater awareness of his own identity. Fifth, interpersonal conflict may be a means for managing the participants' own internal conflicts.

*　*　*

READING　22

THE CONCEPT OF TRANSACTIONAL ANALYSIS

Eric Berne*

STRUCTURAL ANALYSIS

Observation of spontaneous social activity, most productively carried out in certain kinds of psychotherapy groups, reveals that from time to time people show noticeable changes in posture, viewpoint, voice, vocabulary, and other aspects of behavior. These behavioral changes are often accompained by shifts in feeling. In a given individual, a certain set of behavior patterns corresponds to one state of mind, while another set is related to a different psychic attitude, often inconsistent with the first. These changes and differences give rise to the idea of *ego states.*

In technical language, an ego state may be described phenomenologically as a coherent system of feelings, and operationally as a set of coherent behavior patterns. In more practical terms, it is a system of feelings accompanied by a related set of behavior patterns. Each individual seems to have available a limited repertoire of such ego states, which are not roles but psychological realities. This repertoire can be sorted into the following categories: (1) ego states which resemble those of parental figures (2) ego states which are autonomously directed toward objective appraisal of reality and (3) those which represent archaic relics, still-active ego states which were fixated in early childhood. Technically these are called, respectively, exteropsychic, neopsychic, and archaeopsychic ego states. Colloquially their exhibitions are called Parent, Adult and Child, and these simple terms serve for all but the most formal discussions.

*　*　*

* From *Games People Play*, New York: Grove Press, Inc., © 1964 by Eric Berne. Reprinted with permission.

TRANSACTIONAL ANALYSIS

The unit of social intercourse is called a transaction. If two or more people encounter each other in a social aggregation, sooner or later one of them will speak, or give some other indication of acknowledging the presence of others. This is called the *transactional stimulus.* Another person will then say or do something which is in some way related to this stimulus, and that is called the *transactional response.* Simple transactional analysis is concerned with diagnosing which ego state implemented the transactional stimulus, and which one executed the transactional response. The simplest transactions are those in which both stimulus and response arise from the Adults of the parties concerned. The agent, estimating from the data before him that a scalpel is now the instrument of choice, holds out his hand. The respondent appraises this gesture correctly, estimates the forces and distances involved, and places the handle of the scalpel exactly where the surgeon expects it. Next in simplicity are Child-Parent transactions. The fevered child asks for a glass a water, and the nurturing mother brings it.

*   *   *

READING 23

TRANSACTIONAL ANALYSIS FOR MANAGERS, OR HOW TO BE MORE OK WITH OK ORGANIZATIONS

V. P. Luchsinger
L. L. Luchsinger*

A contribution from current nonfiction literature and psychoanalysis that will have a great impact on the management profession is Transactional Analysis. Introduced over a decade ago by Eric Berne, M.D., Transactional Analysis provides the manager with an analytical tool that can help him understand the most complex phenomena in management—the interactions between manager and employee.

* From *MSU Business Topics*, Spring 1974, pp. 5–12. Reprinted by permission of the publisher, Division of Research, Graduate School of Business Administration, Michigan State University.

Many managers have already been exposed to the principles of Transactional Analysis. The subject received much publicity in 1964 when the book *Games People Play* by Dr. Berne climbed to the top of the popular reading lists. A more current title on the best seller lists, *I'm OK—You're OK,* by Thomas A. Harris, M.D., explores the subject of Transactional Analysis in greater depth.

A possible reason for the delay in applying the principles of Transactional Analysis to management has been the fascination and popularity of games, perhaps to the extent of faddism. Dr. Berne wrote *Games People Play* in response to requests for more information about games. Games overshadowed the subject of Transactional Analysis. The more recent book by Dr. Harris is directed at the general public and has not been identified as a manual for managers. Practitioners and scholars of management are looking at the possible contributions of Transactional Analysis to the improved practice of management.

Harris describes Transactional Analysis as a method for examining a transaction between two people "wherein 'I do something to you and you do something back' and determining which part of the multinatured individual is 'coming on.' "[1]

Transactional Analysis (this term will be capitalized when referring to the entire system) can be divided into four component parts: structural analysis, transactional analysis (the analysis of a specific transaction), games analysis, and script analysis. The four areas are briefly described to provide a reference for the language and terms of Transactional Analysis.

STRUCTURAL ANALYSIS

Structural Analysis is concerned with the "segregation and analysis of the ego states."[2] Berne identified the three ego states as the Parent, Adult, and Child. (When referred to as ego states these terms are capitalized.) They are represented in the following diagram and in the literature on Transactional Analysis as P-A-C.

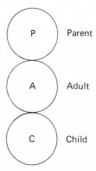

The three ego states are not concepts like Freud's id, ego, and super-ego They are phenomenological realities, based on real world behavior. Although lines separate the ego states, the lines are not barriers. A healthy person is able to move from ego state to ego state.

The Parent ego state is that body of recordings in the brain the reflects the unquestioned events or imposed external re-straints perceived by a person during his early years of life. Characteristics of a person acting in the Parent include being

(P) overprotective, distant, dogmatic, indispensible, and upright. Physical and verbal clues that someone is acting in the Parent include the wagging finger to show displeasure, reference to laws and rules, and reliance on ways that were successful in the past. Parent inputs to behavior are taught.

The Adult, assuming the rationality of man, is the information seeker and processor. It functions as a computer processing new data, making decisions, and updating the data in the original recording of the Parent and Child. The Adult is characterized by

(A) logical thinking and reasoning. This ego state can be identified by verbal and physical signs which include thoughtful concen-tration and factual discussion. Adult inputs to behavior are rea-soned.

The Child ego state is the body of data that is recorded in the brain as a result of experiences during the first five years of life. Characteristics of the Child include creativity, conformity, de-pression, anxiety, dependence, fear, and hate. Physical and ver-

(C) bal clues that a person is acting in the Child are silent compli-ance, attention seeking, temper tantrums, giggling, and coyness. The Child is also characterized by non-logical and immediate actions which result in immediate satisfaction. Child inputs to behavior are laden with feeling and emotion.

ANALYSIS OF TRANSACTION

Analysis of transactions (T.A.) is the technique for examining a transaction or interaction between two people and the ego states involved. Recogniz-ing the ego states of the two people involved in the transaction can help a person communicate and interact more effectively.

Transactions can be classified as complementary or non-complemen-tary. Transactions are complementary when the lines of communication between the two people are parallel. For example, a person in the Parent state interacting with the Child of another person would be involved in a complementary transaction if the response from the second person origi-nates from the Child and is directed to the Parent. Both are acting in the perceived and expected ego states. Complementary transactions are im-

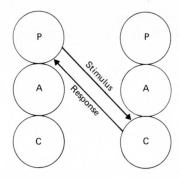

portant because they indicate completed communications or interaction between the two people.

A non-complementary or crossed transaction occurs when the interactions do not have common origination and terminal ego states. The following example shows the stimulus directed from the Adult to the Adult being crossed with a response from the Parent to the Child. In this situation the communication is crossed and ineffective.

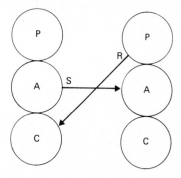

It is possible for the stimulus to originate in any of the three ego states and be directed to any of the three ego states. This produces nine possible types of complementary transactions.

The number of non-complementary transactions varies depending upon how one describes the ego states and the forms of contamination-mixed ego that might appear in an ego state. At this point we turn the subject of non-complementary transactions back to the psychoanalyst and consider only complementary transactions.

GAMES ANALYSIS

Berne defines a game as an ongoing series of complementary ulterior transactions progressing to a well-defined, predictable outcome.[3] Games are basically dishonest and self-defeating as the interactions are not honest requests but gambits or moves in a game.

Some of the games managers play include "You're a Professional Now" and "The Man at the Bench." Articles about the games managers play have been written by Ronald J. Burke (1968),[4] Joe Kelly (1968),[5] and Curits J. Potter (1969).[6] However, a more serious pragmatic approach has been offered by J. V. D. Meininger (1973).[7] The purpose of this article is to avoid the popularity of games and focus upon the analysis of transactions.

SCRIPT ANALYSIS

Script analysis is an examination of transactions and interactions to determine the nature of one's life script. It is a method for uncovering early decisions on how life should be lived. When confronted with a situation, a person acts according to his script which is based on what he expects or how he views his life position. In a sense, man's behavior becomes quasi-programed by the script which emerges out of life experience.

Life Positions

Transactional Analysis uses the four following classifications to describe the life positions that a person holds for himself and others:

I'm not OK, You're OK
I'm not OK, You're not OK
I'm OK, You're not OK
I'm OK, You're OK[8]

A person lives his life in one of these life positions. Such a life position or view of himself and others affects how he will interact with them. Only the "I'm OK, You're OK" position is considered healthy.

MANAGER-EMPLOYEE INTERACTION

Managers and employees continually interact with each other. Accepting the idea that the manager initiates most of the interactions and transactions, examples of the nine complementary transactions are used to illustrate manager-employee interactions.

Manager in the Parent Ego State

The manager in the Parent is typified by the "I'm OK, You're not OK" life style. He will be a source of admonitions, rewards, rules, criticisms, and praise. He can be expected to thrive on power and use personal successes or the failures of others as justification for a course of action.

Parent-Parent Transaction The Parent-Parent transaction can be beneficial in cases where the employee joins forces with the manager and supports the manager. An executive secretary who dictates orders in the absence of the manager provides an excellent example of the co-operative or supportive Parent-Parent transaction. There are disadvantages to this type of transaction. Consider the situation in which the manager and employee are competing for the position of "Best" Parent. In such a situation the employee will promote his own ideas and orders rather than those of the manager.

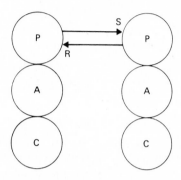

If the manager and employee have opposing recordings in the Parent, they will work against each other.

Another disadvantage can be found when the employee communicates with the manager. In the example below the employee is agreeing with the Parent in the manager without really engaging in a meaningful dialogue.

Manager: "An effective maintenance repair program always reduces costs."

Employee: "I always say that a stitch in time saves nine."

Both the Manager and employee agree on a basic philosophical issue that a maintenance program can save money. No facts were mentioned or introduced in this transaction.

Parent-Adult Transaction The manager in the Parent ego state will have difficulty with the employee in the Adult ego state. In such transactions the manager will be frustrated because the employee will not perform as directed. The manager may consider the employee an incorrigible smart aleck. The employee will be condemned for not respecting the voice of authority and experience.

The employee will be frustrated by the manager's failure to act in the Adult.

The dialogue below provides an example of this transaction:

Manager: "An effective maintenance repair program always reduces costs."

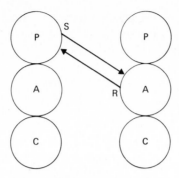

Employee: "The problem is the new supplier. Maintenance and production records show that his parts don't last as do the parts from Acme Company."

The manager, using the standard cliche about effective maintenance, finds himself confronted with facts. In the Parent he is not able to accept this "smart alecky" reply and the idea that his successful method from the past may be wrong. The employee will not be able to accept a slogan in place of facts and records. Due to the mutual frustration, such a relationship will not be productive or long lasting.

Parent-Child Transaction   Perhaps the ideal situation when the manager is in the Parent is for the employee to be in the Child. The manager will find this advantageous in that he will have a loyal and dutiful employee who will respect him and follow his orders.

This ideal situation has disadvantages. The manager may feel that his employees are incapable of assuming responsibility. The manager continually lives with the possibility that someday one or more of the employees in the Child will change from compliance to tantrums.

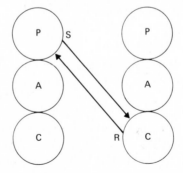

The employee finds such a transaction advantageous in that it eliminates much responsibility and pressure. Acting in the Child prevents much conflict and provides for ease in operation. The employee suffers from this interaction in that he must surrender his Adult. He doesn't think and his job must be routine so he performs only as directed. The example below uses the same stimulus used in the previous example:

Manager: "An effective maintenance repair program always reduces costs."
Employee: "Yes, sir."

In this transaction there is no meaningful feedback for the manager except that he has a loyal employee who agrees. Although a real problem may exist, the employee finds it easier to perform as directed than to bring the factual information to the attention of the manager.

A closing note on the Parent: The Parent is not the best ego state for the manager to exercise in his daily interactions with employees. The limitations outweigh the advantages. Although it may be useful and required in some situations, it limits effectiveness and denies the use of current facts.

Manager in the Adult Ego State

The manager in the Adult tries to reason out issues, clarifies and informs employees of issues, and has concern for facts, figures, and human needs. His life style generally is the "I'm OK, You're OK" position.

Adult-Parent Transaction   While the manager attempts to use the information he has processed, the employee in the Parent prefers to use cliches and rules of the past. Citing past successes or proven methods, the employee will not favor change or progress even when it is based on facts, figures, and logic.

In such a transaction the employee will try to control and dominate the manager by using the Parent ego state. This transaction style can be effective only on a temporary basis. It can be used to help a new manager understand the rules and guidance under which the employees operate. The employee in the Parent can be accepted for the facts that he can provide.

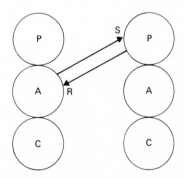

There are many disadavantages to this transaction style. The classic example is the Parent's resentment of the young college graduate in a managerial position. The older and experienced employees who know what is to be done and how to do it do not want the newcomers to change the ways of old. The manager in this situation must remain in the Adult. He must not compete by entering his Parent nor retreat by entering the Child. The manager must remind the employee who is the manager and who is the employee.

The employee in the Parent can create other difficulties for the manager if other employees in the Child recognize and accept the employee in the Parent. The employee in the Parent may have better interaction with the other employees. Acting in the Parent the employee may discount all of the benefits that management attempts to use while introducing change. An employee in the Parent can create hostile feelings toward managers in the Adult.

A typical Adult-Parent transaction is provided below:

Manager; "The new supplier's parts will last if we make the adjustments as directed in his technical instructions."
Employee: "We never had this problem with the old supplier. You just can't beat the old reliable supplier."

In this example the manager is attempting to communicate with facts and logic. The employee is not concerned with facts or instructions but with past success. Although there may be valid reasons for changing suppliers, the employee in the Parent refuses to accept facts or technical instruction.

Adult-Adult Transaction An ideal manager-employee relationship exists in the Adult-Adult. Complementary transactions in these states are very effective because both persons are acting in a rational and businesslike manner. Data is processed, decisions are made, and both parties are working toward the solution. Satisfaction is gained from the solution rather than the manager having a dutiful employee or the employee only trying to please her boss.

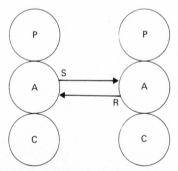

There are some inherent disadvantages to the Adult-Adult transactions. The elimination of the Child can make the transactions dull due to the lack of stimulation that the child can provide. The Adult-Adult level may prevent decisions from being reached due to the rational data-processing procedures. This may prevent the manager and employee from meeting deadlines. When a decision has to be made but cannot be reached because of lengthy discussions, the manager may have to make the decision in the Parent.

An example of the manager in the Adult directing a stimulus to an employee who responds in the Adult demonstrates the exchange of facts.

Manger: "The new supplier's parts will last if we make the adjustments as directed in his technical instructions."

Employee: "We found that using his recommended tension level reduced our product acceptance by 6 percent."

Such a transaction, based on facts and figures, may help the manager and the employee identify the real problem. Both the manager and the employee want a solution based on facts.

Adult-Child Transaction   The Adult-Child interaction can be effective if the manager is aware of the ego state of the employee. In such interactions the manager can allow the employee in the Child to be creative.

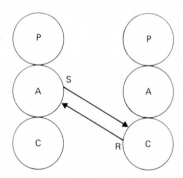

The manager in the Adult often assumes that his employees are also in the Adult. Very often this assumption prevents the manager from recognizing that the employee is in the Child ego state. This creates a situation that will be frustrating to the manager and the employee. The manager will find himself assigning more responsibility than the employee can handle. The manager becomes frustrated when the work is not done and the employee becomes discouraged because he cannot do the work.

Another disadvantage is the irrational responses that an employee in the Child will give to the manager in the Adult. An example is provided.

Manager: "The new supplier's parts will last if we make the adjustments as directed in his technical instructions."

Employee: "I hate to make that darn adjustment. I get my hands dirty."

In this example we can see the Child rebelling against the factual Adult.

A closing note on the Adult: The Adult is capable of providing efficient analysis of information. The efficiency of the Adult must be increased when it is supported by the strength of the Parent and the creativity of the Child.

Manager in the Child Ego State

The manager in the Child ego state will have very little to contribute in the form of effective management. Although creativity is one of the characteristics of the Child, the role of manager requires more than just creativity. Creativity alone does not offset the disadvantages of being anxious, fearful, conforming, and acting on whims.

The manager in the Child is defensive. He assumes the basic "I'm not OK, You're OK" life position.

Child-Parent Transaction   An employee acting in the Parent will control the manager in the Child. The Parent will be strong and overbearing on the Child. The manager will yield to the employee. If the Child in the manager objects or does something that is not approved by the employee in the Parent, the manager is punished. The employee holds threats of punishment over the manager. The threats may be of ridicule, loss of popularity, or demotion.

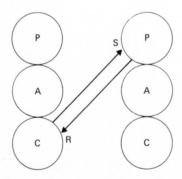

An example of the manager and employee illustrates the Child-Parent transaction.

Manager: "I'll show them that we cannot operate with inferior parts. Stop the machines."

Employee: "If you stop the machines the men don't get paid. The men will not like you if they stop getting paid."

The manager in the Child state, seeking an immediate solution, decides on an irrational course of action. The employee in the Parent condemns the manager. The Child in the manager might be expected to ask the employee, in the Parent, what to do. This results in the employee making the decisions.

Child-Adult Transaction Sometimes it is possible for an Adult employee to control the manager in the Child. More often, the employee will become discouraged by the manager. The manager who makes his decision on whims, fancies, and emotions will pose a threat to the employee who wants to interact with the manager in terms of facts. A major disadvantage of this transaction style is that the organization may lose many good employees.

The following example provides an Adult response to a Child stimulus.

Manager: "I'll show them that we cannot operate with inferior parts. Stop the machines."

Employee: "Stopping the machines will not solve the problem. Our repair and production records should be shown to the purchasing department."

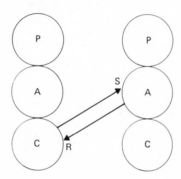

In this example the manager's Child has provided a solution to the problem. The employee, responding in the Adult, attempts to present a solution based on facts.

Child-Child Transaction The manager in the Child interacting with an employee in the Child will not last very long in an organization that reviews performance. The manager is not capable of leading or directing and the employee is not able to follow. The manager will act on whim and fancy and the employee will be the same. The chances for effective transactions and performance are as great as might be observed with two small children building sand castles. All will go well as long as all is going well.

The effectiveness of the Child-Child transaction can be seen in the example below:

Manager: "I'll show them that we cannot operate with inferior parts. Stop the machines.

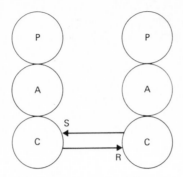

Employee: "Good. We will have a good time with real long coffee breaks."

The manager is taking action that will halt production. In his Child he is having a tantrum. The employee, also in the Child, appreciates the immediate satisfaction.

A closing note on the Child: The manager in the Child ego state may prove to be a liability to the organization. In the Child a person cannot be expected to make decisions or provide the direction and guidance that is expected of a manager.

Hints for Managers

The effective manager should be able to analyze transactions with employees. Transaction Analysis provides him with a theoretical framework within which to examine the interactions with employees. The manager should be able to identify the ego states from which both parties are interacting. A better understanding of himself, employees, and interactions with others will make the manager more comfortable, confident, and effective. He will be aware of ego states and seek the proper ego states when interacting with employees.

Transactional Analysis is a managerial tool. It should help the manager in his daily transactions with employees.

REFERENCES

1 Thomas A. Harris, M.D., *I'm OK—You're OK* (New York: Harper & Row Publishers, Inc., 1967), pp. 12–13.
2 Eric Berne, *Transactional Analysis in Psychotherapy* (New York: Grove Press, 1961), p. 22.
3 Eric Berne, M.D., *Games People Play* (New York: Grove Press, 1964), p. 48.
4 Ronald J. Burke, "Games Managers Play," *Personnnel Administration,* September 1968, pp. 52–57.
5 Joe Kelly, "Executive Defense Mechanisms and Games," *Personnel Administration,* July 1968, pp. 30–35.
6 Curtis J. Potter, "Games Managers Play," *Supervisory Management,* April 1969, pp. 29–33.
7 J. V. D. Meininger, *Success Through Transactional Analysis* (New York: Grosset & Dunlap, Inc., 1973).
8 Harris, *I'm OK—You're OK,* p. 43.

CHAPTER 6
LEADERSHIP AND SUPERVISION

READING 24

LEADERSHIP IN ORGANIZATIONS OF THE FUTURE

Paul R. Lawrence

Jay W. Lorsch*

The viable multi-organization, like the effective organizations of today, will require strong leadership to provide direction to the enterprise. Unlike many of today's effective organizations (*e.g.,* the high-performing container organization), however, the effective multi-organization will require not just a few such leaders, but many of them. All the evidence of this and other research points to the need for multiple leadership in these complex organizations. As they cope with heterogeneous and dynamic environments, the issues and knowledge involved become too complicated for only a few leaders to understand. Simpler organizations dealing with more homogeneous and stable environments can be led by a few great men, and this gives these leaders great prominence. They fit the picture of the romantic hero. The fact that the multi-organization needs many leaders may reduce the unique prominence of any of them, but this must not obscure the importance of each. All these leaders will have to face the tensions of making commitments of great consequence. These will be the modern heroes, even if they are not conspicuous to the general public.

*   *   *

*From *Organization and Environment: Managing Differentiation and Integration* (Homewood, Ill.: Richard D. Irwin, Inc., 1967), pp. 243–244. Copyright 1967. Reprinted with permission.

READING   25

HOW DO YOU MAKE LEADERS MORE EFFECTIVE? NEW ANSWERS TO AN OLD PUZZLE

Fred E. Fiedler*

Let's begin with a basic proposition: The organization that employs the leader is as responsible for his success or failure as the leader himself. Not that this is a new insight—far from it. Terman wrote in 1904 that leadership performance depends on the situation, as well as on the leader. Although this statement would not be questioned by anyone currently working in this area, it also has been widely ignored. Practically all formal training programs attempt to change the individual; many of them assume explicitly or implicitly that there is one style of leadership or one way of acting that will work best under all conditions. Most military academies, for example, attempt to mold the individual into a supposedly ideal leader personality. Others assume that the training should enable the individual to become more flexible or more sensitive to his environment so that he can adapt himself to it.

Before going further let's define a few terms. I will confine my discussion to *task groups* rather than the organization of which the group is a part. Furthermore, we will assume that anyone who is placed in a leadership position will have the requisite technical qualifications for the job. Just as the leader of a surgical team obviously has to have medical training, so a manager must know the essential administrative requirements of his job. We will here talk primarily about training *as a leader* rather than training as a specialist. The effectiveness of the leader will be defined in terms of how well his group or organization performs the primary tasks for which the group exists. We measure the effectiveness of a football coach by how many games his team wins and not by the character he builds, and the excellence of an orchestra conductor by how well his orchestra plays, not by the happiness of his musicians or his ability as a musicologist. Whether the musicians' job satisfaction or the conductor's musicological expertness

*Reprinted by permission of the publisher from *Organizational Dynamics*, Autumn, 1972, pp. 3–18. © 1972 by AMACOM, a division of American Management Association, Inc.

do, in fact, contribute to the orchestra's excellence is an interesting question in its own right, but it is not what people pay to hear. Likewise, the performance of a manager is here measured in terms of his department's or group's effectiveness in doing its assigned job. Whether the accomplishment of this job is to be measured after a week or after five years depends, of course, upon the assignment the organization gives the group, and the accomplishments the organization considers important.

When we think of improving leadership, we almost automatically think of training the individual. This training frequently involves giving the man a new perspective on his supervisory responsibilities by means of role playing, discussions, detailed instructions on how to behave toward subordinates, as well as instruction in the technical and administrative skills he will need in his job. A training program might last a few days, a few months, or as in the case of college programs and military academies, as long as four years. What is the hard evidence that this type of training actually increases organizational performance?

Empirical studies to evaluate the effectiveness of various leadership training programs, executive development, and supervisory workshops have been generally disappointing. Certainly, the two field experiments and two studies of ongoing organizations conducted by my associates and me failed to show that training increases organizational performance.

The first experiment in 1966 was conducted at a Belgian naval training center. We chose 244 Belgian recruits and 48 petty officers from a pool of 546 men. These men were assembled into 96 three-men groups: 48 groups had petty officers and 48 groups had recruits as leaders. The recruits ranged in age from 17 to 24, and none had been in the service longer than six weeks. The petty officers ranged in age from 19 to 45 years, and had an average of ten years' experience. All petty officers had received a two-year technical and leadership training course at petty officer candidate school. Since most successful graduates enlist for a 20-year term, Belgian petty officers are not only well-trained but they are also truly motivated and committed careermen.

The petty officers were matched with the recruit leaders on intelligence and other relevant scores. Each group worked on four cooperative tasks which were considered fair samples of the type of work petty officers might perform. One task consisted of writing a recruiting letter urging young men to join the Belgian navy as a career; the second and third tasks required the groups to find the shortest route for a convoy first through ten and then through twelve ports; the fourth task required the leader to train his men without using verbal instructions in the disassembling and reassembling of a .45-caliber automatic pistol.

Despite the fact that the recruits had had no leadership experience or training, their groups performed as well as those led by petty officers.

To test whether these results were not simply due to the chance or to a fault in our experimental design, we conducted a second experiment at a leadership training workshop for officers of Canadian military colleges. This study compared the performance of groups led by captains and majors with groups led by enlisted men who had just finished their eight weeks of basic training. All of the officers were, themselves, graduates of a Canadian military college. In addition, the officers had from 5 to 17 years of leadership experience and training after graduation. The 32 enlisted men were basic trainees between 19 and 22 years of age, and their intelligence scores were substantially below those of the officers. To reduce the possibility that they might feel anxious or inhibited by working with officers, the officers wore casual clothes and the enlisted men were told that they would work with civilian instructors.

The officers and men worked as three-men groups on three different tasks. They were asked to (a) write a fable, (b) find the shortest route for a truck convoy, and (c) draw bar graphs from score distributions that first had to be converted from one scale to another. As in the Belgian study, the tasks were designed so that all three group members had to participate in the work. As in the Belgian study, the groups led by the trained and experienced officers performed no better than the groups led by untrained and inexperienced enlisted men.

It is, of course, possible that experimental tasks do not give realistic results. For this reason we further checked in real-life situations whether the amount of training influenced performance by a study of 171 managers and supervisors in U.S. post offices. The performance of each of these supervisors was rated by two to five of his superiors. Amount of training ranged from zero hours of training to three years, with a median of 45 hours. The number of hours of supervisory training received by these managers was totally unrelated to their rated performance. We also investigated whether the post offices with highly trained supervisors were more effective on such objective post office performance measures as target achievement in number of first-class pieces handled, indirect costs, mail processing, etc. However, 12 of the 15 correlations were slightly *negative;* none was significant. Thus, training apparently did not improve organizational performance.

Another study related the amount of training received by police sergeants with the performance ratings made by their supervisors and other sergeants. Here again, training was unrelated to performance. Thus, neither the two controlled experiments nor the two field studies provide any basis for assuming that leadership training of the type given in these institutions, or in the training programs taken by postal managers or police sergeants, contributed to organizational performance.

I repeat that these findings are by no means unusual. Empirical studies to determine whether or not leadership training improves organizational performance have generally come up with negative findings. Newport, after surveying 121 large companies, concluded that not *one* of the companies had obtained any scientifically acceptable evidence that the leadership training for their middle management had actually improved performance.

T-group and sensitivity training, which has become fashionable in business and industry, has yielded similarly unsatisfactory results. Reviews of the literature by Campbell and Dunnette and by House found no convincing evidence that this type of training increased organizational effectiveness, and a well-known study at the International Harvester Company by Fleishman, Harris, and Burtt on the effects of supervisory training concluded that the effects of supervisory training in modifying behavior were very short-lived and did not improve performance.

EFFECT OF EXPERIENCE ON LEADERSHIP

Let us now ask whether supervisory experience improves performance. Actually, since leadership experience almost always involves on-the-job training, we are dealing with a closely related phenomenon.

Interestingly enough, the literature actually contains few, if any, studies which attempt to link leadership experience to organizational effectiveness. Yet, there seems to be a firmly held expectation that leadership experience makes a leader more effective. We simply have more trust in experienced leaders. We can infer this, for example, from the many regulations that require time in grade before promotion to the next higher level, as well as the many specifications of prior job in hiring executives for responsible positions.

We have already seen that the experienced petty officers and military academy officers did not perform more effectively than did the inexperienced enlisted men, nor did the more experienced officers or petty officers perform better than the less experienced.

In addition, we also analyzed data from various other groups and organizations. These included directors of research and development teams at a large physical research laboratory, foremen of craftshops, general foremen in a heavy machinery manufacturing company, managers of meat, and of grocery markets in a large supermarket chain as well as post office supervisors and managers, and police sergeants. For all these managers we could obtain reliable performance ratings or objective group effectiveness criteria. None of the correlations was significant in the expected direction. The median correlation relating leadership experience to leadership performance for all groups and organizations was $-.12$—certainly not significant in the positive direction!

To summarize the findings, neither orthodox leadership training nor leadership experience nor sensitivity training appear to contribute across the board to group or organizational effectiveness. It is, therefore, imperative first that we ask why this might be so, and second that we consider alternative methods for improving leadership performance.

THE CONTINGENCY MODEL

The "Contingency Model," a recent theory of leadership, holds that the effectiveness of group performance is contingent upon (a) the leader's motivational pattern, and (b) the degree to which the situation gives the leader power and influence. We have worked with a leadership motivation measure called the "Esteem for the Least Preferred Coworker," or LPC for short. The subject is first asked to think of all the people with whom he has ever worked, and then given a simple scale on which he describes the one person in his life with whom he has been able to work *least well*. This "least preferred coworker" may be someone he knows at the time, or it may be someone he has known in the past. It does not have to be a member of his present work group.

In grossly oversimplified terms, the person who describes his least preferred coworker in relatively favorable terms is basically motivated to have close interpersonal relations with others. By contrast, the person who rejects someone with whom he cannot work is basically motivated to accomplish or achieve on the task, and he derives satisfaction from being recognized as having performed well on the task. The task-motivated person thus uses the task to obtain a favorable position and good interpersonal relations.

CLASSIFYING LEADERSHIP SITUATIONS

The statement that some leaders perform better in one kind of situation while some leaders perform better in different situations is begging a question. "What kinds of situations are best suited for which type of leader?" In other words, how can we best classify groups if we wish to predict leadership performance?

We can approach this problem by assuming that leadership is essentially a work relationship involving power and influence. It is easier to be a leader when you have complete control than when your control is weak and dependent on the good will of others. It is easier to be the captain of a ship than the chairman of a volunteer group organized to settle a school bussing dispute. The *job* may be more complex for the navy captain but *being in the leadership role* is easier for him than for the committee chairman. It is, therefore, not unreasonable to classify situations in terms of how much power and influence the situation gives the leader. We call this "situational favorableness." One simple categorization of groups on their situational favorableness classifies leadership situations on the basis of three major dimensions:

1 *Leader-member relations.* Leaders presumably have more power and influence if they have a good relationship with their members than if they have a poor relationship with them, if they are liked, respected, trusted, than if they are not. Research has shown that this is by far the most important single dimension.

2 *Task structure.* Tasks or assignments that are highly structured, spelled out, or programmed give the leader more influence than tasks that are vague, nebulous and unstructured. It is easier, for example, to be a leader whose task it is to set up a sales display according to clearly delineated steps than it is to be a chairman of a committee preparing a new sales campaign.

3 *Position power.* Leaders will have more power and influence if their position is vested with such prerogatives as being able to hire and fire, being able to discipline, to reprimand, and so on. Position power, as it is used here, is determined by how much power the leader has over his subordinates. If the janitor foreman can hire and fire, he has more position power in his own group than the chairman of a board of directors who, frequently, cannot hire or fire—or even reprimand his board members.

Using this classification method we can now roughly order groups as being high or low on each of these three dimensions. This gives us an eight-celled classification (Figure 1). This scheme postulates that it is easier to be a leader in groups that fall into Cell 1 since you are liked, have position power, and have a structured task. It is somewhat more difficult in Cell 2 since you are liked, have a structured task, but little position power, and so on to groups in Cell 8 where the leader is not liked, has a vague, unstructured task, and little position power. A good example of Cell 8 would be the disliked chairman of the volunteer committee we mentioned before.

The critical question is, "What kind of leadership does each of these different group situations call for?" Figure 2 summarizes the results of 63 analyses based on a total of 454 separate groups. These included bomber and tank crews, antiaircraft artillery units, managements of consumer cooperative companies, boards of directors, open-hearth shops, basketball and surveying teams, and various groups involved in creative and problem-solving tasks.

The horizontal axis of the graph indicates the "situational favorableness," namely, the leader's control and influence as defined by the eightfold classification shown in Figure 1. The vertical axis indicates the relationship between the leader's motivational pattern, as measured by the LPC score, and his group's performance. A median correlation above the midline shows that the relationship-motivated leaders tended to perform better

Figure 1   Cells or "Octants"

	Very favorable			Intermediate in favorableness			Unfavorable	
	1	2	3	4	5	6	7	8
Leader-member relations	Good	Good	Good	Good	Poor	Poor	Poor	Poor
Task structure	High	High	Low	Low	High	High	Low	Low
Position power	Strong	Weak	Strong	Weak	Strong	Weak	Strong	Weak

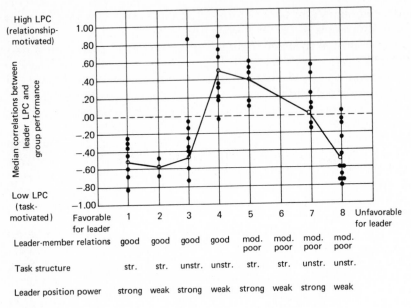

Figure 2

than the task-motivated leaders. A correlation below the midline indicates that the task-motivated leaders performed better than the relationship-motivated leaders. Figure 3 shows the predictions that the model would make in each of the eight cells.

These findings have two important implications for our understanding of what makes leaders effective. First, Figure 2 tells us that the task-motivated leaders tend to perform better than relationship-motivated leaders in situations that are very favorable and in those that are unfavorable. Relationship-motivated leaders tend to perform better than task-motivated leaders in situations that are intermediate in favorableness. Hence, both the relationship- and the task-motivated leaders perform well under some conditions and not under others. It is, therefore, not correct to speak of any

Figure 3   Prediction of the Performance of Relationship- and Task-motivated Leaders

	1	2	3	4	5	6	7	8
High LPC (relationship-motivated)				Good	Good	Some-what better	Some-what better	
Low LPC (task-motivated)	Good	Good	Good					Good

person as generally a good leader or generally a poor leader. Rather, a leader may perform well in one situation but not in another. This is also borne out by the repeated findings that we cannot predict a leader's performance on the basis of his personality traits, or even by knowing how well he performed on a previous task unless that task was similar in situational favorableness.

Second, the graph on Figure 2 shows that the performance of a leader depends as much on the situational favorableness as it does on the individual in the leadership position. Hence, the organization can change leadership performance either by trying to change the individual's personality and motivational pattern or by changing the favorableness of the leader's situation. As we shall see, this is really what training is all about.

Before we go further, we must ask how valid the Contingency Model is. How well does it predict in new situations? There have been at least 25 studies to date that have tested the theory. These validation studies included research on grocery and meat markets, a physical science laboratory, a machinery plant, a hospital, an electronics company, and teams of volunteer public health workers in Central America, as well as various experimentally assembled groups in the laboratory. Of particular importance is a large experiment that used cadets at West Point to test the entire eight cells of the model. This study almost completely reproduced the curve shown on Figure 2. In all studies that were recently reviewed, 35 of the 44 obtained correlations were in the predicted direction—a finding that could have occurred by chance less than one time in 100. An exception is Cell 2, in which laboratory experiments—but not field studies—have yielded correlations showing the relationship-motivated leaders perform better than task-motivated leaders.

EFFECT OF LEADERSHIP TRAINING?

The main question of this paper is, of course, how we can better utilize leadership training and experience to improve leadership performance. While appropiate leadership training and experience apparently do not increase organizational performance, there is considerable evidence that they do affect the manager's attitudes, behavior, and of course, his technical skills and administrative know-how. These programs teach the leader better methods of getting along with his subordinates, more effective handling of administrative routines, as well as technical background required for the job. In other words, the leader who is trained or experienced will have considerably greater control and influence over his job and his subordinates than one who is untrained and inexperienced.

In contrast, the inexperienced and untrained leader confronts numerous problems that are new to him, and for which he does not have a ready answer. As a result, he cannot give clear and concise instructions to his subordinates. Moreover, since so many situations are novel, he will be more anxious and less sure of himself, which will tend to make him more dependent upon his group and others in the organization. Not even the most detailed manual of operating instructions will enable a new manager to step into his job and behave as if he had been there for years. Thus, situations will be correspondingly less favorable for the untrained and inexperienced leader than for the trained and experienced leader.

What we are really saying here is that leadership training and experience primarily improve the favorableness of the leadership situation. But, if the Contingency Model is right, a more favorable situation requires a different type of leadership than a less favorable situation. Hence, leadership training and experience that will improve the performance of one type of leader *will decrease the performance of the other.* On the average, it will have little or no measurable effect on organizational performance. This is schematically shown in Figure 4. The arrows indicate that effect of training and experience in improving the favorableness of the leadership situation.

The headings on Figure 4 indicate the situational favorableness for the already trained or experienced leader. The untrained or inexperienced leader obviously would face a correspondingly less favorable situation. Thus, while the situation at the left of the table is very favorable for the trained leader, it is likely to be intermediate for the leader who lacks training and experience.The training or experience, as indicated by the arrow, would then change the untrained leader's situation from one which is intermediate to one which is very favorable. Likewise, if the trained leader's situation is intermediate in favorableness, the untrained leader's situation would be unfavorable. Training would, then, improve the untrained leader's situation from an unfavorable one to a situation which is intermediate in favorableness.

But why should an inexperienced and untrained leader perform better than someone with training and experience? Under certain conditions this is not too difficult to see. An individual who is new on the job is likely to seek good interpersonal relations with his coworkers so that he can enlist their full cooperation. He is not likely to throw his weight around and he will, therefore, be less likely to antagonize his group members. In other words, the proposition is far from absurd, and it is quite compatible with the behav-

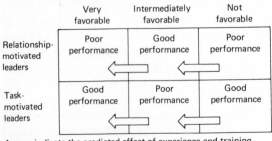

Arrows indicate the predicted effect of experience and training.

Figure 4 Favorableness of the situation for the trained or experienced leader.

ior of the manager who learns to rely on his staff of experts in making various decisions.

The proof of this theoretical pudding lies in various studies that bear out our suppositions.

STUDY OF SCHOOL PRINCIPALS

One study was conducted by McNamara on principals of rural elementary schools and of urban secondary schools in Canada. The performance of elementary principals was evaluated by means of ratings obtained from school superintendents and their staffs. The performance of secondary school principals was measured on the basis of province-wide achievement tests given to all students in the 11th grade. The average test score was used as the measure of the principal's effectiveness.

McNamara divided his group into task- and relationship-motivated principals, and again into inexperienced principals who had been on their job less than two years and those with three or more years of experience.

Let us now consider the favorableness of the leadership situation of elementary school principals. Their position power is reasonably high, and their task is fairly structured. The schools in McNamara's sample were quite small, the curricula of these schools are determined by the authorities of the province and by the school superintendent's office, and the elementary school principal typically is not called upon to make many policy decisions or innovations. His task is, therefore, structured. Hence, the experienced principal will have a very favorable leadership situation, and we would expect the task-motivated principals to perform better than the relationship-motivated principals.

The inexperienced principal faces a considerably less favorable situation. While his position power is high, he does not know his teachers well, and many of the administrative problems that arise will have to be handled in a manner that is new to him. We would predict that his task is unstructured and that the situation is intermediate. Without much experience the relationship-motivated principals will, therefore, perform better than their task-motivated colleagues. That this is the case is shown on Figure 5.

The secondary principal also has high position power. However, his organization is considerably more complex. In McNamara's sample, the schools had from 25 to 40 teachers who, in turn, were supervised by department heads. Thus, the principal's control over the teachers is less direct. In addition, of course, the curriculum of a high school varies from school to school and the high school principal generally has to make a considerable number of policy decisions about the teaching program, his staff, as well as the activities and disciplinary problems of his students. For this reason, the experienced principals of secondary schools were judged to have a situation of intermediate favorableness. Relationship-motivated principals should perform best. The inexperienced high school principal

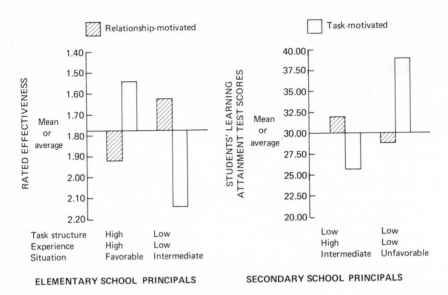

ELEMENTARY SCHOOL PRINCIPALS   **SECONDARY SCHOOL PRINCIPALS**

Figure 5

will have to set new precedents and he will have to think through many of the problems for the first time as they arise. Hence, the situation will be relatively unfavorable. We would predict, therefore, that the task-motivated principals with less than two-years' experience will perform best in these situations. Here again, the data will follow the prediction. (See Figure 5.)

It is particularly important to note that the relationship-motivated elementary school principal with longer experience actually performed *less well* than the relationship-motivated elementary school principal with less experience. Likewise, the task-motivated secondary school principal with more experience had significantly *poorer* performance than the task-motivated principal with considerably less experience. Thus, for these particular administrators, the more extensive experience not only failed to improve their performance but actually decreased their effectiveness.

STUDY OF CONSUMER COOPERATIVES

Another study that illustrates the effect of training and experience was conducted some years ago on 32 member companies of a large federation of consumer cooperatives. The federation used two indices for measuring company effectiveness and managerial performance. These were (a) the operating efficiency of the company, that is, roughly the proportion of overhead to total sales, and (b) the proportion of net income to total sales. We used the three-year average of these measures for our study.

In a reanalysis of these data, the managers were divided into those with task- and relationship-motivated leadership patterns, and of these, the ten with the most and the ten with the least years of experience in the organization. Since the federation of the companies maintained a strong management development program, managers with long experience also tended to have the most extensive training.

The leadership situation for the experienced managers was judged to be relatively favorable. They had considerable position power, and their job was relatively structured. As in the case of the school administrators, the inexperienced and less well trained managers would, of course, face a larger number of problems that they had not encountered before, and the task would, therefore, be correspondingly less structured. Hence, for the inexperienced managers the situation would be intermediate in favorableness.

The Contingency Model would then predict that the experienced managers with task-oriented leadership patterns would perform better, as would the inexperienced managers with relationship-motivated leadership patterns. That this was the case is shown on Figure 6 for operating efficiency. Somewhat weaker results were obtained for the net income criterion. It is again apparent that the experienced and trained relationship-motivated managers performed less well than did the relatively inexperienced and untrained managers who are relationship-motivated.

We have also studied the effect of training and experience on the performance of the post office managers and supervisors, police sergeants, and formal and informal leaders of company boards. These studies have yielded essentially similar results.

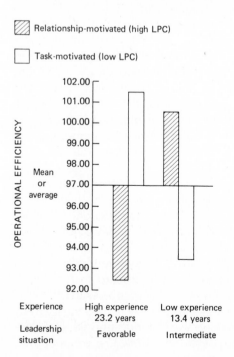

Figure 6 Performance of relationship- and task-motivated managers with relatively high and relatively low levels of experience.

NEW STUDIES OF MILITARY LEADERSHIP

Two studies were recently conducted specifically for the purpose of testing the hypothesis on completely new data. These were of field artillery sections and navy aircraft maintenance shops. Training and experience data were available for the noncommissioned officers in charge of these groups. In these studies, groups were assigned to cells 1, 3, 5, and 8 of the model. (See Figure 7.) Just as predicted, the task-motivated leaders performed best in cells 1, 3, and 8, while the relationship-motivated leaders performed best in cell 5. All findings were statistically significant.

TO TRAIN OR NOT TO TRAIN

What does all this mean for improving managerial performance, and how can we apply the findings that we have described?

In sum, if we want to improve leadership performance, we can either change the leader by training, or we can change his leadership situation. Common sense suggests that it is much easier to change various aspects of a man's job than to change the man. When we talk about leadership behavior, we are talking about fairly deeply ingrained personality factors and habits of interacting with others. These cannot be changed easily, either in a few hours or in a few days. In fact, as we have seen, not even four years of military academy and 5 to 17 years of subsequent experience enable a leader to perform significantly better on different tasks than someone that has had neither training nor experience.

We have seen that a leader's performance depends not only on his personality, but also on the organizational factors that determine the leader's control and influence, that is, the "situational favorableness." As we have shown, appropriate training and experience improve situational favorableness. Whether or not they improve performance depends upon the match between the leader's motivational pattern and the favorableness of the situation. This means that a training program that improves the leader's control and influence may benefit the relationship-motivated managers, but it will be detrimental to the task-motivated managers, or vice versa, depending upon the situation.

The idea that we can improve a leader's performance by increasing the favorableness of his situation is, of course, far from new. A poorly performing manager may be given more authority, more explicit instructions, more congenial coworkers in the hope that it will help him do a better job. Moreover, decreasing the favorableness of the situation in order to improve a manager's performance is also not quite as unusual as it might appear at first blush. If a man becomes bored, stale, or disinterested in his job, a frequent remedy is to transfer him to a more challenging job. As it turns out, "challenging" is just another way of saying that the job is less structured, has less position power, or requires working with difficult people. It is certainly well known that some men perform best under pressure and that they

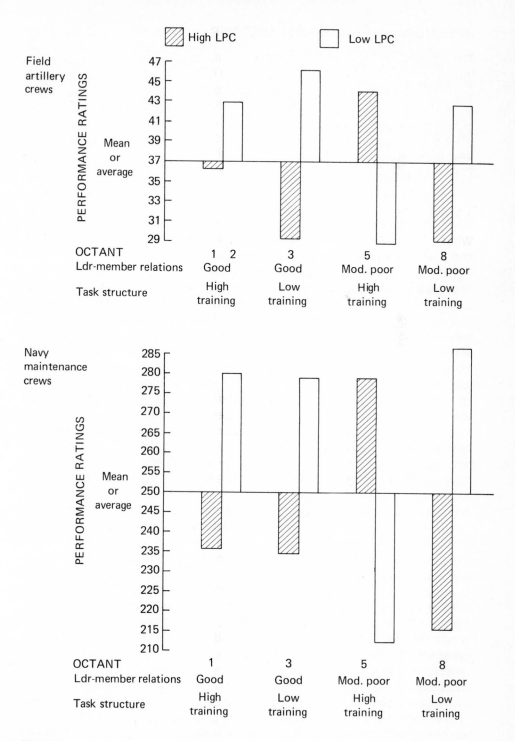

Figure 7

get into difficulty when life is too calm. These are the trouble shooters who are dispatched to branch offices or departments that need to be bailed out.

What, then, can an organization do to increase managerial performance? As a first step, it is necessary to determine which of the managers are task- and which are relationship-motivated. This can be accomplished by means of a short scale. Second, the organization needs to categorize carefully the situational favorableness of its managerial jobs. (Scales are available in Fiedler, F. E., *A Theory of Leadership Effectiveness,* McGraw-Hill, 1967.) Third, the organization can decide on a number of options in its management of executive personnel.

The least expensive and probably most efficient method is to develop a careful program of managerial rotation that moves some individuals from one job to another at a faster rate than it moves others. For example, it will be recalled that the relationship-motivated elementary school principals on the average became less effective after two years on the job. Moving these men to new jobs probably would have made them more effective than leaving them at the same school for many more years. Likewise, moving the task-motivated secondary school principals after two years probably would have increased their performance. In the case of the consumer cooperatives, it took 15 to 20 years in the organization (as employee and assistant manager, as well as manager) before the relationship-motivated managers began to go stale. How long a man should stay on a particular job must, of course, be determined empirically in each organization.

A second major option is management training. The problem here is whether to train only some people or all those who are eligible: training a task-motivated manager who is accepted by his group and has a structured task is likely to improve his performance; training a relationship-motivated manager for the same job is likely to make him less effective. The organization would, therefore, be better off if it simply did not train relationship-motivated managers for these particular jobs. On the other hand, the relationship-motivated but not the task-motivated managers should be trained for jobs in which the situational favorableness is intermediate.

Leadership training should devote more effort to teaching leaders how to modify their environment and their own job so that they fit their style of leadership. We must get rid of the implicit assumption that the environment and the organization, or a particular leadership position, are constant and unchanging. In addition to changes which occur as the leaders gain experience, they also continuously modify their leadership positions. They often speak of showing their men who is boss, presumably to assert their position power or of "being one of the boys" to deemphasize it; they speak of getting to know their men, presumably to establish better relations with them; they speak of different approaches to their work; they look for certain types of assistants who complement their abilities; they demand more authority, or they play down the authority they already have; they ask for certain types of assignments and try to avoid others. The theory that has here been described merely provides a basis for a more rational modification of the leadership job.

How can we train leaders to determine the conditions under which they are most likely to succeed or fail, and how can they learn to modify their own leadership situation? The frequently negative relationship between leadership experience and leader performance undoubtedly stems in part from the difficulties in obtaining feedback about one's own leadership effectiveness. As research has shown, unless the group fails utterly in its task, most leaders are unable to say with any degree of accuracy how well their group performed in comparison with other groups.

Leadership training away from the organization should provide the prospective leader with a wide range of leadership situations in which he can get immediate feedback on how well he has performed. On the basis of these experiences, he must learn to recognize which situations fit his particular style of leadership and how he can best modify situations so that they will enable him to perform effectively. This may involve the development of six to eight leadership tasks and situations, or adequately measured organizational tasks, in which each trainee is required to lead. He must then be given an objective appraisal of how well his group's performance compared with the performance of others under the same conditions.

The closest approximation to the all-around good leader is likely to be the individual who intuitively or through training knows how to manage his environment so that the leadership situation best matches his leadership style.

It may be desirable for various reasons to train all managers of a certain level, especially since being sent to executive training programs has in many organizations become a symbol of success. Men are sent to these training programs not because they need to learn, but because they need to be rewarded. If this is the case, the organization might do well to place the manager who completes the training program into a position that matches his leadership motivation pattern. For example, in the consumer cooperative companies, the relationship motivated managers might have been given staff jobs, or jobs with troubled companies at the conclusion of an extensive training program.

CONCLUSION

As a consequence of our research, we have both discredited some old myths and learned some new lessons.

The old myths:

- That there is one best leadership style, or that there are leaders who excel under all circumstances.
- That some men are born leaders, and that neither training, experience, or conditions can materially affect leadership skills.

The lessons, while more pedestrian and less dogmatic, are more useful. We know that people differ in how they respond to management situations. Furthermore, we know that almost every manager in an organization can perform effectively, providing that we place him in a situation that matches his personality, providing we know how to match his training and experience to the available jobs—and providing that we take the trouble.

READING   26

PATH-GOAL THEORY OF LEADERSHIP

Robert J. House
Terence R. Mitchell[*]

An integrated body of conjecture by students of leadership, referred to as the "Path-Goal Theory of Leadership," is currently emerging. According to this theory, leaders are effective because of their impact on subordinates' motivation, ability to perform effectively and satisfactions. The theory is called Path-Goal because its major concern is how the leader influences the subordinates' perceptions of their work goals, personal goals and paths to goal attainment. The theory suggests that a leader's behavior is motivating or satisfying to the degree that the behavior increases subordinate goal attainment and clarifies the paths to these goals.

HISTORICAL FOUNDATIONS

The path-goal approach has its roots in a more general motivational theory called expectancy theory.[1] Briefly, expectancy theory states that an individual's attitudes (e.g., satisfaction with supervision or job satisfaction) or behavior (e.g., leader behavior or job effort) can be predicted from: (1) the degree to which the job, or behavior, is seen as leading the various outcomes (expectancy) and (2) the evaluation of these outcomes (valences). Thus, people are satisfied with their job if they think it leads to things highly valued, and they work hard if they believe that effort leads to things that are highly valued. This type of theoretical rationale can be used to predict a variety of phenomena related to leadership, such as why leaders behave they way they do, or how leader behavior influences subordinate motivation.[2]

* Reprinted with permission of the *Journal of Contemporary Business*. Copyright, Autumn 1974, pp. 81–97.

This latter approach is the primary concern of this article. The implication for leadership is that subordinates are motivated by leader behavior to the extent that this behavior influences expectancies, e.g., goal paths and valences, e.g., goal attractiveness.

Several writers have advanced specific hypotheses concerning how the leader affects the paths and the goals of subordinates.[3] These writers focused on two issues: (1) how the leader affects subordinates expectations that effort will lead to effective performance and valued rewards, and (2) how this expectation affects motivation to work hard and perform well.

While the state of theorizing about leadership in terms of subordinates' paths and goals is in its infancy, we believe it is promising for two reasons. First, it suggests effects of leader behavior that have not yet been investigated but which appear to be fruitful areas of inquiry. And, second, it suggests with some precision the situational factors on which the effects of leader behavior are contingent.

The initial theoretical work by Evans asserts that leaders will be effective by making rewards available to subordinates and by making rewards contingent on the subordinate's accomplishment of specific goals.[4] Evans argued that one of the strategic functions of the leader is to clarify for subordinates the kind of behavior that leads to goal accomplishment and valued rewards. This function might be referred to as path clarification. Evans also argued that the leader increases the rewards available to subordinates by being supportive toward subordinates, i.e., by being concerned about their status, welfare and comfort. Leader supportiveness is in itself a reward that the leader has at his or her disposal, and the judicious use of this reward increases the motivation of subordinates.

Evans studied the relationship between the behavior of leaders and the subordinates' expectations that effort leads to rewards and also studied the resulting impact on ratings of the subordinates' performance. He found that when subordinates viewed leaders as being supportive (considerate of their needs) and when these superiors provided directions and guidance to the subordinates, there was a positive relationship between leader behavior and subordinates' performance ratings.

However, leader behavior was only related to subordinates' performance when the leader's behavior also was related to the subordinates' expectations that their effort would result in desired rewards. Thus, Evans' findings suggest that the major impact of a leader on the performance of subordinates is clarifying the path to desired rewards and making such rewards contingent on effective performance.

Stimulated by this line of reasoning, House, and House and Dessler advanced a more complex theory of the effects of leader behavior on the motivation of subordinates.[5] The theory intends to explain the effects of four specific kinds of leader behavior on the following three subordinate attitudes or expectations: (1) the satisfaction of subordinates, (2) the subordinates' acceptance of the leader and (3) the expectations of subordinates

that effort will result in effective performance and that effective performance is the path to rewards. The four kinds of leader behavior included in
the theory are: (1) directive leadership, (2) supportive leadership, (3) participative leadership and (4) achievement-oriented leadership. Directive leadership is characterized by a leader who lets subordinates know what is
expected of them, gives specific guidance as to what should be done and
how it should be done, makes his or her part in the group understood,
schedules work to be done, maintains definite standards of performance
and asks that group members follow standard rules and regulations. Supportive leadership is characterized by a friendly and approachable leader
who shows concern for the status, well-being and needs of subordinates.
Such a leader does little things to make the work more pleasant, treats
members as equals and is friendly and approachable. Participative leadership is characterized by a leader who consults with subordinates, solicits
their suggestions and takes these suggestions seriously into consideration
before making a decision. An achievement-oriented leader sets challenging goals, expects subordinates to perform at their highest level, continuously seeks improvement in performance *and* shows a high degree of confidence that the subordinates will assume responsibility, put forth effort and
accomplish challenging goals. This kind of leader constantly emphasizes
excellence in performance and simultaneously displays confidence that
subordinates will meet high standards of excellence.

     A number of studies suggest that these different leadership styles can
be shown by the same leader in various situations.[6] For example, a leader
may show directiveness toward subordinates in some instances and be
participative or supportive in other instances.[7] Thus, the traditional method
of characterizing a leader as either highly participative and supportive *or*
highly directive is invalid; rather, it can be concluded that leaders vary in
the particular fashion employed for supervising their subordinates. Also,
the theory, in its present stage, is a tentative explanation of the effects of
leader behavior—it is incomplete because it does not explain other kinds of
leader behavior and does not explain the effects of the leader on factors
other than subordinate acceptance, satisfaction and expectations. However, the theory is stated so that additional variables may be included in it
as new knowlege is made available.

PATH-GOAL THEORY

General Propositions

The first proposition of path-goal theory is that leader behavior is acceptable and satisfying to subordinates to the extent that the subordinates see
such behavior as either an immediate source of satisfaction or as instrumental to future satisfaction.

     The second proposition of this theory is that the leader's behavior will
be motivational, i.e., increase effort, to the extent that (1) such behavior

makes satisfaction of subordinate's needs contingent on effective performance and (2) such behavior complements the environment of subordinates by providing the coaching, guidance, support and rewards necessary for effective performance.

These two propositions suggest that the leader's strategic functions are to enhance subordinates' motivation to perform, satisfaction with the job and acceptance of the leader. From previous research on expectancy theory of motivation, it can be inferred that the strategic functions of the leader consist of: (1) recognizing and/or arousing subordinates' needs for outcomes over which the leader has some control, (2) increasing personal payoffs to subordinates for work-goal attainment, (3) making the path to those payoffs easier to travel by coaching and direction, (4) helping subordinates clarify expectancies, (5) reducing frustrating barriers and (6) increasing the opportunities for personal satisfaction contingent on effective performance.

Stated less formally, the motivational functions of the leader consist of increasing the number and kinds of personal payoffs to subordinates for work-goal attainment and making paths to these payoffs easier to travel by clarifying the paths, reducing road blocks and pitfalls and increasing the opportunities for personal satisfaction en route.

Contingency Factors

Two classes of situational variables are asserted to be contingency factors. A contingency factor is a variable which moderates the relationship between two other variables such as leader behavior and subordinate satisfaction. For example, we might suggest that the degree of structure in the task moderates the relationship between leaders' directive behavior and subordinates' job satisfaction. Figure I shows how such a relationship might look. Thus, subordinates are satisfied with directive behavior in an unstructured task and are satisfied with nondirective behavior in a structured task. Therefore, we say that the relationship between leader directiveness and subordinate satisfaction is contingent upon the structure of the task.

The two contingency variables are (a) personal characteristics of the subordinates and (b) the environmental pressures and demands with which subordinates must cope in order to accomplish the work goals and to satisfy their needs. While other situational factors also may operate to determine the effects of leader behavior, they are not presently known.

With respect to the first class of contingency factors, the characteristics of subordinates, path-goal theory asserts that leader behavior will be acceptable to subordinates to the extent that the subordinates see such behavior as either an immediate source of satisfaction or as instrumental to future satisfaction. Subordinates' characteristics are hypothesized to partially determine this perception. For example, Runyon[8] and Mitchell[9] show that the subordinate's score on a measure called Locus of Control moder-

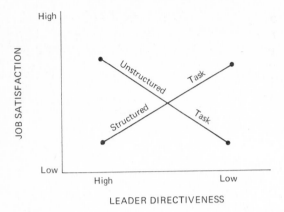

Figure 1 Hypothetical relationship between directive leadership and subordinate satisfaction with task structure as a contingency factor.

ates the relationship between participative leadership style and subordinate satisfaction. The Locus-of-Control measure reflects the degree to which an individual sees the environment as systematically responding to his or her behavior. People who believe that what happens to them occurs because of their behavior are called internals; people who believe that what happens to them occurs because of luck or chance are called externals. Mitchell's findings suggest that internals are more satisfied with a participative leadership style and externals are more satisfied with a directive style.

A second characteristic of subordinates on which the effects of leader behavior are contingent is subordinates' perception of their own ability with respect to their assigned tasks. The higher the degree of perceived ability relative to task demands, the less the subordinate will view leader directiveness and coaching behavior as acceptable. Where the subordinate's perceived ability is high, such behavior is likely to have little positive effect on the motivation of the subordinate and to be perceived as excessively close control. Thus, the acceptability of the leader's behavior is determined in part by the characteristics of the subordinates.

The second aspect of the situation, the environment of the subordinate, consists of those factors that are not within the control of the subordinate but which are important to need satisfaction or to ability to perform effectively. The theory asserts that effects of the leader's behavior on the psychological states of subordinates are contingent on other parts of the subordinates' environment that are relevant to subordinate motivation. Three broad classifications of contingency factors in the environment are:

- The subordinates' tasks
- The formal authority system of the organization
- The primary work group

Assessment of the environmental conditions makes it possible to predict the kind and amount of influence that specific leader behaviors will have on the motivation of subordinates. Any of the three environmental factors could act upon the subordinate in any of three ways: first, to serve as stimuli that motivate and direct the subordinate to perform necessary task operations; second, to constrain variability in behavior. Constraints may help the subordinate by clarifying expectancies that effort leads to rewards or by preventing the subordinate from experiencing conflict and confusion. Constraints also may be counterproductive to the extent that they restrict initiative or prevent increases in effort from being associated positively with rewards. Third, environmental factors may serve as rewards for achieving desired performance, e.g., it is possible for the subordinate to receive the necessary cues to do the job and the needed rewards for satisfaction from sources other than the leader, e.g., coworkers in the primary work group. Thus, the effect of the leader on subordinates' motivation will be a function of how deficient the environment is with respect to motivational stimuli, constraints or rewards.

With respect to the environment, path-goal theory asserts that when goals and paths to desired goals are apparent because of the routine nature of the task, clear group norms or objective controls of the formal authority systems, attempts by the leader to clarify paths and goals will be both redundant and seen by subordinates as imposing unnecessary, close control. Although such control may increase performance by preventing soldiering or malingering, it also will result in decreased satisfaction (see Figure I). Also with respect to the work environment, the theory asserts that the more dissatisfying the task, the more the subordinates will resent leader behavior directed at increasing productivity or enforcing compliance to organizational rules and procedures.

Finally, with respect to environmental variables the theory states that leader behavior will be motivational to the extent that it helps subordinates cope with environmental uncertainties, threats from others or sources of frustration. Such leader behavior is predicted to increase subordinates' satisfaction with the job context and to be motivational to the extent that it increases the subordinates' expectations that their effort will lead to valued rewards.

These propositions and specification of situational contingencies provide a heuristic framework on which to base future research. Hopefully, this will lead to a more fully developed, explicitly formal theory of leadership.

Figure II presents a summary of the theory. It is hoped that these propositions, while admittedly tentative, will provide managers with some insights concerning the effects of their own leader behavior and that of others.

EMPIRICAL SUPPORT

The theory has been tested in a limited number of studies which have generated considerable empirical support for our ideas and also suggest

Figure II Summary of Path-Goal Relationships

Leader behavior	and	Contingency factors		Cause	Subordinate attitudes and behavior
1 Directive		1 Subordinate characteristics			1 Job satisfaction
2 Supportive		Authoritarianism		Personal	Job→Rewards
3 Achievement-oriented		Locus of control	*influence*	perceptions	2 Acceptance of leader
4 Participative		Ability			Leader→Rewards
		2 Environmental factors		Motivational	3 Motivational behavior
		The task		stimuli	Effort→Performance
		Formal authority system	*influence*	Constraints	Performance→Rewards
		Primary work group		Rewards	

areas in which the theory requires revision. A brief review of these studies follows.

Leader Directiveness

Leader directiveness has a positive correlation with satisfaction and expectancies of subordinates who are engaged in ambiguous tasks and has a negative correlation with satisfaction and expectancies of subordinates engaged in clear tasks. These findings were predicted by the theory and have been replicated in seven organizations. They suggest that when task, demands are ambiguous or when the organization procedures, rules and policies are not clear, a leader behaving in a directive manner complements the tasks and the organization by providing the necessary guidance and psychological structure for subordinates.[10] However, when task demands are clear to subordinates, leader directiveness is seen more as a hindrance.

However, other studies have failed to confirm these findings.[11] A study by Dessler[12] suggests a resolution to these conflicting findings—he found that for subordinates at the lower organizational levels of a manufacturing firm who were doing routine, repetitive, unambiguous tasks, directive leadership was preferred by closed-minded, dogmatic, authoritarian subordinates and nondirective leadership was preferred by nonauthoritarian, open-minded subordinates. However, for subordinates at higher organizational levels doing nonroutine, ambiguous tasks, directive leadership was preferred for both authoritarian and nonauthoritarian subordinates. Thus, Dessler found that two contingency factors appear to operate simultaneously: subordinate task ambiguity and degree of subordinate authoritarianism. When measured in combination, the findings are as predicted by the theory; however, when the subordinate's personality is not taken into account, task ambiguity does not always operate as a contingency variable as predicted by the theory. House, Burrill and Dessler recently found a similar interaction between subordinate authoritarianism and task ambiguity in a second manufacturing firm, thus adding confidence in Dessler's original findings.[13]

Supportive Leadership

The theory hypothesizes that supportive leadership will have its most positive effect on subordinate satisfaction for subordinates who work on stressful, frustrating or dissatisfying tasks. This hypothesis has been tested in 10 samples of employees,[14] and in only one of these studies was the hypothesis disconfirmed.[15] Despite some inconsistency in research on supportive leadership, the evidence is sufficiently positive to suggest that managers should be alert to the critical need for supportive leadership under conditions where tasks are dissatisfying, frustrating or stressful to subordinates.

Achievement-oriented Leadership

The theory hypothesizes that achievement-oriented leadership will cause subordinates to strive for higher standards of performance and to have more confidence in the ability to meet challenging goals. A recent study by House, Valency and Van der Krabben provides a partial test of this hypothesis among white collar employees in service organizations.[16] For subordinates performing ambiguous, nonrepetitive tasks, they found a positive relationship between the amount of achievement orientation of the leader and subordinates' expectancy that their effort would result in effective performance. Stated less technically, for subordinates performing ambiguous, nonrepetitive tasks, the higher the achievement orientation of the leader, the more the subordinates were confident that their efforts would pay off in effective performance. For subordinates performing moderately unambiguous, repetitive tasks, there was no significant relationship between achievement-oriented leadership and subordinate expectancies that their effort would lead to effective performance. This finding held in four separate organizations.

Two plausible interpretations may be used to explain these data. First, people who select ambiguous, nonrepetitive tasks may be different in personality from those who select a repetitive job and may, therefore, be more responsive to an achievement-oriented leader. A second explanation is that achievement orientation only affects expectancies in ambiguous situations because there is more flexibility and autonomy in such tasks. Therefore, subordinates in such tasks are more likely to be able to change in response to such leadership style. Neither of the above interpretations have been tested to date; however, additional research is currently under way to investigate these relationships.

Participative Leadership

In theorizing about the effects of participative leadership it is necessary to ask about the specific characteristics of both the subordinates and their situation that would cause participative leadership to be viewed as satisfying and instrumental to effective performance.

Mitchell recently described at least four ways in which a participative leadership style would impact on subordinate attitudes and behavior as predicted by expectancy theory.[17] First, a participative climate should increase the clarity of organizational contingencies. Through participation in decision making, subordinates should learn what leads to what. From a path-goal viewpoint participation would lead to greater clarity of the paths to various goals. A second impact of participation would be that subordinates, hopefully, should select goals they highly value. If one participates in decisions about various goals, it makes sense that this individual would select goals he or she wants. Thus, participation would increase the correspondence between organization and subordinate goals. Third, we can see how participation would increase the control the individual has over what happens on the job. If our motivation is higher (based on the preceding two points), then having greater autonomy and ability to carry out our intentions should lead to increased effort and performance. Finally, under a participative system, pressure towards high performance should come from sources other than the leader or the organization. More specifically, when people participate in the decision process they become more ego-involved; the decisions made are in some part their own. Also, their peers know what is expected and the social pressure has a greater impact. Thus, motivation to perform well stems from internal and social factors as well as formal external ones.

A number of investigations prior to the above formulation supported the idea that participation appears to be helpful,[18] and Mitchell presents a number of recent studies that support the above four points.[19] However, it is also true that we would expect the relationship between a participative style and subordinate behavior to be moderated by both the personality characteristics of the subordinate and the situational demands. Studies by Tannenbaum and Allport and Vroom have shown that subordinates who prefer autonomy and self-control respond more positively to participative leadership in terms of both satisfaction and performance than subordinates who do not have such preferences.[20] Also, the studies mentioned by Runyon[21] and Mitchell[22] showed that subordinates who were external in orientation were less satisfied with a participative style of leadership than were internal subordinates.

House also has reviewed these studies in an attempt to explain the ways in which the situation or environment moderates the relationship between participation and subordinate attitudes and behavior.[23] His analysis suggests that where participative leadership is positively related to satisfaction, regardless of the predispositions of subordinates, the tasks of the subjects appear to be ambiguous and ego-involving. In the studies in which the subjects' personalities or predispositions moderate the effect of participative leadership, the tasks of the subjects are inferred to be highly routine and/or nonego-involving.

House reasoned from this analysis that the task may have an overriding effect on the relationship between leader participation and subordinate responses, and that individual predispositions or personality characteristics of subordinates may have an effect only under some tasks. It was assumed that when task demands are ambiguous, subordinates will have a need to reduce the ambiguity. Further, it was assumed that when task demands are ambiguous, participative problem solving between the leader and the subordinate will result in more effective decisions than when the task demands are unambiguous. Finally, it was assumed that when the subordinates are ego-involved in their tasks they are more likely to want to have a say in the decisions that affect them. Given these assumptions, the following hypotheses were formulated to account for the conflicting findings reviewed above:

- When subjects are highly ego-involved in a decision or a task and the decision or task demands are ambiguous, participative leadership will have a positive effect on the satisfaction and motivation of the subordinate, *regardless* of the subordinate's predisposition toward self-control, authoritarianism or need for independence.
- When subordinates are not ego-involved in their tasks and when task demands are clear, subordinates who are not authoritarian and who have high needs for independence and self-control will respond favorably to leader participation and their opposite personality types will respond less favorably.

These hypotheses were derived on the basis of path-goal theorizing; i.e., the rationale guiding the analysis of prior studies was that both task characteristics and characteristics of subordinates interact to determine the effect of a specific kind of leader behavior on the satisfaction, expectancies and performance of subordinates. To date, one major investigation has supported some of these predictions[24] in which personality variables, amount of participative leadership, task ambiguity and job satisfaction were assessed for 324 employees of an industrial manufacturing organization. As expected, in nonrepetitive, ego-involving tasks, employees (regardless of their personalty) were more satisfied under a participative style than a nonparticipative style. However, in repetitive tasks which were less ego-involving the amount of authoritarianism of subordinates moderated the relationship between leadership style and satisfaction. Specifically, low authoritarian subordinates were *more satisfied* under a participative style. These findings are exactly as the theory would predict, thus, it has promise in reconciling a set of confusing and contradictory findings with respect to participative leadership.

SUMMARY AND CONCLUSIONS

We have attempted to describe what we believe is a useful theoretical framework for understanding the effect of leadership behavior on subordinate satisfaction and motivation. Most theorists today have moved away from the simplistic notions that all effective leaders have a certain set of personality traits or that the situation completely determines performance. Some researchers have presented rather complex attempts at matching certain types of leaders with certain types of situations. But, we believe that a path-goal approach goes one step further. It not only suggests what type of style may be most effective in a given situation—it also attempts to explain *why* it is most effective.

We are optimistic about the future outlook of leadership research. With the guidance of path-goal theorizing, future research is expected to unravel many confusing puzzles about the reasons for and effects of leader behavior that have, heretofore, not been solved. However, we add a word of

caution: the theory, and the research on it, are relatively new to the literature of organizational behavior. Consequently, path-goal theory is offered
more as a tool for directing research and stimulating insight than as a
proven guide for managerial action.

FOOTNOTES

1 T. R. Mitchell, "Expectancy Model of Job Satisfaction, Occupational Preference and Effort: A Theoretical, Methodological and Empirical Appraisal," *Psychological Bulletin*
   (1974, in press).
2 D. M. Nebeker and T. R. Mitchell, "Leader Behavior: An Expectancy Theory Approach,"
   Organization Behavior and Human Performance, 11(1974), pp. 355–367.
3 M. G. Evans, "The Effects of Supervisory Behavior on the Path-Goal Relationship," *Organization Behavior and Human Performance,* 55(1970), pp. 277–298; T. H. Hammer and
   H. T. Dachler, "The Process of Supervision in the Context of Motivation Theory," Research Report No. 3 (University of Maryland, 1973); F. Dansereau, Jr., J. Cashman and G.
   Graen, "Instrumentality Theory and Equity Theory as Complementary Approaches in Predicting the Relationship of Leadership and Turnover among Managers," *Organization
   Behavior and Human Performance,* 10(1973), pp. 184–200; R. J. House, "A Path-Goal
   Theory of Leader Effectiveness, *Administrative Science Quarterly,* 16, 3(September 1971),
   pp. 321–338; T. R. Mitchell, "Motivation and Participation: An Integration," *Academy of
   Management Journal,* 16, 4(1973), pp. 160–179; G. Graen, F. Dansereau, Jr. and T. Mina-
   mi, "Dysfunctional Leadership Styles," *Organization Behavior and Human Performance,*
   7(1972), pp. 216–236;———, "An Empirical Test of the Man-in-the-Middle Hypothesis
   among Executives in a Hierarchical Organization Employing a Unit Analysis," *Organization Behavior and Human Performance,* 8(1972), pp. 262–285; R. J. House and G. Dessler,
   "The Path-Goal Theory of Leadership: Some Post Hoc and A Priori Tests," to appear in J.
   G. Hunt, ed., *Contingency Approaches to Leadership* (Carbondale, Ill.: Southern Illinois
   University Press, 1974).
4 M. G. Evans, "Effects of Supervisory Behavior";———, "Extensions of a Path-Goal Theory
   of Motivation," *Journal of Applied Psychology,* 59(1974), pp. 172–178.
5 R. J. House, "A Path-Goal Theory"; R. J. House and G. Dessler, "Path-Goal Theory of
   Leadership."
6 R. J. House and G. Dessler, "Path-Goal Theory of Leadership"; R. M. Stogdill, *Managers,
   Employees, Organization* (Ohio State University, Bureau of Business Research, 1965); R.
   J. House, A. Valency and R. Van der Krabben, "Some Tests and Extensions of the Path-
   Goal Theory of Leadership" (in preparation).
7 W. A. Hill and D. Hughes, "Variations in Leader Behavior as a Function of Task Type,"
   Organization Behavior and Human Performance (1974, in press).
8 K. E. Runyon, "Some Interactions between Personality Variables and Management
   Styles," *Journal of Applied Psychology,* 57, 3(1973), pp. 288–294; T. R. Mitchell, C. R.
   Smyser and S. E. Weed, "Locus of Control: Supervision and Work Satisfaction," *Academy
   of Management Journal* (in press).
9 T. R. Mitchell, "Locus of Control."
10 R. J. House, "A Path-Goal Theory";——— and G. Dessler, "Path-Goal Theory of Leadership"; A. D. Szalagyi and H. P Sims, "An Exploration of the Path-Goal Theory of Leadership in a Health Care Environment," *Academy of Management Journal* (in press); J. D.
   Dermer, "Supervisory Behavior and Budget Motivation" (Cambridge, Mass.: unpublished,
   MIT, Sloan School of Management, 1974); R. W. Smetana, "The Relationship between
   Managerial Behavior and Subordinate Attitudes and Motivation: A Contribution to a Behavioral Theory of Leadership" (Ph.D. diss, Wayne State University, 1974).

11 S. E. Weed, T. R. Mitchell and C. R. Smyser, "A Test of House's Path-Goal Theory of Leadership in an Organizational Setting" (paper presented at Western Psychological Assoc., 1974); J. D. Dermer and J. P. Siegel, "A Test of Path-Goal Theory: Disconfirming Evidence and a Critique" (unpublished, University of Toronto, Faculty of Management Studies, 1973); R. S. Schuler, "A Path Goal Theory of Leadership: An Empirical Investigation" (Ph.D. diss, Michigan State University, 1973); H. K. Downey, J. E. Sheridan and J. W. Slocum, Jr., "Analysis of Relationships among Leader Behavior, Subordinate Job Performance and Satisfaction: A Path-Goal Approach" (unpublished mimeograph, 1974); J. E. Stinson and T. W. Johnson, "The Path-Goal Theory of Leadership: A Partial Test and Suggested Refinement," *Proceedings* (Kent, Ohio: 7th Annual Conference of the Midwest Academy of Management, April 1974), pp. 18–36.

12 G. Dessler, "An Investigation of the Path-Goal Theory of Leadership" (Ph.D. diss, City University of New York, Bernard M. Baruch College, 1973).

13 R. J. House, D. Burrill and G. Dessler, "Tests and Extensions of Path-Goal Theory of Leadership," (unpublished, in process).

14 R. J. House, "A Path-Goal Theory";——— and G. Dessler, "Path-Goal Theory of Leadership"; A. D. Szalagyi and H. P. Sims, "Exploration of Path-Goal"; J. E. Stinson and T. W. Johnson, *Proceedings;* R. S. Schuler, "Path-Goal: Investigation"; H. K. Downey, J. E. Sheridan and J. W. Slocum, Jr., "Analysis of Relationships"; S. E. Weed, T. R. Mitchell and C. R. Smyser, "Test of House's Path-Goal."

15 A. D. Szalagyi and H. P. Sims, "Exploration of Path-Goal."

16 R. J. House, A. Valency and R. Van der Krabben, "Tests and Extensions of Path-Goal Theory of Leadership, II" (unpublished, in process).

17 T. R. Mitchell, "Motivation and Participation."

18 H. Tosi, "A Reexamination of Personality as a Determinant of the Effects of Participation," *Personnel Psychology,* 23(1970), pp. 91–99; J. Sadler, "Leadership Style, Confidence in Management and Job Satisfaction," *Journal of Applied Behavioral Sciences,* 6(1970), pp. 2–19; K. N. Wexley, J. P. Singh and J. A. Yukl, "Subordinate Personality as a Moderator of the Effects of Participation in Three Types of Appraisal Interviews," *Journal of Applied Psychology,* 83, 1(1973), pp. 54–59.

19 T. R. Mitchell, "Motivation and Participation."

20 A. S. Tannenbaum and F. H. Allport, "Personality Structure and Group Structure: An Interpretive Study of Their Relationship through an Event-Structure Hypothesis," *Journal of Abnormal and Social Psychology,* 53(1956), pp. 272–280; V. H. Vroom, "Some Personality Determinants of the Effects of Participation," *Journal of Abnormal and Social Psychology,* 59(1959), pp. 322–327.

21 K. E. Runyon, "Some Interactions between Personality Variables and Management Styles," *Journal of Applied Psychology,* 57, 3(1973), pp. 288–294.

22 T. R. Mitchell, C. R. Smyser and S. E. Weed, "Locus of Control."

23 R. J. House, "Notes on the Path-Goal Theory of Leadership" (University of Toronto, Faculty of Management Studies, May, 1974).

24 R. S. Schuler, "Leader Participation, Task Structure and Subordinate Authoritarianism" (unpublished mimeograph, Cleveland State University, 1974).

READING 27

PERCEPTIONS OF LEADERSHIP BY MANAGERS IN A FEDERAL AGENCY

Harold C. White*

Management includes the functions of planning, organizing, staffing, directing, and controlling. Leadership, considered as being synonymous with directing, is the concern of this report. Leadership may be defined as the act of providing incentives to motivate others by satisfying their needs to perform in some desired manner.

In his book, *Human Relations at Work,* Keith Davis says: "Leadership is something a person does, not something he has." R. Tannenbaum and W. Schmidt, in their article, "How to Choose a Leadership Pattern" (*Harvard Business Review,* Mar.-Apr. 1958), have suggested the variety of behavior patterns a manager may perform as a leader. These behaviors can range from one extreme by which the manager makes all decisions and announces them to the subordinates in the form of an order (autocratic leadership), through increasing amounts of subordinate involvement, to a point where the subordinates make decisions jointly with their manager on topics which affect them.

Experienced managers, when considering various alternative leadership styles, typically recognize that they have used a variety of styles, and have observed their fellow managers using them, at one time or another. They have concluded there is not one right way to lead effectively. Rather there is the appropriate way to lead, depending on the circumstances. The challenge for the manager is to identify accurately which leadership style is most appropriate for a given set of variables.

PARTICIPATIVE LEADERSHIP

However, it is participative leadership that is most supported by research reported in the literature. The participative manager, when faced with the responsibility for making decisions which affect his subordinates, identifies objectives and establishes guidelines. Within these constraints he includes his immediate subordinates in the problem-solving and decision-making process. It is group, not individual, decision-making.

*From *Personnel Administration and Public Personnel Review,* July–August 1972, pp. 51–56. Reprinted with permission.

In actual practice, as contrasted with the autocratic manager, the participative manager displays consideration for the feelings, attitudes, and needs of his subordinates, supervises less closely, and spends a greater amount of time increasing his subordinates' feelings of freedom and self-responsibility.

Where it can be applied, participative leadership is most effective—it is motivating—because it is more likely to provide satisfaction of the needs of the greatest number of employees. The need for security may be satisfied by keeping the subordinates informed and by allowing them to be involved in decisions which affect their own work. Social need is satisfied because the participative process is social in nature. Decision-making is a team effort. There is status satisfaction in having one's ideas sought by an organizational superior and by having those ideas presented and discussed. There is personal growth (self-actualization) in being made aware of the total situation, in solving problems, and in carrying out decisions one has been involved in making.

The purpose of this study was to discover what leadership style, autocratic or participative, was viewed by managers as being most effective.

THE RESEARCH

Selected managers from one federal agency are the source for the data in this study. The agency employs approximately 20,000 persons: 1,000 in the national office and the remainder in offices in nearly every county in the United States. The study was conducted prior to an extensive management training program within the agency.

One group of respondents was composed of both line and staff personnel, mainly GS 12–14, located in the national office in Washington, D.C. The other group, GS 9–11, was composed of county office managers of a state in the Rocky Mountain region, each supervising from one to a dozen employees. The majority of managers in both groups supervise mainly office employees; work in the county offices involves considerable contact with the public.

Thirty-three questions were asked of each manager, a selection of which is summarized in the following tables. Each respondent selected the most *effective* manager he personally knew in the agency and answered the questionnaire with that manager in mind. Next, each respondent answered the same questions for the *weakest* (least effective) manager known personally, in the agency. Neither the terms "effective" nor "weak" were defined. Each respondent was required to base the selection of managers evaluated on criteria he considered appropriate.

Each question contained three possible answers, which, in turn, were divided into three units, providing a nine-point scale. On the questionnaire, scales were alternated from right to left and left to right at random to reduce the possibility of a pattern developing in responding. For purposes of clarity, all scales on the following tables read from left (least desirable, 1) to right (most desirable, 9).

Numbers above the scales in the tables refer to responses of managers from the national office (indicated by an N to the left of the scale); numbers below the scales refer to the responses of the county office managers (indicated by a C). Numbers on the scale preceded by E refer to mean (average) responses for effective managers; numbers preceded by a W refer to mean responses for weak managers. The differences in responses between effective and weak managers are significant to at least the 5 percent level of confidence.

ATTITUDES OF SUBORDINATES

Approximately half the questions dealt with attitudes and behaviors of the subordinates whom the evaluated managers supervised. The results will not be discussed in depth here, but a summary of the responses is of interest.

As perceived by the federal managers completing this questionnaire, the effective managers, compared to the weak managers, supervise employees who:

1 Have more favorable attitudes toward other members in their own work unit and toward the organization as a whole.

2 Cooperate more effectively with other employees.

3 Communicate more effectively with other employees.

4 Have a greater feeling of responsibility for reaching organizational goals.

5 Have greater trust and confidence in their manager.

6 Are more accepting of information from their manager.

7 Feel greater freedom in discussing job-related problems with their manager.

8 Are more accurate in reporting their performance.

Employees of effective managers were perceived as performing effectively on most or all of the items measured; employees of weak managers tended to display inappropriate behaviors on most items.

LEADERSHIP STYLES

It might well be pointed out that a manager who supervises employees possessing appropriate behaviors and attitudes is more likely to be effective than a manager who supervises employees with inappropriate behaviors and attitudes.

However, there is evidence to suggest that this is not accidental, or luck. It is the leadership style of the manager that influences the attitudes and responses of the subordinates—a cause and effect relationship exists. Subordinates of effective managers possess attitudes and behaviors that are more desirable than subordinates of weak managers because the leadership style of the effective manager is more appropriate.

Table 1 provides information on the responses related to the leadership styles of effective and weak managers. Autocratic leadership is associated with the left-hand portion of each scale; participative leadership with the right-hand portion.

Question 1: Obtains unit members' ideas on job-related problems.
Question 2: Uses special knowledge of unit members in making decisions.

EFFECTIVE MANAGER

The effective manager, more than the weak manager, is perceived as seeking ideas and recommendations from his subordinates, and is more likely to use their ideas and special knowledge in making decisions. Encouraging upward communication is a rather continuous practice of the effective manager. The weak manager utilizes the ideas and special knowledge of his subordinates on a much more infrequent basis. Subordinates of effective managers are, therefore, more inclined to feel their interests are being considered and that the final decision of the managers will be fair and appropriate. They are more likely to develop a commitment to, and contribute effort toward, the success of the decisions.

Question 3: Aware of unit members' problems before making decisions.

Respondents perceive the effective manager is well aware of his subordinates' problems. The weak manager is frequently unaware. The effective manager is effective, perhaps in part, because he is better informed as to the needs and problems of his subordinates before making decisions.

Question 4: Adequacy and accuracy of information for unit members to make decisions.
Question 5: Shares information with unit members.

COMMUNICATION

Not only is the effective manager more likely than the weak manager to encourage upward communication from his subordinates, he is more likely to practice downward communication through keeping his subordinates informed. Such communication is seen as being both accurate and adequate. At best, the weak manager provides only partial information to his subordinates.

Table 1   Perceived Behaviors of Effective and Weak Managers

1 Obtains unit members' ideas on job related problems

	Never	Occasionally	Always
N	W3.2		E7.6
C	W3.7		E7.4

2 Uses special knowledge of unit members in making decisions

	Seldom or never	Little	Completely
N	W4.2		E7.8
C	W4.2		E7.4

3 Aware of unit members' problems before making decisions

	Seldom aware or totally unaware	Occasionally not aware	Well aware
N	W3.2		E7.7
C	W3.8		E7.4

4 Adequacy and accuracy of information for unit members to make decisions

	Mostly in-accurate and inadequate	Partially accurate and adequate	Mostly accurate and adequate
N	W3.9		E7.5
C	W3.8		E7.3

5 Shares information with unit members

	Little or not at all	Provides mini-mum the manager feels they need	Shares most or all
N	W3.6		E7.5
C	W4.1		E7.5

6 Provides support to unit members

	None	Occasionally	Completely
N	W3.9		E7.7
C	W4.1		E7.5

7 Trust and confidence in unit members

	Little or none	Some, not complete	Complete
N	W3.7		E7.1
C	W3.9		E7.5

8 Means of motivating unit members

	Fear, threats, punishment	Rewards, some involvement, some punishment	Rewards and in-volvement
N	W3.9		E7.3
C	W3.9		E7.3

9 Use of control measures as productivity, costs, etc.

	For policing, punishment	Policing, little punishment, emphasis on rewards	For unit members as a form of guidance
N	W3.8		E7.1
C	W3.7		E7.0

N = Responses from selected managers in the national office.
C = Responses from selected county managers in one state.
E = Effective manager.
W = Weak manager.
Number of respondents: N = 38, C = 41.

Typically, the manager, more than anyone else in the unit, by his own practices establishes standards and patterns of behavior for other members in the unit. If the manager communicates openly with his subordinates, they are more likely to be open with him.

Question 6: Provides support to unit members.

SUPPORTIVE ATTITUDE

One of the strongest behaviors of the effective manager is his supportive attitude toward his subordinates. The weak manager is perceived as providing only occasional support. Support comes from a variety of sources, such as the feeling of freedom to discuss problems openly with their manager, and from the practice of the manager of asking for advice and suggestions (questions 1 and 2).

Question 7: Trust and confidence in unit members.

Respondents perceive the effective manager as having considerably greater confidence in his subordinates than does the weak manager. This factor could explain, in part, the greater willingness of the effective manager to share information with his subordinates and to seek their ideas. The manager who displays a trusting attitude is more likely to receive trust in return.

Question 8: Means of motivating unit members.

REWARDS AND INVOLVEMENT

The effective manager is more disposed to motivate his subordinates through rewards and involvement thereby developing their interest in the job. The weak manager uses fear as a motivating force to obtain performance and punishment in response to poor performance. Emphasis of the effective manager is on positive motivators; emphasis of the weak manager is on negative motivators.

Question 9: Use of control measures as productivity, costs, etc.

Consistent with the mode of motivation is the use of control measures. The effective manager is more ready to reward desirable performance and is more likely to use reports of poor performance as a basis for instruction and guidance for improvement rather than as a basis for punishment. Although the weak manager may offer some rewards for desired performance, he is inclined to impose punishment for poor performance.

Additional observations: From additional data not shown on Table 1, it has been found that effective managers, as a group, are more similar in their leadership practices than are the weak managers. The effective managers tend to be participative in all behavior measures. While weak managers tend to be autocratic generally, few of them are perceived as being autocratic in all their practices. However, as the averages on the scales suggest, they are not consistent among each other as to which practices they have chosen to be participative.

DECISION-MAKING

As noted in Table 1, effective managers tend to display behaviors which are characteristic of the participative leadership style. Weak managers tend to display characteristics more associated with the autocratic leadership style. Further analysis is called for. The truly participative manager permits, indeed encourages, his subordinates to share decision-making with him. Table 2 is concerned with the amount of subordinate decision-making permitted by the managers.

Question 1: Decisions made in the unit.

Effective managers are perceived as sharing decision-making with their subordinates more than that permitted by the weak manager. Most

Table 2   Perceived Participation Permitted by Effective and Weak Managers

		By manager only		Mostly by manager, some by unit members		Fairly equally shared by manager with unit members	
1	Decisions made in unit						
	N		W3.5		E5.9		
	C		W3.7		E5.5		

		By manager only		By manager after questions and comments by unit members		Mostly jointly by manager and total unit	
2	Goal setting						
	N	W3.2			E6.5		
	C	W2.8				E6.6	

		Highly concentrated in the manager		Mainly with the manager, some delegated control		Shared equally by manager and unit members	
3	Concentration of review and control functions						
	N		W3.6		E6.1		
	C		W3.4		E5.6		

N = Responses from selected managers in the national office.
C = Responses from selected county managers in one state.
E = Effective manager.
W = Weak manager.
Number of respondents: N = 38, C = 41.

weak managers make all decisions themselves. It is to be noted, however, that while the effective manager is more participative, he does not share all decision-making with his subordinates.

Question 2: Goal-setting.

The effective manager does not appear to be as reluctant to share goal-setting as he is to share decision-making. Nonetheless, goal-setting is not completely shared by all effective managers. They do tend, however, to seek information and ideas from their subordinates before establishing goals. It is in goal-setting that the average weak manager is the most auto-cratic. The average responses for the weak manager are lower for this question than for any item in either Tables 1 or 2.

Question 3: Concentration of review and control functions.

The effective manager generally limits the sharing of reviewing work and establishing controls. He does tend to delegate at least some of the functions. By comparison, the average weak manager tends to hold all such functions to himself with no delegation.

FINAL DECISIONS

Additional observations: All average responses for effective managers in Table 2 are lower than all average responses in Table 1. Even though these managers are more sharing and open with their subordinates, they have retained most of the final decision-making to themselves. It is important to note, however, that the weak managers tend even more to make all final decisions themselves.

Again, while not shown on the Table, the range of responses for both effective and weak managers is much greater for the questions in Table 2 than for those in Table 1. That is, some effective managers are perceived as being fairly autocratic even though most tend to be more participative. Also, there are some weak managers whom the respondents perceive to be tending toward participation even though the majority are highly autocratic.

SUMMARY

In general the federal manager is perceived as being more effective through:

1 Seeking ideas and knowledge from, and understanding the prob-lems of, his subordinates, and utilizing this information in his decision-mak-ing process.

2 Sharing information with his subordinates.

3 Providing support to his subordinates.

4 Displaying trust and confidence to his subordinates.

5 Using rewards and involvement as incentives for motivation rather than fear and threats; emphasizing corrective measures rather than punitive measures.

Effective managers, on the average, however, are not completely participative in decision-making, goal-setting, or in establishing of control. The explanation may be that complete participation is not appropriate in the governmental agency surveyed. Another explanation may be that even some of the more effective managers may not be aware of the potential available through even greater participation by their subordinates.

It is important to note that these managers, although employed in the same agency, are at different levels in the organization, are assigned different duties, and are separated in location by nearly a continent, have provided responses for which the means on almost all items are nearly identical. By their own experience and observation, they have identified *effective managers* as being relatively *participative* in their leadership style and *weak managers* as being relatively *autocratic*.

CHAPTER 7
PARTICIPATIVE MANAGEMENT

READING 28

PARTICIPATIVE MANAGEMENT*

In redesigned worksettings one finds the workers participating in decisions on:

- Their own production methods
- The internal distribution of tasks
- Questions of recruitment
- Questions regarding internal leadership
- What additional tasks to take on
- When they will work

Not all of the work groups make all of these decisions, but the list provides the range within which the workers are participating in the management of the business or industry. Participative management does *not* mean participation through representatives, for, as experience has shown, that kind of participation may foster alienation through the inevitable gap between expected and actual responsiveness of the representatives. Nor does this kind of participation mean placing workers or union representatives on the board of directors of a corporation. Where workers have so served (in Norway, for example), neither participation by the rank and file nor productivity has increased, and worker alienation has not decreased.[10]

Participative management means, as the examples above illustrate, that workers are enabled to control the aspects of work intimately affecting their lives. It permits the worker to achieve and maintain a sense of personal worth and importance, to grow, to motivate himself, and to receive recognition and approval for what he does. It gives the worker a meaningful voice in decisions in one place where the effects of his voice can be immediately experienced. In a broader sense, it resolves a contradiction in our Nation—between democracy in society and authoritarianism in the workplace.

Not all of a company's decisions, of course, are turned over to the workers when they participate in management. Upper-level managers continue to run the company, handle major financial transactions, and coordinate all the functions. Although they are no longer involved in planning the

---

* Adapted from *Work in America,* Report of a Special Task Force to the Secretary of Health, Education, and Welfare, Cambridge, Mass.: The MIT Press, 1973, pp. 103–104.

[10] Louis E. Davis and Eric Trist, "Improving the Quality of Work Life: Experience of the Socio-Technical Approach," Management and Behavioral Science Center, University of Pennsylvania, 1972.

details of every operation in the company, they serve as expert consultants to the teams of workers.

*   *   *

READING   29

PARTICIPATIVE MANAGEMENT—A PRACTICAL EXPERIENCE

Frederick B. Chaney
Kenneth S. Teel*

In recent years, increasing numbers of employees have pressured for greater involvement and relevance in their day-to-day, on-the-job activities. Like today's college students, many have openly resisted authoritarian, "do as you're told" management practices. Instead, they have demanded a voice in determining what they are to do, how they are to do it, and even how they are to be evaluated. In short, more and more employees have insisted on being in on decisions that affect them and on being involved in what they consider to be meaningful work.

To meet these demands, many companies have adopted participative management practices. Some, like Harwood and Texas Instruments, have been highly successful. Others, not so well publicized, have been unsuccessful. Most, undoubtedly, have fallen somewhere between the two extremes. To show how participative management techniques can be successfully introduced and used on a continuing basis, this article describes the authors' four years of experience in implementing and applying such techniques at Autonetics, a division of North American Rockwell.

Before describing how to use participative management techniques, it seems appropriate to discuss briefly why a company might wish to use them. Obviously, no profit-oriented company exists solely to satisfy its employees' personal needs; rather, it has at least two fundamental goals—to survive and to make a profit. Effective use of participative management techniques can help reach these goals. When employees have "a piece of

* Reprinted by permission of the publisher from *Personnel*, November–December 1972, pp. 8–18. © 1972 by AMACOM, a division of American Management Associations.

the action," they identify more closely with the company; they develop greater esprit de corps; and, perhaps most important, they work harder to achieve goals they have helped to establish. In other words, participative management can bring about increased employee motivation.

At the same time, involving employees in identifying and solving production problems can result in improved technical solutions. Employees who face problems on a day-to-day basis often develop a clearer understanding of the nature of the problems and sounder ideas of how they might be solved than do experts brought in to deal with them. Providing a supportive environment in which employees are encouraged to express their ideas can make available to the company a reservoir of previously untapped technical expertise.

Despite these logical and persuasive theories and apparent advantages, at Autonetics it was decided that pilot studies should be conducted before any systematic attempt to introduce participative management throughout the production facility.

THE PILOT STUDIES: QUALITY ASSURANCE

The first study was conducted in an electronics inspection department. There, supervisors of two equivalent groups were given six hours of instruction in principles and techniques of employee motivation and performance improvement, supplemented by one hour of individual counseling by the staff psychologist on the specific goal-setting techniques to be used.

After this training, the supervisors met with their subordinates and encouraged them to establish goals for a reduction in paperwork errors, which were excessive and were causing delays in shipping the end product. One supervisor met with his inspectors as a group for approximately one hour each week for four weeks; the second supervisor held a series of short individual conferences during the same period. Both participative techniques resulted in establishment of goals of 50 percent reductions in paperwork errors, but, during the three-month evaluation period, reductions in errors of approximately 75 percent were obtained by the first group, whereas the second group showed no significant improvement.

Experience gained in this study indicated that it was impossible to make a clear-cut distinction between group and individual goal setting. Employees were generally reluctant to establish individual goals until they knew how their own performance compared with the department average. So, in reality, goals set in individual supervisor-employee conferences were strongly influenced by the performance of the group as a whole. Furthermore, both supervisors indicated a strong preference for the group procedure, because it required less time to cover the same number of employees and it provided an opportunity for employees to exchange ideas on how the goals might be met. These findings, along with the apparent superiority of the group goal-setting process, led to a decision to use the group process in all subsequent studies.

One other finding that emerged from this initial study: It was extremely difficult and somewhat artificial to try to get employees to establish more challenging goals without discussing the factors that limited group performance. Group problem solving seemed to be a prerequisite to goal setting—employees must be given a chance to identify and solve problems inhibiting performance before they could be expected to set and meet more ambitious goals.

THE PILOT STUDIES: MANUFACTURING

The second study was carried out to evaluate the combined effectiveness of group problem solving and goal setting in a typical manufacturing operation. Five supervisors in electronics assembly took an eight-hour training course in participative management, covering traditional topics such as principles of motivation, performance measurement, feedback, and communications, as well as the group problem-solving and goal-setting processes. The supervisors were also given practice in the use of discussion leadership techniques and individual counseling by staff psychologists after each meeting.

Next, each supervisor conducted a series of eight biweekly, half-hour meetings with his employees. Quantitative data on quantity and quality of production were obtained for three of the five groups. (Similar data were not available for the other two.) Two months after initial goal setting, one group had increased its output from 12 to 17 cables per week and had reduced its defect rate from eight to less than three per cable. A second group, by changing from a stationized assembly line, in which each person performed a series of specialized tasks, to an individual-build approach, in which each built the complete circuit board, reduced production time from 5.5 to 4.2 hours per board and defect rates by 50 percent. A third group reduced assembly time per system by 50 percent and defect rates by 40 percent. Improved performance by this group alone resulted in a saving of approximately $20,000 in five months.

GETTING THE BUGS OUT OF THE PROGRAM

Even though these early attempts in manufacturing were quite successful, several problems were noted:

- The supervisors appeared to need more individual guidance in conducting their initial sessions than had originally been assumed. Several found that they were unable to create the proper atmosphere or to supply the information requested by their subordinates during their first few group meetings. Two commented that they would have stopped the meetings after the first two or three if they had not received additional counseling by the staff psychologist for an average of two hours per week.

• The formal classroom instruction seemed to be of little value in preparing supervisors for the group sessions. Instead, the most effective training seemed to occur in the group meetings themselves—"learning by doing"—and in the individual supervisor-psychologist coaching sessions held immediately after each training session.

• All of the participating supervisors stated that their superiors did not fully understand and therefore did not adequately support the use of participative techniques. As a matter of fact, some of the superiors openly expressed doubts about the value of the meetings and questioned whether supervisors should pull their employees off the production line to take part in such meetings. This finding clearly demonstrated that more effort was needed to orient higher levels of management before any attempt to introduce participative management at lower levels.

To overcome these deficiencies, the implementation program was modified before participative management was launched throughout most of the production areas, and in some engineering organizations. The key elements in the revised program were these:

• Management orientation
• Supervisory seminars
• Supervisor-group meetings, emphasizing performance measurement, problem solving, and goal setting
• Coaching of supervisors by staff psychologists
• Management follow-up

Since the revised program proved to be markedly successful, the discussion that follows might be considered a how-to guide for an organization interested in establishing its own participative management program.

Step 1: Management Orientation

Two informal discussion meetings were held by staff psychologists with the managers to whom the supervisors participating in the program reported, to ensure that the managers both understood and supported the program. The rationale underlying the use of participative management was described; the successful pilot studies were detailed; the concepts to be presented to the supervisors were reviewed; the overall program was outlined; suggestions were solicited as to how the program might be tailored to meet the special needs of each department; and questions were answered.

It was emphasized that (1) change occurs slowly and the managers, therefore, should not expect overnight "miracles," and (2) the supervisors would have to devote considerable time to preparing for, holding, and following up on the group meetings and might need temporary help during the early phases of the program. An attempt was made to get the managers to agree to support the program for three months and postpone evaluating it until the end of that period.

In over 90 percent of the cases, this step resulted in a management commitment to support the program. In the few cases where it did not, no further attempt was made to implement the program in the managers' bailiwicks.

Step 2:   Supervisory Seminars

In four informal, one-hour seminars, a staff psychologist and five to eight supervisors discussed in depth the principles and techniques of effective communications, leadership, problem solving, and goal setting. The psychologist served primarily as a discussion leader, encouraging the supervisors to raise questions and to offer suggestions about making participative management work for them. He also attempted to set an example by conducting the seminars in the way he hoped the supervisors would conduct their own group meetings; to underscore that point, part of the final seminar was devoted to a critique of the techniques the psychologist had used as discussion leader.

Step 3:   Supervisor-Group Meetings

Next, each supervisor met with his employees, as a group, once a week for 12 weeks, even though some of the supervisors still felt inadequately prepared to conduct group meetings. There were two reasons for this go-ahead: First, previous research had clearly shown that supervisors, like almost anyone else, learn best by doing. Second, if the supervisors had been given the option of having additional training until they felt fully ready to start the new program, some might have chosen an excessive amount, thereby causing serious delays and accompanying administrative complications.

To help the supervisors feel more secure, a staff psychologist attended each group meeting, serving strictly as a resource person and observer. He answered questions directed to him by the supervisor, but always referred group members' questions to the supervisor, to reinforce the fact that the supervisor was not just the designated, but the actual, discussion leader. He also made detailed notes on the supervisor's and the group's behavior, which he used as the basis for his individual coaching session with the supervisor after each meeting.

After the initial 12 weekly meetings, supervisors were encouraged to continue them, although less frequently, as meaningful problem-solving sessions, rather than routine get-togethers. Most supervisors held monthly or quarterly meetings, or scheduled them on an as-needed basis.

The first two or three group meetings were devoted primarily to identifying possible ways in which group performance could be measured objectively and quantitatively, and to selecting the most appropriate ones for tracking subsequent performance. Thus, the group members themselves played the major role in determining how their work would be evaluated.

The selected measures were used to identify areas in which group performance was above, at, or below expectations, and several meetings were then devoted to in-depth analyses of problem areas. Group members were encouraged to identify factors inhibiting production, suggest ways in which they might be handled, and, with the help of industrial engineers who served as consultants, select modifications of work methods and procedures to be adopted on a trial basis. As feedback became available on the success of the modified approaches, further changes were made if they were indicated; thus, problem solving continued through all of the meetings, and the group members remained alert to the significance of the problem identification-problem solving-feedback loop.

By the sixth or seventh meeting, most groups had established goals calling for significant improvements in performance; in those groups that had not, the staff psychologist urged the supervisor to try to get the group to agree on firm goals by the ninth meeting, for several reasons. After all, performance data had been available on a weekly basis from the third meeting on, so each group had ample information on which to base its goals. Furthermore, long-time research had pretty well proved that participation gets sound performance results only when a group makes decisions and sets firm goals. However, research had also shown that people work harder and perform better when they shoot for goals that are within their reach. Thus, it was up to the supervisor both to encourage his group to set goals and to see that the goals set were attainable. (Actually, most supervisors found themselves having to hold back the group from setting "pie in the sky," instead of realistic, goals.)

Step 4: Coaching of Supervisors

Before and after each of the first 12 group meetings, the supervisor and staff psychologist met privately for a coaching-critique session. Before the meeting, the psychologist reviewed the supervisor's performance in previous meetings, suggested ways in which he might improve his effectiveness as a discussion leader, discussed the specific purposes of the forthcoming meeting, and answered any questions the supervisor had. In short, he served as a personal professional adviser in helping the supervisor prepare for the meeting. Immediately after the meeting he went over the supervisor's performance, pointing out what he had done well or poorly and suggesting ways in which he might do better next time.

The supervisors and the staff psychologists agreed that this individual coaching-feedback was the most valuable single element in preparing the supervisors, both intellectually and attitudinally, for effective use of participative management techniques. They also agreed, however, that after the first 12 meetings, the psychologist should attend subsequent meetings and provide further coaching only at the invitation of the supervisor. As far as the authors are aware, this participative management implementation program at Autonetics is the only one that gives so much emphasis to the systematic use of coaching.

Step 5:   Management Follow-up

After the first 12 group meetings, a second meeting was held with the managers to whom the supervisors reported. With the help of a staff psychologist, the supervisors described their experiences in the group meetings, explained changes that had been made to improve performance, reviewed the goals that had been set, showed the progress that had been made toward those goals, described their own and their employees' reactions to the program, and answered questions raised by the managers. In this way, the meeting effectively closed the loop, providing direct feedback to the managers on how well participative management had worked in their own organizations, and a suitable occasion for the managers to reinforce the behavior of the supervisors by public praise of those who had successfully used participative techniques.

HOW WELL DID THE PROGRAM WORK—AND WHY?

During the four years the authors were involved in the Autonetics program, quantitative performance data were obtained for 40 groups. Of these, 27 showed statistically significant performance gains; 12 showed no significant changes; and one showed a significant decline. The 27 averaged 20–30 percent increases in production, along with 30–50 percent decreases in errors, and they also exhibited more positive attitudes (via a questionnaire survey) toward the company after being involved in the program. It therefore seems reasonable to conclude, generally, that the overall program was successful. Participative management is no panacea. It will not solve all management problems; it may not achieve any gains at all in some cases. Nevertheless, the two-out-of-three batting average reported here suggests that the odds are heavily in favor of a well-planned and carefully conducted implementation program. Furthermore, the dollar value of the gains achieved in the successful groups should, as it did in this instance, far exceed the total cost of the program for all groups, successful or not-so-successful.

Detailed analyses of the data and observations of the individual groups lead to a number of more specific conclusions:

* *A little no better than none.*   Unless the supervisor succeeds in generating a fairly high level of participation in his group, the chances of achieving worthwhile performance gains are extremely low—a prediction borne out by a study conducted by one of the authors as part of the overall implementation program at Autonetics.

Six groups were ranked by level of participation, on the basis of observations made independently by two staff psychologists. The two rankings were identical, so the top two groups were categorized as high in participation, the next two as medium, and the last two as low. Performance and attitude data were also obtained for two equivalent groups in the same organization in which participative techniques were not used. Attitude measures for all groups were obtained by computing the percentage of positive responses to a 30-item job-related questionnaire.

It was found that medium to high levels of participation resulted in significant improvements in both attitudes and performance. Even low levels of participation resulted in more positive attitudes, but they did not evince any tangible performance benefits over the three-month period covered by the study. Expressed positive attitudes showed an almost linear improvement with increased participation, ranging from 35 percent for the no-participation groups to 80 percent for the high. On the other hand, performance showed no noteworthy changes for the no- and low-participation groups, but highly significant improvements for both the medium and high groups. The gains achieved by the high-participation groups, however, were almost twice as great as those of the medium groups.

• *Supervisors the key element.* Observation of both those groups in which participation was successful and those in which it was not revealed that the individual supervisor was the crucial factor. His attitudes and behavior strongly influenced the level of participation achieved; the level of participation, in turn, determined the extent of the gains achieved.

The "successful" supervisors by words and actions made clear their genuine interest in the employee ideas and feelings. They created an open, supportive atmosphere; they identified areas where they needed help; they actively solicited employee comments; they listened attentively to those comments, without making snap judgments; and they provided feedback at every meeting about what they were doing to implement employee suggestions.

Most of the "unsuccessful" supervisors, on the other hand, went through the motions of asking for employee comments and suggestions but actually did not pay much attention to them. Employees were quick to see that they were simply taking part in another exercise and typically offered only superficial or negative comments.

Discussions with several of these supervisors brought out two major reasons for their ineffective use of participative techniques. Some had used authoritarian management techniques for so long that they were convinced that they had sole responsibility for making decisions affecting the group; under pressure from higher management, they apparently subscribed to the participation idea, but did not really involve their employees in the decision-making process. The other reason was that a few who were relatively new to supervision felt insecure and were reluctant to reveal their own weaknesses by asking their employees for help in solving work-group problems.

As was pointed out earlier, participative management is not for every-one. If the supervisor is not sold on participation or if he is insecure, he would probably be better off using other management techniques.

- *It helps, but participation doesn't have to start with the boss.* All of the supervisors in this program were at the first level, and most of them, particularly in the factory, worked for superiors who used rather authoritar-ian management techniques. Nevertheless, as we have seen, two out of three were able to obtain significant improvements in employee perform-ance and attitudes by using participative techniques, and several of their bosses have since begun to follow the participative approach. Thus, suc-cessful implementation occurred from the bottom up, rather than in the more traditional top-down direction. (Of course, the management orienta-tion at the outset established at least a hands-off, wait-and-see manage-ment commitment to what the supervisors were about to try.)

A top-down program undoubtedly would have been faster, and it might have been more effective, but it might also have had only token accept-ance, which would have died out as soon as another management tech-nique received the blessing of top executives. At Autonetics, demonstrat-ing the value of the program at the first level proved to be highly effective in enlisting strong top-level support for continuing and expanding it.

- *Group goal setting not a must.* Under certain circumstances—for example, when firm contractual commitments have already been estab-lished—it may not be possible to allow a group to set its own production goals. Even then, though, participation can be used both to gain group acceptance of the predetermined goals and to identify ways in which those goals can best be met. In one such case, the supervisor personally set a new production goal at the level demanded by contract but succeeded in obtaining a high level of participation by explaining fully why that goal had to be met, by showing a real interest in getting the employees' help in identifying and solving the problems facing the group, and by putting into effect many of their suggestions for changes in work methods and proce-dures. The success of his approach was evidenced by the fact that his employees surpassed a goal that was twice what their production had aver-aged during the two and a half months prior to the first group meeting.

It is evident that group goal setting is not a requisite for successful use of participation. What is a requisite, however, when the supervisor sets the goals—and perhaps particularly then—is his positive attitude in dealing with the group.

- *Participative vs. permissive management.* Some critics of partici-pative management have contended that it is too permissive, that it results in the supervisor's abandoning his prerogatives and relegating his respon-sibilities to the group. Apparently, these critics have confused participative with laissez-faire management. True participative management requires that the supervisor work closely and actively with his employees to plan, organize, coordinate, and control the work of the group. The supervisor shares his responsibilities with the group—he does not surrender them.

Furthermore, he often has to provide firm guidelines to keep group meetings focused on appropriate topics; he has to provide information on requirements imposed on the group by the larger organization of which it is a part; he has to take the lead in deciding which of the group's suggestions should be implemented and in seeing that they are implemented; and he has to establish a system for providing regular feedback on how well the group is doing.

In short, true participative management is an active, goal-oriented process in which the supervisor works *together* with his employees to identify and solve the problems they share. By so doing, he makes them feel more important and thereby creates an environment in which they not only produce more but also are more satisfied with their work.

A PROGNOSIS OF CAUTIOUS OPTIMISM

The implementation program described here was successful in a large majority of the cases in one large company. With management commitment and perhaps some minor modifications to meet the requirements of a particular organization, it should be just as successful in other companies, regardless of their size.

Participative management offers no simple, easy solution to all organizational problems; for managers and supervisors who are willing to work hard at it, however, it does offer high probabilities of payoff in both increased production and improved employee attitudes. Participative management is a practical way of integrating individual and organizational goals. It gives employees opportunities to play active roles in planning, coordinating, and controlling their own work, and thus makes employees' work more meaningful and relevant. For the modern manager having to deal with a workforce demanding more voice in shaping its own activities and destiny, participative management seems to offer a promising route to the satisfaction of employee needs and, at the same time, increased company profits. Who can fault that combination?

READING   30

THE NON-LINEAR SYSTEMS EXPERIMENT IN PARTICIPATIVE MANAGEMENT

Erwin L. Malone*

I   INTRODUCTION

The human relations theory of management states that man's psycholog-ical needs are at least as important as his physiological needs. This theory holds that employee satisfaction and increased productivity and creativity are obtained under conditions where employees have high security and maximum opportunities for self-direction and self-control.

Non-Linear Systems, Inc., of Del Mar, California, went to unusual lengths to apply human relations concepts to a functioning business. The experiment drew the attention of scientists, writers, educators, engineers, consultants, and representatives of governments and industries from all parts of the world, although most of the evaluative reporting of the experi-ment was incomplete or simply erroneous. This paper reports many details of the experiment for the first time and throws new light on its outcome.[1]

II   THE COMPANY'S HISTORY

Non-Linear Systems, Inc. (which hereafter will be designated as NLS) was established in Del Mar, California, in 1952 and incorporated in California in 1953. Its entire corporate stock was held by Andrew F. Kay, president, and his family until recently, when some distribution to employees was made. The company principally manufactures a complete line of digital electrical measuring instruments, ranging in price from $500 to over $20,000 per unit, which are also tailored to specific requirements of such customers as U.S. governmental agencies, universities, and, through subcontractors, utilities, petroleum, chemical, textile, and other industries. The company grew from

* From *The Journal of Business,* January 1975, pp. 52–64. Copyright 1975 by the Univer-sity of Chicago. Reprinted with permission.

[1] The author spent 2 weeks at Non-Linear Systems shortly after the termination of the experiment in 1965. There, at the invitation of the company, he interviewed directors, officers, managers, and operative employees and was given free access to all correspondence, rec-ords, and employees in and out of the plant. Since then, he has been in frequent contact with important actors in and observers of the experiment.

an initial five employees in 1952 to a high of 340 (75 percent of them male) in the 1960s; it now employs one-third that number. Dun and Bradstreet rated the company as a $6 million enterprise. For years NLS was the leader in an industry where it and six competitors took 95 percent of the available business and some 50 others shared the remaining 5 percent.

The company had been in business for 8 years and was firmly established in its field before the experiment in "participative management" was initiated in 1960–61. There never had been unionization in any department of the company. The experiment was completely voluntary on the part of the company. It was set up by a liberal-minded president whose early life observations of the critical impact of working policies and conditions on his parents, himself, and others generated an insatiable interest in methods to better human relations in industry and develop each individual's potential to the full. The experiment was instituted after years of deliberation and long conferences with professional scientists and industrialists who professed similar interests and after many months of discussion with employees and with their full consent.

III   ELEMENTS OF THE PARTICIPATIVE MANAGEMENT EXPERIMENT

The general theory of the Non-Linear Systems experiment drew on the writings of behavioral scientists, most of whom were identified with the human relations approach. These included Peter F. Drucker, Douglas McGregor, and A. H. Maslow.[2] The view of human nature and worker motivation drawn from these writers included the following points:

1   Work is as natural as play or rest, and if made a source of satisfaction it will be performed willingly and voluntarily.

2   In the service of objectives to which he is committed, man requires little or no external direction or control. He will exercise self-direction and self-control. The degree of his self-control will depend upon the degree to which he is committed to these objectives.

3   Commitment to objectives is a function of rewards associated with their achievement, these rewards being those which go to satisfy man's physiological, psychological, safety, social, ego, and self-actualization needs.

4   Many humans not only are ready to accept responsibility, they seek to shoulder it. Avoidance of responsibility, lack of ambition, and emphasis on security are not inherent human characteristics.

[2] Peter F. Drucker, *The Practice of Management* (New York: Harper & Row, 1954), pp. 125–36; Douglas McGregor, *The Human Side of Enterprise* (New York: McGraw-Hill Book Co., 1960), pp. 33–48; A. H. Maslow, "A Theory of Human Motivation," *Psychological Review* 50, no. 4 (July 1943): 370–96.

5 The powers of imagination, ingenuity, and creativity are more widely distributed throughout the population than most executives admit. They simply await the proper time, place, stimulus, and atmosphere of receptivity to pour forth.

6 Under the conditions of modern industrial life, man's intellectual potentialities are only partially realized.

To apply these beliefs to the day-to-day operations of a business required that they be translated into specific objectives and then into changes in the structure and procedures of the firm. These changes were as follows:

Wages   Human relations theory states that wages can satisfy human needs for security, safety, and status, but that hourly and piecework wages are not needed to evoke employee effort. To eliminate the punishment-reward psychology of hourly wages, toward the end of 1960 all hourly rated employees (who were already being paid higher-than-average area wages of $1.90 an hour, or $76 a week) were advanced $0.60 an hour and placed on a straight salary of $100 a week. Thereafter no deductions were made for arriving late, for leaving early, for cleanup or wash-up time in any amount, or for fatigue or coffee breaks taken at the employee's convenience. No records were kept of these or of any other work absences.

Not long after the new salary scale was put into effect, older employees requested the president of NLS to start new employees at the rate of $85 a week instead of at the $100 a week rate and that salary scale was adopted, with the increase to $100 a week coming after a probationary period of flexible length. There never was a specific plan other than this for merit or length-of-service increases; such increases were proposed by managers of departments and acquiesced in by the president; they were few in number and moderate in amount. Salaries of technicians, draftsmen, and other employees were advanced in 1960–61 wherever revision was deemed desirable in order to keep their remuneration reasonably commensurate with the increases given hourly rated employees.

Organization Human relations theory, with its emphasis on self-direction, argues for making the staff an advisory rather than an authoritarian administrative body. Prior to the experiment, NLS operated with a traditional "vertical" organization: a board of directors; president; vice-presidents; managers for production, sales, accounting, inspection, quality, purchasing, engineering, and shipping; engineers; superintendents; technicians; draftsmen; foremen; inspectors; assemblers; shippers; and miscellaneous workers. In the experiment, although the corporate-level structure remained the same, the organization structure shown on charts distributed throughout the plant was vastly different. In the new setup there were three "zones":

Zone 1: trustee management   This consisted of the four members of the board of directors of the company, including Andrew F. Kay, chairman of the board. Responsibilities: to determine the basic policies and the basic course of the business.

Zone 2: general management   This was an eight-member Executive Council consisting of seven members chosen by the president, plus the president himself. The council was to establish operating policies; plan, coordinate, and control the business as a whole; and appraise results. The seven members held titles indicating prime interest in certain areas of operation: vice-president—innovation; vice-president—productivity; vice-president—physical and financial resources; vice president—profitability; vice-president—manager performance and development; vice-president—marketing; vice-president—legal council and public responsibility. (Note that in the organization charts the office of president was eliminated: the president was a member of the Executive Council and that was the level at which he functioned.) The Executive Council was to operate as a unit, never directing or controlling. Decisions were to be advisory, by mutual consent of the members present at any meeting.

Zone 3: departmental management.   At this level were the 30 department units, also called project teams. Each consisted of three to 12 employees, including the department manager. They were to "manage the business of their departments for the objectives defined and authorized by the Executive Council." Department unit managers had been chosen by the president with the aid of the former works manager who became an Executive Council vice-president. Department managers were responsible for day-to-day methods, operations, and procedures in their units. Typical of these numerous department units were: project team (designing and developing company products); industrial engineering; materials; fabrications (assembling instruments from parts supplied to these units in kits coming from the warehouse); instrument assembly (nonkit assembly); systems; distribution (receiving and filling customers' orders and also invoicing outgoing material); plant facilities; personnel services; sales promotion; regional sales (numerous such units, each responsible for sales in a specified territory).

Executive Council meetings were held daily for a period, then weekly. Managers of project and production teams met daily or as needed. Managers of other departments met irregularly.

Production Setup   Prior to the time of change, two assembly lines produced two basic models of digital voltmeters. Relatively slight changes or additions adapted these two basic models to specific needs of individual customers. These assembly lines were discontinued in 1960–61. They were replaced by departmental units of three to 12 people, each in a separate room, each headed by a manager, each responsible for creating completed instruments from parts brought to it from the stockroom. Each group assembled, calibrated, inspected, packed its instruments, usually making five to 10 instruments at a time. Each group worked at its own pace, making its own decisions as to whether each man would make a complete instrument from start to finish or whether the group would operate on an assembly-line basis with each person contributing certain operations to the line. Each group worked out its own internal problems of tardiness, absences, jealousies, breaks, and grievances; only in rare instances did such problems reach the Executive Council. Groups made their own rules of procedure. If they kept any records it was because they chose to do so. Records were not required.

The manager of a group was well qualified from his previous work experience to lead the group, but he was not a "boss" or a disciplinarian. Since the members of his group had the authority to do about what they wished, when, as, and how they wished, his job was one of consultation, direction, and advice at this lowest level. The group (unit) managers reported to the Executive Council as a whole, not to any individual member.

Indoctrination Programs   At the start of the experiment, every effort was made to acquaint each member of the organization, individually, with the new policy of the company and to inform one department after another of the potential benefits as the details of operation were described. The president personally addressed employees en masse, in groups, and individually, answering all questions freely and accepting suggestions.

The Executive Council was lectured to by many of the very prominent persons in the field of human and industrial relations, among whom were James V. Clark, Richard E. Farson, Abraham H. Maslow, Vance Packard, Carl Rogers, Robert Tannenbaum, and Frances Torbert.

A Los Angeles personnel-testing service interviewed every employee in the company in behalf of the program. Industrial relations counselors were retained on a permanent consulting basis to counsel employees, interview new applicants, and help indoctrinate them when they became employees of the company.

Training Procedures   Each new employee was first thoroughly informed as to the company's policies and operations. He then received an on-the-job training of some length. Thereafter, any employee, male or female, could have almost any type of job training he or she desired, inside or outside the plant. Courses of study taken outside the company premises were paid for in full by the company upon their completion.

Time Clocks   Punching a time clock is held to be degrading by most people who work in factories. They feel it implies mistrust. Time clocks were eliminated from all departments of the plant.

Record Keeping Douglas McGregor had stated that keeping performance records would vitiate the principle of self-control,[3] inasmuch as records could be used by management to control a subordinate and as a check on his performance. So far as production and personnel records were concerned, NLS became a company that operated essentially on a "put nothing in writing" basis. Because of this, statistical data of almost every sort are lacking; the data cited hereafter are from the personal knowledge, recollection, and papers of the board of directors, of Andrew F. Kay in his capacity as an Executive Council member, other members of the Executive Council, and company employees who were intimately in touch with operations from 1960 to 1965.

Accounting The Accounting Department as a unit was eliminated. Accountants were dispersed to purchasing, shipping, and personnel where separate books were kept, balances being reported to the treasurer at intervals.

Inspection The Inspection Department, as such, was eliminated. Each separate production unit was made responsible for the quality of its work, the members of each unit deciding how and when the inspection, or inspections, would be made on the product the unit made.

IV TERMINATION OF THE EXPERIMENT

For 5 years those who visited the plant at Del Mar, to witness firsthand this pioneering test of a new theory, came, saw, and departed unaware of any serious defects in the firm's operations. Although critical kinds of quantitative information were not furnished to these visitors, they generally concluded that the experiment was proceeding smoothly and could be expected to continue indefinitely. Yet early in 1965, NLS introduced modification so extensive and extreme as to signify the end of the experiment in participative management. These included the following:

1 "Line" organization procedures were reestablished at the top levels.
2 Direct supervision was provided.
3 Specific duties and responsibilities were assigned.
4 Standards of performance and quality were reestablished.
5 Authority was delegated commensurate with responsibility.
6 Records were reinstituted and maintained.
7 Remuneration was related to effort.
8 Factory department units were accorded a large measure of autonomy to schedule work within their units in the fashion they wished. In this

[3] McGregor, p. 160.

respect the department units function reasonably closely to the manner in which they operated during the years of the experiment.

The state of the firm at that point was as follows:

1 Sales volume was not measuring up to expectations; and, for the actual volume of sales, administrative and sales costs were heavy.
2 Organization restlessness had been developing at management levels.
3 Productivity as a whole remained unchanged.
4 Employee layoffs began in 1963. Other layoffs occured in 1964 and 1965.
5 Competition in the industry was multiplying.
6 The sales force resisted efforts to decrease sales costs.
7 The company was finding itself becoming progressively less profitable the longer it continued with participative management. The question was arising: how long would the company be able to afford the luxury of pursuing a theory of operation which bid fair to bring about its demise?

V   WHY DID THE EXPERIMENT FAIL?

The numerous reports published during the experiment generally fail to prepare the reader for the failure acknowledged by the company's turnabout in 1965. This section quotes some of these and also refers to opinions of behavioral scientists (some of whom were employed by NLS to counsel the firm and its employees) as these were made during the experiment and afterward. It also presents evaluations of these statements and explanations.

Business Conditions

It has been said that the firm made overoptimistic predictions of sales, leading to excessive increases in personnel in sales, advertising, development, engineering, and in other outlays. Thus, when the error was realized (in 1965) the firm was forced to jettison all but the most essential programs and tighten cost controls in every possible way.

Actually, in the period from 1953 to 1960 the company had experienced a phenomenal rate of growth, with sales doubling year after year. It cannot be said, now or then, that such a trend would not have continued. The management did anticipate that the sales mix might change from the 90 percent government and indirect-government sales of 1960 to the 60 percent which it became in 1965, and so it provided both a larger sales force and additional employees to take care of far greater sales.

Sales volume did increase each year from 1960 to 1963, but the rate of increase diminished. Late in 1963 and again in 1965 sales dropped sharply.

At these times orthodox management would have reduced plant employ-ment in line with the incoming order rate, but such an action would have been in conflict with the goals of job and personal security. Layoffs were not given the degree of serious consideration that was warranted until long after the problem of diminishing sales first arose, although the costs of retaining this manpower reserve were tremendous and were depleting the firm's treasury. Even when layoffs did occur, the higher-salaried engineer-ing and research personnel were shifted to lower-rated production jobs without the usual downward salary adjustment, in the belief that this would keep them available when improved conditions warranted their services.

Organization and Autonomy

The form of organization adopted under the experiment in participative management left many former administrators restless and frustrated be-cause they no longer had specific operating responsibilities. The Executive Council comprised seven vice-presidents plus the company president. The seven vice-presidents formerly had been vigorously active in the midst of daily problems and were more or less expert in their individual specialties. Under participative management these men were practically immobilized as "sideline consultants." Their duties were not well defined. New organi-zation charts every 6 months or so often changed their designations, for example, to "vice-presidents function virtually as assistant presidents," but without outlining specific duties or authority. In council meetings they were always in danger of being overwhelmed by the brilliant, mercurial thinking of President Kay, whose ability to originate new ideas on the spur of the moment, or to change direction, was astounding. It also was disconcerting. It is difficult to see how this group could be other than restless and frus-trated.

Department managers were heads of units engaged in production, sales, design, development, personnel, plant facilities, order distribution, etc. They managed their departments as well as they could. When technical problems arose and they went to the Executive Council for advice perhaps only one, or, at the most, two council members had the proficiency in the specific matters to be able to advise. When these men were not available, others could not make decisions that would be meaningful. So either the department managers made up their own minds or frustration developed as the problems remained unsolved. And since the questions had been asked verbally—nothing needed to be put in writing—there were no permanent records for future take-up at subsequent council meetings.

Each department manager oversaw the work of employees in his de-partment, to whom he was adviser, coordinator, consultant. With a modi-cum of experience behind them, numerous of these managers had need of the guidance and training they normally would have received had they worked directly under individually responsible supervisors. Under partici-

pative management they were chiefly on their own. Many found it disquiet-
ing to have to seek aid from the Executive Council as a whole. And no
matter how well experienced, young men in subordinate positions appear
to want some measure of authoritative direction—someone else to help
shoulder some of their problems.

Wages, Production, and Productivity

After the end of the experiment, a number of NLS executives told the author that the wage increase from $76 to $100 per week was a substantial
burden on the company. Yet, during the experiment, reports such as these
were common in the press: "Man-hours devoted to building each instrument have been cut in half—enabling Non-Linear to offer the highest pay in
the community."[4] "Production man-hours have been sliced in half, while
production is 30% higher than it ever has been."[5] "Within six months productivity began to rise. It's now averaging 50% more for each of the 350
employers."[6] "Productivity in man-hours per instrument has steadily improved. Today it is 30% better than at any period in the company's history."[7]

Actually, no production records were kept from 1960 to 1965 which
would show whether productivity increased or decreased. President Kay
and the members of the Executive Council who were interviewed in July
1965 were in complete agreement with the statement that "on some items
there may have been a productivity increase, but on other items there may
have been a productivity decrease. In the plant as a whole, there probably
was no change in productivity." It is very probable that productivity (the
output per individual in any given time) remained the same at the $100 per
week salary as it was at the $76 per week wage, since there appears to have
been no decrease in the man-hours required per instrument assembled.
(Note: the 31–32 percent increase in direct labor cost increased the sales
cost less than 5 percent.)

Quite a different matter is that of increased production (the output of
the factory in any given time). In 1963 the output from the factory was in the
neighborhood of 30 percent more than it was in 1960. But the number of
employees rose from 240 to 340, an increase of 42 percent over the same
period. (The NLS officers agree with the figures given here.) Even allowing
for a greater number of models of more intricate design, there is no indication of NLS ever having increased its plant efficiency during the entire run
of the experiment.

---

[4] Vance Packard, "A Chance for Everyone to Grow," *Readers Digest* (November 1963),
p. 115.

[5] "No-Assembly-Line Plan Gets Nothing But Results," *Steel*, May 25, 1964, p. 90.

[6] "Non-Conformity at Non-Linear," *Quality Assurance* (August 1964), p. 28.

[7] Authur H. Kuriloff, "An Experiment in Management—Putting Theory Y to the Test,"
Personnel (November–December 1963), p. 14.

Layoffs

At least one outside consultant to NLS has told the author that, if the company had possessed greater financial resources, standard instruments could have been stocked in a warehouse during periods when sales were low and employee layoffs avoided.

From 1952, when the company first began to operate, to 1960, when the experiment started, models of digital computers were sufficiently similar so that they could be made on two assembly lines. By 1965 specifications were more individualistic and more complicated—so much so that with 200 different models (counting adaptations) made annually, there could be no certainty that any instrument put into inventory would move out within 6 months or over. Models obsolesce quickly. Though the principle of inventory buildup during slack periods would supplement the participate management theory, it hardly can apply at NLS where a total of perhaps 10 instruments would have comprised a maximum salable inventory. Working capital was sufficient for NLS's needs, and total assets were well in line with sales. It was not due to lack of working capital that no appreciable inventory of instruments was carried.

Sales-Force Behavior and Competition

Over the period of the experiment (and since), there was an increase in the number and vigor of competitors, many of them offering reduced prices. To increase a company's sales in such a market, the company must provide something extra in the way of design, operation, adaptability, quality, service, or delivery. Beginning in 1960 NLS anticipated this by the creation of an expanded research and development staff and an augmented sales force covering the nation, and was quite successful in retaining its leadership with a major share of the market.

The company had employed sales representatives from 1953 to 1959. During 1960, 19 sales offices were opened throughout the country, and, in keeping with the human relations emphasis on security of income, staffed by salaried salesmen. Each district office was given a flat yearly sum to cover salaries, expenses for travel and entertainment, the purchase of new cars every 2 years, and office expenses. Each district office ran its own affairs, had its own bank account, paid its own bills, and sent the paid receipts to the home office. Sales reports and salesmen's expense books were not required.

Sales increased, but unfortunately the increased sales volume was not commensurate with the increased sales costs, and there were great differences in the ratios of costs to sales among districts with similar potential. In 1964 an attempt was made to lower sales costs by requesting each sales district to service its own customers rather than have servicemen sent out from the home office. A number of salesmen—some competent to service and others not—refused to service instruments, although the practice was not unusual in the industry. Instead of welcoming this opportunity to be of service to their customers, many salesmen took it as a lowering of their status and quit the company. In 1965, after the experiment's end, salaried salesmen were replaced by commission sales agents. This constituted a major policy change.

Product Quality

The quality of work was acceptable. What at one time had been thought to be a work-quality problem, which plagued the company for many months, was discovered to be caused by damage in transit at a particular transfer point; when shipments were routed around this point, the problem was solved.

Yet, because no company records were kept from 1960 to 1965, there is no statistical basis for published reports like these, which could only have been based on general impressions or wishful thinking: "Customer complaints fell 70%."[8] "Complaints from customers have dropped 90%."[9] "The number of complaints from the field: these are now 70% fewer than they were three years ago."[10] "Improvements in quality steadily reduced the number of complaints from the field. Though the business doubled in the four years after the assembly lines were dismantled, the number of complaints diminished by over 70% during that time."[11]

Job Satisfaction

Employee satisfaction with a job at NLS depended on the employee's position. Shop workers at the factory level obtained higher wages, greater autonomy and a voice in the production process, extensive opportunities to increase competence through training at company expense, and the numerous psychological benefits which undoubtedly followed from these. For them, NLS was a good place to work, and there was always a long list of applicants waiting to be hired. Employees brought in their relatives: 18 percent were related in 1965. Absenteeism was 2.8 percent in 1960 and 2.5 percent in 1965, and labor turnover was 4–5 percent in both years, about normal for manufacturing plants in the Del Mar area. Morale was high and grievances were few.

At the lower management level, department managers, many of them engineers and technicians, experienced a drop in morale during the course of the experiment. These technically skilled employees had often remained working at the plant long after quitting time. Toward the end they departed promptly after putting in an 8-hour day, and their offices were deserted on Saturdays, Sundays, and holidays as never before. Despite

---

[8] "When Workers Manage Themselves," *Business Week*, March 20, 1965, p. 94.
[9] See Packard.
[10] See Kuriloff.
[11] Arthur H. Kuriloff, *Reality in Management* (New York: McGraw-Hill Book Co., 1966), p. 44.

"ideal" working conditions and high salaries, 13 of the 30 department managers who were with the company in 1962 were not with NLS in 1965: the company ran out of work for three specialists, two had personality problems, one became discouraged, one resented the company's sales policy, one was permitted to resign because of inability to produce sales, four left for better jobs, and one went with a product division that NLS disposed of to another company.

For the seven executives who, with President Kay, made up the Executive Council, the experiment seems to have been highly unsatisfactory. The Executive Council did not prove to be effective in working out, or even in raising policy differences, and the seven subordinate executives felt that participative management had restricted rather than widened their horizons. They made constant, rather unsuccessful, attempts to define specific duties for their individual members.

Initially, three of the seven had favored the plan, two had cooperated even though unconvinced of its merit, and three had cooperated while privately believing that it could not succeed. During the 5 years of the experiment, one new member was added, and one was dismissed and then later rehired. After the end of the experiment in 1965 three were given long advance notice of employment termination, a fourth left of his own volition after refusing a salary reduction, and death overtook two.

Creativity

It had been hoped that participative management would encourage latent powers of imagination and creativity and uncover incipient managerial ability and provide the proper medium for its development. While it is difficult to conceptualize and measure these qualities, there is no evidence of an unusual development of human potential. During the 5 years of the experiment, many men were helped by the training and instruction they received, and many enlarged their work skills. But only two gave indications of greatness, and in 5 years any plant with 300 or more employees should expect to find two men of well-above-average caliber.

In addition, NLS was far from being an ordinary plant. Factory workers had at least a full high school education and were well trained, well adjusted, multitested, and highly screened by professional personnel experts who were generally sympathetic to the goals and methods of the human relations movement. Such a group may well be unique. But its accomplishments cannot be shown to have been especially high under participative management, whether accomplishment is measured by average performance or by the development of unusually productive individuals.

Profitability

When NLS initiated participative management in 1960, it looked forward to increasing the prosperity and well-being of everyone concerned. No thought may have been given to raising profits above the 1959–60 level reached prior to the experiment, but it hardly could have been expected that profits, which had increased yearly from 1953 to 1960, would begin in 1961 to spiral downward until the losses sustained compelled abandonment of the experiment in 1965. In retrospect, it is surprising now to read: "We feel we are well launched on an exciting experiment that ultimately will not only pay off in larger profits for the company, but will also contribute in some small measure toward the betterment of our industrial society."[12] "The company's unique experiment has attracted considerable national attention from management specialists, production people, and educators. Company morale has been examined by many outsiders and termed sky-high—and company profits have climbed too—even though the electronics industry as a whole has suffered a major price let-down."[13] "The program, under way now for five years, is beginning to show gains that sharpen NLS's competitive edge. . . .   A. H. Maslow, Brandeis University psychologist, believes NLS's experiment shows the way to the future."[14]

In contrast to these hopeful statements, all made more than halfway through the experiment, we have the much more recent remark by a behavioral scientist who had been employed on the NLS experiment since its inception: "I think we know now that Human Relations don't have a lot to do with profit and productivity."[15]

VI   AFTERMATH: WHAT DID THE EXPERIMENT SHOW?

In 1965 NLS retreated, in the face of overwhelming financial pressure, to the relatively conventional management methods described in Section IV above. The results are described by a long-time director with considerable business experience: "Both management and factory workers appear not dissatisfied with these changes. The company probably avoided bankruptcy by abandoning the experiment and returning to orthodox methods of management; it is now operating with a small profit and expanding into other, but related, fields."[16] Beyond this, the question remains of what the NLS experiment shows about the validity of the human relations and participative management approaches. Some of those who are familiar with the NLS experiment have suggested that much of the outcome was due to the unique personality of the president, Andrew F. Kay, and that a less powerful and less experimentally oriented individual might have produced results much more favorable to these theories. Of course, only an individual of Mr. Kay's unusual qualifications and position would have considered risking a

---

[12] Kuriloff, "An Experiment in Management," p. 17.

[13] See n.6.

[14] See n.8.

[15] Richard Farson, quoted in "Where Being Nice to People Didn't Work," *Business Week*, January 20, 1973, p. 94.

[16] Ludwig Weindling, management consultant, L. Weindling & Co., Rancho Santa Fe, California, and director, Non-Linear Systems, in letter to the author, April 1974.

thriving, multimillion-dollar business to test a theory previously untested on anything like this scale, and, in any case, we need to make the most of such a large and costly experiment, no matter how imperfect its design. In that spirit, the following conclusions are offered as being reasonably supported by the evidence:

1 The removal of the high-level NLS executives from their individual responsibilities for planning, directing, and controlling specific areas of operations was not successful. Whatever Kay may have done to make their problems more difficult, there is little reason to believe that these individuals could have achieved high productivity and job satisfaction within the rules of the experiment, regardless of who was president. It remains to be seen whether any individuals organized as a collective of advisers can perform successfully and, if so, what sorts of persons and training programs are required.

2 Quite similar conclusions apply to the lower levels of management, where productivity and job satisfaction dropped as a result of the experiment. These department managers wanted and needed more direction than the Executive Council was able to give, either collectively or as individuals. It remains to be seen whether any individuals could have performed the department manager functions productively and with satisfaction and, if so, how such individuals should be selected and trained.

3 At the level of the shop floor, job satisfactions increased, but there was no marked welling up of energy and creativity, much less a productivity improvement sufficient to overcome the loss of productivity at the executive levels, and none should be expected.

4 Over all, the sort of thoroughgoing adoption of human relations theories tried at NLS may be possible only while a firm enjoys an unusually profitable, protected market and has owners who are willing to accept unusually high frustrations and negligible or negative future returns. Smaller, more limited applications of a vastly modified participative management–human relations approach may continue to be considered in frameworks which retain effective supervision and rewards. But in a competitive market a company must receive from its employees enough in return to offset the extra costs of higher wages, additional benefits, lower work standards, better work conditions, and less efficient operations. If it does not, it soon will cease to exist.

CHAPTER 8
JOB ENRICHMENT

READING 31

SOME CAUSES OF JOB MOTIVATION

Martin Patchen*

WORK DIFFICULTY

Results of our study at TVA indicate that jobs of moderate difficulty, as compared with jobs of lesser challenge, lead to stronger motivation—as reflected by stronger interest in work innovation and by fewer absences. These results are consistent with laboratory studies which have shown motivation to increase in situations of moderate task difficulty. They suggest that there are important motivational advantages to be gained by trying to structure job content in a way that introduces some elements of problem solving and challenge into what might tend to be routine work. Our results also indicate that the higher motivation of those in moderately difficult jobs is *not* accompanied by greater symptoms of stress. This may not be the case in all work situations. For example, where individuals feel that their abilities are not adequate to meet the difficulties posed by the work, they may become tense, angry, or depressed. However, the present findings do suggest that, in a fairly wide range of job situations, the motivational advantages that come with the challenge of some difficulty are not bought at the expense of greater psychological stress.

CONTROL OVER METHODS

Results concerning job features relevant to achievement incentive also indicate the great importance of employees' control over work methods as a determinant of work motivation. The more control employees have over work methods, the greater their general job interest and their interest in work innovation, and the fewer their absences. These results are consistent with the general trend of results from other studies which usually show a positive association between employee influence on work methods and work performance. What is particularly impressive and noteworthy in the present results is that, when the effects of a large number of factors affecting job motivation are compared (each controlled for the effect of other factors), control over work methods emerges as the one factor which has sizeable associations with all indicators of job motivation. These results emphasize the advantages of designing job specifications and assigning responsibilities, insofar as technology allows, in such a way that employees are not greatly constrained by procedural rules or by supervisory instructions. Where, instead, employees are encouraged, within the limits of their training and abilities, to decide themselves (or in consultation with others) how their work shall be done, their motivation to do the work well is likely to be considerably enhanced.

*   *   *

READING 32

JOB ENRICHMENT LESSONS FROM AT&T

Robert N. Ford*

There is a mounting problem in the land, the concern of employed persons with their work life. Blue-collar workers are increasingly expressing unhappiness over the monotony of the production line. White-collar workers want to barter less of their life for bread. More professional groups are unionizing to fight back at somebody.

The annual reports of many companies frequently proclaim, "Our employees are our most important resource." Is this a statement of conviction or is it mere rhetoric? If it represents conviction, then I think it is only fair to conclude that many business organizations are unwittingly squandering their resources.

The enormous economic gains that sprang from the thinking of the scientific management school of the early 1900's—the time-and-motion study analysts, the creators of production lines—may have ended insofar as they depend on utilizing human beings more efficiently. Without discarding these older insights, we need to consider more recent evidence showing that the tasks themselves can be changed to give workers a feeling of accomplishment.

The growing pressure for a four-day workweek is not necessarily evidence that people do not care about their work; they may be rejecting their work in the form that confronts them. To ask employees to repeat one small task all day, at higher and higher rates of speed, is no way to reduce the pressure for a shorter workweek, nor is it any longer a key to rising productivity in America. Work need not be so frequently a betrayal of one's education and ability.

*From *Harvard Business Review*, January–February, 1973, pp. 96–106. © 1973 by the President and Fellows of Harvard College; all rights reserved. Used with permission.

Author's note: I wish to acknowledge the collaboration of Malcolm B. Gillette of AT&T and Bruce H. Duffany of Drake-Beam & Associates in the formulation of the job enrichment strategy discussed in this article.

From 1965 to 1968 a group of researchers at AT&T conducted 19 formal field experiments in job enrichment. The success of these studies has led to many company projects since then. From this work and the studies of others, we have learned that the "lifesaving" portion of many jobs can be expanded. Conversely, the boring and unchallenging aspects can be reduced—not to say eliminated.

Furthermore, the "nesting" of related, already enriched jobs—a new concept—may constitute another big step toward better utilization of "our most important resource."

First in this article I shall break down the job enrichment strategy into three steps. Then I shall demonstrate what we at AT&T have been doing for seven years in organizing the work beyond enrichment of individual jobs. In the course of my discussion, I shall use no illustrations that were not clearly successful from the viewpoint of both employees and the company.

While obviously the functions described in the illustrations differ superficially from those in most other companies, they are still similar enough to production and service tasks in other organizations to permit meaningful comparison. It is important to examine the nature of the work itself, rather than the external aspects of the functions.

Moreover, in considering ways to enrich jobs, I am not talking about those elements that serve only to "maintain" employees: wages, fringe benefits, clean restrooms, a pleasant atmosphere, and so on. Any organization must meet the market in these respects or its employees will go elsewhere.

No, employees are saying more than "treat me well." They are also saying "use me well." The former is the maintenance side of the coin; the latter is the work motivation side.

ANATOMY OF ENRICHMENT

In talking about job enrichment, it is necessary to go beyond such high-level concepts as "self-actualization," "need for achievement," and "psychological growth." It is necessary to specify the steps to be taken. The strategy can be broken down into these aspects—improving work through systematic changes in (a) the module of work, (b) control of the module, and (c) the feedback signaling whether something has been accomplished. I shall discuss each of these aspects in turn.

Work Module

Through changing the work modules, Indiana Bell Telephone Company scored a striking success in job enrichment within the space of two years. In Indianapolis, 33 employees, most of them at the lowest clerical wage level, compiled all telephone directories for the state. The processing from clerk to clerk was laid out in 21 steps, many of which were merely for verification. The steps included manuscript reception, manuscript verification, keypunch, keypunch verification, ad copy reception, ad copy verification, and so on—a production line as real as any in Detroit. Each book is issued yearly to the customers named in it, and the printing schedule calls for the appearance of about one different directory per week.

In 1968, the year previous to the start of our study, 28 new hires were required to keep the clerical force at the 33-employee level. Obviously, such turnover had bad consequences. From every operating angle, management was dissatisfied.

In a workshop, the supervisors concluded that the lengthy verification routine, calling for confirmation of one's work by other clerks, was not solving the basic problem, which was employee indifference toward the tasks. Traditional "solutions" were ineffective. They included retraining, supervisor complaints to the employees, and "communicating" with them on the importance to customers of error-free listing of their names and places of business in the directories. As any employee smart enough to be hired knows, an incorrect listing will remain monumentally wrong for a whole year.

The supervisors came up with many ideas for enriching the job. The first step was to identify the most competent employees, and then ask them, one by one, if they felt they could do error-free work, so that having others check the work would be pointless. Would they check their own work if no one else did it?

Yes, they said they could do error-free work. With this simple step the module dropped from 21 slices of clerical work to 14.

Next the supervisory family decided to take a really big step. In the case of the thinner books, they asked certain employees whether they would like to "own" their own books and perform all 14 remaining steps with no verification unless they themselves arranged it with other clerks— as good stenographers do when in doubt about a difficult piece of paperwork. Now the module included every step (except keytape, a minor one).

Then the supervisors turned their attention to a thick book, the Indianapolis directory, which requires many hands and heads. They simply assigned letters of the alphabet to individuals and let them complete all 14 steps for each block of letters.

In the past, new entries to all directories had moved from clerk to clerk; now all paperwork connected with an entry belonging to a clerk stayed with that clerk. For example, the clerk prepared the daily addenda and issued them to the information or directory assistance operators. The system became so efficient that most of the clerks who handled the smaller directories had charge of more than one.

Delimiting the Module   In an interview one of the clerks said, It's a book of my own." That is the way they felt about the books. Although not all modules are physically so distinct, the idea for a good module is usually there. Ideally, it is a slice of work that gives an employee a "thing of my own." At AT&T I have heard good modules described with pride in various ways:

- "A piece of turf" (especially a geographic responsibility).
- "My real estate" (by engineers responsible for a group of central offices).
- "Our cradle-to-grave modem line" (a vastly improved Western Electric switching-device production line).
- "Our mission impossible team" (a framemen's team, Long Lines Department).

The trouble with so much work processing is that no one is clearly responsible for a total unit that fails. In Indianapolis, by contrast, when a name in a directory is misspelled or omitted, the clerk knows where the responsibility lies.

Delimiting the module is not usually difficult when the tasks are in production, or at least physically defined. It is more difficult in service tasks, such as handling a telephone call. But modules make sense here, too, if the employee has been prepared for the work so that nobody else need be involved—in other words, when it is not necessary to say to the caller, "Let me connect you with my supervisor about that, please" or "May I give you our billing department, please?"

It is not always true that any one employee can handle a complete service. But our studies show that we consistently erred in forming the module; we tended to "underwhelm" employees. Eventually we learned that the worker can do more, especially as his or her experience builds. We do not have even one example from our business where job enrichment resulted in a *smaller* slice of work.

In defining modules that give each employee a natural area of responsibility, we try to accumulate horizontal slices of work until we have created (or recreated) one of these three entities for him or her:

1   A customer (usually someone outside the business).
2   A client (usually someone inside the business, helping the employee serve the customer).
3   A task (in the manufacturing end of the business, for example, where, ideally, individual employees produce complete items).

Any one of these three can make a meaningful slice of work. (In actuality, they are not separated; obviously, an employee can be working on a task for a *customer*.) Modules more difficult to differentiate are those in which the "wholeness" of the job is less clear—that is, control is not complete. They include cases where—

- the employee is merely one of many engaged in providing the ultimate service or item;
- the employee's customer is really the boss (or, worse yet, the boss's boss) who tells him what to do;
- the job is to help someone who tells the employee what is to be done.

While jobs like these are harder to enrich, it is worth trying.

Control of the Module

As an employee gains experience, the supervisor should continue to turn over responsibility until the employee is handling the work completely. The reader may infer that supervisors are treating employees unequally. But it is not so; ultimately, they may all have the complete job if they can handle it. In the directory-compilation case cited—which was a typical assembly-line procedure, although the capital investment was low—the supervisors found that they could safely permit the employee to say when sales of advertisements in the yellow pages must stop if the ads were to reach the printer on time.

Employees of South Central Bell Telephone Company, who set their own cutoff dates for the New Orleans, Monroeville, and Shreveport phone books, consistently gave themselves less time than management had previously allowed. As a result, the sale of space in the yellow pages one year continued for three additional weeks, producing more than $100,000 in extra revenue.

But that was only one element in the total module and its control. The directory clerks talked *directly* to salesmen, to the printer, to supervisors in other departments about production problems, to service representatives, and to each other as the books moved through the production stages.

There are obvious risks on the supervisors' side as they give their jobs away, piece by piece, to selected employees. We have been through it enough to advise, "Don't worry." Be assured that supervisors who try it will say, as many in the Bell System have said, "Now, at last, I feel like a manager. Before I was merely chief clerk around here."

In other studies we have made, control has been handed by the supervisor to a person when the employee is given the authority to perform such tasks as these:

- Set credit ratings for customers.
- Ask for, and determine the size of, a deposit.
- Cut off service for nonpayment.
- Make his or her own budget, subject to negotiation.
- Perform work other than that on the order sheet after negotiating it with the customer.

- Reject a run or supply of material because of poor quality.
- Make free use of small tools or supplies within a budget negotiated with the supervisor.
- Talk to anyone at any organizational level when the employee's work is concerned.
- Call directly and negotiate for outside repairmen or suppliers (within the budget) to remedy a condition handicapping the employee's performance.

Feedback

Definition of the module and control of it are futile unless the results of the employee's effort are discernible. Moreover, knowledge of the results should go directly to where it will nurture motivation—that is, to the employee. People have a great capacity for mid-flight correction when they know where they stand.

One control responsibility given to excellent employees in AT&T studies is self-monitoring; it lets them record their own "qualities and quantities." For example, one employee who had only a grade-school education was taught to keep a quality control chart in which the two identical parts of a dry-reed switch were not to vary more than .005 from an ideal dimension. She found that for some reason too many switches were failing.

She proved that the trouble occurred when one reed that was off by .005 met another reed that was off by .005. The sum, .010, was too much in the combined component and it failed. On her own initiative, she recommended and saw to it that the machine dies were changed when the reeds being stamped out started to vary by .003 from the ideal. A total variance of .006 would not be too much, she reasoned. Thus the feedback she got showed her she was doing well at her job.

This example shows all three factors at work—the module, its control, and feedback. She and two men, a die maker and a machine operator, had the complete responsibility for producing each day more than 100,000 of these tiny parts, which are not unlike two paper matches, but much smaller. How can one make a life out of this? Well, they did. The six stamping machines and expensive photometric test equipment were "theirs." A fork-lift truck had been dedicated to them (no waiting for someone else to bring or remove supplies). They ordered rolls of wire for stamping machines when they estimated they would need it. They would ship a roll back when they had difficulty controlling it.

Compared with workers at a plant organized along traditional lines, with batches of the reeds moving from shop to shop, these three employees were producing at a fourfold rate. Such a minigroup, where each person plays a complementary part, is radically different psychologically from the traditional group of workers, where each is doing what the others do.

(In the future, when now undreamed-of computer capacities have been reached, management must improve its techniques of feeding performance results directly to the employee responsible. And preferably it should be done *before* the boss knows about it.)

IMPROVING THE SYSTEM

When a certain job in the Bell System is being enriched, we ask the supervisory family, "Who or what is the customer/client/task in this job?" Also, "How often can the module be improved?" And then, "How often can control or feedback be improved? Can we improve all three at once?"

These are good questions to ask in general. My comments at this stage of our knowledge must be impressionistic.

The modules of most jobs can be improved, we have concluded. Responsibilities or tasks that exist elsewhere in the shop or in some other shop or department need to be combined with the job under review. This horizontal loading is necessary until the base of the job is right. However, I have not yet seen a job whose base was too broad.

At levels higher than entrance grade, and especially in management positions, many responsibilities can be moved to lower grade levels, usually to the advantage of every job involved. This vertical loading is especially important in mature organizations.

In the Indianapolis directory office, 21 piecemeal tasks were combined into a single, meaningful, natural task. There are counterparts in other industries, such as the assembly of an entire dashboard of an automobile by two workers.

We have evidence that two jobs—such as the telephone installer's job and the telephone repairman's job—often can make one excellent "combinationman's" job. But there are some jobs in which the work module is already a good one. One of these is the service representative, the highly trained clerk to whom a customer speaks when he wants to have a telephone installed, moved, or disconnected, or when he questions his telephone bill. This is sometimes a high-turnover job, and when a service representative quits because of work or task dissatisfaction, there goes $3,450 in training. In fact, much of the impetus for job enrichment came through efforts to reduce these costs.

In this instance the slice of work was well enough conceived; nevertheless, we obtained excellent results from the procedures of job enrichment. Improvements in the turnover situation were as great as 50%. Why? Because we could improve the control and feedback.

It should be recognized that moving the work module to a lower level is not the same as moving the control down. If the supervisor decides that a customer's account is too long overdue and tells the service representative what to do, then both the module and the control rest with the supervisor. When, under job enrichment procedures, the service representative makes the decision that a customer must be contacted, but checks it first with the supervisor, control remains in the supervisor's hands. Under full job enrichment, however, the service representative has control.

Exhibit I shows in schematic form the steps to be taken when improving a job. To increase control, responsibility must be obtained from higher levels; I have yet to see an instance where control is moved upward to enrich a job. It must be acknowledged, however, that not every employee is ready to handle more control. That is especially true of new employees.

Moreover, changing the control of a job is more threatening to supervisors than is changing the module. In rejecting a job enrichment proposal, one department head said to us, "When you have this thing proved 100%, let me know and we'll try it."

As far as feedback is concerned, it is usually improvable, but not until the module and control of it are in top condition. If the supervisory family cannot come up with good ways for telling the employee how he or she is doing, the problem lies almost surely in a bad module. That is, the employee's work is submerged in a total unit and he or she has no distinct customer/client/task.

When the module is right, you get feedback "for free"; it comes directly from the customer/client/task. During the learning period, however, the supervisor or teacher should provide the feedback.

When supervisors use the performance of all employees as a goad to individual employees, they thwart the internalization of motivation that job enrichment strives for. An exception is the small group of mutually supporting, complementary workers, but even in this case each individual needs knowledge of his or her own results.

These generalizations cannot be said to be based on an unbiased sample of all jobs in all locations. Usually, the study or project locations were

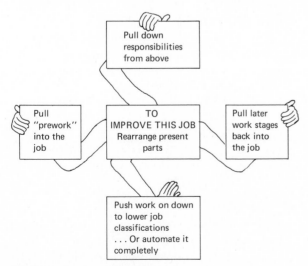

Exhibit I Steps in improving a job.

not in deep trouble, nor were they the best operating units. The units in deep trouble cannot stand still long enough to figure out what is wrong, and the top performers need no help. Therefore, the hard-nosed, scientifically trained manager can rightfully say that the jury is still out as to whether job enrichment can help in all work situations. But it has helped repeatedly and consistently on many jobs in the Bell System.

JOB 'NESTING'

Having established to its satisfaction that job enrichment works, management at AT&T is studying ways to go beyond the enriching of individual jobs. A technique that offers great promise is that of "nesting" several jobs to improve morale and upgrade performance.

By way of illustration I shall describe how a family of supervisors of service representatives in a unit of Southwestern Bell Telephone Company improved its service indexes, productivity, collection of overdue bills, and virtually every other index of performance. In two years they moved their Ferguson District (adjacent to St. Louis) from near the bottom to near the top in results among all districts in the St. Louis area.

Before the job enrichment effort started, the service representatives' office was laid out as it appears in *Exhibit II*. The exhibit shows their desks in the standard, in-line arrangement fronted by the desks of their supervisors, who exercised close control of the employees.

As part of the total job enrichment effort, each service rep group was given a geographical locality of its own, with a set of customers to take care

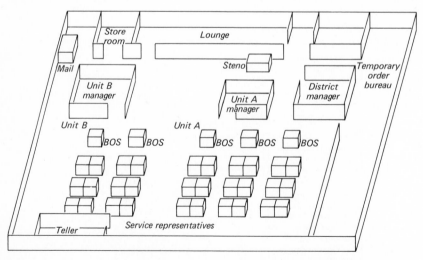

BOS — Business office supervisor

Exhibit II   Ferguson District service representatives' office layout before job enrichment.

of, rather than just "the next customer who calls in" from anywhere in the district. Some service reps—most of them more experienced—were detached to form a unit handling only the businesses in the district.

Then the service representatives and their business office supervisors (BOS) were moved to form a "wagon train" layout. As *Exhibit III* shows, they were gathered into a more-or-less circular shape and were no longer directly facing the desks of the business office supervisors and unit managers. (The office of the district manager was further removed too.)

Now all was going well with the service representatives' job, but another function in the room was in trouble. This was the entry-level job of service order typist. These typists transmit the order to the telephone installers and the billing and other departments. They and the service order reviewers—a higher-classification job—had been located previously in a separate room that was soundproofed and air-conditioned because the TWX machines they used were noisy and hot. When its equipment was converted to the silent, computer-operated cathode ray tubes (CRTs), the unit was moved to a corner of the service reps' room (see *Exhibit III*).

But six of the eight typists quit in a matter of months after the move. Meanwhile, the percentage of service orders typed "on time" fell below 50%, then below 40%.

The reasons given by the six typists who quit were varied, but all appeared to be rationalizations. The managers who looked at the situation, and at the $25,000 investment in the layout, could see that the feeling of

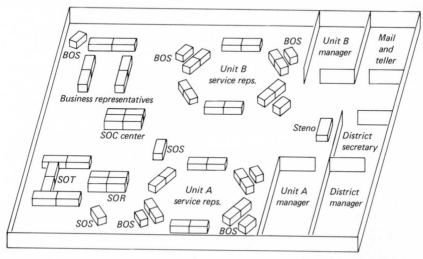

SOS — Service order supervisor
SOC — Service order control
SOR — Service order reviewers
SOT — Service order typists

Exhibit III Service representatives' office layout after job enrichment program was implemented.

physical isolation and the feeling of having no "thing" of their own were doubtless the real prime factors. As the arrangement existed, any service order typist could be called on to type an order for any service representative. On its face, this seems logical; but we have learned that an employee who belongs to everybody belongs to nobody.

An instantly acceptable idea was broached: assign certain typists to each service rep team serving a locality. "And while we're at it," someone said, "why not move the CRTs right into the group? Let's have a wagon train with the women and kids in the middle." This was done (over the protest of the budget control officer, I should add).

The new layout appears in *Exhibit IV*. Three persons are located in the station in the middle of each unit. The distinction between service order typist and service order reviewer has been abolished, with the former upgraded to the scale of the latter. (Lack of space has precluded arranging the business customer unit in the same wagon-train fashion. But that unit's service order review and typing desks are close to the representatives' desks.)

Before the changes were started, processing a service request involved ten steps—and sometimes as many persons—not counting implementation of the order in the Plant Department. Now the procedure is thought of in terms of people, and only three touch a service order on its way through the office. (See *Exhibit V*.) At this writing, the Ferguson managers hope to eliminate even the service order completion clerk as a specialized position.

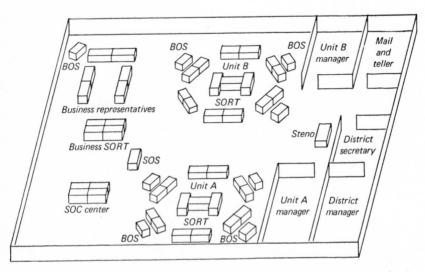

SORT — Service order review and typing

Exhibit IV Office layout after service order typists were "nested."

Has the new arrangement worked? Just before the typists moved into the wagon train, they were issuing only 27% of the orders on time. Half a year later, in one particular month, the figure even reached 100%.

These results were obtained with a 21% jump in work load—comparing a typical quarter after "nesting" with one before—being performed with a net drop of 22 worker-weeks during the quarter. On a yearly basis it is entirely reasonable to expect the elimination of 88 weeks of unnecessary work (conservatively, 1½ full-time employees). Unneeded messenger service has been dispensed with, and one of two service order supervisor positions has been eliminated. The entire cost has been recovered already.

The service order accuracy measurement, so important in computerization, has already attained the stringent objectives set by the employees themselves, which exceeded the level supervisors would have set. Why are there fewer errors? Because now employees can lean across the area and talk to each other about a service order with a problem or handwriting that is unclear. During the course of a year this will probably eliminate the hand preparation of a thousand "query" slips, with a thousand written replies, in this one district.

And what of the human situation? When on-time order issuance was at its ebb, a supervisor suggested having a picnic for the service representatives and the typists. They did, but not a single typist showed up. Later, when the on-time order rate had climbed over 90%, I remarked, "Now's the time for another picnic." To which the supervisor replied facetiously, "Now we don't need a picnic!"

The turnover among typists for job reasons has virtually ceased. Some

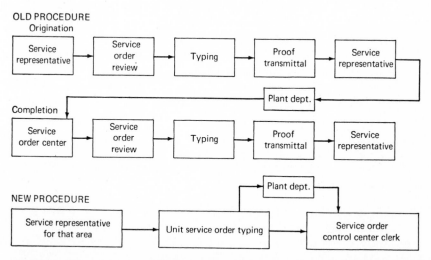

Exhibit V Old and new processing procedures in request for service department.

are asking now for the job of service representative, which is more demanding, more skilled, and better paid. Now, when the CRTs or the computer is shut down for some reason, or if the service order typist runs out of
work, supervisors report that typists voluntarily help the service reps with
filing and other matters. They are soaking up information about the higher-
rated jobs. These occurrences did not happen when the typists were 100
feet away; then they just sat doing nothing when the work flow ceased.
(Because of this two-way flow of information, incidentally, training time for
the job of service representative may drop as much as 50%.)

As the state general manager remarked when the results were first
reported, "This is a fantastic performance. It's not enough to enrich just
one job in a situation. We must learn how to put them together."

Different Configuration

While the Ferguson District supervisory family was making a minigroup out
of the service reps and their CRT typists, a strikingly different minigroup
was in formation in the Northern Virginia Area of the Chesapeake and Poto-
mac Telephone Company. There the family hit on the idea of funneling to
selected order typists only those orders connected with a given central
office, such as the Lewinsville frame. Soon the typists and the framemen—
those who actually make the changes as a result of service orders—became acquainted. The typists even visited "their" framerooms. Now some
questions could be quickly resolved that previously called for formal interdepartmental interrogations through supervisors.

At the end of the first eight months of 1972, these 9 CRT typists were
producing service order pages at a rate one third higher than the 51 service order typists in the comparison group. The absence rate in the experimental unit was 0.6%, compared with 2.5% for the others, and the errors
per 100 orders amounted to 2.0 as against 4.6 in the comparison group.

The flow of service orders is from (a) service rep to (b) service order
typist to (c) the frameroom. The Ferguson District enjoyed success when it
linked (a) and (b), while productivity for the Lewinsville frame improved
when (b) and (c) were linked. Obviously, the next step is to link (a), (b), and
(c). We are now selecting trial locations to test this larger nesting approach.

LESSONS LEARNED

In summary fashion, at the end of seven years of effort to improve the work
itself, it is fair to say that:

• Enriching existing jobs pays off. To give an extreme example, consider the fact that Illinois Bell Telephone Company's directory compilation
effort reduced the work force from 120 persons to 74. Enriching the job
started a series of moves; it was not the only ingredient, but it was the
precipitating one.

- Job enrichment requires a big change in managerial style. It calls for increasing modules, moving control downward, and dreaming up new feedback ideas. There is nothing easy about a successful job enrichment effort.

- The nesting or configuring of related tasks—we call it "work organization"—may be the next big step forward after the enrichment of single jobs in the proper utilization of human beings.

It seems to produce a multiplier effect rather than merely a simple sum. In the Ferguson District case the job modules were not changed; the service representatives were not asked to type their own orders on the cathode ray tubes, nor were the typists asked to take over the duties of the service representatives. The results came from enriching other aspects (control and feedback) and, more important, from laying out the work area differently to facilitate interaction among responsible people.

- While continuing job enrichment efforts, it is important not to neglect "maintenance" factors. In extending our work with job nesting, for example, we plan to experiment with "office landscaping," so called. The furniture, dividers, planters, and acoustical treatment, all must add to the feeling of work dedication. By this I mean we will dedicate site, equipment, and jobs to the employees, with the expectation that they will find it easier to dedicate themselves to customer/client/task. Especially in new installations, this total work environmental approach seems a good idea for experimentation. We will not be doing it merely to offset pain or boredom in work. The aim is to facilitate work.

- A "pool" of employees with one job (typing pool, reproduction pool, calculating pool, and so on) is at the opposite extreme from the team or "minigroup" which I have described. A minigroup is a set of mutually supporting employees, each of whom has a meaningful module or part in meeting the needs of customer/client/task. What is "meaningful" is, like a love affair, in the eye of the beholder; at this stage, we have difficulty in describing it further.

A minigroup can have several service representatives or typists; one of each is not basic to the idea. The purpose is to set up a group of employees so that a natural, mutual dependence can grow in providing a service or finishing a task. It marks the end of processing from person to person or group to group, in separate locations or departments and with many different supervisors.

The minigroup concept, however, still leaves room for specialists. In certain Scandinavian auto plants, for example, one or two specialists fabricate the entire assembly of the exhaust pollution control system or the electrical system. Eventually, a group of workers may turn out a whole engine. In the United States, Chrysler has given similar trial efforts a high priority. The idea is to fix authority at the lowest level possible.

- Experience to date indicates that unions welcome the kind of effort described in our studies. Trouble can be expected, of course, if the economics of increases in productivity are not shared equitably. In the majority of cases, the economics can be handled even under existing contracts, since they usually permit establishment of new jobs and appropriate wage grades between dates of contract negotiation.

An employee who takes the entire responsibility for preparing a whole telephone directory, for example, ought to be paid more, although a new clerical rating must be established. Job enrichment is not in lieu of cash; good jobs and good maintenance are two sides of the same coin.

- New technology, such as the cathode ray tube, should enable us to break free of old work arrangements. When the Ferguson District service order typists were using the TWX machines, nesting their jobs was impractical because the equipment would have driven everybody to distraction. Installation of the high-technology CRTs gave the planners the opportunity to move together those employees whose modules of work were naturally related. This opportunity was at first overlooked.

Everyone accepts the obvious notion that new technology can and must eliminate dumb-dumb jobs. However, it probably creates more, rather than fewer, fragments of work. Managers should observe the new module and the work organization of the modules. This effort calls for new knowledge and skills, such as laying out work so attractively that the average employee will stay longer and work more effectively than under the previous arrangement.

Moreover, technology tends to make human beings adjuncts of machines. As we move toward computerized production of all listings in the white pages of the phone books, for example, the risk of an employee's losing "his" or "her" own directories is very great indeed. (Two AT&T companies, South Central Bell and Pacific Northwest Bell, are at this stage, and we must be certain the planned changes do not undermine jobs.) Making sure that machines remain the adjunct of human beings is a frontier problem which few managers have yet grappled with.

- Managers in mature organizations are likely to have difficulty convincing another department to make pilot runs of any new kind of work organization, especially one that will cause the department to lose people, budget, or size. Individual job enrichment does not often get into interdepartmental tangles, but the nesting of jobs will almost surely create problems of autonomy. This will call for real leadership.

- When the work is right, employee attitudes are right. That is the job enrichment strategy—get the work right.

READING   33

DOES JOB ENRICHMENT REALLY PAY OFF?

William E. Reif
Fred Luthans*

During the last few years, behavior-oriented management scholars and practitioners have generally extolled the virtues of Frederick Herzberg's job enrichment approach to employee motivation. Much of the management literature, especially journals aimed at the practicing manager, propose that "Job Enrichment Pays Off."[1] Lately, it has become commonplace for behavioral scientists to criticize Herzberg's research methodology but then admit the overall motivational value of the technique of job enrichment.[2] Only in a few instances have scholars or, especially, practitioners, seriously questioned the motivating effect of job enrichment. It is widely felt to be an excellent way of motivating employees in today's organizations.

In the mad dash to modernize and get away from the Theory X (Douglas McGregor) or Systems I and II (Rensis Likert) or Immaturity (Chris Argyris) or 9,1 (Robert Blake and Jane Mouton) approaches to the management of people, both professors of management and practicing managers may be guilty of the same thing: blindly accepting and overgeneralizing about the first seemingly local, practical and viable alternative to old style management—Herzberg's job enrichment. It now seems time to take a step back, settle down, and take a hard look at the true value that job enrichment has for motivating employees. Does job enrichment really pay off or is it merely a convenient crutch used by professors and practitioners to be modern in their approach to the management of human resources? This article attempts to provide another point of view and play the devil's advocate in critically analyzing job enrichment.

ENRICHMENT OR ENLARGEMENT?

The logical starting point in the analysis would be to see how, if at all, job enrichment differs from the older job enlargement concept. Although Herzberg, M. Scott Myers, Robert Ford and others portray job enrichment as one step beyond job enlargement, the real difference may lie more in the eyes of the definer than any actual differences in practice. The distinction

*© 1972 by The Regents of the University of California. Reprinted from *California Management Review,* vol. XV, no. 1, pp. 30–37, by permission of The Regents.

between the terms becomes even cloudier when concepts such as job extension and job rotation enter the discussion. The differences between these various terms can perhaps best be depicted on a continuum of variety, responsibility, and personal growth on the job. Most job enrichment advocates carefully point out that enrichment, relative to rotation, extension, and enlargement, infers that there is greater variety, more responsibility, and increased opportunity for personal growth. Yet, for practical purposes, the differences, especially between enlargement and enrichment, may be more semantic than real. Researchers who have studied job enlargement define their term almost exactly the same way that Herzberg defines job enrichment.

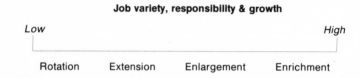

CONCLUSIONS FROM RESEARCH

To develop a framework of analysis for job enrichment, conclusions from research must first be summarized. William Reif and Peter Schoderbek's 1965 study revealed that 81 percent of the firms which responded to a mailed questionnaire survey were not using job enlargement. Of the 19 percent (forty-one firms) who were using the concept, only four indicated their experience was "very successful."[3] A more recent National Industrial Conference Board study disclosed that even though 80 percent of the responding companies expressed interest in the behavioral sciences, that even though 90 percent replied that their executives read books and articles about the behavioral sciences, and that more than 75 percent sent their executives to outside courses and seminars dealing with behavioral science concepts, there were very few firms which indicated they had put such concepts into actual practice.[4] Although a number of companies stated they were engaged in some form of job design activity, the N.I.C.B. study revealed that few have made any *sustained* effort in redesigning jobs.

The two companies which are cited most often in discussions of job enrichment are Texas Instruments and American Telephone and Telegraph. The two are given as examples of the outstanding success that can be attained when applying the job enrichment concept. However, one may question what constitutes "success." For example, Mitchell Fein, a long-time industrial engineer, assessed the Texas Instruments' job enrichment program as follows:

> Texas Instruments' management was probably more dedicated to job enrichment than any other company in the world. They earnestly backed their managing philosophies with millions of dollars of efforts.

After 15 years of unrelenting diligence, management announced in its 1968 report to the stockholders its program for "increasing human effectiveness," with the objective: "Our goal is to have approximately 10,000 TI men and women involved in team improvement efforts by the end of 1968 or 1969." Since TI employed 60,000, the program envisioned involving only 16 percent of its work force. The total involved was actually closer to 10 percent.[5]

In another instance, Robert Ford, who has been primarily responsible for implementing job enrichment in AT&T, reports, "Of the nineteen studies, nine were rated 'outstandingly successful,' one was a complete 'flop,' and the remaining nine were 'moderately successful.'"[6] Even more noteworthy perhaps is the fact that although Ford does not hesitate to generalize from the nineteen studies, he appears at one point to question his own optimism over the applicability of and benefits derived from job enrichment. He states: No claim is made that these 19 trials cover a representative sample of jobs and people within the Bell system. For example, there were no trials among the manufacturing or laboratory employees, nor were all operating companies involved. There are more than a thousand different jobs in the Bell system, not just the nine in these studies.[7]

In an early study (1958), James Kennedy and Harry O'Neill published findings on the effects job enlargement had had on the opinions and attitudes of workers whose jobs were highly routine, unskilled, and paced by the assembly line, and on utility men whose jobs were quite varied. The results showed no statistical difference between the two sets of scores. This finding led Kennedy and O'Neill to conclude:

> If job content is a factor in determining how favorably workers view their supervisors and their work situation, the difference in content apparently must be along more fundamental dimensions than those observed in this study.[8]

In 1968, Charles Hulin and Milton Blood conducted an in-depth study of job enlargement. They concluded that, "The case for job enlargement has been drastically overstated and over-generalized. . . .Specifically, the argument for larger jobs as a means of motivating workers, decreasing boredom and dissatisfaction, and increasing attendance and productivity is valid only when applied to certain segments of the work force—white-collar and supervisory workers and nonalienated blue-collar workers."[9]

Unfortunately, these studies are not widely cited in the management literature. Instead, a number of widely known and quoted management oriented behavioral scientists, among them Herzberg, McGregor, Likert, Argyris, and Blake and Mouton, are most often interpreted, sometimes wrongly, to advocate the opposite.[10] The popular position is that job enrichment is a key to successful motivation and productivity and many scholars, consultants, and practitioners actively campaign for its widespread use in modern organizations. McGregor summed up the feelings of job enrichment advocates when he said, "Unless there is opportunity *at work* to satisfy these high level needs (esteem and self-actualization), people will be deprived, and their behavior will reflect this deprivation."[11] In other words, the predominant conclusion is that people have a need to find fulfillment in their work and job enrichment provides them with the opportunity.

Why the wide divergence on the conclusions about job enrichment? Why the differences of opinion not only among scholars but also among practitioners, and between scholars and practitioners, about the efficacy of job enrichment? These are questions that the article tries to answer. The approach taken is to critically analyze the three most important concepts in job enrichment: (1) worker motivation, (2) job design, and (3) resistance to change.

WORKER MOTIVATION: ONE MORE TIME

The stated purpose of early job enlargement programs was to provide job satisfaction for unskilled blue-collar and low level white-collar (clerical) workers whose jobs were highly standardized and repetitive, operated on a short time cycle, required little knowledge and skill, and utilized only a few low-order abilities. Only a cursory review of management literature reveals that the majority of job enlargement programs in existence today are concerned with enriching the jobs of highly skilled workers, technicians, professionals, supervisors and managers, not unskilled blue- and white-collar employees. For example, in the William Paul, Keith Robertson, and Frederick Herzberg article on job enrichment in British companies, *none* of the employees in the studies could be classified as blue-collar workers.[12] Fein reports, "My experience in numerous plants has been that the lower the skills level, the lower the degree to which job enlargement can be established to be meaningful to the employees and management."[13]

The Reif and Schoderbek study discovered that of the firms using job enlargement, 73 percent used it at the supervisory level, 51 percent used it to enlarge clerical jobs, and 49 percent used it in the production area. Of the firms practicing job enlargement in the plant, 35 percent replied that the employees were primarily skilled, while only 15 percent classified the employees on enlarged jobs as unskilled.[14] In follow-up interviews three major reasons clearly emerged why it was more difficult to get unskilled workers to accept job enlargement than skilled or semi-skilled workers: (1) the unskilled prefer the status quo, (2) the unskilled seem to prefer highly specialized work, and (3) the unskilled show a lack of interest in improvements in job design which require learning new skills or assuming greater responsibility. A representative comment was: "Most unskilled workers prefer the routine nature of their jobs, and it has been my experience that they are not eager to accept responsibility or learn new skills."

In a parallel manner, the most frequent response to another question, "What are the major considerations taken into account in determining the particular job(s) to be enlarged?" was "The potential skills of employees." The survey respondents noted that in their experience, the higher the skill level of employees, the greater the probability of success with the enlarged job. Another question was, "What do you consider to be the major disadvantages of job enlargement?" The second most frequent response was that some workers were just not capable of growing with the enlarged job that was designed for them. Follow-up interviews indicated that the workers referred to by the respondents were primarily unskilled and semi-skilled blue-collar workers. Of particular interest was the response from a number of company spokesmen that in their experience many workers seemed capable of growing with the job but simply were not willing to do so. This observation was confirmed in interviews with a number of workers who had declined the opportunity to work on enlarged jobs.

The above results seem to directly contradict the commonly held motivational assumptions made by well-known behavioralists. It has become widely accepted that:

1 *Man seeks and needs meaningful work.*   Many behaviorists would contend that man's psychological well-being is dependent upon his ability to find expression and challenge in his work.

2 *Motivation is a function of job satisfaction and personal freedom.*—As was noted in a comprehensive N.I.C.B. study on job design: "Satisfaction with job content and the freedom to work on a self-sufficient independent basis are viewed as the crucial variables in the motivation to work."[15]

3 *Job content is related to job satisfaction.*—This major assumption is primarily derived from Herzberg's two-factor theory of motivation which provides the foundation for job enrichment. Herzberg implies that people are capable and desirous of greater responsibility and can be positively motivated by work which provides "meaning" to them.

These motivational assumptions do not account for why some workers show little or no interest in job enlargement. Beside the overall social and cultural impact on the values toward work, there are other specific but less widely held assumptions about worker motivation. One possible alternative assumption is that some people actually prefer highly routine, repetitive jobs. Numerous studies have pointed out that repetitive work can have positively motivating characteristics for some workers.[16] For example, Maurice Kilbridge found that assembly line workers in a television factory did not necessarily regard repetitive tasks as dissatisfying or frustrating. Also, the mechanical pacing of the conveyors was not necessarily distasteful to most workers. The Reif and Schoderbek study found that some workers preferred routine tasks because there was little thinking involved, and as a result, they were free to socialize and daydream without impairment to their productivity.[17]

Do these results suggest that workers' attitudes toward work and their ideas of what constitute satisfactory working conditions have gradually conformed to the technical requirements of our modern, industrialized society? For decades scholars and practitioners have been concerned with changing the design of work in order for it to be compatible with the psychological make-up of today's workers. In the meantime, is it possible that scholars and managers alike have failed to observe adaptation of the worker to his environment or, even more important, fundamental changes in the psychological need structure of the individual? Is there any tangible evidence which would give positive support to these intriguing possibilities?

Although not widely known to students of management, there is a small but significant literature which contradicts and is in opposition to the widely held assumptions made by job enrichment advocates. The study by Hulin and Blood is a good example. After closely analyzing practically all relevant research, they conclude that the effects of job enrichment on job satisfaction and worker motivation are generally overstated and in some cases unfounded.[18] Their study raises a number of interesting questions about the popular assumptions of worker motivation and the relationship between job enrichment, job satisfaction, and motivation. They argue that many blue-collar workers are not alienated from the work environment but are alienated from the work norms and values of the middle class. The middle class norms include: (a) positive effect for occupational achievement, (b) a belief in the intrinsic value of hard work, (c) a striving for the attainment of responsible positions, and (d) a belief in the work-related aspects of the Protestant ethic. On the other hand, these blue-collar workers do follow the norms of their own subculture. The implications are that workers who are alienated from middle class values do not actively seek meaning in their work and therefore are not strongly motivated by the job enlargement concept.

Fein's study of blue-collar and white-collar worker motivation came up with essentially the same conclusion. He states:

> Workers do not look upon their work as fulfilling their existence. Their reaction to their work is the opposite of what the behavioralists predict. It is only because *workers choose not to find fulfillment in their work* that they are able to function as healthy human beings. By rejecting involvement in their work which simply cannot be fulfilling, workers save their sanity.[19]

Fein goes on to say:

> . . . the concepts of McGregor and Herzberg regarding workers' needs to find fulfillment through their work are sound *only for those workers*

who choose to find fulfillment through their work. In my opinion, this includes about 15–20% of the blue-collar work force. These behavioralists' concepts have little meaning for the others. Contrary to their postulates, the majority of workers seek fulfillment outside their work.[20]

Whether one agrees or disagrees with the above observation, it does raise an interesting point. One could speculate that Fein's 15 to 20 percent is about the proportion of the worker population that David McClelland and David Winter would regard as high achievers.[21] Assuming this percentage were accurate, it would be vitally important to the analysis of job enrichment. It would follow that high achievers are essentially self-motivated and would not require the external stimulus of job enrichment to perform well. By the same token, the low-achievers would not respond to job enrichment because work holds too little meaning for them to be motivated by it. They find satisfaction outside the work place.

Another interesting parallel is provided by Hulin and Blood's analysis of William F. Whyte's study of rate busters.[22] They contend that Whyte's rate busters rejected the norms of their peer group and accepted the norms of management whereas the "quota restricters" retained their peer group norms. One might safely speculate that Whyte's quota restricters belong to the group known as the "alienated from the work norms of the middle class" workers or McClelland's low-achievers or Fein's 80 to 85 percent. Thus, a plausible answer to the question, "Why isn't job enrichment used more extensively on jobs of blue-collar and low-level white-collar workers?" is that a majority of these workers may not be positively motivated by an enriched job content with the accompanying motivators. Instead, they may be willing to exchange their minimum efforts on the job so that they can live satisfactorily outside the job.

A RE-EXAMINATION OF JOB DESIGN

Louis Davis defines job design as the "specification of the contents, methods, and relationships of jobs in order to satisfy technological and organizational requirements as well as the social and personal requirements of the job holder."[23] Traditionally, the technological requirements of work were given primary consideration in designing a job. For example, Frederick W. Taylor's work improvement efforts were directed at the task. Adjustments between technology and human needs were made in terms of the individual's adjustment to the system rather than designing the system to meet human needs. Because of the recent influence of the behavioralists, more emphasis has been devoted to the human aspects of job design. Today, the commonly expressed purpose of job design is to create more meaningful and satisfying work with the assumption being that productivity can be increased not so much by improving the technology as by improving the motivational climate.

Job enrichment is very compatible with "work is a human as well as a technical process" approach to job design. The conceptual similarity between job enrichment and the human approach to job design is very evident in the two factor motivation theory of Frederick Herzberg.[24] According to Herzberg, motivation is intrinsic to the job and the true rewards (achievement, recognition, work itself, responsibility, advancement, growth) come from doing the work, from performing effectively on the job. Many other behaviorally oriented theorists are in agreement with Herzberg's emphasis on job content, notably Argyris and McGregor who both express the desire to redesign jobs so they are capable of fulfilling esteem and self-actualization needs.

If Herzberg is correct, why hasn't job enrichment been more readily implemented into modern organizations? Possibly one of the major reasons is the failure to fully understand the significance of that part of job design which is concerned with meeting the social and personal requirements of the job holder. Everyone agrees that work is a social activity and probably most would agree that the framework for social interaction is largely an outgrowth of technology, the specific task, and the authority relationships prescribed by the formal organization. As a result, the social system or informal organization is usually structured along the lines of plant layout, machine processes, job specifications, the physical proximity of workers to each other, and operating policies and procedures. Finally, most would agree that the social system is an important means of fulfilling workers' needs for companionship, affection, reputation, prestige, respect, and status; of providing for interpersonal communication; and of helping protect the integrity and self-concept of the individual. This conclusion is brought out in a classic statement by Chester Barnard:

> The essential need of the individual is association, and that requires local activity or immediate interaction between individuals. Without it the man is lost. The willingness of men to endure onerous routine and dangerous tasks which they could avoid is explained by this necessity for action at all costs in order to maintain the sense of social integration, whether the latter arises from "instinct," or from social conditioning, or from physiological necessity, or all three.[25]

It is entirely possible that for many blue-collar workers, the affiliation motive is much stronger than the Herzberg "motivators" to which job enrichment is aimed. Enriched job designs that reduce the opportunities for social interaction may have a negative rather than positive impact on worker satisfaction and productivity. The Reif and Schoderbek study found a number of workers dissatisfied with the job enrichment program for this reason. A typical response was: "I don't see my old friends anymore except during coffee breaks and at lunch. On the line a bunch of us used to talk and tell jokes all the time."[26] For these workers the only satisfaction they had experienced at work was their interaction and identification with other members of their primary group. It should not be surprising that they expressed an unwillingness to give up their group membership for the promise of more meaningful work through job enrichment. To them, a newly enriched job which threatened to destroy the established social pattern was unacceptable.

RESISTANCE TO CHANGE:
THE DILEMMA OF JOB ENRICHMENT

In the Reif and Schoderbek study, the most frequent reply (almost half of firms using job enlargement) to the inquiry "What are the major problems encountered in applying job enlargement?" was "overcoming resistance to change." By far the most frequent response to another question, "What are the major problems experienced by the workers in adjusting to job enlargement?" was "adjustment to increased duties."[27] It became clear during follow-up interviews that the two answers were related. This led to a specific investigation of why workers would resist the opportunity to work on enlarged jobs. Four basic reasons emerged as to why workers resisted job enlargement:

• First, there was anxiety expressed by some workers who felt they would not be able to learn the new and modified skills required by the job enlargement design. Was this lack of confidence in one's ability to perform efficiently on the new job justified? The answer appeared to be yes. Most of the routine jobs did not require a great amount of skill and initiative. The very routine nature of a job reduced the possibility that an employee could ever develop the necessary knowledge and skills required by the enlarged or enriched job design.

• Closely related to the feeling of inadequacy was the fear of failure. Many workers spend years developing the skills which make them highly proficient at their present jobs. Why change now? Why give up a job which affords a relatively high degree of security for one which requires learning new skills, adjusting to unfamiliar methods and operating procedures, and establishing new working relationships? Furthermore, it should be recognized that over time most workers become highly competent in performing specialized, routine tasks. Despite the seemingly unchallenging nature of a job, the worker develops a sense of pride in knowing he can execute his job better than anyone else. This feeling of accomplishment, however limited it may appear to academicians and managers, may give the employee cause to decline an offer, or react negatively, to an enriched job.

• Third, employees' attitudes toward change can be influenced by their relationship with superiors. As workers become highly proficient in their jobs, they require less direct supervision and, as a result, achieve a high degree of freedom and independence. This feeling can be quite satisfying to the worker. Initially, the move to an enriched job would require closer and more frequent supervision, especially if the worker has to rely on his supervisor for the training necessary to master new and often more difficult job skills. Going from a state of independence to even a temporary state of dependence may not be welcomed by the worker.

- A fourth reason for resisting job enrichment is characteristic of any change, at work or otherwise, and is commonly known as psychological habit.

Originally Chester Barnard, and since, many others, believed that psychological habit is a major cause of resisting change. Barnard noted that "Another incentive . . . is that of customary working conditions and conformity to habitual practices and attitudes. . . .It is taken for granted that men will not or cannot do well by strange methods or under strange conditions. What is not so obvious is that men will frequently not attempt to cooperate if they recognize that such methods or conditions are to be accepted."[28] Barnard's argument seems to directly apply to the modern job enrichment technique.

CONCLUSIONS

The preceding discussion of worker motivation, job design, and resistance to change was geared toward answering the question of whether job enrichment really pays off. Obviously, there is no simple answer. On the other hand, the preceding analysis of job enrichment has raised some very significant but badly neglected points that need emphasis. These include the following:

1   There seems to be a substantial number of workers who are not necessarily alienated from work but are alienated from the middle class values expressed by the job enrichment concept. For these workers, job content is not automatically related to job satisfaction, and motivation is not necessarily a function of job satisfaction. These alienated workers are capable of finding need satisfaction outside the work environment. If they do experience satisfaction at work, it is not strictly the result of job content or formal job design but instead is largely influenced by social interactions with other primary group members. Job enrichment may not motivate this type of worker.

2   For some workers, improved job design by job enrichment is not seen as an even trade for the reduced opportunity for social interaction. The present job may be considered unpleasant and boring, but breaking up existing patterns or social isolation is completely unbearable.

3   The introduction of a job enrichment program may have a negative impact on some workers and result in feelings of inadequacy, fear of failure, and a concern for dependency. For these employees, low level competency, security, and relative independence are more important than the opportunity for greater responsibility and personal growth in enriched jobs.

These three points do not negate nor are they intended to be a total indictment of the job enrichment concept. On the other hand, they are intended to emphasize that job enrichment is not a cure-all for all the human problems presently facing modern management. This word of caution seems very appropriate at the present time. Many management professors and practitioners have jumped on the job enrichment bandwagon without carefully considering the research and analysis that is reported in this article. If nothing else, both professors and practitioners should take another hard look at their position on job enrichment as a method of motivating workers.

Like all sound management programs, job enrichment must be used *selectively* and with due consideration to situational variables such as the characteristics of the job, the organizational level, and the personal characteristics of the employees. Finally, job enrichment probably works best in organizations which have a supportive climate for innovation and change and a management which is genuinely interested in achieving greater job satisfaction for *its own sake.* Under these conditions, job enrichment can be practiced successfully and can offer great potential for the future, not only in terms of enriching the work experience for countless organizational participants, but also for increased productivity and organizational goal accomplishment.

REFERENCES

1 See William J. Paul, Jr., Keith B. Robertson, and Frederick Herzberg, "Job Enrichment Pays Off," *Harvard Business Review* (March–April, 1969), pp. 61–78.
2 See Valerie M. Bockman, "The Herzberg Controversy," *Personnel Psychology* (Vol. 24, No. 2, 1971), pp. 155–189.
3 See Peter P. Schoderbek and William E. Reif, *Job Enlargement* (Ann Arbor, Michigan: Bureau of Industrial Relations, Graduate School of Business Administration, The University of Michigan, 1969).
4 Harold M. F. Rush, "Behavioral Science—Concepts and Management Application," *Studies in Personnel Policy, No. 216* (New York: National Industrial Conference Board, 1969).
5 Mitchell Fein, *Approaches to Motivation* (Hillsdale, N.J.: 1970), p. 20.
6 Robert N. Ford, *Motivation through the Work Itself* (New York: American Management Association, Inc., 1969), p. 188.
7 *Ibid.*, p. 189.
8 James E. Kennedy and Harry E. O'Neill, "Job Content and Workers' Opinions," *Journal of Applied Psychology* (Vol. 42, No. 6, 1958), p. 375.
9 Charles L. Hulin and Milton R. Blood, "Job Enlargement, Individual Differences, and Worker Responses," *Psychological Bulletin* (Vol. 69, No. 1, 1968), p. 50.
10 See Frederick Herzberg, *Work and the Nature of Man* (Cleveland: The World Publishing Company, 1966); also, Douglas McGregor, *Leadership and Motivation* (The MIT Press, 1966); and Rensis Likert, *The Human Organization* (New York: McGraw-Hill Book Company, 1967); also Chris Argyris, *Personality and Organization* (New York: Harper & Row, Publishers, 1957); also Chris Argyris, *Integrating the Individual and the Organization* (New York: John Wiley & Sons, Inc., 1964); and Robert Blake and Jane Mouton, *Corporate Excellence through Grid Organizational Development* (Houston: Gulf Publishing Company, 1968).

11 Douglas McGregor, *op. cit.*, p. 40.

12 Paul, Robertson, and Herzberg, *op. cit.*

13 Mitchell Fein, *op. cit.*, p. 15.

14 Peter P. Schoderbek and William E. Reif, *op. cit.*, pp. 41–72.

15 Harold M. F. Rush, *Job Design for Motivation, Conference Board Report, No. 515* (New York: The Conference Board, Inc., 1971), p. 10.

16 Patricia C. Smith, "The Prediction of Individual Differences in Susceptibility to Industrial Monotony," *Journal of Applied Psychology* (Vol. 39, No. 5, 1955), pp. 322–329; also Patricia C. Smith and Charles Lem, "Positive Aspects of Motivation in Repetitive Work: Effects of Lot Size upon Spacing of Voluntary Work Stoppages," *Journal of Applied Psychology* (Vol. 39, No. 5, 1955), pp. 330–333; also Maurice D. Kilbridge, "Do Workers Prefer Larger Jobs?" *Personnel* (Sept.–Oct., 1960), pp. 45–48; also Wilhelm Baldamus, *Efficiency and Effort: An Analysis of Industrial Administration* (London: Tavistock Publications, 1967); also Victor H. Vroom, *Some Personality Determinants of the Effects of Participation* (Englewood Cliffs: Prentice-Hall, Inc., 1960); also Arthur N. Turner and Amelia L. Miclette, "Sources of Satisfaction in Repetitive Work," *Occupational Psychology* (Vol. 36, No. 4, 1962), pp. 215–231; and Arthur W. Kornhauser, *Mental Health of the Industrial Worker: A Detroit Study* (New York: John Wiley & Sons, Inc., 1965).

17 William E. Reif and Peter P. Schoderbek, "Job Enlargement: Antidote to Apathy," *Management of Personnel Quarterly* (Spring, 1966), pp. 16–23.

18 Hulin and Blood, *op. cit.*

19 Mitchell Fein, *op. cit.*, p. 31.

20 *Ibid.*, p. 37.

21 David C. McClelland and David J. Winter, *Motivating Economic Achievement* (New York: The Free Press, 1969).

22 Hulin and Blood, *op. cit.*, p. 49.

23 Louis E. Davis, "The Design of Jobs," *Industrial Relations* (October, 1966), pp. 21–45.

24 Herzberg, *op. cit.*

25 Chester I. Barnard, *The Functions of the Executive* (Cambridge, Mass.: Harvard University Press, 1938), p. 119.

26 Reif and Schoderbek, *op. cit.*, pp. 16–23.

27 *Ibid.*, pp. 64–70.

28 Chester I. Barnard, *op. cit.*, p. 77.

CHAPTER 9
REWARD SYSTEMS

READING   34

THE SCANLON PLANT-WIDE INCENTIVE PLAN —A CASE STUDY*

In 1971, a plant-wide incentive system, designed to increase productivity and improve job satisfaction, was put into operation at one of the nine Desoto, Inc. Chemical Coatings plants. . . .

Over a three-year period, this incentive plan, better known as the "Scanlon Plant-wide Incentive Plan," produced measurable gains in productivity (as high as 41 per cent) as well as extremely high levels of satisfaction with the plan. . .expressed by both plant management and workers.

SCANLON PLAN—BACKGROUND

The Scanlon Plan is based on the principles developed by the late Joseph N. Scanlon, former union official. The original plan was developed with the concept in mind that the employee, employer and the union had much in common. Scanlon felt. . ."Every employee has a contribution to make concerning improvements on the job and that any improvements that could be made on the job would someday help solidify the company's business in the marketplace and, in turn, would provide increased job security."

Union-management cooperation is the basic philosophy behind the Scanlon Plan, with teamwork promoted in the belief that workers have information to share with management and management, in turn, has something to share with the workers. This sharing provides workers with the means to collaborate . . . with management leading and labor actively participating.

The Scanlon Plant-wide Incentive Plan is of particular interest since it represents a form of management/labor cooperation built around the many issues of improved productivity practices . . .and it also features a financial reward appearing in the form of a monthly bonus.

In the nonadversary atmosphere of Scanlon committee meetings, workers and management share technical and financial information of value to both. Wages, hours, grievances and other classic union concerns are reserved for the bargaining table and must have no part in the proceed-

* Reproduced by special permission from the February 1976 *Training and Development Journal*, pp. 50–53. Copyright 1976 by the American Society for Training and Development, Inc.

Editor's note: The following information was excerpted from the report, "A Plant-wide Productivity Plan in Action: Three Years of Experience with the Scanlon Plan" (May 1975) prepared by Dr. Brian Moore for the National Commission On Productivity and Work Quality.

ings where the focus is on improving the overall productivity of the organization.

Although the Plan began as a means for "saving" a threatened plant or
company, it has more recently been adopted by "healthy" organizations as
a means for releasing the productivity potential of a generation of better
educated and more sophisticated management and labor. Continued success with the Plan in the last 20 years seemed to be confined to small
proprietary companies. . . . However, in recent years, it has appeared and
grown in large, diversified manufacturing concerns with matured policies
of decentralization.

In some of the most successful industrial settings, the Scanlon Plan is
seen as the first step in a series of continuing innovations that are changing
the character of industrial relations and productivity in the most advanced
plants of Western Europe, Japan and the United States.

PRODUCTIVITY MEASURES

A basic formula, relating total personnel or labor costs to the sales value of
production is one of the Plan's key elements. This baseline measure is
necessary in order to pay out bonuses for increases in productivity levels.
The ratio is the relationship between total labor costs and the market value
of goods and services produced as a result of labor. (See Figure 1.)

This relationship between the human resources cost and the value of
production is the *normal ratio of labor to productivity*. . . . Any increases in
the denominator relative to the numerator represent increases in productivity in excess of the base ratio. This increase comes in the form of a financial
bonus to be paid to the participating payroll.

Therefore, with the entire organization focusing its attention on this
relationship of human resource investment to productivity, the formula encourages learning of more productive behavior . . . in order to improve the
base ratio.

PRODUCTIVITY OUTCOME

Figure 2 represents the average bonus per cent of annual pay from 1971 to
1974. The range of average annual bonus was from slightly less than four
per cent to almost 11 per cent, with the average of all Desoto plants being
six per cent. This bonus is usually paid as a per cent of pay earned in a
given month. It should also be remembered that it is *organization-wide* . . .

Figure 1   The Formula

$$\text{Base ratio} = \frac{\text{total personnel costs of items to be included}}{\text{sales and inventory changes (finished and work in process inventories)}}$$

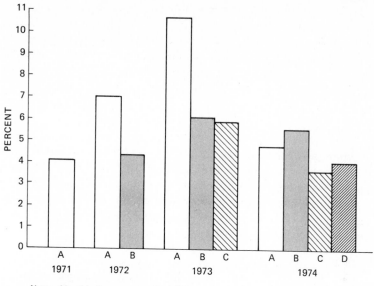

Note: Monthly bonus range = 0 to 18%
         Months a bonus earned = 70%

Figure 2   Average bonus percent of pay by year.

with managers, clerical workers, technicians and hourly employees included.

The monthly bonus range in Desoto plants was 0 to 18 per cent, which means that one plant, in a highly productive period, was able to provide a bonus of 18 per cent to everyone based on each person's monthly pay plus overtime.

Care must be exercised in any measure of productivity since output per work hour can be influenced by many factors. Obviously, the Scanlon Plan is only one factor. Nevertheless, Desoto management believes that the tangible benefits of the Plan are measurable. Unfortunately, productivity also depends on demand. . . . Thus, softening consumer markets compounded by rapidly rising prices for raw materials have had an effect on the productivity picture.

Large and rapid changes in the prices for raw materials is a special issue associated with the productivity formula . . . equity of the formula is disturbed. Management must adjust the ratio to keep it closely tied to true productivity. However, if the formula is constantly being changed, employee trust will diminish.

Another kind of problem that Desoto had to overcome was the mix in labor costs. As in many manufacturing concerns, some products are "buy outs" . . . with much or all of the product produced elsewhere and only *handled* by Desoto. Thus, the labor content in buy-out products is lower than produced products.

Clearly, if the object of the formula is to reward cooperative efforts and true productivity, then equity for both management and labor is important. Labor must trust management's construction and calculation of the bonus formula! On the other hand, management must not feel that the formula is a "give-away." One of management's concerns about the Plan has been the efficacy of the bonus formula. . . . It proves to be an empirical problem . . .answerable when accounting data are assembled.

SUGGESTION SYSTEM

At Desoto, a committee structure was superimposed on the organization to facilitate communication, evaluation and disposition of a *suggestion sys-tem*. . .another key element of the Scanlon Plan. Two kinds of committees were established: *production committees* which are formed in each work-ing unit or department and consisted of elected workers; and *screening committees* that include management and elected members of production committees.

Each department or functional area elects members to its own produc-tion committee. The supervisor automatically becomes a member. Sugges-tions are solicited, reviewed and evaluated by the production committee, with ground rules established whereby the committee can only accept sug-gestions and implement them if they (1) do not cost over a certain amount, and (2) do not affect other departments.

The screening committees are made up of 50 per cent management and 50 per cent elected representatives of the production committees, with the purpose being to deal with those suggestions that are beyond the scope of the production committees. Thus, suggestions involving signifi-cant expenditures or changes in methods across two or more departments are reviewed by the screening committee.

Production committees meet *at least* once a month. The screening committee meets monthly to evaluate suggestions and to discuss the goals and progress of the company. As a part of the discussion, the productivity data are reviewed and the bonus . . . or lack of it . . . is announced. Minutes are kept for both committee meetings, documenting the disposition of each suggestion and the accounting information supporting the productivity for-mula.

Whatever the organizational climate and managerial style, the process of group suggestion-making involves the entire organization. It is of interest to note that, at Desoto, rates of interaction increased . . . worker to work, worker to supervisor and worker to management. The content of these interactions is assumed to focus on productivity-related suggestions.

One point raised about the structure of the suggestion has been the amount of time spent on committee meetings. All four plants spend one to two hours per month in the screening committee—about 12 to 24 worker hours monthly. Production committees meet formally at least once a month for 10 minutes to one hour. Meetings are scheduled at slow periods—about 24 worker hours each month per plant. However, breaks, lunch periods and even car pools provide opportunities for discussing suggestions. Many suggestions are made by groups . . . culminating after much "pilot testing" behavior.

What, then, is the economic impact of the group suggestion system? From the experience with Desoto, it is clear that many suggestions have modest economic impact. Nevertheless, each plant can point with pride to suggestions which have or may have very high economic impact. Many of these quality suggestions are group authored. This type of behavior rarely happens under individual suggestion systems. Again, the economic measure is perceived by all to be reflected in the productivity bonus formula.

INTANGIBLE BENEFITS

Whether the tangible benefits of the Plan can be measured to the satisfaction of everyone is debatable. Intangible benefits have been reviewed by management of four Desoto plants. Here is their synopsis after seven years of collective experience:

1 Probably the most important intangible benefit is the feeling all employees have of actively participating in the management of their department and the plant.
2 This gives the employees a mechanism to contribute ideas that are documented and receive consideration of the production committee within their department. Eventually a decision must be made on each suggestion. It cannot be allowed to die by the employee's supervisor. At the same time, the worth of a suggestion is evaluated and often turned down by fellow employees.
3 Because of Scanlon, management receives a greater number of suggestions from all levels of employees. The Plan encourages employees to be more outspoken in advancing ideas.
4 Many suggestions result in savings to management that are not directly related to productivity. Examples are:
   a Helps develop employees at all levels.
   b Identifies employees with potential for work leader or supervisor positions.
   c Educates employees of the need to justify capital budget requests.
   d Where suggestions result in the addition of a capital item, the employees have a greater interest in getting the unit operating faster or overcoming start-up difficulties.
   e Increase knowledge of total plant operations—not just a single department. This can contribute to a fresh approach to improving plant safety and housekeeping.

CONCLUSIONS

Productivity across four Desoto plants appears to be enhanced by the Plan. The bonus formula, which measures productivity, shows an average payroll bonus of six percent. When this result is combined with a careful accounting of output labor costs and hours worked, the gains to productivity are as high as 41 per cent.

Construction of the formula raises special problems of employing sufficient techniques to maintain equity and mutual trust. The decision to use a simple, one-ratio formula rather than a complex one depends on the complexity of the organization and how important worker understanding of the formula is to management.

The analysis of the suggestion system reveals that irritants with the working environment can be expected as a common source of suggestions. As learning occurs, productivity-related suggestions dominate . . . especially those focusing on quantity. However, suggestion-making behavior is affected by productivity itself, with slack-period suggestions reflecting ideas not associated with productivity.

Job satisfaction, as measured, increased from already high levels. After nine-months' experience with the Plan, probably as a function of the bonus, feelings about increased responsibilities and involvement with work increased also.

Costs associated with operating the Plan at Desoto, such as time spent in meetings, appear to be outweighed by the benefits, both tangible and intangible. Indeed the benefits of the Plan appear to be the reason it has remained viable through the years. It could be that times are catching up to the Plan. As the quality of the labor force consistently improves, industrial culture is more conducive to this form of sharing benefits from productivity improvement.

Finally, there are a number of key considerations of which decision-makers should be aware in the installation and maintenance of the Scanlon Plant-wide Incentive Plan in other organizations. Based on available knowledge and the results of this multiplan evaluation, the following recommendations can be made:

- Key people in managerial and working ranks who understand the formula act as filters of trust for others in the organization. Key people must be identified and exposed to the mechanics of the formula very early in its formulation or installation. Good distribution and circulation of these individuals enhance acceptance of the Plan.
- Complaints or dissatisfiers are the most likely type of suggestion to be received. Managers must anticipate these nonproductive suggestions in a way to (a) instruct production committees that the nonproductive suggestions will not influence the bonus and (b) deal with the substance of the nonproductive suggestions by encouraging union leadership to handle them. If there is no union, then management still must deal with the nonpro-

ductive suggestions on a basis which is perceived to be *outside of the Plan.* If some of these nonproductive suggestions should be processed as suggestions, i.e., accepted and implemented, they should be reviewed later as nonproductive suggestions and be processed (in terms of policy) outside of the Plan.

- Another related issue is the decline of suggestions over time. All organizational leaders should prepare for this decline. Managers must seek opportunities to "feed the system" and direct efforts toward new areas. *One role in the organization most suited for this task is the controller or chief cost accountant.* By participating in production committee meetings, he can indicate high cost services or operations, inform the committee of apparent redundancies in services or operations, or point out cyclical costs with the objective of smoothing the production processes.

- Front-line supervisors may feel threatened by new types of participation and high rates of suggestions from their departments (including grievances). Managers and consultants must work with the supervisors by counseling and reassuring them. There may be some turnover at this level of supervision. However, the suggestion system also serves to identify promotable individuals and can assist in solving this problem.

- Information must be provided so that an individual has a clear picture of the relationship between behaviors and rewards.

- Since individuals differ in the ability to process information about a new reward system, it is often necessary to individualize the communication. That is, the communication must be tailored to the ability of the employee to receive the information.

- All too frequently the Plan is presented as a structure or formula which will produce greater cooperation and productivity. This emphasis ignores the *process of participation* in favor of the structure. Basic human values and attitudes about work, coworkers, the organization, and our economic system are at stake. There is no substitute for organizational policies built on trust and mutual dependence. The process of participation can be enhanced by supportive training in interpersonal skills for all members of the organization. This type of training helps smooth the process of group interaction so central to the Plan's success.

READING 35

INTRINSIC VERSUS EXTRINSIC REWARDS: RESOLVING THE CONTROVERSY

William E. Reif*

In his foreword to *Work in America,* Elliot Richardson included the following quote from Richard Nixon's 1971 Labor Day Address:

> In our quest for a better environment, we must always remember that the most important part of the quality of life is the quality of work, and the new need for job satisfaction is the key to the quality of work.[1]

Although some might question the belief that work is a central life force, the statement does serve to illustrate the great amount of attention that working life has recently received. The growing concern for meaningful work, due largely to the accumulation of evidence that the quality of working life is poor for many blue-collar, clerical, professional and managerial employees, has persuaded an increasing number of academicians and managers to investigate what can be done to make work a more personally satisfying experience.

While the concept of meaningful work appeals to the humanitarian instincts of most managers, their primary concern continues to be productivity; in terms of human resources, their focus is on how to promote effective work behavior. In an attempt to integrate the two seemingly divergent themes of meaningful work and productivity many firms have adopted an organization development (OD) approach, which encourages managers to take the steps necessary to create an organizational climate that can sustain a high level of individual needs (job) satisfaction and concurrently support the organization's requirements for effectiveness.

STRATEGIES FOR EFFECTIVE WORK BEHAVIOR

Two strategies have received widespread acclaim for their ability to create a work situation that is capable of integrating individual and organizational objectives. The first strategy is based on the assumption that workers are motivated by intrinsic rewards, also known as job content variables or motivators, and is the approach taken by the proponents of job design/enrichment. The second basic strategy assumes that workers respond more readily to extrinsic rewards, also known as job context or hygiene variables, and argues that they will be productive if factors such as working conditions, pay and fringe benefits, job security and work rules are provided in sufficient amounts to warrant their best efforts.*

One of the reasons that the question of extrinsic versus intrinsic motivation continues to be hotly debated is that there is not substantial support for either side. The debate is often more emotional than rational; arguments are frequently based on personal experience (a single case study) and "seasoned judgement." The purpose of this article is to reconcile several of the key issues presented by the two sides by reporting the results of a study that was designed to record worker's perceptions of the importance and degree of satisfaction with selected intrinsic and extrinsic variables that typically constitute an organization's reward system. It was intended that the findings would reveal the extent to which management can rely on either intrinsic or extrinsic rewards to provide the motivational climate necessary to sustain job satisfaction and productivity.

RESEARCH METHOD

Thirty-three items were selected to represent the reward system that is usually available to management for influencing worker behavior. The individual items were classified as direct economic rewards, indirect economic rewards, and psychosocial rewards.

A Porter-Lawler type of research instrument was used because of its ability to record perceptions of "importance" and "satisfaction with" the variables in question.[2] The questionnaire consisted of two parts. Part I included fifteen items of which eleven were used to represent four intrinsic reward categories and four to represent three extrinsic reward categories:

1 Social needs
   opportunity to help people
   opportunity for friendship
2 Esteem needs
   feeling of self-esteem
   prestige inside company
   prestige outside company
3 Autonomy needs
   opportunity for independent thought and action
   authority in position
   opportunity to participate in goal setting

* See boxed insert on intrinsic and extrinsic rewards at the end of this discussion.

4 Self-actualization needs
   opportunity for growth and development
   feeling of self-fulfillment
   feeling of worthwhile accomplishment
5 Compensation
   direct pay
   fringe benefits
6 Working conditions
   working conditions associated with the job
7 Security needs
   security in job

Part II of the questionnaire consisted of eighteen direct and indirect economic rewards that were selected by the author on a judgement basis from a comprehensive list of over seventy-five benefits consistently appearing in the wage and salary literature. The rewards that were chosen for inclusion were considered to be the ones most representative of an organization's compensation package. They included:

Direct Economic Rewards	*Indirect Economic Rewards*
overtime pay	retirement benefits
salary/wages	stock purchase plan
profit sharing plan	life insurance benefits
incentive plans	health insurance benefits
cost of living adjustment	disability insurance benefits
	sick or absence pay benefits
	vacation policy
	lunch, rest and break time
	educational opportunities
	recreation program
	holidays
	shorter work week
	flexible scheduling of hours

Figure 1 is an example of the series of three questions asked of each respondent for each of the thirty-three items on the questionnaire. The degree of dissatisfaction with a particular reward was computed by subtracting the answer for question (a) from question (b). For example, if the respondent circled 1 for question (a) and 5 for question (b) he had a dissatisfaction score of 4 for that item. Larger scores indicate a greater degree of dissatisfaction.

Figure 1 Sample Question   Min $<—>$ Max

The direct pay for my position:
  (a) How much is there now?   1 2 3 4 5 6 7
  (b) How much should there be?   1 2 3 4 5 6 7
  (c) How important is this to me?   1 2 3 4 5 6 7

The perceived importance of each reward item was determined by the number the respondent circled for question (c). If, for example, he recorded a 7 for the sample question, it would indicate that he considered direct pay to be an important reward—one that would have potential as a modifier of job-related behavior.

Six organizations participated in the study: an electronic component manufacturer, printing company, mobile home manufacturer, savings and loan association, heavy equipment distributor, and a city government. They varied in size from $3,000,000 to $50,000,000 (sales or budget) and employed from 100 to 600 employees. Three hundred and fifty-four employees (252 men and 102 women), representing all organizational levels and functional areas, were selected from the six organizations by a systematic stratified sampling procedure.

Statistical analyses of the data included the following:

1 Calculation of the overall importance and need dissatisfaction means for each of the thirty-three items and for the nine major reward categories.

2 Application of two-tailed *t* tests to determine if significant differences existed between importance and need dissatisfaction means for the nine reward categories.

3 Application of correlation analysis and the F test of significance to the correlation coefficients to determine the relationship between four moderating variables—age, education, organizational status and salary/wages—and the importance and need dissatisfaction means for each of the nine reward categories.

RESEARCH RESULTS

The overall importance and need dissatisfaction means for each reward item are shown in Table 1. The same information for the nine reward categories is shown in Table 2. Analysis of Table 1 reveals that the correspondents perceived direct and indirect economic (extrinsic) rewards to be more important than intrinsic rewards. Four of the top five and six of the top ten are extrinsic rewards: salary/wages, direct pay, health insurance benefits, working conditions, cost of living adjustment and security. This finding is not consistent with the popular notion that employees are primarily concerned with higher-order needs, or what Herzberg refers to as motivators.

The ten items with which respondents were most dissatisfied are all extrinsic reward (salary and fringe benefits). The first intrinsic reward item to appear on the list of dissatisfiers is personal growth and development, which ranks thirteenth. The three rewards that appear on both top ten lists—that is, the ones respondents perceived as most important and most dissatisfying—are all extrinsic variables: cost of living adjustment, salary/wages and direct pay. (Salary/wages and direct pay are synonymous terms and were used as a validity check.)

Table 1 Importance and Need Dissatisfaction Means for Each Reward Item
(Ranked in Order of Importance)

Reward item	Importance Mean	Importance Rank	Need dissatisfaction Mean	Need dissatisfaction Rank
Salary/wages	6.514	1	2.401	6
Direct pay	6.463	2	2.266	7
Self-esteem	6.398	3	1.127	29
Health insurance benefits	6.395	4	1.969	11
Working conditions	6.354	5	1.828	14
Worthwhile accomplishment	6.353	6	1.435	23
Cost of living adjustment	6.316	7	3.480	1
Security	6.274	8	1.452	22
Self-fulfillment	6.254	9	1.534	18
Personal growth and development	6.229	10	1.907	13
Independent thought and action	6.195	11	1.209	28
Vacation policy	6.167	12	1.384	24
Disability insurance benefits	6.076	13	2.138	9
Sick or absence pay benefits	6.068	14	2.150	8
Fringe benefits	6.045	15	1.992	10
Life insurance benefits	5.997	16	1.760	17
Opportunity to help others	5.890	17	0.831	31
Holidays	5.845	18	1.506	19(tie)
Retirement benefits	5.828	19	2.653	4
Participation in goal setting	5.678	20	1.774	16
Educational opportunities	5.675	21	1.935	12
Lunch, rest and break time	5.551	22	0.723	32
Opportunity to develop friendships	5.503	23	0.492	33
Prestige inside the organization	5.486	24	1.322	26
Authority	5.376	25	1.350	25
Incentive plans	5.362	26	2.760	2
Profit sharing plans	5.246	27	2.692	3
Prestige outside the organization	5.181	28	0.879	30
Overtime pay	5.003	29	1.506	19(tie)
Shorter work week	4.975	30	1.494	21
Flexible scheduling of work hours	4.960	31	1.308	27
Stock purchase plan	4.308	32	2.630	5
Recreation programs	4.113	33	1.780	15

Table 2, which consolidates the thirty-three items into nine reward categories, shows that three of the four categories judged most important are working conditions, security and compensation. The only intrinsic reward category in the top four is self-actualization. Only one of the five categories with which respondents were most dissatisfied is considered an intrinsic motivator, and that is self-actualization which ranks fifth. The two reward categories that are in the top four on both lists—working conditions and compensation—are two of Fein's extrinsic determinants of job satisfaction.

Table 2   Importance and Need Dissatisfaction Means by Reward Category
(Ranked in Order of Importance)

Reward category	Importance		Need dissatisfaction	
	Mean	Rank	Mean	Rank
Working conditions	6.384	1	1.828	4
Self-actualization	6.279	2	1.625	5
Security	6.274	3	1.452	6
Compensation	6.254	4	2.219	2
Autonomy	5.750	5	1.444	7
Social	5.696	6	0.661	9
Esteem	5.688	7(tie)	1.109	8
Direct economic benefits	5.688	7(tie)	2.568	1
Indirect economic benefits	5.535	9	1.880	3

Further analysis of the data was conducted by applying the two-tailed t test to the importance and need dissatisfaction means for each of the nine reward categories to see if statistically significant differences existed between them. Two distinct clusters were found along the importance dimension. Working conditions, self-actualization, security and compensation form one cluster and are all significantly different from the other five reward categories that comprise the second cluster.[3] It may be concluded that, with the exception of self-actualization, the respondents viewed extrinsic rewards as more important than intrinsic rewards.

In terms of need dissatisfaction, the t tests indicated a significant difference between five reward clusters: (1) direct economic benefits, (2) compensation, (3) indirect economic benefits, working conditions, self-actualization, security and autonomy, (4) esteem, and (5) social.[4] Esteem and social needs, frequently mentioned as two strong motivators, were viewed by respondents as highly need satisfying, and according to Abraham Maslow's concept of prepotency satisfied needs do not serve as active motivators.

The reward categories were then arranged in a modified need hierarchy to see how the results of this study compared to Maslow's theory of motivation. Figure 2 shows that the respondents regarded self-actualization and security as most important. Also, they expressed greater dissatisfaction with security and self-actualization than with the other three reward categories.

These findings do not confirm the widely held notion that lower-order needs (represented by security in the modified need hierarchy) have to be reasonably well satisfied before individuals turn their attention to higher-level need gratification. Furthermore, assuming that Maslow was correct in his premise that satisfied needs do not serve as active motivators, and

Figure 2   Reward Hierarchy

| | Importance | | Need dissatisfaction | |
Reward	Mean	Rank	Mean	Rank
Self-actualization	6.279	1	1.625	2
Autonomy	5.750	3	1.444	3
Esteem	5.688	5	1.109	4
Social	5.696	4	0.661	5
Security*	5.907	2	1.932	1

* The four reward categories working conditions, security, direct economic benefits and indirect economic benefits were combined to form the composite category of security.

supposing that rewards perceived as both most important and most dissatisfying are strong motivators, the results of this study would support the proposition that security and self-actualization are the two areas where management should place primary emphasis. Applying the same reasoning, rewards that are considered to be relatively unimportant and at the same time well satisfied (e. g., social needs) are weak motivators and probably would not have a great effect on increasing worker satisfaction and performance.

To complete the analysis of the data, correlation coefficients were computed and the F test of significance was applied to determine what relationships, if any, existed between the importance and need dissatisfaction means for the nine reward categories and the key variables of age, education, organizational status (as determined by position or level in the organizational hierarchy), and salary/wages. Results were considered significant at the .05 level.

Age

Significant positive correlations were found between the security and esteem categories and age along the importance dimension, indicating that these two rewards were considered more important by the older respondents. Significant negative correlations were found between esteem, self-actualization, compensation, working conditions, direct economic benefits, indirect economic benefits and age along the need dissatisfaction dimension. In other words, older respondents were more satisfied than younger respondents with six of the nine reward categories. The findings indicate that younger workers are less concerned with security and esteem and generally more dissatisfied with the whole organizational reward system.

Education

Significant negative correlations were found between the security, working conditions, direct and indirect economic benefits categories and education along the importance dimension, indicating that the higher level of formal education the less important these rewards were to the respondents. Significant negative correlations were found between security, compensation and education along the need dissatisfaction dimension; in other words, the more education the respondent had the less dissatisfied he tended to be with security and compensation. To summarize, the more highly educated repondents viewed intrinsic motivators as more important than those with less education and were more satisfied with the basic extrinsic motivators of security and compensation.

Organizational Status

Significant positive correlations were found between the social, esteem, autonomy and self-actualization categories and organizational status along the importance dimension, which confirms the generally held belief that people at higher organizational levels are more oriented toward instrinsic rewards than people in lower-level (predominately blue-collar and white-collar clerical) jobs. A negative correlation was found between direct economic benefits and organizational status; that is, the higher an individual is in his organization the less important are direct economic benefits. Significant negative correlations were found between *all* reward categories and organizational status along the need dissatisfaction dimension, which means that the higher a person climbs in his organization the more satisfied he becomes with all types of organizational rewards.

Salary/Wages

Significant positive correlations were found between the esteem, autonomy, and self-actualization categories and salary/wages along the importance dimension. In other words, as a person makes more money the intrinsic motivators of esteem, autonomy and self-actualization become more important. Significant negative correlations were found between eight of the nine reward categories (the exception being autonomy) and salary/wages along the need dissatisfaction dimension. This infers that employees who command high salaries are generally more satisfied with all types of organizational rewards.

It is evident that all workers do not perceive organizational rewards alike and that certain needs are much more prominent with some groups than others. If one were to draw a general conclusion from the findings it would be that younger, more highly educated workers who receive acceptable salaries and are in higher-level jobs are likely to be more motivated by intrinsic than extrinsic rewards and are prime candidates for job design/enrichment. Taking a look at the other end of the scale, older, less educated workers in relatively low paying, low status jobs are probably more concerned with the extrinsic determinants of job satisfaction and may respond more readily to working conditions, job security, compensation and fringe benefits.

Implications and Conclusions

The purpose of this study was to empirically test the sharply contrasting assumptions that intrinsic rewards or extrinsic rewards are the primary determinants of job satisfaction and productivity. It is evident by now that neither position is all right nor all wrong, but that a third strategy is warranted. The results of this research suggest that what is needed is a contingency approach that takes into consideration the needs of the workers, the characteristics of their work environment, and the requirements of the organization.

An organizational reward system based solely on money as the motivator, or at the other extreme intrinsic motivation through job enrichment, is not likely to lead to an optimum utilization of human resources. This study clearly shows that what constitutes a meaningful work experience is a composite of many things—chief among them security (which is a function of working conditions, job security and compensation) and self-actualization, which is realized through well-designed jobs that provide job holders the opportunity to be autonomous, demonstrate competence, further develop capabilities, and experience feelings of self-fulfillment and worthwhile accomplishment.

Although much easier said than done, the key to administering an organizational reward system is to know what combination of motivators is effective with particular workers or work groups. The findings presented here support the argument that most individuals have a multi-faceted need structure and that few, if any, are driven by an all-consuming desire to satisfy a single need. It is highly unlikely, for example, that anyone can be motivated to perform well on the job by appealing only to his need for job security or by paying attention only to the one job dimension of autonomy. It is more realistic to assume that most workers have a need hierarchy, similar in concept to that in Figure 2, and have assigned weights to a set of rewards that they perceive as need satisfying.

If this is true, and if organizations are going to be effective, management must become more knowledgeable of workers and how they identify with their work situation. Managers must be more holistic in their approach to identifying the determinants of job satisfaction and must adopt a contingency approach to designing and administering the organizational reward system. Job dissatisfaction and poor performance cannot be extinguished by a decision rule that says "enrich all jobs" anymore than by the more traditional method of literally paying off workers to perform dull, repetitive, routine jobs—unless, of course, the worker does not mind performing a meaningless task and is willing to trade-off an unsatisfying work experience for pleasure he can buy outside of the work environment.

Diagnostic tools, such as the questionnaire used in this study, are available to assist managers in evaluating reward preferences and analyzing productive work behavior. Once management knows what should constitute an organizational climate that supports worker effectiveness it is in a better position to utilize human resources in a manner that satisfies both individual and organizational needs. For several years everyone has been talking about "enlightened" management. Now is the time to begin practicing it.

REFERENCES

1 *Work in America,* Report of a Special Task Force to the Secretary of Health, Education, and Welfare, Cambridge, The MIT Press, pp. vii–viii.
2 Lyman W. Porter and Edward E. Lawer, III, *Managerial Attitudes and Performance,* Homewood, Illinois, Richard D. Irwin, Inc., 1968.
3 Results were considered significant at the .001 level for d. f. = 353. The very conservative .001 level of significance was used in order to compensate for the large number of *t* tests conducted. Use of the .001 level enabled the researcher to maintain an experimentwise confidence level of approximately .96.
4 The significant difference between the two similar categories, *direct economic benefits* and *compensation,* was due to the fact that three of the five items that comprised direct economic benefits—cost of living adjustment, incentive plans and profit sharing plans—are the three rewards with which the respondents were most dissatisfied.

THE CASE FOR INTRINSIC MOTIVATION

For the last fifteen years the leading advocate of intrinsic motivation has been Frederick Herzberg.[1] Herzberg's two-factor theory of motivation states that there are two rather distinct sets of job-related variables: job content variables, or motivators, and job context, or hygiene, variables. The motivators include achievement, recognition, interesting (challenging) work, responsibility, advancement and growth in competence. These need satisfiers are intrinsic to the job, meaning needs are satisfied through performance of the work itself. The hygiene variables are extrinsic to the job, meaning they are not necessarily related to job performance. They include company policy and administration, the worker's relationship with his boss and peers, working conditions, salary and fringe benefits.

The key to applying Herzberg's theory of motivation is his contention that it is the motivators that are primarily responsible for increasing job satisfaction and performance. If the hygiene variables are not present in sufficient quantity to meet workers' expectations, the result will be a highly dissatisfied work force. However, if they meet or even exceed workers' demands the result is not job satisfaction, at least not for long, but merely no job dissatisfaction. For example, as salary is increased to a level that meets or exceeds expectations workers will no longer be dissatisfied. At the same time they will probably not be motivated to improve their job performance. To put it simply, they may be happier but they will not be more productive, and they may not even be happier if they regard the salary increase as something that they deserved all along.

Recent research by Hackman, Lawler, Oldham and others generally supports the case for intrinsic rewards.[2] Hackman and Lawler predicted and found that when jobs are high on four core dimensions—autonomy, feedback, task identity and variety—employees who are desirous of higher order need satisfaction (e. g., esteem, autonomy, self-actualization) tend to have high motivation and high job satisfaction, are absent from work infrequently, and are rated by their supervisors as doing high quality work.

Hackman and Oldham hypothesized that three psychological states—experienced meaningfulness, experienced responsibility, and knowledge of results—are critical in determining a person's motivation on the job. When these conditions are present a worker tends to feel very good about himself when he performs well. This feeling is referred to as internal motivation, which is defined as "being turned on to one's work because of the positive internal feelings that are generated by doing well, rather than being dependent on external factors (such as incentive pay or compliments from the boss) for the motivation to work effectively."[3] When all three psychological states are high the consequences are high internal work motivation, high job satisfaction, high quality of work, and low absenteeism and turnover.

Hackman and Oldham concluded from their research that there are five dimensions (job characteristics) that constitute an enriched job: skill variety, task identity, task significance, autonomy, and feedback from the job. A job with a high "motivating potential score" must be high on at least one of the three dimensions that lead to experienced meaningfulness (skill variety, task identity, and task significance), and high on both autonomy and feedback.

Their findings did point out one very important qualifier. They found that not everyone can be turned on by his work, even when the motivating potential score for his job is very high. Consistent with the earlier research by Hackman and Lawler they found that workers who are high in growth needs—that is, a strong desire for personal accomplishment, for learning and further development and for being stimulated and challenged—are the ones most likely to become internally motivated by jobs that possess the five core dimensions. They generally concluded:

> We believe that job enrichment has moved beyond the stage where it can be considered 'yet another fad.' As experience using diagnostic and work re-design procedures . . . accumulates, the oft-espoused goal of achieving basic organizational change through the redesign of work may come increasingly within reach. Job enrichment, we believe, is growing up.[4]

The case for intrinsic motivation also receives strong support from a growing number of companies that have been well satisfied with their investment in job design/enrichment; among them AT&T, Texas Instruments, the Maytag Company, Motorola, Corning Glass, Proctor and Gamble, The Travelers Insurance Companies, Bankers Trust Company, Donnelly Mirrors, Inc., and the General Foods Pet Food plant in the U. S.; Volvo and Saab in Sweden; and Philips N. V. in the Netherlands.

To summarize the argument for intrinsic motivation, if management wants to motivate workers it must concentrate on improving their jobs.

THE CASE FOR EXTRINSIC REWARDS

One of the prominent spokesmen for extrinsic rewards is Mitchell Fein, who has denounced the optimistic pronouncements of job enrichment researchers and practitioners and taken the position that workers for the most part are satisfied with the nature of their work. What they find particularly dissatisfying are pay, job security and the many work rules that dictate their behavior on the job. He states his case as follows:

> My own observation, and my analysis of such data as are available, convince me that enriched work will not bring greater job satisfaction to alienated workers, nor cause them to become more involved with their work. I am inclined to the thought that most workers work in order to eat; they exchange their skills, efforts and time for what they can buy back outside of the work place.[5]

His solution to worker dissatisfaction is simple. "Management must provide the basic conditions which will motivate workers to raise productivity: job security, good working conditions, good pay and financial incentives.''[6]

A careful reading of Fein reveals that his argument is not against job enrichment *per se,* but the fact that intrinsic motivators appeal to a very small segment of the total work force (somewhere around 8–12%). He contends that the majority of workers are motivated to perform by good pay, working conditions and job security. Consistent with the findings of Hackman and Lawler and Hackman and Oldham, Fein would argue that workers who are high in growth needs probably will respond positively to jobs that have high motivating potential scores. However, he is convinced that it is not worth management's time to try and convince the other 90% that job redesign/enrichment will create a more meaningful work experience.

Fein, of course, is not the only advocate of extrinsic motivation. The unions traditionally have taken a bargaining position that strongly emphasizes economic rewards (salary and fringe benefits), working conditions, job security, and work rules. Furthermore, the management literature abounds with arguments for money as a motivator.

REFERENCES

1 Frederick Herzberg, *Work and the Nature of Man,* Cleveland, The World Publishing Company, 1966. For a brief review of two-factor theory see Frederick Herzberg, ''One More Time: How Do You Motivate Employees?'' *Harvard Business Review,* January–February, 1968, pp. 53–67.
2 See J. Richard Hackman and Edward E. Lawler, III, ''Employee Reactions to Job Characteristics,'' *Journal of Applied Psychology Monograph,* June 1971, pp. 259–286; J. Richard Hackman and Greg R. Oldham, *Motivation through the Design of Work: Test of a Theory.* T. R. No. 5, Department of Administrative Sciences, Yale University, 1974; and J. Richard Hackman and Greg R. Oldham, ''A New Strategy for Job Enrichment,'' Prepublication draft, March 1974.
3 Hackman and Oldham, ''A New Strategy for Job Enrichment,'' p. 3.
4 Hackman and Oldham, ''A New Strategy,'' p. 27.
5 Mitchell Fein, ''The Real Needs and Goals of Blue Collar Workers,'' *The Conference Board Record,* February, 1973, p. 33.
6 Mitchell Fein, ''Job Enrichment: A Reevaluation,'' *Sloan Management Review,* Winter, 1974, p. 87.

CHAPTER 10
ORGANIZATIONAL DEVELOPMENT AND CHANGE

READING 36

THE DIFFICULTY OF CHANGE

Niccolò Machiavelli*

It must be considered that there is nothing more difficult to carry out, nor more doubtful of success, nor more dangerous to handle, than to initiate a new order of things. For the reformer has enemies in all those who profit by the old order, and only lukewarm defenders in all those who would profit by the new order, this lukewarmness arising partly from fear of their adversaries, who have the laws in their favour; and partly from the incredulity of mankind, who do not truly believe in anything new until they have had actual experience of it. Thus it arises that on every opportunity for attacking the reformer, his opponents do so with the zeal of partisans, the others only defend him halfheartedly, so that between them he runs great danger.

*   *   *

*From *The Prince,* written in approximately 1513. Translation by Luigi Ricci, revised by E. R. P. Vincent (New York: New American Library of World Literature, Inc., 1952), p. 55.

READING 37

ORGANIZATIONS, DINOSAURS, AND ORGANIZATION DEVELOPMENT

Warren G. Bennis†

McGregor may have been overly optimistic about the death of authoritarianism, but he was unerring, as usual, in putting his finger on the right issue. Given the retroactive insight of almost 20 years, we can say that organization development is essentially an evolutionary process. It asserts

†From *Organization Development: Its Nature, Origins, and Prospects* (Reading, Mass.: Addison-Wesley Publishing Company, Inc., 1969), pp. 76–77. Copyright 1969. Reprinted with permission.

that every age develops an organizational form and life style most appropriate to the genius of that age. Most organizations reflect the uneasiness of transition for they were built upon certain assumptions about man and his environment. The environment was thought to be placid, predictable, and uncomplicated. Man was thought to be placid, predictable, and uncomplicated. Organizations based on these assumptions will fail, if not today, then tomorrow. They will fail for the very same reasons that dinosaurs failed: the environment changes suddenly at the peak of their success.

The environment now is busy, clogged, and dense with opportunities and threats; it is turbulent, uncertain and dynamic. The people who work for organizations are more complicated than ever before. They have needs, motives, anxieties, and to make matters even more complicated, they bring higher expectations than ever before to our institutions. The institutions themselves are changing, through the press of environmental challenges and the internal demands of its people. Organization development is a response to these complex challenges, an educational strategy which aims to bring about a better fit between the human beings who work in and expect things from organizations and the busy, unrelenting environment with its insistence on adapting to changing times.

*   *   *

READING   38

A DEFINITION AND HISTORY OF ORGANIZATION DEVELOPMENT: SOME COMMENTS

Wendell L. French

Cecil H. Bell*

A DEFINITION OF ORGANIZATION DEVELOPMENT

Although a literal interpretation of the words "organization development" could refer to a wide range of strategies for organization improvement, the phrase has come to take on some fairly specific meanings in the behavioral science literature and in practice. We say "fairly specific" because the boundaries are not entirely clear, perceptions of different authors and practitioners vary somewhat, and the field is evolving.

In the behavioral science and perhaps ideal sense of the term, *organization development is a long-range effort to improve an organization's problem-solving and renewal processes, particularly through a more effective and collaborative management of organization culture—with special emphasis on the culture of formal work teams—with the assistance of a change agent or catalyst and the use of the theory and technology of applied behavioral science, including action research.*

By the term "culture" in our definition we mean prevailing patterns of activities, interactions, norms, sentiments (including feelings), attitudes, values, and products [1]. By including products we include technology in our definition, although changes in technology tend to be secondary in organization development efforts. However, technology—if one includes procedures and methods along with equipment—is almost always influenced, and is an influence, in organization development activities.

Our use of the term "culture" includes the notion of the "informal system" which includes feelings, informal actions and interactions, group norms, and values. In some ways the informal system is the hidden or suppressed domain of organizational life—the covert part of the "organization-

---

*From *Proceedings of the Thirty-first Annual Meeting,* Academy of Management, Boston,1972, pp. 146–153. Copyright 1972. Reprinted with permission.

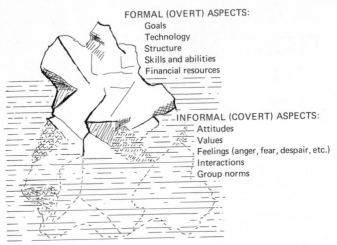

FORMAL (OVERT) ASPECTS:
Goals
Technology
Structure
Skills and abilities
Financial resources

INFORMAL (COVERT) ASPECTS:
Attitudes
Values
Feelings (anger, fear, despair, etc.)
Interactions
Group norms

Figure 1 Organizational iceberg. (*Adapted from an address by Stanley N. Herman, TRW Systems, at an organization development conference sponsored jointly by the Industrial Relations Management Association of British Columbia and NTL Institute for Applied Behavioral Science, Vancouver, B.C., Canada, 1970.*)

al iceberg" as shown in Figure 1. Traditionally, this hidden domain is either not examined at all or is only partially examined. Organization development efforts focus on both the formal and the informal systems, but the initial intervention strategy is usually through the informal system in the sense that attitudes and feelings are usually the first data to be confronted.

By "collaborative management" of the culture we mean a shared kind of management—not a hierarchically imposed kind. Who does what to whom is an important issue in organization development, and we want to stress that management of group culture must be "owned" as much by the subordinates as it is by the formal leader.

Our definition recognizes that the key unit in organization development activities is the on-going work team, including both superior and subordinates. This is different from more conventional organizational interventions. To give only one example, in most management development activities the focus is on the individual manager or supervisor—not his work group. Traditionally he has participated in the learning experience in isolation from the dynamics of his work situation. Although we are emphasizing a focus on relatively permanent work groups to differentiate OD from traditional management development, in comprehensive OD programs extensive attention is also paid to temporary work teams, to overlapping team memberships, and to intergroup relations, as well as to total system implications.

The notion of the use of a "change agent" or "catalyst" as one of the distinguishing characteristics of OD has a purpose in our definition. We are somewhat pessimistic about the optimal effectiveness of OD efforts which are "do-it-yourself" programs. In the early phases, at least, the services of a third party who is not a part of the prevailing organization culture are essential. This does not mean that the third party cannot be a member of the organization but that he at least be external to the particular subsystem which is initiating an OD effort.

And finally, the basic intervention model which runs through most organization development efforts is "action research." To oversimplify, the action research model consists of (1) a preliminary diagnosis, (2) data gathering from the client group, (3) data feedback to the client group, (4) data exploration by the client group, (5) problem diagnosis, (6) action planning, and (7) action. Parenthetically, because of the extensive applicability of this model to organization development, another definition of organization development could be *organization improvement through action research.*

The above characteristics of organization development depart substantially from the features of traditional change programs, which Bennis categorizes as follows: "(1) exposition and propagation, (2) elite corps, (3) psychoanalytic insight, (4) staff, (5) scholarly consultations, and (6) circulation of ideas to the elite." [2] Bennis states that "exposition and propagation" are "possibly the most popular" and cites as illustrations the impact of the ideas of philosophers and scientists. The "elite corps" method is basically the infusion of scientists into key power and decision-making posts in organizations. "Psychoanalytic insight" as a change method is similar to the elite corps method, but refers to effective change occurring through the medium of executives who have high self-insight and considerable "psychiatric wisdom" relative to subordinates. The "staff" strategy refers to the employment in organizations of social scientists who analyze situations and make policy recommendations. "Scholarly consultations" is a method of change involving ". . . exploratory inquiry, scholarly understanding, scholarly confrontation, discovery of solutions, and finally, scientific advice to the client." The final method described by Bennis is "circulation of ideas to the elite." One of the illustrations given is the Council of Correspondence, a chain letter which linked rebel leaders in the American Revolution [3].

Organization development efforts depart substantially from these methods of organizational change. Of particular relevance are the two organizational consultation methods as categorized by Bennis, "staff" and "scholarly consultations." In both strategies an inside or external expert studies a situation and makes recommendations; this is the traditional way of consulting. Organization development efforts are different. To oversimplify, the OD consultant does *not* make recommendations in the traditional sense; he intervenes in the on-going processes of the organization.

We see, then, seven characteristics which we think differentiate organizational development intervention from more traditional interventions: (1) an emphasis, although not exclusive, on group and organizational processes in contrast to substantive content; (2) an emphasis on the work team as the key unit for learning more effective modes of organizational behavior; (3) an emphasis on the collaborative management of work team culture; (4) an emphasis on the management of the culture of the total system and total system ramifications; (5) the use of the "action research" model; (6) the use of a behavioral scientist "change agent" or catalyst; and (7) viewing the change effort as an on-going process. Another characteristic, (8), a primary emphasis on human and social relationships, does not necessarily differentiate OD from other change efforts, but is nevertheless an important feature.

If we agree that these seven characteristics do differentiate OD from other kinds of interventions, how do we classify programs like "management by objectives" (MBO) and "job enrichment"? Increasingly, these terms are used under the umbrella of "organization development," and, we think, erroneously. They *can* be part of, or an outcome of, OD efforts, but to equate them has the consequence of confusing or misleading people about what OD is about.

"Management by Objectives," it seems to us, is an extension of, or part of, the OD "ball park" providing it grows out of action research—i.e., gathering data about the problems being experienced by the client group, data feedback to the group involved, and careful diagnosis as to the nature of those problems. Our hunch is that most MBO programs are imposed by line managers and/or personnel departments and without much joint diagnosis. Further, our hunch is that most MBO programs do not use a team approach, that they do not provide for sufficient acknowledgement of interdependency between jobs, and rather than helping examine team culture, tend to reinforce a one-to-one leadership style. Incidentally these are some of the basic faults pointed out by Harry Levinson in his recent *Harvard Business Review* article [4].

"Job enrichment" is another kind of program aimed at improving organizations and which frequently does not square with the characteristics of OD as described earlier. Like MBO, it *can* be highly congruent with organization development. For example, some job enrichment is inherent in the action-research model—the minute subordinates are asked to help prepare an agenda for a problem-solving workshop, their jobs are being enriched. Further, job enrichment may very well be the consequence of the action plans which are a part of the action-research cycle. But, again, job enrichment can be an imposed program which is not based on a collaborative diagnosis. As a matter of fact, Herzberg et al., almost seems to say that job enrichment *should* be imposed from top-side:

> . . . So far as the process of job enrichment itself is concerned, experimental constraints in the studies dictated that there could be no participation by jobholders themselves in deciding what changes were to be made in their jobs. The changes nevertheless seemed to be effective. On the other hand, when people were invited to participate—not in any of the reported studies—results were disappointing. In one case, for example, a group of personnel specialists suggested fewer

than 30 fairly minor changes in their jobs, whereas the managers had compiled a list of over 100 much more substantial possibilities.

It seems that employees themselves are not in a good position to test out the validity of the boundaries of their jobs. So long as the aim is not to measure experimentally the effects of job enrichment alone, there is undoubtedly benefit in the sharing of ideas. . . . [5].

However, before we would conclude that Herzberg's experiments really were all that unilateral, we would want to know much more about the preliminary stages of his job enrichment programs. There may be more joint diagnosis and joint planning involved than is immediately evident.

Our purpose here is not to quarrel with the successes or failures of programs like MBO or job enrichment, but simply to state that sometimes they may be highly congruent with organization development and sometimes quite different. In the main, whether such programs are OD in nature depends upon what processes are used in their adoption and utilization.

Given these comments about what we think OD is, we now turn to a history of those kinds of organization improvement programs which fit our definition or organization development.

A HISTORY OF ORGANIZATION DEVELOPMENT

Systematic organization development activities have a fairly short history and, to use the analogy of a tree, have at least two important trunk stems. One stem is the application of laboratory training insights to industrial organizations. The other stem is survey research and feedback methodology.

The Laboratory Training Stem

The first stem, laboratory training, essentially unstructured small-group situations in which organizationally unrelated participants learn from their own interactions and the evolving dynamics of the group, began to evolve about 1946 from various experiments in the use of group discussions to achieve changes in behavior in back-home situations.

Over the next ten or twelve years, as trainers in the laboratory training and group dynamics movement began to work with social systems of more permanency and complexity than T-groups, they began to experience considerable frustration in transferring laboratory training skills and insights into the solution of problems in these organizations. Skills learned in the T-group simply were very difficult to transfer to complex organizations. The late Douglas McGregor, working with Union Carbide beginning about 1957, is considered to be one of the first behavioral scientists to begin to talk systematically about and to help implement the application of laboratory training skills to a complex organization [6]. In collaboration with McGregor, John Paul Jones, with the support of the Union Carbide's executive vice president and director, Birny Mason, Jr. (later president of the corporation), established a small internal consulting group which in large part used behavioral science knowledge in assisting line managers. Jones' organization was later called an "organization development group" [7].

During the same year, Herbert Shepard joined the Employee Relations Department of Esso Standard Oil as a research associate on organization. In 1958 and 1959 he launched three experiments in organization development at major Esso refineries: Bayonne, Baton Rouge and Bayway. At Bayonne an interview survey and diagnosis were made and discussed with top management, followed by a series of three-day laboratories for all members of management. Paul Buchanan, who had been using a somewhat similar approach in Republic Aviation, collaborated with Shepard at Bayonne, and subsequently joined the Esso staff.

At Baton Rouge, Robert Blake joined Shepard, and they conducted a series of two week laboratories attended by all members of "middle" management. At first, an effort was made to combine the case method with laboratory method, but the designs soon became similar to NTL Institute's present Management Work Conferences which emphasize T-groups, organizational exercises, and relevant lectures. One innovation in this training program was an emphasis on intergroup as well as interpersonal relations. Although working on interpersonal problems affecting work performance clearly had organizational overtones, between-group problem solving had even more organization development implications in that a broader and more complex segment of the organization was involved.

At Baton Rouge, efforts to involve top management failed, and as a result follow-up resources for implementing organization development were not made available. By the time the Bayway program started, two fundamental OD lessons had been learned: the requirement of active involvement in and leadership of the program by top management, and the need for on-the-job application.

At Bayway there were two significant innovations. First, Shepard, Blake, and Murray Horwitz utilized the instrumented laboratory, which Blake and Jane Mouton had been developing in social psychology classes at the University of Texas, and which they later developed into the Managerial Grid approach to organization development [8]. (An essential dimension of the instrumented lab is the use of feedback based on scales and measurements of group and individual behavior during sessions.) [9] Secondly, at Bayway more resources were devoted to team development, consultation, intergroup conflict resolution, etc., than were devoted to laboratory training of "cousins," i.e., organization members from different departments [10].

As Robert Blake stated, "It was learning to *reject* T-group stranger-type labs that permitted OD to come into focus." As he has further commented, it was intergroup projects, in particular, which "triggered real OD" [11]. As is evident from the Esso and Union Carbide activities, Shepard, Blake, McGregor and others were clearly trying to build on the insights and learnings of laboratory training toward more linkage with and impact on the problems and dynamics of on-going organizations.

It is not entirely clear who coined the term, organization development, but in all probability it was Robert Blake, Herbert Shepard and Jane Mouton [12]. The phrase "development group" had earlier been used by Blake and Mouton in connection with human relations training at the University of Texas and appeared in their 1956 document, "Training for Decision Making in Groups," which was distributed for use in connection with the Baton Rouge experiments [13]. (The same phrase appeared in a Mouton and Blake article first published in the journal, *Group Psychotherapy,* in 1957.) [14] The Baton Rouge T-Groups were called "Development Groups," [15] and this terminology, coupled with the insights which were emerging, undoubtedly culminated in the concept of organization development.

It is of considerable significance that the emergence of organization development efforts in the first two firms to be involved, Union Carbide and Esso, included employee relations-industrial relations people seeing themselves in new roles. At Union Carbide, John Paul Jones, who had come up through industrial relations, now saw himself in the role of a behavioral science consultant to other managers [16]. At Esso, the headquarters human relations research division began to view itself as an internal consulting group offering services to field managers rather than as a research group developing reports for top management [17]. Thus, in history of OD, we see both external consultants and internal staff departments departing from traditional roles and collaborating in quite a new approach to organization improvement.

The Action Research-Survey Feedback Stem

Of particular importance to the history of organization development is a specialized form of action research which we will call survey research and feedback, which refers to the use of attitude surveys and data feedback in workshop sessions. Survey research and feedback constitutes the second major stem in the history of organization development.

The history of this stem, in particular, revolves around the experience which staff members at the Research Center for Group Dynamics, founded in 1945 by Kurt Lewin, were gaining over a period of years in action research. The Center was first established at the Massachusetts Institute of Technology and subsequently moved to the University of Michigan after Lewin's death in 1957. A few of the key figures involved at M.I.T. in addition to Lewin were Marian Radke, Leon Festinger, Ronald Lippitt, Douglas McGregor, John R. P. French, Jr., and Dorwin Cartwright [18]. Names conspicuous in the work at Michigan in recent years include Floyd Mann and Rensis Likert.

One example of the action research approach is the 1948 project at the Detroit Edison Company where researchers began systematic feedback of data from a company-wide employee and management attitude survey [19]. In this project, data from an attitude survey were fed back to participating accounting departments in what Mann calls an "interlocking chain of conferences" [20]. Some of the insights which emerged from this process have a very contemporary OD ring. To illustrate, in drawing conclusions from the Detroit Edison Study, Baumgartel stated:

> The results of this experimental study lend support to the idea that intensive group discussion procedure for utilizing the results of an employee questionnaire survey can be an effective tool for introducing positive change in a business organization. It may be that the effectiveness of this method, in comparison to traditional training courses, is that it deals with the system of human relationships as a whole (superior and subordinate can change together) and it deals with each manager, supervisor, and employee in the context of his own job, his own problems, and his own work relationships" [21].

Kurt Lewin

If the people involved in laboratory training and survey research constitute the two main stems in the organization development tree, then certainly Kurt Lewin and his work in developing a field theory of social psychology was the taproot. His passionate interest in applied behavioral science was the main thrust to both laboratory training and survey research. Lewin was a central figure in the origin of both the National Training Laboratories (now NTL-Institute for Applied Behavioral Science) and the Research Center for Group Dynamics. Although Lewin died only two years after the founding of the Research Center and just before the first formal session of NTL, he had a profound influence on both organizations and the people associated with them, and his influence continues today [22].

CONCLUDING COMMENTS

In conclusion, what we are calling organization development has a number of unique characteristics and a unique history which differentiates it from other change programs. In particular, it should not be confused with MBO or job enrichment, although such programs can be outcomes of, and can be highly congruent with, organization development.

The history of organization development, as we have defined it, has emerged largely from the social psychology of Kurt Lewin and his associates. One main stem, laboratory training, which is largely the history of NTL, culminated in the pioneering industrial applications of Douglas McGregor, Herbert Shepard, Robert Blake, Jane Mouton, and others, in which actual organizational problems of work teams and broader systems were encountered. Part of that history includes organizational staff departments viewing themselves in new roles.

Another stem, survey feedback, emerged from the Center for Group Dynamics and the subsequent work of Floyd Mann and others in the use of attitude surveys and working with overlapping work teams in the utilization of the survey data.

If there is one central technique in all of this history, it is the action-research model. If this feature, plus some others which have been mentioned above are not present, a change effort may be an organization improvement program but it is not "organization development" in the historical meaning of the term.

REFERENCES

1 Kroeber and Kluckhohn cite 164 definitions of culture: our above definition is congruent with their synthesis: "Culture consists of patterns, explicit and implicit, and for behavior acquired and transmitted by symbols, constituting the distinctive achievement of human groups, including their embodiments in artifacts; the essential core of culture consists of traditional (i.e., historically derived and selected) ideas and especially their attached values; culture systems may, on the one hand, be considered as products of action, on the other as conditioning elements of further action." See A. L. Kroeber and Clyde Kluckhohn, *Culture: A Critical Review of Concepts and Definitions* (New York: Vintage Books, originally published 1952), pp. 291, 357.

2 Warren G. Bennis, "A New Role for the Behavioral Sciences: Effecting Organizational Change," *Administrative Science Quarterly*, 8:130 (September, 1963).

3 Ibid., pp. 130–134.

4 Harry Levinson, "Management by Whose Objectives?" *Harvard Business Review*, 48:125–134 (July–August, 1970).

5 William Paul, Keith Robertson, and Frederick Herzberg, "Job Enrichment Pays Off," *Harvard Business Review*, 47:75 (March–April, 1969).

6 Richard Beckhard, W. Warner Burke, and Fred I. Steele, "The Program for Specialists in Organization Training and Development," p. ii, mimeographed paper, NTL Institute for Applied Behavioral Science, December 1967, and John Paul Jones, "What's Wrong with Work?" in *What's Wrong with Work?* (New York: National Association of Manufacturers, 1967), p. 8.

7 Gilbert Burck, "Union Carbide's Patient Schemers," *Fortune*, 72:147–149 (December 1965). For McGregor's account, see "Team Building at Union Carbide" in Douglas McGregor, *The Professional Manager* (New York: McGraw-Hill Book Co., 1967), pp. 106–110.

8 Correspondence from Robert Blake and Herbert Shepard.

9 See Robert Blake and Jane Srygley Mouton, "The Instrumented Training Laboratory," in Irving R. Weschler and Edgar M. Schein, eds., *Selected Readings Series Five: Issues in Training* (Washington, D.C.: National Training Laboratories, 1962), pp. 61–85. In this paper, Blake and Mouton credit Muzafer and Carolyn Sherif with important contributions to early intergroup experiments. Reference is also made to the contributions of Frank Cassens of Humble Oil and Refinery in the early phases of the Esso program.

10 Much of the historical account in the above four paragraphs is based on correspondence with Herbert Shepard, with some information added from correspondence with Robert Blake.

11 Based on correspondence from Robert Blake to the authors.

12 Blake correspondence.

13 Blake correspondence.

14 Jane Srygley Mouton and Robert R. Blake, "University Training in Human Relations Skills," *Selected Readings Series Three: Forces in Learning* (Washington, D.C.: National Training Laboratories,1961), pp. 88–96, reprinted from *Group Psychotherapy,* 10:342–345 (1957).

15 Shepard and Blake correspondence.

16 Gilbert Burcsk, op. cit., p. 149.

17 Harry D. Kolb, "Introduction" to *An Action Research Program for Organization Improvement* (Ann Arbor: Foundation for Research on Human Behavior, 1960), p. i. The term organization development is used several times in this monograph based on a 1959 meeting about the Esso programs, and written by Kolb, Shepard, Blake, and others.

18 For part of this history, see Alfred J. Marrow, *The Practical Theorist: The Life and Work of Kurt Lewin* (New York: Basic Books, 1969), Ch. 19.

19 Floyd C. Mann, "Studying and Creating Change," in Warren Bennis, Kenneth Beene and Robert Chin, *The Planning of Change* (New York: Holt, Rinehart and Winston, 1961), pp. 605–613. Another early project which had some overtones of organization development, but was not published for many years was the "Tremont Hotel Project." See William Foote Whyte and Edith Lentz Hamilton, *Action Research for Management* (Homewood, Ill.: Richard D. Irwin, 1965), pp. 1–282.

20 Floyd Mann, op. cit., p. 609.

21 Howard Baumgartel, "Using Employee Questionnaire Results for Improving Organizations: The Survey 'Feedback' Experiment," *Kansas Business Review,* 12:2–6 (December, 1959).

22 For an excellent and detailed account of Lewin's life and influence, see Alfred J. Marrow, op. cit., Parts I–III.

READING   39

ORGANIZATION EXCELLENCE THROUGH EFFECTIVE MANAGEMENT BEHAVIOR

Robert R. Blake
Jane Srygley Mouton*

When the word "moon" is mentioned today, a listener is far less likely to think of green cheese, what the cow jumped over, or June and spoon than about launching pads and space capsules. Just so, "management" no longer conjures up a picture of an ogre, a big rich corporate tycoon, or the

*From *Manage* magazine, vol. 20, no. 2, pp. 42–47. Copyright 1967 by the National Management Association. Reprinted with permission.

"robber barons" so much as the scientific knowledge a modern manager uses to organize his work and work of others.

APPLYING "SCIENCE"

Many new scientific ideas about management have evolved during the past decade from research findings in the behavioral sciences. One new approach to management has been hailed as a scientific "breakthrough" and is being used by many leading companies in the United States and Canada as well as Great Britian, Australia, and Japan. It is known as the Managerial Grid. (See Figure 1.)

The Grid is based on research into practical use of behavioral science in business. It is more than just a theory. It is a framework in which a variety of findings about behavior of managers can be fitted. It is a behavioral road map.

Companies that have used Grid learning say that it has improved management. Some can even show its direct influence on their profit and loss statements. They have realized better output when their managers understand what lies behind their styles of behavior and the effects it has on others. The Grid makes it possible for all managers and whole organizations to learn better ways to manage.

PHILOSOPHY CHANGE

Until 20 years or so ago, good managers were thought to have a born talent. It took quite a few experiments to discover exactly what it is that makes a good manager. Every man, whether he knows it or not, has deeply imbedded theories about behavior that are reflected in his style of managing. Once a man has a clear, explicit idea or theory about how to manage, a theory about how to work with others, how to integrate people and production, he finds it possible to become a better and better manager in countless ways.

He not only knows how to direct people's work, but how to put to work the good that can come out of the disagreements that invariably arise. He can make conflict useful as well as resolve it. Furthermore, when all managers in a company share ideas about the soundest ways to manage, the work climate takes on a whole new atmosphere. It is an atmosphere of fact finding, trust, and confidence among members of the organization, and problem solving by thrashing through problems to resolution, not by simply giving in, horse trading, smoothing over differences, or pushing one's own solutions on a take-it-or-leave-it basis.

WHAT IS IT?

The Grid is an 81-squared framework on which styles of behavior can be plotted. A manager has to think about two things—how to get the work

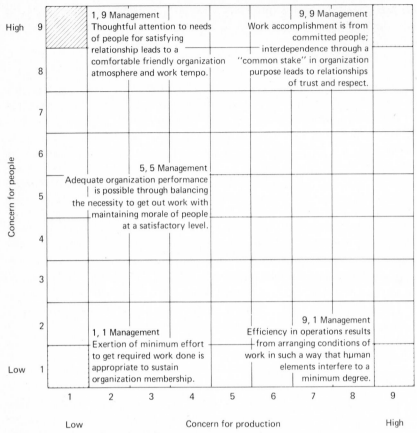

Figure 1   The managerial grid.

done and the people who are going to do the work. Some managers have production on their minds more than people; others, people more than production. On the horizontal axis of the Grid, which goes from 1 to 9, the 9 represents high concern for output, the 1 low concern for output. On the vertical axis, the 9 represents high concern for people and the 1 low concern for people.

GRID THEORIES USED

In the lower right-hand corner, "9,1" represents a great deal of concern for output but very little for the people who are expected to produce. At the opposite corner of the Grid is "1,9" representing much concern for people and little for the output needed in a healthy business.

Another Grid corner is 1,1. It seems almost impossible that a manager could have little or no concern for either people or production, but these are the ones in an organization who go through the motions of being a part of it but are invisible though present. They are not participators or doers but free-riders. They have not quit the organization, but they have done a mental walkout.

Still another possibility is in dead center of the Grid. This is the 5,5 style. A manager with this approach is on a seesaw. He says to his people, "Let's get to work but don't kill yourself, and don't rush around, but find yourself a comfortable tempo." He tells himself not to push too much or he will be seen as hardnosed, and not to let people off too easy or he will be seen as soft, to be "fair but firm." He is the "organization man."

UPPER RIGHT

The upper right-hand corner, the 9,9 position, denotes a high concern for both production and people and involves some new and useful ideas. A man with a 9,9 orientation emphasizes fact finding for problem solving. When conflict arises, the facts are dug into and thrashed through to solution of a problem. The 9,9 position is characterized by commitment of organization members to accomplishment of work which contributes to organization goals. They recognize an interdependence through a common stake in the outcome of their work.

Furthermore, managers have been found to use at least two theories, a dominant and a backup. Pressure brings out a manager's backup theory. For example, a man may display a 5,5 style most of the time, but when he is under pressure, he may shift to a 9,1 style of managing, calling upon his authoritative backup theory for a way to get something accomplished. Or a man may have a 1,1 backup style. He may function regularly as a 9,1 production oriented manager but backed into a corner, when he is not able to get his own way, he may move down into the "to-heck-with-it-I-quit" 1,1 position. It is a widely recognized fact that fatigue pushes a manager down toward the 9,1 corner and finally into the 1,1 corner. Overindulgence in alcohol is a sure path to 1,1.

HOW CAN IT HELP?

When managers from the same company study the Grid, it gives them two things—a set of ideas for thinking about production-people problems and a language for describing and talking about them. It provides them with ideas for studying their own practices and attitudes and for changing their own behavior. With this framework, an organization's procedures can be revised. Indeed the whole organization culture can be changed to achieve a 9,9 climate.

TEXTBOOK PLUS . . .

The Grid is not learned from a textbook, alone. Rather, managers study theories of the Grid in week-long seminars. These seminars include personal study by each man of his managerial style, and measurement of his team effectiveness as he works on a team with others. A high point of the seminar is when each person receives a critique of his managerial style from the other members of his team based on his behavior during the week. The emphasis is on his style of managing, not on his character traits or personality. Another high point is when managers discuss the style of their organization cultures and begin to consider steps for increasing the effectiveness of their companies.

PREWORK INVOLVED

The seminars require about 30 hours of "prework" before the actual study week begins. The seminar usually starts on Saturday afternoon, and participants study morning, noon, and night through noon the following Friday. The seminars are self-taught, since the method of instruction is by instruments—questionnaires and measurement tasks. But the study is not classroom study so much as it is the study of action.

ORGANIZATIONAL BENEFITS

A Grid seminar week is the foundation for six-phase Grid Organization Development, an approach to improving the effectiveness of an entire organization. A second step is to apply learnings back on the job within one's own work team, an on-the-job extension of Grid learning called Work Team Development. Each work team investigates how it works, and decides how to get the most effective 9,9 approach to work problems. It starts with top executives and moves down through the organization. Team members probe for facts, listen, maintain attitudes of self-examination, and get better relationships with one another by facing up to conflict and solving it on the spot. Each man also receives an action critique of how he works from other team members.

The last four phases of Grid Organization Development are built upon the first two. They enable managers to work toward developing the culture and the business practices of the whole organization. In Phase 3 the emphasis shifts from managers to groups in the organization, focusing on better co-ordination among departments or divisions. Phase 4 involves the top team's design of the soundest possible blueprint for the business operations of the corporation, Phase 5, carrying it out, and Phase 6, stabilizing and strengthening results. This is the Grid pattern for moving a whole company ahead toward excellence.

HAS IT WORKED?

This is the Grid pattern. What have been the results in companies that have followed it—studying the Managerial Grid and moving on into Grid Organization Development? Thousands of managers in many countries as well as the U.S. have studied the Grid and hundreds of companies are holding in-company Grid Seminars and working toward completing all the phases. Some have gone much further and extended the Grid to their wage ranks. Some firms have arranged for outside researchers from universities to evaluate their development efforts to see if there have been positive changes that can be traced specifically to Grid learning. The answer in each case is "yes."

The results have shown that Grid trained managers bring in a new perspective to their work—no longer asking, "Are we doing better than last year?" or "Are we doing better than competitors?" but "What's the best we can do, not only now but in the future?" They have a whole new set of optimistic *expectations* once they learn how they can manage an organization's culture instead of letting it manage them.

And they have developed new *values*—understanding the use of participation, getting commitment instead of operating by old-fashioned methods of supervision, and using experimentation and critique to learn, to change, and to improve. They are not only able to face up to conflict, but even make constructive use of disagreement, seeing it as valuable in the search for sound operational decisions.

READING 40

APPLICATION OF SYSTEM 4 IN AN AUTOMOBILE ASSEMBLY PLANT

Rensis Likert
Jane Gibson Likert*

The basic proposition of this [discussion] is that the management of conflict can be improved substantially by replacing the traditional structure and processes of organizations with those based on a more effective social system, namely System 4T.** The degree of improvement in conflict man-

* From Rensis Likert and Jane Gibson Likert, *New Ways of Managing Conflict,* New York: McGraw-Hill Book Company, 1976, pp. 71–77. © by McGraw-Hill, Inc. Reprinted with permission.

** *Editor's note:* System 4T represents "System 4, Total," meaning that an organization has approximately System 4 conditions on all variables in the System 4 model of participative-supportive management.

agement which can be expected from the proposed action depends, of course, on the magnitude of the superiority of the new social system over the one it replaces. This chapter will examine briefly some of the available data dealing with this issue.

In 1969 The University of Michigan's Institute for Social Research undertook a project for the General Motors Corporation. One of the objectives of this project was to test the System 4T theory. Did two assembly plants in the same labor market that differed substantially in productivity, costs, quality, and labor relations display the differences in the human organizational measurements that would be expected from the theory? The results for salaried employees (see fig. 5–1) show that they did. Plant A, the highest-producing assembly plant, has a substantially more favorable profile than does plant B, the lowest-producing, highest-cost plant. The measurements were obtained in October and November, 1969. Tables 5–1 and 5–2 briefly define the human organizational variables based on the items used to measure them. The questionnaire is described fully in Taylor and Bowers (1972).

A second objective of the General Motors–Institute for Social Research project was to test whether the knowledge and skills were available to help the managements of the two plants—and especially the poorer plant—shift closer to the System 4T model and, if these shifts were successful, whether the performance data of the plants would show corresponding improvement.

In October, 1969, the president of General Motors asked the Institute director whether shifting the manager of the high-producing plant to be-

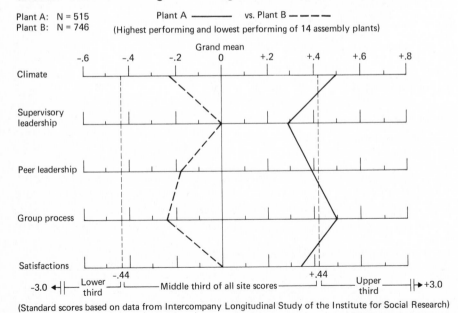

Plant A: N = 515
Plant B: N = 746

Plant A ———— vs. Plant B — — — —
(Highest performing and lowest performing of 14 assembly plants)

(Standard scores based on data from Intercompany Longitudinal Study of the Institute for Social Research)

Figure 5–1 Human organizational scores for all salaried personnel in November, 1969.

Table 5-1   Items Used to Measure Human Organizational Causal Variables

---

Supervisory (Managerial) Leadership
- *Support.* Friendly; pays attention to what you are saying; listens to subordinates' problems.
- *Team building.* Encourages subordinates to work as a team; encourages exchange of opinions and ideas.
- *Goal emphasis.* Encourages best efforts; maintains high standards.
- *Help with work.* Shows ways to do a better job; helps subordinates plan, organize, and schedule; offers new ideas, solutions to problems.

Organizational Climate
- *Communication flow.* Subordinates know what's going on; superiors are receptive; subordinates are given information to do jobs well.
- *Decision-making practices.* Subordinates are involved in setting goals; decisions are made at levels of accurate information; persons affected by decisions are asked for their ideas; know-how of people of all levels is used.
- *Concern for persons.* The organization is interested in the individual's welfare; tries to improve working conditions; organizes work activities sensibly.
- *Influence on department.* From lower-level supervisors and from employees who have no subordinates.
- *Technological adequacy.* Improved methods are quickly adopted; equipment and resources are well managed.
- *Motivation.* Differences and disagreements are accepted and worked through; people in organization work hard for money, promotions, job satisfaction, and to meet high expectations from others and are encouraged to do so by policies, working conditions, and people.

---

come the plant manager of the poor-producing plant would cause any difficulty in carrying out the objectives of the project. When assured that this shift would have advantages rather than disadvantages, the change was made. This high-producing manager was employing the kinds of principles that our organizational theory (System 4T) indicated would yield the best performance. The Institute staff felt that the measurements and organizational model could help this manager more rapidly achieve a sizable improvement in the poor plant after he took it over.

Figure 5–2 shows the kind of management this manager was seen to be providing to the high-producing plant prior to his transfer. These data are based on the perceptions of the top 52 managers in that plant. As the profile for his current (now) behavior shows, he is seen to be a System 4 manager. In addition, he had high performance goals, high technical competence, and scored high on "help with work." Therefore, his scores on all these dimensions showed that he was a System 4T manager.

This man made extremely good use of our survey measurements when he took over as plant manager of the poor plant. The data helped him understand his problems and how best to proceed. He saw to it that the managers and supervisors reporting to him were aided by the survey-feedback organizational improvement process and coaching. He provided the foremen with assistants (utility trainers) to train workers, chase stock, and do similar tasks, thereby freeing the foremen to spend time on the human

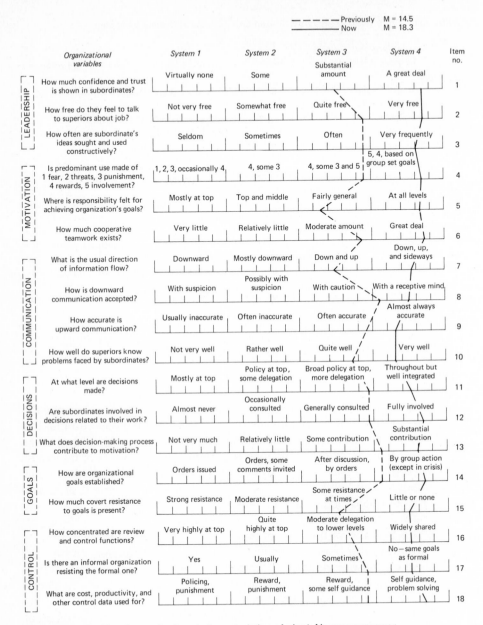

Figure 5-2 Profile of organizational characteristics of plant A's new manager.

problems. As Figure 5–3 shows, he made usually rapid progress in bringing about substantial improvement in the human organization and its productive capability, as reflected in the measurements of the human organization.

Table 5-2   Items Used to Measure Human Organizational Intervening Variables

Peer Leadership
- *Support.* Friendly; pays attention to what others are saying; listens to others' problems.
- *Goal emphasis.* Encourages best efforts; maintains high standards.
- *Help with work.* Shows ways to do a better job; helps others plan, organize, and schedule; group shares with each other new ideas, solutions to problems.
- *Team building.* Encouragement from each other to work as a team: emphasis on team goal; exchange of opinions and ideas.

Group Process
- Planning together; coordinating efforts.
- Making good decisions; solving problems.
- Knowing jobs and how to do them well.
- Sharing information.
- Wanting to meet objectives.
- Having confidence and trust in other members.
- Ability to meet unusual work demands.

Satisfaction
With other workers, superiors, jobs, this organization compared with others, pay, progress in the organization up to now, chances for getting ahead in the future.

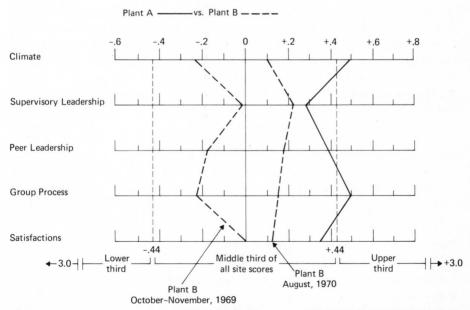

Figure 5-3 Human organization scores for salaried personnel in November, 1969, and August, 1970.

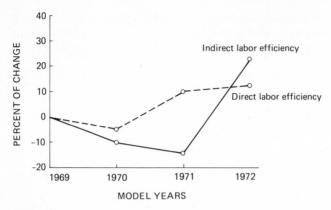

Figure 5-4 Percent of change in operating efficiency at an assembly plant (plant B).

From November, 1969, to August, 1970, he had moved the human organization scores for the 750 salaried employees about one-half the distance from the poorest to the best plant.

The data in Figure 5-4 show the pattern that we typically find: improvement in productivity and costs lags in time behind improvement in the human organization. Even though the human organization scores (Fig. 5-3) showed a sizable improvement by the end of the 1970 model year (August, 1970), both direct and indirect labor costs continued to *deteriorate* rather than improve. Costs were increasing even though there was an improvement in the human organization. The deterioration in indirect labor costs continued for one more year. Direct labor efficiency showed a sizable improvement in the 1971 model year and continued this trend in the 1972 year. Indirect labor efficiencies, however, did not improve until the 1972 model year when a sizable improvement occurred. Figure 5-5 shows some of the the improvement attained by the 1972 model year. The improvement in labor efficiency alone represents a $5 million saving. In addition, there were various other savings, such as a reduction in tool breakage and an improvement in quality. There was also a sizable improvement in employee satisfaction which has been found to be associated with employee health, both physical and mental.

It usually requires substantially more time for a new plant manager to begin to show improvement in productivity and costs after taking over a poor plant than was required by this manager in improving plant B. Two

Figure 5-5 Plant B Performance 1972 vs. 1969

Direct labor efficiency	14% improvement
Indirect labor efficiency	23% improvement
Monitored quality index	10% improvement
Grievances per 100 employees	60% decrease
(January–April)	

and three years are not uncommon. The survey-feedback organizational improvement process enabled the plant B manager to achieve much more rapid improvement than would have been likely without this resource.

REFERENCE

Taylor, J. C. & Bowers, D. G. *Survey of organizations: Toward a machine-scored, standardized questionnaire instrument.* Ann Arbor: University of Michigan, Institute for Social Research, 1972.

CHAPTER 11
ORGANIZATIONS AND ORGANIZATIONAL DESIGN

READING   41

THE NECESSITY FOR ENLIGHTENED MANAGEMENT POLICIES

Abraham H. Maslow*

People are growing and growing, either in their actual health of personality, or in their aspirations, especially in the United States, and especially women and underprivileged groups. The more grown people are, the worse authoritarian management will work, the less well people will function in the authoritarian situation, and the more they will hate it. Partly this comes about from the fact that when people have a choice between a high and a low pleasure, they practically always choose the high pleasure if they have previously experienced both. What this means is that people who have experienced freedom can never really be content again with slavery, even though they made no protest about the slavery *before* they had the experience of freedom. This is true with all higher pleasures; those people who have known the feeling of dignity and self-respect for the first time can never again be content with slavishness, even though they made no protest about it before being treated with dignity.

*   *   *

*From *Eupsychian Management: A Journal* (Homewood, Ill.: Richard D. Irwin, Inc. and The Dorsey Press, 1965), p. 261. Copyright 1965. Reprinted with permission.

READING   42

AN ORGANIZATION
AS A SYSTEM

Paul R. Lawrence
Jay W. Lorsch*

At the most general level we find it useful to view an organization as an open system in which the behaviors of members are themselves interrelated. The behaviors of members of an organization are also interdependent with the formal organization, the tasks to be accomplished, the personalities of other individuals, and the unwritten rules about appropriate behavior for a member. Under this concept of system, the behavior of any one manager can be seen as determined not only by his own personality needs and motives, but also by the way his personality interacts with those of his colleagues. Further, this relationship among organization members is also influenced by the nature of the task being performed, by the formal relationships, rewards, and controls, and by the existing ideas within the organization about how a well-accepted member should behave. It is important to emphasize that all these determinants of behavior are themselves interrelated.

*   *   *

*From *Organization and Environment: Managing Differentiation and Integration* (Homewood, Ill.: Richard D. Irwin, Inc., 1967), p. 6. Copyright 1967. Reprinted with permission.

READING   43

MECHANISTIC VS. ORGANIC ORGANIZATIONS: WHAT DOES THE FUTURE HOLD?

C. Ray Gullett*

Organizations are reflections of the environments in which they function, at least in the long run. Environment means all those external forces that influence an organization, including the actions of competitors, technological developments, legal restrictions, customer preferences and society's expectations. Any external influence on an organization can be included as a part of its environment. If an organization is not able to accommodate itself to the constraints and challenges that its environment poses, that organization will eventually cease to exist. Environmental adaptation is a fundamental law in biology; it should be given equal importance in the understanding of organizations. Corporate "dinosaurs" are no more likely to survive than their prehistoric counterparts. Of course, adaptation is a two-way street. An organization also has an impact on its environment. But ultimately, an organization must adapt to some extent or face ruin.

When we look into the future and attempt to make predictions about tomorrow's organizational forms we have to begin with a discussion of tomorrow's environment for organizations. This is a risky task at best.

Even though the future is far from clear, most who will hazard a guess about tomorrow emphasize that it will be more turbulent than today. Product life cycles will continue to shorten. International competition will increase. Technological complexities will require longer lead times for product development.

ORGANIC ORGANIZATION

Faced with such environmental conditions, organizations are seen by many as developing along "organic" lines. Organic organizations are those which have most, if not all, of the following characteristics:

---

*From *The Personnel Administrator*, November 1975, pp. 17–19 and 49. Copyright 1975 by The American Society for Personnel Administration. Reprinted with permission.

1　There is a de-emphasis on job descriptions and specialization. Persons become involved in problem solving when they have knowledge or skill that will help to solve the problem. Concern is chiefly with organization-wide objectives rather than those of a sub-specialty. There is a great deal of emphasis on the authority of knowledge.

2　It is not assumed that persons holding higher positions are necessarily better informed than at lower levels. In fact, the reverse may be true with regard to a specific work problem.

3　Horizontal and lateral organizational relationships are given as much or more attention as vertical relationships. Departmental boundaries are not rigid. Problem solving teams made up of several departments are commonly used.

4　Status and rank differences are de-emphasized. Strict superior-subordinate relationships are replaced with a more collegial atmosphere.

5　The formal structure of the organization is less permanent and more changeable.

Organizations of this sort are not unheard of today. In certain industries they are the norm rather than the exception. The electronics, aerospace and computer technology fields are examples. Indeed, where the environment is rapidly changing, these flexible organizational designs appear to be much more efficient than so-called "mechanistic" structures. Their major attraction is their ability to adjust rapidly to external changes.

MECHANISTIC ORGANIZATION

In contrast to the organic format, the "mechanistic" organizational design emphasizes structure and stability. Among its characteristics are the following:

1　Activities are specialized into clearly defined jobs and tasks. Each person is concerned primarily with his work and not that of the organization as a whole.

2　Persons of higher rank typically have greater knowledge of the problems facing the organization than those at lower levels. Unresolved problems are thus passed up the hierarchy until someone with appropriate knowledge is found to solve them.

3　Standardized policies, procedures, and rules guide much of the decision making in the organization. "Managing by the book" is often emphasized.

4　Rewards are chiefly obtained through obedience to instructions from superiors. Most communication flows upward and downward in the structure rather than laterally or horizontally.

The mechanistic organizational form is a classic bureaucracy. Coordination of activities is largely achieved through the vertical hierarchy. Emphasis is placed on stability, predictability and uniformity of action.

Are structures of this sort defunct? Clearly not, as of today. To some extent, these characteristics exist in most organizations. A certain amount of emphasis on authority levels and routine is necessary, even in organizations on the organic end of the scale. In some industries, however, the mechanistic approach is clearly the superior one. An automobile manufacturing plant and the clerical processing unit of a large insurance company are more efficient and effective when structured mechanistically. Because their environments are stable, they could profit little from an organic design.

But what of the future? Will the mechanistic form of organization design become a thing of the past or will it survive? Those who foresee an increasingly turbulent environment plus increasing employee demands for autonomy have said that the death of bureaucracy is inevitable. Organic structures are seen as the dominant form of structural design in the not-too-distant future. And, indeed this appears reasonable if one agrees that future environments will simply not support organizations built on the assumption of stability or slow change.

But reality is seldom as simple as such a view would have us believe. Two problems are associated with the position. First of all, the rate of change of the environment is not the same for all organizations. Secondly, different parts of the same organization often face different sub-environments and must structure themselves accordingly.

While undoubtedly there is some movement or change taking place in the environments of all organizations, the rate at which this change is occurring is not uniform. Competitive pressures, the pace of innovation in the industry, customer expectations and technologies used for the production of goods and services are all variable. Even if we assume that all environments will be more dynamic in future years than they are today, it is a safe bet that some will continue to be more stable than others.

As an example of uneven rates of change we can take a brief look at the pace of product development. In the past 15 years the research breakthroughs that have occurred in the aerospace industry have been astounding. The industry has been marked by rapid-fire innovation in space vehicles and support equipment. It is no accident that matrix organization design and project management has been used so extensively by firms in this dynamic industry.

By contrast, design and performance changes in automobiles are relatively slow, with only slight variations often occurring from year to year. The efforts of government and environmentalists along with the fuel crisis have forced more fundamental changes in weight, safety equipment, engine efficiency and exhaust emissions, but even these changes have come at a gradual speed. With such a standardized product produced in large quantities, the more mechanistic form of structure is probably most efficient. Mass production technology calls for a relatively stable, bureaucratic structure. It is a reflection of a low change rate in the organization's external world.

The point of this example is that environments are not equally vairable or stable, nor are they changing at the same rate. Some environments will remain much more stable than others. And organization designs are likely to reflect these differences. The more stable or slowly changing the environment, the better a more mechanistic structure is likely to fit an organization's needs. Even with faster change rates in the future, some environments will probably remain fairly stable.

One assumption that much of our discussion has made so far is that an organization faces a single, clearly-defined environment. Prescriptions for the formal design of the structure are thus based on the identification of either a stable or unstable environment for the organization as a whole.

While a single environment sometimes confronts an organization, quite often it faces several different environments at once. Some parts of the organization may be operating under conditions of rapid change while others may be functioning under relatively stable conditions.

In their research Lawrence and Lorsch found that the research units in the plastics industry faced a very dynamic and uncertain sub-environment. Product innovation was a necessity for a firm to stay competitive. New products could rapidly make existing ones obsolete. In such a sub-environment the research departments of successful firms were designed and operated along organic lines.

In the same firms, production units were another story. Their sub-environments were fairly stable. Once new products were developed it was the production units' task to produce them in standardized and low-cost fashion. Concern was chiefly for meeting customer delivery dates and maintaining product standards. Consequently, successful firms in the industry designed their production units along mechanistic lines.

Additional research by Lawrence and Lorsch and by others indicates that the more diverse the sub-environments of an organization, the more diverse must be its structure. Success is related to creating the proper amount of diversity among organizational units. Thus a single organization could be both organic and mechanistic depending on the sub-environments faced by different parts of the organization.

This diversity is likely to be one key to the design of tomorrow's organizations. The turbulent environments foreseen for the future are more likely to change at different rates. The result may mean that few organizations can expect a uniform set of external conditions for all organizational units. Different departments are likely to experience different change rates.

In turn, structural differences among departments may grow. Attitudinal differences of employees and managers are also likely to be more pronounced. Those who function in free-form, organically designed units may have orientations much different than those who are part of more mechanistically designed sub-units. Differences in time perspectives, in personal satisfactions obtained from the work and in work objectives being sought may increase.

As a result, managers will have to concern themselves more than ever with effective coordination. Linking organizational sub-units together so that they contribute to common objectives is a major purpose of organization and management. And the more diverse the sub-units, the more difficult the coordination becomes.

In a stable environment with little diversity, coordination of departments can be achieved primarily through supervision by a common superior. But with greater environmental variation and with subsequent variation in organizational sub-units, reliance on the organizational hierarchy for coordination will often be insufficient. As a result of such diversity, a common superior will have a great deal of difficulty knowing all he needs to know to adequately integrate the various sub-units' activities.

Because of this complexity and diversity, more of the coordination will take place at the level of operating problems. This will mean more reliance on team relationships and cross-functional specialists to coordinate the activities among departments. Persons or groups acting as an interface between and among diverse sub-units will become a necessity in more of tomorrow's organizations. While hierarchy will not vanish, greater emphasis will be placed on managing through horizontal and lateral relationships. Integrative sub-units such as the one shown in Figure I will grow in importance.

What then does the future hold for organizational design? Although we are painting in only broad brush strokes, we can foresee more diversity and turbulence in external environments confronting organizations and their sub-units. This will mean greater diversity within the organization itself. Some parts may be relatively mechanistic while others will be organic in design. Many intermediary positions are also likely.

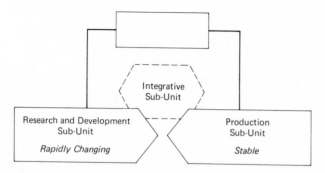

Figure 1 For organizations facing diverse environments, one or more integrative sub-units will be necessary to coordinate varied activities.

MANAGING DIVERSITY

As a result of this diversity coordination problems will increase. While hierarchy will not vanish, it will be less important as the way to coordinate sub-unit activities. More emphasis will be placed on team relationships, specialists who act as integrators and even departments whose mission is to effectively link the activities of sub-units.

Project managers operating in a matrix relationship with functional departments provide a prototype for future organizational designs. Traditional structures will be increasingly overlayed with horizontal and lateral flows of authority and influence. Those who operate as "integrators" will become increasingly important to the success of the organization's activities. They will be in touch with many operating problems on a "real-time" basis. Theirs will be the responsibility of insuring that special interests are directed toward the accomplishment of overall organizational objectives. They will take on many of the responsibilities traditionally reserved for higher-level management. Indeed, such positions may become the training ground for top management posts.

In summary, we can note that the typical organization of tomorrow is likely to be an even more complex entity than today. Hierarchy and bureaucracy will not vanish. In selected parts of many organizations it will thrive. At the same time, more organic, free-form structural formats will co-exist in other sub-units. Overlayed on this diversity will be individuals and groups whose mission will be to "bring it all together" so that unity toward organizational objectives will be achieved.

Those organizations that can successfully adapt to tomorrow's world will be the ones which prosper. And since the future belongs to those who prepare for it, managers should begin thinking and planning now for this future and its impact on their organizations.

READING   44

CORPORATE PROFITS AND EMPLOYEE SATISFACTION: MUST THEY BE IN CONFLICT?

Edward E. Lawler III

J. Richard Hackman*

> The Vice President reacted with an ominous start. Incredulity, mistrust, and then hostility crossed his face. Gathering himself up to full vice-presidential stature, he croaked in response: *Are you suggesting that we sacrifice company profits just to make our employees happy?*

The Vice-President was reacting to a suggestion that corporations should be more concerned about the satisfaction of their employees. And his response to the suggestion is not unusual. Many executives believe that it is difficult for most organizations to have both high profits and satisfied employees. They have heard about the human relations movement and Theory Y. They recognize the importance of treating employees with respect and the value of having satisfied employees. Still they often feel that a choice between satisfaction and profits is necessary and, not surprisingly, most feel that they must choose to maximize profits.

Why are high satisfaction and high profits often seen as incompatible goals by many executives? We believe that one of the most important reasons stems from many executives' perceptions of the way work has to be designed so as to maximize corporate profits. Since the rise of "scientific management" early in the century, it has been widely assumed that profits could be increased by simplifying, standardizing, and specializing the work that is done in an organization. Consistent with this assumption, there has been a pervasive tendency in organizations to break work down into very small segments, and to standardize the procedures for performing these work segments. As Frederick W. Taylor suggested more than fifty years ago:

> The work of every workman is fully planned out by the management at least one day in advance, and each man receives in most cases complete written instructions, describing in detail the task which he is to accomplish. . . . This task specified not only what is to be done but how it is to be done and the exact time allowed for doing it.[1]

*© 1971 by The Regents of the University of California. Reprinted from *California Management Review*, vol. XIV, no. 1, pp. 46–55, by permission of The Regents.

A number of economic advantages are expected to accrue from such work simplification and standardization. Simple jobs can be filled with unskilled people. It is much easier to recruit an unskilled worker off the street than it is to locate a highly skilled person; thus recruitment costs (and perhaps even salaries) can be minimized. Further, small, simple jobs are learned very quickly, decreasing the need for expensive training programs and training staffs. Since training is not an important problem it also becomes economically feasible to interchange workers among different jobs as day-to-day staffing needs change. If a worker is absent, if he is fired or quits, production can go on.

Many standardized, specialized jobs have the additional advantage that they can be mechanically paced. Presumably, this creates conditions under which quality can be carefully controlled and production can be predicted because each worker is doing a simplified job in a standardized way. Mistakes are unlikely, it is reasoned, because each worker is doing one part of the production process—and only one part—in the best possible way. This should lead to high quality because every worker can easily become an expert in the job he does. Production becomes more predictable because it is determined by the speed at which the machine runs, and this is controlled by management.

Jobs designed to be machine-paced, standardized, and simplified give management more control over the workers. A supervisor need only glance at a worker to know whether he is performing correctly. Assuming the worker is at his machine or machine station and is doing the simple repetitive task he has been trained to do, production should proceed according to plan.

Finally, since the company has little training equity in the worker, workers can be replaced without a great deal of expense to the organization. This serves to increase the company's power over the labor force, since the threat of being fired can be very real and immediate to most workers.

In summary, a solid rational case can be made for the economic advantage of having simple, standardized, and relatively routine jobs. The only problem seems to be, as both managers and behavioral science researchers have noted, that many employees dislike such jobs intensely. Workers find the work monotonous, boring, noninvolving, and tiring. And there is a growing body of social science knowledge which shows that the more jobs are simplified and routinized, the more workers experience these dissatisfactions while at work.[2]

It would appear, therefore, that a case can be made for the contention that an organization cannot simultaneously optimize both profits and employee satisfaction. If the work is designed to be most "efficient" as outlined above, profits should rise—but morale should drop. Can a company reasonably be asked to arrange the work of its employees in an "inefficient" way, merely to increase employee satisfaction? Let's listen to the answer given by one manager interviewed by the authors: "Yes, I made the job more boring in order to get higher productivity, but after all isn't productivity what business is all about?''

A PSEUDO-DILEMMA

The wisdom of choosing to simplify and standardize jobs rests on the validity of one very important assumption. The assumption is that the *economic benefits that derive from the simplification of work more than offset any possible costs associated with having dissatisfied employees.* If contemporary industrial practice has any validity as an indicator, it appears that many corporations are willing to accept and act on this assumption. We are not convinced, however, that the assumption necessarily is valid.

A substantial body of research literature has grown up over the past twenty years indicating that organizations may incur some substantial—albeit indirect—costs when the sole criterion for how work is designed is ''production efficiency.'' Many of these costs are based on a lack of ''fit'' between employees and the jobs they are given to perform. The psychological costs to employees of simplified, standardized jobs have been well documented. Walker and Guest, for example, showed the employees working on assembly line jobs—the archetypes of technologically efficient work design—tended to experience strongly negative psychological reactions to their work.[3] More recently, Argyris has pointed out and documented in some detail that there is a basic incongruence between the needs and personality dispositions of the mature adult and the demands of simple, standardized jobs.[4]

There is little question about the research findings which point up the psychological costs to workers of performing jobs designed solely to be technologically efficient, but the degree to which these psychological costs are translated into organizational costs is still open to question. Our view is that there are substantial hidden costs associated with efficient, albeit dissatisfying, jobs—costs which can and often do more than offset the savings expected to accrue from a ''scientific management'' approach to work design.

HIDDEN COSTS

Turnover Is High

Employees want to do things that satisfy their needs as fully as possible. Money is an important need for most people, and routinized jobs often pay quite well.[5] Despite the many well-paying jobs in contemporary society, workers have other needs that money cannot satisfy. If a worker finds a boring, repetitive, nonmeaningful job sufficiently frustrating of his other needs, he may decide to quit—and many workers do quit, for just these reasons. Some companies are now reporting turnover in excess of 100 percent per year for their assembly line jobs. If too many workers leave, even minimal training costs begin to become significant, thereby countering some of the expected economic advantages of simplified jobs. Further, a number of other costs go up as turnover increases—such as the expenses of recruitment, selection, payroll accounting, having inexperienced workers on the job, and supervision. When all of these costs are totalled up, turnover can turn out to be quite a significant cost for an organization. In many organizations it costs as much as $2,000 to replace even a lower level employee. Thus, it is not surprising that many large organizations estimate that turnover costs them many millions of dollars each year.

Absenteeism Is High

Closely related to turnover is absenteeism, another factor that is caused by job dissatisfaction and that is acute on routinized jobs. Like labor turnover, absenteeism is expensive, for it means that extra workers must be maintained on a standby basis. It also means that each employee is likely to use all of his paid sick leave and vacation time. As a result, the organization usually gets a relatively small return for the dollars it spends on wages.

Wages Are High, Not Low

An anticipated advantage of simple and technically efficient jobs is employing cheap unskilled labor. However, because the work is basically dissatisfying, companies are often forced to pay high wages just to get workers to accept routine, simplified jobs. In view of their skills, many assembly-line workers are paid at least a dollar an hour more than they could earn on other jobs.

Design Costs Are Greater

When we asked one engineer to identify the most difficult part of his product design job, he responded, "Making the product assembly-line proof." To him this meant designing the product so that it could be assembled in only one way—no matter how hard a worker might try to assemble it in another. Why was this important? It seems that workers, frequently mesmerized by the boredom and monotony of assembly-line work, become unaware of what they are doing. As a result, they assemble parts incorrectly even though—or perhaps because—they are only performing a simple, repetitive task. Part of the problem also undoubtedly stems from a conscious effort to vary the way in which the parts are assembled in order to add an element of variety to their jobs. There are numerous stories about auto workers ingeniously varying the name they put on the hoods and trunks of cars simply to relieve the boredom that comes from spending all day, every day, in putting the same few letters on passing autos.

Another type of design problem is also typically present when organizations use assembly lines. It is very difficult to set up a "balanced" line, that is, a line where every job takes the same length of time to do. Because of this companies with assembly lines have to have industrial engineers who spend a great deal of time designing "balanced" lines. Every time demand for the product fluctuates and the number of people on the lines changes, the line has to be balanced again. This is time-consuming and often quite expensive. Even where lines are well balanced, not every one has equal tasks. Some workers thus spend time waiting for preceding workers to finish their task. This can result in more direct labor time being required for assembly-line production of products than for individualized production.

Quality Tends to Decrease

Since many jobs are not "assembly-line-proof," and since many workers are what might be termed "consciously irresponsible," the assembly-line concept of production is no guarantee of high-quality products. It does eliminate some of the quality problems that normally occur due to insufficient knowledge on the part of the workers. But at the same time, it creates an entirely different set of nearly insoluble quality problems that can be attributed to lack of motivation and personal involvement in the job.

The traditional handling of this problem has been to hire more quality-control inspectors and to use increasingly sophisticated control procedures and closer supervision. These practices can be helpful, but they are very costly—and they have their own set of psychological costs. Most workers do not like having a foreman or inspector looking over their shoulders—it smacks of distrust.

Indeed, management may *not* trust them, and with very good reasons, given some of the less-than-above-board activities that employees engage in when working on routine, boring jobs. Reactions to mistrust can range from psychological withdrawal from the job to trying to beat the system in order to satisfy those needs which they cannot satisfy by doing the job in the specified way. Whatever the response, it is not likely to enhance either the quantity or the quality of the employee's work, and further costs to the organization eventually accrue.

In summary, it is not at all clear that designing jobs which are "efficient" from an engineering point of view—standardized, specialized, simplified—will result in higher productivity and higher profits. There are so many direct and indirect costs to the company associated with how employees react to such jobs that the "efficient job" may indeed be the *less* profitable one in many cases.

Four relationships are possible between the employee's ability to satisfy his needs and the organization's ability to satisfy its need for profits. Scientific management, originally thought to produce low individual satisfaction but high organization satisfaction, is shown by our analysis to produce neither. The Human Relations movement grew out of managers' dissatisfaction with scientific management. It stressed the importance of developing high employee satisfaction and emphasized that high satisfaction will lead to high productivity. However, subsequent research has shown that high satisfaction does not lead to high productivity. All managers would of course like to have both high satisfaction and high productivity. The challenge is to create those conditions under which they will both be present.

Toward both employee satisfaction and organizational goals, how do you make a person satisfied? The general answer is straightforward: give him something he wants, or, in psychological terms, provide a reward that will satisfy one or more of his needs.

But how do you at the same time encourage a person to contribute effectively to the achievement of *organizational* goals? Again, the general answer is fairly straightforward: arrange things so that the individual is *most likely* to obtain rewards that are important to him *when he is contributing to organization goals*—e.g., by working effectively. A large number of research studies in organizations have documented the validity of this general principle of motivation.

The arguments we have been giving in this paper against highly simplified and routinized jobs can be summarized in terms of the above motivational principle. Our view is that when jobs are simple, routine, and repetitive, the harder a person works on the job, the *less* chance he has of obtaining rewards that are important to him. All he may get from a day of hard work on the assembly line is a headache, a backache, and a generally unpleasant disposition.

If monetary rewards are tied to quantity of performance on such jobs, individuals may feel some incentive to work harder on the job. But even when incentive plans "work" moderately smoothly, they may put the employee into a motivational bind. He can get something he wants—money—by working hard on the job, but in the process he may suffer some negative consequences. Examples of these consequences include not only the backaches and headaches, but also a sense of personal frustration, feelings that he is not really doing anything meaningful or worthwhile with his work life, and a general loss of his sense of personal worth. The reaction of many employees in our relatively affluent society is to decide that the money simply is not worth the personal costs it takes to earn it—and the incentive plan loses effectiveness.

Thus, we are arguing that most employees are likely to experience more feelings of being punished than being rewarded when they work especially hard on traditional simplified jobs. Indeed, we might even say that such jobs can induce a state of "negative" motivation in employees. And trying to "patch up" an inherently bad state of affairs with such external prods as piece rate incentive systems is not likely to improve the situation very much.

How could some of the negative consequences of hard work on simple jobs be reduced? One approach that some organizations have applied, especially for assembly-line jobs, is to make the setting pleasant—providing carpeting, music, a congenial atmosphere, and so on. But again, the motivational principal suggests that this approach is not likely to succeed. The fact still remains that working hard on simplified jobs has large consequences for the individual, and the harder he works the more of these negative consequences he receives. Putting a rug on the floor or a Muzak in the ear is going to do little if anything to change that state of affairs. It may encourage him to come to work by making the total work experience more pleasant. However, it may also serve as an additional mild incentive for an employee to work less hard so that he can enjoy his surroundings, the good company, and the music.

Recently a number of behavioral scientists have stressed that job enlargement or job enrichment may hold the answer to creating conditions that will allow for maximizing both individual satisfaction and organization profits. Argyris stressed this approach during the 1950s. More recently Herzberg has reported on a number of successful experiments where job enlargement has been tried.[6] These data suggest that indeed job enlargement can under certain conditions create jobs that will satisfy people and contribute to corporate profits. There are, however, a number of critical unanswered questions about the job-enlargement or job-enrichment approach.

It is not clear just what the properties of an enriched or enlarged job have to be for it to be motivating and satisfying. Herzberg has stressed the importance of enlarging jobs vertically—giving more autonomy and responsibility—while others have emphasized that both horizontal—more tasks—and vertical enlargement is necessary. However, most studies that have enlarged jobs have changed them in a number of ways, increasing the variety, autonomy, and responsibility associated with them.

Some studies of job enlargement have pointed out that not everyone responds positively to a new enlarged job. It is not clear, however, just who these employees are or why they do not respond positively. It is also not clear how enlargement affects employee behavior. Does it lead to higher productivity? Higher quality work? Lower indirect costs? Or all of these?

Finally, little attention has been paid to the problems that arise when attempts are made to enlarge jobs. How do superiors react? What kind of blocks are there to the idea of enlarging jobs?

To answer these questions about job design and in particular to see if we could specify more exactly the effects of different job characteristics, we conducted a series of studies over the last three years. We began by first trying to determine what kinds of conditions must exist if a worker is to find particular job accomplishments rewarding. The results of this initial research, together with a body of relevant social science literature, suggest that adults experience intrinsic satisfaction as a result of task accomplishment when the following three conditions exist:

1 *What is accomplished is through the individual's own efforts.* For an employee to have truly *personal* feelings of accomplishment at work, he must know that the work he does is his own, and that he is personally responsible for whatever successes or failures occur because of his efforts. If every time there is a crisis a supervisor rushes to take over, the worker will not feel that the results are due largely to his own efforts—and the possibilities for his developing internal motivation on the job will be severely diminished.

The job dimension autonomy would seem to tap the degree to which the work accomplished is the result of an employee's own effort. In jobs with high autonomy, workers tend to feel that what they do is "theirs"; in low autonomy jobs where supervision is always right at hand and where procedures are minutely specified, it is very rare for an employee to feel that he personally has been very important in accomplishing the work.

2 *What is accomplished is meaningful to the individual.* If a worker does not feel that his work makes much difference to anybody, himself included, it is unlikely that he will feel especially good if he does it well. Thus, neither the worker who mass-produces trinkets for bubble-gum machines nor a telephone operator baby-sitting for a tardy computer is a very strong candidate for developing internal motivation in his work.

There are at least two ways for work to be experienced as meaningful by employees. One way is for an employee's work to be intrinsically and obviously important. This often happens when an employee's job is high in task identity—when he does an entire or "whole" piece of work, the outcomes of which are recognizable.

A second way work comes to take on personal meaning to an individual is for the job to require him to use a variety of valued skills and abilities—pretty much regardless of the broader significance of what is done. Thus, a golfer feels good when he hits a good tee shot because his golfing skills are on the line when he steps to the tee and those skills are important to him.

3 *The individual finds out how he is performing as he works.* Even if the two general conditions discussed above are met, an employee will not be able to reward himself for good performance unless he gets feedback. The feedback may come from the task itself; it may also come from another employee. But it *must* come.

What, then, are likely to be the characteristics of a job from which a person will obtain meaningful personal satisfaction when he performs well? Jobs high on variety, autonomy, task identity, and feedback—the four "core dimensions." And the harder and better an individual performs on a job which is high on these four core dimensions, the more satisfaction he is likely to experience.

The core dimensions deal exclusively with the task performance and achievement of employees at work. In addition, of course, people have social needs. It may be that by providing opportunities for social interaction at work jobs can be more satisfying. Thus, dimensions reflecting the degree to which employees have opportunities to develop informal friendships on the job must be considered.

We have recently completed a study of fourteen jobs in one organization that examines the relationships between job characteristics and employee satisfaction, motivation, absenteeism, and performance effectiveness.[7] More than 200 employees and 50 supervisors filled out questionnaires describing their jobs and their job reactions. Several recent studies have involved experimentally changing the design of jobs. Six job dimensions were used in these studies. These dimensions, which were suggested by the discussion above and by the large-scale research study of job effects by Turner and Lawrence,[8] are defined as follows:

1 *Variety.* The degree to which a job requires employees to perform a wide range of operations in their work or to use a variety of equipment and procedures on the job. Our data show that jobs which have high variety also are seen as very challenging in that employees must draw on a wide range of their skills and abilities to complete the work successfully.

2 *Autonomy.* The degree to which employees have a major "say" in scheduling their work, in selecting the equipment they will use, and in deciding on procedures to be followed.

3 *Task identity.* The degree to which employees do an entire or "whole" piece of work and can clearly identify the results of their efforts.

4 *Feedback.* The degree to which employees as they are working receive information which reveals how well they are performing.

5 *Dealing with others.* The degree to which a job allows employees to talk with one another on the job and to establish informal relationships.

6 *Friendship opportunities.* The degree to which a job allows employees to make friends at work.

FOUR CORE DIMENSIONS: TOWARD INTERNAL MOTIVATION

Our results confirm that the way jobs are structured can make differences in employee satisfaction, motivation, performance, and absenteeism. We are therefore in a position to draw some strong conclusions about the effect of various job-design approaches on individual satisfaction and motivation.

1 *The core dimensions seem to affect work quality more strongly than productivity.* The greater the core dimensions, the more employees reported feeling internal pressures to pay close attention to their work, and pressures to try to do work of especially high quality. When variety, autonomy, and task identity are high, employees perform better: their supervisors rate them as doing higher quality work but not necessarily as being more productive.

The data provide a clue about why the core dimensions relate so well to internal pressure to do high quality work. The employees indicated that when they perform well on jobs high on the core dimensions, they experience positive feelings—and that when they do poorly, they feel badly. Apparently something about jobs which are high on the four dimensions makes it possible for workers to obtain personally rewarding experiences by doing well on the job. Further, it appears that these experiences are linked primarily to doing high *quality* work—since the core dimensions do not relate either to felt pressure for quantity, or to the actual quantity of work produced.

2 *The core dimensions strongly affect satisfaction, involvement, and absenteeism.* They also are strongly and positively related to overall job satisfaction and to the degree of personal involvement employees feel in their work. And, given that employees whose jobs are high on the four core dimensions report that they like their jobs and are personally involved in them, it is not surprising to find that these workers tend to have better attendance records as well. Work is apparently a very good place to be for employees with jobs which are high on the four, and one way they show that they like it is by coming to work regularly.

3 *The interpersonal dimensions have little impact.* The two dimensions assessing the interpersonal components of jobs—dealing with others and friendship opportunities—do not relate consistently or strongly either to employee satisfaction or to performance.

Employees do report stronger internal pressures to be pleasant and helpful, to put a lot of effort and energy into their work, and to come to work regularly when dealing with others is an important characteristic of the job. The finding is reasonable: if a large portion of my day is spent dealing with other people, being pleasant and helpful, it may make my own work day a more pleasant one. Further, when my work directly involves other people I may feel relatively more pressure to come to work regularly and to work hard on the job because I do not want to let other people down. Unfortunately, these felt pressures are apparently not often translated into actual behavior: there is no relationship between dealing with others and any measure of performance or absenteeism.

The effects of "friendship opportunities" are negligible. The only relationship between the amount of friendship opportunities a job affords and felt pressures is negative: the more friendship opportunities on the job, the less employees feel pressure to produce large quantities of work. Friendship opportunities also do not relate to the level of internal motivation employees experience, or to any measure of performance or absenteeism.

Finally, there are moderate positive relationships between the two interpersonal dimensions and job satisfaction—although these relationships are not nearly as large as those involving the four core dimensions.

4 *One is not enough, nor is two or three. All four core dimensions must be present.* Our studies show that it is important for a job to be at least moderately high on all four of the core dimensions. Typically, a job high on three of the four was clearly better than one low on all four, but it still was not a good job. It did not lead to employees feeling satisfaction when they performed well. Some jobs were found, for example, that were high on feedback, autonomy, and task identity, but so low on variety that people were not challenged. More common, however, were jobs that were low on more than just one dimension. These jobs, of course, served neither to satisfy the holders nor to motivate them to perform. The important point to remember about these jobs is that improving them so they are high on one more dimension is not enough. They must be high on all four of the dimensions; that is, they must be enlarged both vertically and horizontally.

5 *There are large individual differences in how employees react to jobs high on the core dimensions.* It is clear from the results of our studies that not everyone responds with high satisfaction and high motivation to jobs high on the core dimensions. Those employees who did not desire higher-order-need satisfaction on their job did not respond; that is, people who were not concerned with self-actualization, personal growth, and self-fulfillment. People from urban backgrounds tended more frequently to fall in this category than people from rural backgrounds. This fits with the frequently stated view that urban workers are much more alienated from middle-class norms and values than are rural workers.[9]

Figure 1 shows how people with different degrees of desire for growth-need satisfaction react to jobs. It shows that good organizational outcomes result only when there is a fit between the needs of the person and the design of the job. It is not surprising that people who do not desire higher-order-need satisfaction did not respond to jobs that are high on the core dimensions. In fact, it is consonant with our view that jobs affect motivation and satisfaction because of their potential role in satisfying these needs. There is no reason to expect job changes to affect the motivation and satisfaction of employees who do not value the rewards that their jobs have to offer.

6 *Many managerial jobs and white-collar jobs are low on the core dimensions.* At the start of our research we did not expect many production-line jobs to be high on our core dimensions, and none were. But we did expect many managerial jobs and many white-collar jobs to be high on them. Since our original study we have looked at a number of jobs and found that many white-collar jobs are about as low as are the assembly-line jobs. This is a highly significant point since it suggests that many people who have focused on doing job enlargement for assembly-line workers have had too narrow a focus. Our data suggest that many jobs in organiza-

Figure 1   Relationship of Job and Employee Needs

Job's standing on core dimensions	Employees' growth needs	
	Low	High
Low	Congruence in the "classical" mode. Predict adequate performance—use of pay to motivate.	Workers feel underutilized and over-controlled. React with frustration, dissatisfaction, aggression. High absenteeism and turnover.
High	Individual overwhelmed, confused. Poor performance and psychological withdrawal.	Congruence. High quality performance. High satisfaction, low absenteeism and turnover.

tions are low on what it takes to be a good job and that they are ripe candidates for change.

7 *Supervisors often misperceive the jobs of their subordinates.* A tendency appeared for the bosses to see the jobs as much higher on the four core dimensions than the subordinates see them. Further, in some recent studies where we have made changes in lower-level jobs the supervisors have tended to see the changes as much greater and more significant than have the workers. This is a particularly disturbing finding because it suggests that supervisors are often not aware of just how bad their subordinates' jobs are, that they blissfully go along wondering why their subordinates are not as involved and committed as they are themselves, never suspecting that the nature of their subordinates' jobs makes this impossible. A good example of this is found in the news story about a recent strike at the British Columbia Telephone Company during which executives did the low-level jobs in the organization. According to President J. E. Richardson, the executives found the work "incredibly dull." As a result, Mr. Richardson went on, "We're going to look at all the repetitive jobs and make them more interesting, less frustrating, and give the junior employees a broader experience."

8 *The supervisor is often the major block to job enrichment.* Where we have been concerned with experimentally changing the characteristics of jobs, we have usually found the greatest resistance to be centered among the supervisors. Part of this resistance seems to stem from their failure to recognize just how bad their subordinates' jobs are.

If supervisors are to be even minimally committed to changing their subordinates' jobs toward being higher on the four core dimensions the superiors need to be helped to see these jobs realistically. Not every company is "fortunate" enough to have a strike that demands the managers work on their subordinates' jobs and thereby realize just how bad they are.

One way of helping superiors to see jobs as their subordinates see them is to gather systematic attitude data from the subordinates. We developed and used an appropriate questionnaire. It provides data that allow organizations to assess how each of their jobs stand on the four core dimensions as seen by the job holders. It can be used to show executives where the weak jobs are in the organization as well as what is missing in the jobs. Data from it can also bring home to superiors just how bad their subordinates perceive their jobs to be. The impact of this is particularly dramatic where the superior fills out the questionnaire before he sees his subordinates' answers. Faced with the difference between his view and the subordinates' he is often forced to reassess.

A second reason why supervisors often resist enlarging their subordinates' jobs has to do with the world in which they must live. As was pointed out, if the supervisor's job is not enlarged, he does not have enlargement to give. The supervisor can act as an insulator between the rest of the organization and his subordinates, living with tight controls and low autonomy in his job, but not passing them on to subordinates. However, this obviously is a difficult role to play and few managers can perform it. Because of this, large-scale job enlargement is impossible in many organizations. One way to improve the climate for job enlargement in an organization may be to start job enlargement at the top and work down. Given that many managers don't have enlarged jobs, is it any wonder that they may block enlarging their subordinates' jobs?

Vertical enlargement can be very threatening to the supervisor since this usually involves giving some of his tasks to his subordinates. This can force the supervisor to redefine his job and puts pressure on him to manage in a different way. In one study we found that vertical enlargement led to the superior's having less to do and to his using his free time to supervise more closely, thus reducing the positive effects of the enlargement that had taken place.

9 *Job enlargement begets desires for more enlargement which begets desires for more enlargement.* There is evidence to suggest that once people have experienced jobs high on the core dimensions they may want even further job enrichment. It has been pointed out by many psychologists that the needs for competence and self-fulfillment are insatiable. If this is true it would follow that some people will be unable to get enough autonomy, feedback, task identity, and variety in their jobs and this seems to be true. In one study it was found that most people were satisfied after their jobs had been significantly enlarged, but some wanted more and more. Organizations should be on the lookout for these people and try to provide them with opportunities for further growth.

IMPLICATIONS FOR THE DESIGN OF JOBS IN ORGANIZATIONS

Many jobs in organizations could profit from enlargement or enrichment, but not everyone will respond to an enlarged job. Thus, the correct strategy for an organization wanting to maximize both profits and satisfaction is not to enlarge all jobs, but to fit all jobs to the people who hold them.

Our research suggests that there are simply not enough jobs high on the core dimensions. Unless some jobs are changed, this misfit is likely to get worse since the educational level is increasing and, along with it, concern for things like self-fulfillment. But, again, enlarging all jobs will not necessarily create a good fit. This will happen only if jobs are designed around the needs and capabilities of people. This requires careful attention to the personnel selection process and the redesign of a number of jobs so that they will be high on the core dimensions. Taylor himself recognized the importance of fitting the person to the job as the following quote illustrates:

> Now one of the very first requirements for a man who is fit to handle pig iron as a regular occupation is that he shall be so stupid and so phlegmatic that he more nearly resembles in his mental make-up the ox than any other type. The man who is mentally alert and intelligent is for this very reason entirely unsuited to what would, for him, be the grinding monotony of work of this character.[10]

What is required to make a significant number of jobs high on the core dimensions? In many cases it demands major surgery. It demands that technology and automation become our servants. It demands that instead of automatically simplifying and automating every job we ask if automation is appropriate. In thinking about this it is useful to look at jobs as being on an automation continuum. At one end of the continuum is unit production performed by individual craftsmen. At the other end is the process or completely automated production facility, where the worker controls vast amounts of automated equipment. Mass production or assembly-line jobs fall at the middle—neither highly automated nor highly individualized. Unit production is quite satisfying, involving, and motivating to the worker. It provides him with responsibility for production of an entire product. It enables him to take justifiable pride in his work.

Jobs in automated plants can be satisfying and involving because high skill levels are required. Moreover, the workers—even at the lower skill level—feel that they are controlling the production process. Thus, despite their basic differences, jobs at both ends of the automation continuum seem high on the core dimensions.

For a person who desires self-fulfillment, the assembly line has the worst features of both the unit and the automated production processes. For example, the assembly line has the physical working-with-the-product that is characteristic of unit production, but this work is so simplified that it provides no variety or challenge. Similarly, the assembly line provides the worker with little or no control over the machines. The machine controls him.

This suggests that many jobs should be moved away from the center of the continuum toward either end, an approach that would often involve reversal of the historic movement from unit production toward process production, and of the movement from whole jobs to specialized jobs. The kinds of changes that any organization could make would, of course, be dictated by its products and the nature of its work force. In the production of automobiles, a move toward greater automation may be needed in many cases although unit production may be possible in some others. In the manufacture of electronic instruments, however, it would make good sense in many instances to move from mass production to unit production. In an organization where most of the workers come from urban settings and do not desire higher-order-need satisfaction, however, jobs in the center of the continuum should be developed or maintained.

The important point is that once a zone on an automation continuum has been developed for a product, decisions as to how it is to be produced should be a matter of choosing the production method that best fits the people who are available to do the work. In some cases this may involve moving the job from the center of the continuum to the unit production end. This would seem to be a particularly good strategy when:

1   There is low capital investment in the machinery associated with the present method of production.

2   The employees who are doing the jobs as presently designed are clearly overqualified and desire more challenging work.

3   Problems of low job satisfaction, high absenteeism and poor work quality have been present for quite a while.

4   No union exists or if one does exist it is willing to collaborate in redesigning the work.

TOWARD A TWO-CLASS SOCIETY?

At this point, it seems ironic how easily we have fallen into the trap of believing that corporate profits and employee satisfaction are conflicting. Our research suggests that they naturally go together when a systematic effort is made to fit the characteristics of jobs to the needs of the employees who do them. Thus, it would seem that a desire to maximize profits should cause organizations to become more oriented toward designing jobs to fit the needs of employees. From the point of view of the society as a whole it may be very important that just this happens. As John Gardner has pointed out:

> Of all the ways society serves the individual, few are more meaningful than providing individuals with decent jobs. And it is not likely to be a decent society for any of us until it is for all of us. If our sense of responsibility fails us, our sheer self-interest should come to the rescue.[11]

Perhaps the most obvious impact of the scientific management approach is that it has produced a large group of people who have no profession or marketable skill. The assembly-line worker, for example, has no real skill he can market. He doesn't have a real craft. Rather than seeing his work as a part of him or an expression of himself he sees it as a place to remain as short a time as possible and to earn as much money as possible so that life off the job can be made enjoyable. Unions are supporting this view by demanding shorter and shorter work weeks, and early retirement as if to say to management, you can make work unpleasant, but we will do everything we can to see that our members spend a minimum of time working.

Many executives, however, seem to be working the same long hours they always have. They are highly involved in their jobs and, if anything, seem to let nonwork activities suffer. The danger is that this split between workers and managers will widen and we will end up with a two-class society—classes not distinguished by their wealth, but by their relationship to their work—one class made up of those uninvolved workers who hold routine jobs, and a second class made up of those involved employees who have exciting, stimulating jobs. The involved class would work long hours and presumably see little separation between work and leisure. Many, but not all, of these people would hold managerial positions. One sociologist has suggested that the uninvolved class (which presumably would include some managers and many white- and blue-collar workers) might work only three days a week and actually live in the country the rest of the week. They would come to work in the cities and live in dormitories for the days they work. Their families would stay in the country, thus completing the separation between work and leisure.

Can a society thrive with this kind of class system? We don't know, but there are some obvious problems that would arise if it were to exist. It is not clear that people can handle large amounts of leisure well. Tied in with this is the impact on them of working on a meaningless job. There is reason to believe this can do significant psychological damage. John Gardner summarizes the plight of the uninvolved pleasure seeker as follows:

It is one of the amusing errors of human judgment that the world habitually feels sorry for overworked women and men—and doesn't feel a bit sorry for the women and men who live moving from one pleasure resort to the next. As a result, the hard workers get not only all the real fun but all the sympathy too, while the resort habitues scratch the dry soil of calculated diversion and get roundly criticized for it. It isn't fair.[11]

REFERENCES

1 F. W. Taylor, *The Principles of Scientific Management* (New York: Harper, 1911).
2 R. Blauner, *Alienation and Freedom* (Chicago: University of Chicago Press, 1964).

3 C. R. Walker and R. Guest, *Man on the Assmebly Line* (Cambridge, Mass.: Harvard University Press, 1952).

4 C. Argyris, *Personality and Organization* (New York: Harper, 1957).

5 E. E. Lawler, *Pay and Organizational Effectiveness* (New York: McGraw-Hill, 1971).

6 Argyris, *Personality and Organization,* W. J. Paul, Jr., K. B. Robertson, and F. Herzberg, "Job Enrichment Pays Off," *Harvard Business Review,* 47 (March–April 1969), 61–78.

7 J. R. Hackman and E. E. Lawler, "Employee Reactions to Job Characteristics," *Journal of Applied Psychology,* (in press).

8 A. N. Turner and P. R. Lawrence, *Industrial Jobs and the Worker: An Investigation of Response to Task Attributes* (Boston: Harvard University, Graduate School of Business Administration, 1965).

9 C. L. Hulin and M. R. Blood, "Job Enlargement, Individual Differences, and Worker Responses," *Psychological Bulletin 69* (1968), 41–55.

10 Taylor, *Principles of Scientific Management.*

11 J. W. Gardner, *No Easy Victories* (New York: Harper and Row, 1968).

CHAPTER 12
SOCIOTECHNICAL SYSTEMS

READING   45

CHARACTERISTICS OF AN ORGANIZATION

Douglas McGregor*

An industrial organization is an *open* system. It engages in transactions with a larger system: society. There are inputs in the form of people, materials, and money and in the form of political and economic forces arising in the larger system. There are outputs in the form of products, services, and rewards to its members. Similarly, the subsystems within the organization down to the individual are open systems.

An industrial organization is an *organic* system. It is adaptive in the sense that it changes its nature as a result of changes in the external system around it. The adaptation, however, is not passive; the system affects the larger system as well as being affected by it. It copes with its environment as the individual human being copes with his. It is dynamic in the sense that it undergoes constant change as a result of interaction among the subsystems and with the larger environmental system.

Finally, an industrial organization is a *sociotechnical* system. It is not a mere assembly of buildings, manpower, money, machines, and processes.

The system consists in the *organization* of people around various technologies. This means, among other things, that human relations are not an optional feature of an organization—they are a built-in property. The system exists by virtue of the motivated behavior of people. Their relationships and behavior determine the inputs, the transformations, and the outputs of the system.

CONCLUSIONS

Thinking about an industrial organization as an open, organic, sociotechnical system has several advantages. One of the major ones is that it can represent reality more fully and more adequately than the conventional picture of the formal organization. It provides a better basis for understanding what does go on rather than what ought to go on. It brings the activities of the informal organization into the framework without excluding those of the formal organization. It enlarges and enriches the possibility of understanding the many complex cause-effect relationships constituting an organization. Thus it promises better prediction and better control.

*   *   *

*From *The Professional Manager*, New York: McGraw-Hill Book Company, 1967, pp. 40–41. © 1967 by McGraw-Hill Book Company. Reprinted with permission.

READING 46

HOW TO COUNTER ALIENATION IN THE PLANT

Richard E. Walton*

Managers don't need anyone to tell them that employee alienation exists. Terms such as "blue-collar blues" and "salaried drop-outs" are all too familiar. But are they willing to undertake the major innovations necessary for redesigning work organizations to deal effectively with the root causes of alienation? My purpose in this article is to urge them to do so, for two reasons:

1 The current alienation is not merely a phase that will pass in due time.

2 The innovations needed to correct the problem can simultaneously enhance the quality of work life (thereby lessening alienation) and improve productivity.

In the first part of the article, I shall risk covering terrain already familiar to some readers in order to establish that alienation is a basic, longterm, and mounting problem. Then I shall present some examples of the comprehensive redesign that I believe is required.

I also hope to provide today's managers with a glimpse at what may be the industrial work environment of the future, as illustrated by a pet-food plant which opened in January 1971.

In this facility, management set out to incorporate features that would provide a high quality of work life, enlist unusual human involvement, and result in high productivity. The positive results of the experiment to date are impressive, and the difficulties encountered in implementing it are instructive. Moreover, similar possibilities for *comprehensive* innovations exist in a wide variety of settings and industries.

The word "comprehensive" is important because my argument is that each technique in the standard fare of personnel and organization development programs (e.g., job enrichment, management by objectives, sensi-

*From *Harvard Business Review*, November–December,1972, pp. 70–81. Copyright 1972 by the President and Fellows of Harvard College; all rights reserved. Used with permission.

Author's note: An earlier version of this article was prepared for the Work in America Project, sponsored by the Secretary of the Department of Health, Education and Welfare, as a basis for assessing the nature of problems and potential crises associated with work in the United States.

tivity training, confrontation and team-building sessions, participative decision making) has grasped only a limited truth and has fallen far short of producing meaningful change. In short, more radical, comprehensive, and systemic redesign of organizations is necessary.

ANATOMY OF ALIENATION

There are two parts to the problem of employee alienation: (1) the productivity output of work systems, and (2) the social costs associated with employee inputs. Regarding the first, U.S. productivity is not adequate to the challenges posed by international competition and inflation; it cannot sustain impressive economic growth. (I do not refer here to economic growth as something to be valued merely for its own sake—it is politically a precondition for the income redistribution that will make equality of opportunity possible in the United States.) Regarding the second, the social and psychological costs of work systems are excessive, as evidenced by their effects on the mental and physical health of employees and on the social health of families and communities.

Employee alienation *affects* productivity and *reflects* social costs incurred in the workplace. Increasingly, blue- and white-collar employees and, to some extent, middle managers tend to dislike their jobs and resent their bosses. Workers tend to rebel against their union leaders. They are becoming less concerned about the quality of the product of their labor and more angered about the quality of the context in which they labor.

In some cases, alienation is expressed by passive withdrawal—tardiness, absenteeism and turnover, and inattention on the job. In other cases, it is expressed by active attacks—pilferage, sabotage, deliberate waste, assaults, bomb threats, and other disruptions of work routines. Demonstrations have taken place and underground newspapers have appeared in large organizations in recent years to protest company policies. Even more recently, employees have cooperated with newsmen, Congressional committees, regulatory agencies, and protest groups in exposing objectionable practices.

These trends all have been mentioned in the media, but one expression of alienation has been underreported: pilferage and violence against property and persons. Such acts are less likely to be revealed to the police and the media when they occur in a private company than when they occur in a high school, a ghetto business district, or a suburban town. Moreover, dramatic increases in these forms of violence are taking place at the plant level. This trend is not reported in local newspapers and there is little or no appreciation of it at corporate headquarters. Local management keeps quiet because violence is felt to reflect unfavorably both on its effectiveness and on its plant as a place to work.

Roots of Conflict

The acts of sabotage and other forms of protest are overt manifestations of a conflict between changing employee attitudes and organizational inertia. Increasingly, what employees expect from their jobs is different from what organizations are prepared to offer them. These evolving expectations of workers conflict with the demands, conditions, and rewards of employing organizations in at least six important ways:

1   Employees want challenge and personal growth, but work tends to be simplified and specialties tend to be used repeatedly in work assignments. This pattern exploits the narrow skills of a worker, while limiting his or her opportunities to broaden or develop.

2   Employees want to be included in patterns of mutual influence; they want egalitarian treatment. But organizations are characterized by tall hierarchies, status differentials, and chains of command.

3   Employee commitment to an organization is increasingly influenced by the intrinsic interest of the work itself, the human dignity afforded by management, and the social responsibility reflected in the organization's products. Yet organization practices still emphasize material rewards and employment security and neglect other employee concerns.

4   What employees want from careers, they are apt to want *right now*. But when organizations design job hierarchies and career paths, they continue to assume that today's workers are as willing to postpone gratifications as were yesterday's workers.

5   Employees want more attention to the emotional aspects of organization life, such as individual self-esteem, openness between people, and expressions of warmth. Yet organizations emphasize rationality and seldom legitimize the emotional part of the organizational experience.

6   Employees are becoming less driven by competitive urges, less likely to identify competition as the "American way." Nevertheless, managers continue to plan career patterns, organize work, and design reward systems as if employees valued competition as highly as they used to.

Pervasive Social Forces   The foregoing needs and desires that employees bring to their work are but a local reflection of more basic, and not readily reversible, trends in U.S. society. These trends are fueled by family and social experience as well as by social institutions, especially schools. Among the most significant are:

The rising level of education.   Employees bring to the workplace more abilities and, correspondingly, higher expectations than in the past.

The rising level of wealth and security.   Vast segments of today's society never have wanted for the tangible essentials of life; thus they are decreasingly motivated by pay and security, which are taken for granted.

The decreased emphasis given by churches, schools, and families to obedience to authority. These socialization agencies have promoted individual initiative, self-responsibility and -control, the relativity of values, and other social patterns that make subordinacy in traditional organizations an increasingly bitter pill to swallow for each successive wave of entrants to the U.S. work force.

The decline in achievement motivation. For example, whereas the books my parents read in primary school taught them the virtues of hard work and competition, my children's books emphasize self-expression and actualizing one's potential. The workplace has not yet fully recognized this change in employee values.

The shifting emphasis from individualism to social commitment. This shift is driven in part by a need for the direct gratifications of human connectedness (for example, as provided by commune living experiments). It also results from a growing appreciation of our interdependence, and it renders obsolete many traditional workplace concepts regarding the division of labor and work incentives.

Exhibit 1 shows how these basic societal forces underlie, and contribute to, the problem of alienation and also sums up the discussion thus far. Actually, I believe that protests in the workplace will mount even more rapidly than is indicated by the contributing trends postulated here. The latent dissatisfaction of workers will be activated as (a) the issues receive public attention and (b) some examples of attempted solutions serve to raise expectations (just as the blacks' expressions of dissatisfaction with social and economic inequities were triggered in the 1950's, and women's discontent expanded late in the 1960's).

Revitalization and Reform

It seems clear that employee expectations are not likely to revert to those of an earlier day. As *Exhibit 1* shows, the conflicts between these expectations and traditional organizations result in alienation. This alienation, in turn, exacts a deplorable psychological and social cost as well as causing worker behavior that depresses productivity and constrains growth. In short, we need major innovative efforts to redesign work organizations, efforts that take employee expectations into account.

Over the past two decades we have witnessed a parade of organization development, personnel, and labor relations programs that promised to revitalize organizations:

Job enrichment would provide more varied and challenging content in the work.

Participative decision making would enable the information, judg-

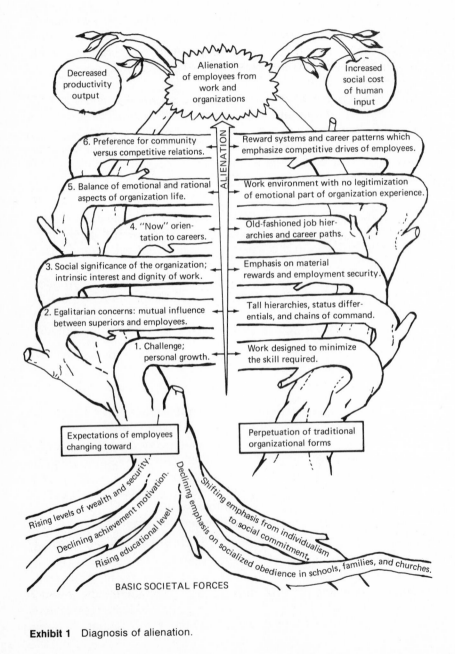

Exhibit 1   Diagnosis of alienation.

ments, and concerns of subordinates to influence the decisions that affect them.

Management by objectives would enable subordinates to understand and shape the objectives toward which they strive and against which they are evaluated.

Sensitivity training or encounter groups would enable people to relate to each other as human beings with feelings and psychological needs.

Productivity bargaining would revise work rules and increase management's flexibility with a quid pro quo whereby the union ensures that workers share in the fruits of the resulting productivity increases.

Each of the preceding programs *by itself* is an inadequate reform of the workplace and has typically failed in its more limited objectives. While application is often based in a correct diagnosis, each approach is only a partial remedy; therefore, the organizational system soon returns to an earlier equilibrium.

The lesson we must learn in the area of work reform is similar to one we have learned in another area of national concern. It is now recognized that a health program, a welfare program, a housing program, or an employment program alone is unable to make a lasting impact on the urban-poor syndrome. Poor health, unemployment, and other interdependent aspects of poverty must be attacked in a coordinated or systemic way.

So it is with meaningful reform of the workplace: we must think "systemically" when approaching the problem. We must coordinate the redesign of the ways tasks are packaged into jobs, the way workers are required to relate to each other, the way performance is measured and rewards are made available, the way positions of authority and status symbols are structured, and the way career paths are conceived. Moreover, because these types of changes in work organizations imply new employee skills and different organizational cultures, transitional programs must be established.

A PROTOTYPE OF CHANGE

A number of major organization design efforts meet the requirements of being systemic and comprehensive. One experience in which I have been deeply involved is particularly instructive. As a recent and radical effort, it generally encompasses and goes beyond what has been done elsewhere.

During 1968, a large pet-food manufacturer was planning an additional plant at a new location. The existing manufacturing facility was then experiencing many of the symptoms of alienation that I have already outlined. There were frequent instances of employee indifference and inattention that, because of the continuous-process technology, led to plant shutdowns, product waste, and costly recycling. Employees effectively worked only a modest number of hours per day, and they resisted changes toward fuller utilization of manpower. A series of acts of sabotage and violence occurred.

Because of these pressures and the fact that it was not difficult to link substantial manufacturing costs to worker alienation, management was receptive to basic innovations in the new plant. It decided to design the plant to both accommodate changes in the expectations of employees and utilize knowledge developed by the behavioral sciences.

Key Design Features

The early development of the plant took more than two years. This involved planning, education, skill training, and building the nucleus of the new organization into a team.

During this early period, four newly selected managers and their superior met with behavioral science experts and visited other industrial plants that were experimenting with innovative organizational methods. Thus they were stimulated to think about departures from traditional work organizations and given reassurance that other organizational modes were not only possible but also more viable in the current social context. While the consultations and plant visits provided some raw material for designing the new organization, the theretofore latent knowledge of the five managers played the largest role. Their insights into the aspirations of people and basically optimistic assumptions about the capacities of human beings were particularly instrumental in the design of the innovative plant. In the remainder of this section, I shall present the nine key features of this design.

1 Autonomous Work Groups Self-managed work teams are given collective responsibility for large segments of the production process. The total work force of approximately 70 employees is organized into six teams. A processing team and a packaging team operate during each shift. The processing team's jurisdiction includes unloading, storage of materials, drawing ingredients from storage, mixing, and then performing the series of steps that transform ingredients into a pet-food product. The packaging team's responsibilities include the finishing stages of product manufacturing—packaging operations, warehousing, and shipping.

A team is comprised of from 7 to 14 members (called "operators") and a team leader. Its size is large enough to include a natural set of highly interdependent tasks, yet small enough to allow effective face-to-face meetings for decision making and coordination. Assignments of individuals to sets of tasks are subject to team consensus. Although at any given time one operator has primary responsibility for a set of tasks within the team's jurisdiction, some tasks can be shared by several operators. Moreover, tasks can be redefined by the team in light of individual capabilities and interests. In contrast, individuals in the old plant were permanently assigned to specific jobs.

Other matters that fall within the scope of team deliberation, recommendation, or decision making include:

- Coping with manufacturing problems that occur within or between the teams' areas of responsibilities.
- Temporarily redistributing tasks to cover for absent employees.
- Selecting team operators to serve on plant-wide committees or task forces.
- Screening and selecting employees to replace departing operators.
- Counseling those who do not meet team standards (e.g., regarding absences or giving assistance to others).

2 Integrated Support Functions Staff units and job specialties are avoided. Activities typically performed by maintenance, quality control, custodial, industrial engineering, and personnel units are built into an operating team's responsibilities. For example, each team member maintains the equipment he operates (except for complicated electrical maintenance) and housekeeps the area in which he works. Each team has responsibility for performing quality tests and ensuring quality standards. In addition, team members perform what is normally a personnel function when they screen job applicants.

3 Challenging Job Assignments While the designers understood that job assignments would undergo redefinition in light of experience and the varying interests and abilities on the work teams, the initial job assignments established an important design principle. Every set of tasks is designed to include functions requiring higher-order human abilities and responsibilities, such as planning, diagnosing mechanical or process problems, and liaison work.

The integrated support functions just discussed provide one important source of tasks to enrich jobs. In addition, the basic technology employed in the plant is designed to eliminate dull or routine jobs as much as possible. But some nonchallenging, yet basic, tasks still have to be compensated for. The forklift truck operation, for example, is not technically challenging. Therefore, the team member responsible for it is assigned other, more mentally demanding tasks (e.g., planning warehouse space utilization and shipping activities).

Housekeeping duties are also included in every assignment, despite the fact that they contribute nothing to enriching the work, in order to avoid having members of the plant community who do nothing but menial cleaning.

4 Job Mobility and Rewards for Learning Because all sets of tasks (jobs) are designed to be equally challenging (although each set comprises unique skill demands), it is possible to have a single job classification for all operators. Pay increases are geared to an employee mastering an increasing proportion of jobs first in the team and then in the total plant. In effect, team members are payed for learning more and more aspects of the total manufacturing system. Because there are no limits on the number of operators that can qualify for higher pay brackets, employees are also encouraged to teach each other. The old plant, in contrast, featured large numbers of differentiated jobs and numerous job classifications, with pay increases based on progress up the job hierarchy.

5 Facilitative Leadership Team leaders are chosen from foreman-level talent and are largely responsible for team development and group decision making. This contrasts with the old plant's use of supervisors to plan, direct, and control the work of subordinates. Management feels that in time the teams will be self-directed and so the formal team leader position might not be required.

6 "Managerial" Decision Information for Operators The design of the new plant provides operators with economic information and managerial decision rules. Thus production decisions ordinarily made by supervisors can now be made at the operator level.

7 Self-Government for the Plant Community The management group that developed the basic organization plan before the plant was manned refrained from specifying in advance any plant rules. Rather, it is committed to letting these rules evolve from collective experience.

8 Congruent Physical and Social Context The differential status symbols that characterize traditional work organizations are minimized in the new plant. There is an open parking lot, a single entrance for both the office and plant, and a common decor throughout the reception area, offices, locker rooms, and cafeteria.

The architecture facilitates the congregating of team members during working hours. For example, rather than following the plan that made the air conditioned control room in the process tower so small that employees could not congregate there, management decided to enlarge it so that process team operators could use it when not on duty elsewhere. The assumption here is that rooms which encourage ad hoc gatherings provide opportunities not only for enjoyable human exchanges but also for work coordination and learning about others' jobs.

9 Learning and Evolution The most basic feature of the new plant system is management's commitment to continually assess both the plant's productivity and its relevance to employee concerns in light of experience.

I believe pressures will mount in this system with two apparently opposite implications for automation:

- On the one hand, people will consider ways of automating the highly repetitive tasks. (There are still back-breaking routine tasks in this plant; for example, as 50-pound bags pile up at the end of the production line, someone must grab them and throw them on a pallet.)
- On the other hand, some processes may be slightly de-automated. The original design featured fully automated or "goof-proof" systems to monitor and adjust several segments of the manufacturing process; yet some employees have become confident that they can improve on the systems if they are allowed to intervene with their own judgments. These employees suggest that organizations may benefit more from operators who are alert and who care than from goof-proof systems.

Implementation Difficulties

Since the plant start-up in January 1971, a number of difficulties have created at least temporary, and in some cases enduring, gaps between ideal expectations and reality.

The matter of compensation, for example, has been an important source of tension within this work community. There are four basic pay rates: starting rate, single job rate (for mastering the first job assignment), team rate (for mastering all jobs within the team's jurisdiction), and plant rate. In addition, an employee can qualify for a "specialty" add-on if he has particular strengths—e.g., in electrical maintenance.

Employees who comprised the initial work force were all hired at the same time, a circumstance that enabled them to directly compare their experiences. With one or two exceptions on each team, operators all received their single job rates at the same time, about six weeks after the plant started. Five months later, however, about one third of the members of each team had been awarded the team rate.

The evaluative implications of awarding different rates of pay have stirred strong emotions in people who work so closely with each other. The individual pay decisions had been largely those of the team leaders who, however, were also aware of operators' assessments of each other. In fact, pay rates and member contributions were discussed openly between team leaders and their operators as well as among operators themselves. Questions naturally arose:

- Were the judgments about job mastery appropriate?
- Did everyone have an equal opportunity to learn other jobs?
- Did team leaders depart from job mastery criteria and include additional considerations in their promotions to team rate?

Thus the basic concepts of pay progression are not easy to treat operation-ally. Moreover, two underlying orientations compete with each other and create ambivalences for team leaders and operators alike:

- A desire for more equality, which tends to enhance cohesiveness.
- A desire for more differential rewards for individual merit, which may be more equitable but can be divisive.

Similar team and operator problems have also occurred in other areas. Four of these are particularly instructive and are listed in the ruled insert at the end of this article.

Management, too, has been a source of difficulty. For example, accept-ance and support from superiors and influential staff groups at corporate headquarters did not always come easily, thus creating anxiety and uncer-tainty within the new plant community.

Management resistance to innovative efforts of this type has a variety of explanations apart from natural and healthy skepticism. Some staff de-partments feel threatened by an experiment in which their functions no longer require separate units at the plant level. Other headquarters staff who are not basically threatened may nevertheless resist an innovation that deviates from otherwise uniform practices in quality control, accounting, engineering, or personnel. Moreover, many managers resent radical change, presuming that it implies they have been doing their jobs poorly.

Evidence of Success

While the productivity and the human benefits of this innovative organiza-tion cannot be calculated precisely, there have nevertheless been some impressive results:

- Using standard principles, industrial engineers originally estimated that 110 employees should man the plant. Yet the team concept, coupled with the integration of support activities into team responsibilities, has re-sulted in a manpower level of slightly less than 70 people.
- After 18 months, the new plant's fixed overhead rate was 33% lower than in the old plant. Reductions in variable manufacturing costs (e.g., 92% fewer quality rejects and an absenteeism rate 9% below the industry norm) resulted in annual savings of $600,000. The safety record was one of the best in the company and the turnover was far below average. New equip-ment is responsible for some of these results, but I believe that more than one half of them derive from the innovative human organization.
- Operators, team leaders, and managers alike have become more involved in their work and also have derived high satisfaction from it. For example, when asked what work is like in the plant and how it differs from other places they have worked, employees typically replied: "I never get

bored." "I can make my own decisions." "People will help you; even the operations manager will pitch in to help you clean up a mess— he doesn't act like he is better than you are." I was especially impressed with the diversity of employees who made such responses. Different operators emphasized different aspects of the work culture, indicating that the new system had unique meaning for each member. This fact confirms the importance of systemwide innovation. A program of job enrichment, for example, will meet the priority psychological needs of one worker, but not another. Other single efforts are similarly limited.

• Positive assessments of team members and team leaders in the new plant are typically reciprocal. Operators report favorably on the greater influence that they enjoy and the open relations which they experience between superiors and themselves; superiors report favorably on the capacities and sense of responsibility that operators have developed.

• While the plant is not without the occasional rumor that reflects some distrust and cynicism, such symptomatic occurrences are both shorter-lived and less frequent than are those that characterize other work organizations with which I am familiar. Similarly, although the plant work force is not without evidence of individual prejudice toward racial groups and women, I believe that the manifestations of these social ills can be handled more effectively in the innovative environment.

• Team leaders and other plant managers have been unusually active in civic affairs (more active than employees of other plants in the same community). This fact lends support to the theory that participatory democracy introduced in the plant will spread to other institutional settings. Some social scientists, notably Carole Pateman, argue that this will indeed be the case.[1]

• The apparent effectiveness of the new plant organization has caught the attention of top management and encouraged it to create a new corporate-level unit to transfer the organizational and managerial innovations to other work environments. The line manager responsible for manufacturing, who initiated the design of the innovative system, was chosen to head this corporate diffusion effort. He can now report significant successes in the organizational experiments under way in several units of the old pet-food plant.

What It Cost

I have already suggested what the pet-food manufacturer expected to gain from the new plant system: a more reliable, more flexible, and lower-cost manufacturing plant; a healthier work climate; and learning that could be transferred to other corporate units.

---

[1] *Participation and Democratic Theory* (Cambridge, England, Cambridge University Press, 1970).

What did it invest? To my knowledge, no one has calculated the extra costs incurred prior to and during start-up that were specifically related to the innovative character of the organization. (This is probably because such costs were relatively minor compared with the amounts involved in other decisions made during the same time period.) However, some areas of extra cost can be cited:

Four managers and six team leaders were brought on board several months earlier than they otherwise would have been. The cost of outside plant visits, training, and consulting was directly related to the innovative effort. And a few plant layout and equipment design changes, which slightly increased the initial cost of the new plant, were justified primarily in terms of the organizational requirements.

During the start-up of the new plant, there was a greater than usual commitment to learning from doing. Operators were allowed to make more decisions on their own and to learn from their own experience, including mistakes. From my knowledge of the situation, I infer that there was a short-term—first quarter—sacrifice of volume, but that it was recouped during the third quarter when the more indelible experiences began to pay off. In fact, I would be surprised if the pay-back period for the company's entire extra investment was greater than the first year of operation.

Why It Works

Listed in the ruled insert on the last page are eight factors that influenced the success of the new pet-food plant. I want to stress, however, that these are merely facilitating factors and are *not* preconditions for success.

For example, while a new plant clearly facilitates the planning for comprehensive plantwide change (Factor 3), such change is also possible in ongoing plants. In the latter case, the change effort must focus on a limited part of the plant—say, one department or section at a time. Thus, in the ongoing facility, one must be satisfied with a longer time horizon for plant-wide innovation.

Similarly, the presence of a labor union (Factor 6) does not preclude innovation, although it can complicate the process of introducing change. To avoid this, management can enter into a dialogue with the union about the changing expectations of workers, the need for change, and the nature and intent of the changes contemplated. Out of such dialogue can come an agreement between management and union representatives on principles for sharing the fruits of any productivity increases.

One factor I do regard as essential, however, is that the management group immediately involved must be committed to innovation and able to reach consensus about the guiding philosophy for the organization. A higher-level executive who has sufficient confidence in the innovative effort is another essential. He or she will act to protect the experiment from premature evaluations and from the inevitable, reactive pressures to bring it into line with existing corporate policies and practices.

Management and supervisors must work hard to make such a system succeed—harder, I believe, than in a more traditional system. In the case of the pet-food group, more work was required than in the traditional plant, but the human satisfactions were also much greater.

THE OTHER INNOVATORS

While the pet-food plant has a unique character and identity, it also has much in common with innovative plants of such U.S. corporations as Procter & Gamble and TRW Systems. Moreover, innovative efforts have been mounted by many foreign-based companies—e.g., Shell Refining Co., Ltd. (England), Northern Electric Co., Ltd. (Canada), Alcan Aluminium (smelting plants in Quebec Province, Canada), and Norsk-Hydro (a Norwegian manufacturer of fertilizers and chemicals). Related experiments have been made in the shipping industry in Scandinavia and the textile industry in Ahmedabad, India. Productivity increases or benefits for these organizations are reported in the range of 20% to 40% and higher, although I should caution that all evidence on this score involves judgment and interpretation.

All of these experiments have been influenced by the pioneering effort made in 1950 in the British coal mining industry by Eric Trist and his Tavistock Institute colleagues.[2]

Procter & Gamble has been a particularly noteworthy innovator. One of its newer plants includes many design features also employed in the pet-food plant. High emphasis has been placed on the development of "business teams" in which organization and employee identification coincides with a particular product family. Moreover, the designers were perhaps even more ambitious than their pet-food predecessors in eliminating first-line supervision. In terms of performance, results are reportedly extraordinary, although they have not been publicized. In addition, employees have been unusually active in working for social change in the outside community.[3]

Progressive Assembly Lines

Critics often argue that experiments like those I have discussed are not transferable to other work settings, especially ones that debase human dignity. The automobile assembly line is usually cited as a case in point.

I agree that different work technologies create different opportunities and different levels of constraint. I also agree that the automotive assembly plant represents a difficult challenge to those who wish to redesign work to

---

[2] See E. L. Trist, G. W. Higgin, H. Murray, and A. B. Pollock, *Organizational Choice* (London, Tavistock Publications, 1963).

[3] Personal correspondence with Charles Krone, Internal Consultant, Procter & Gamble.

decrease human and social costs and increase productivity. Yet serious experimental efforts to meet these challenges are now under way both in the United States and overseas.

To my knowledge, the most advanced projects are taking place in the Saab-Scandia automotive plants in Södertälje, Sweden. Consider, for example, these major design features of a truck assembly plant:

- Production workers have been included as members of development groups that discuss such matters as new tool and machine designs before they are approved for construction.
- Workers leave their stations on the assembly line for temporary assignments (e.g., to work with a team of production engineers "rebalancing" jobs on the line).
- Responsibility for in-process inspection has been shifted from a separate quality-inspection unit to individual production workers. The separate quality section instead devotes all its efforts to checking and testing completed trucks.
- Work tasks have been expanded to include maintenance care of equipment, which was previously the responsibility of special mechanics.
- Individuals have been encouraged to learn several jobs. In some cases, a worker has proved capable of assembling a complete engine.

Encouraged by the results of these limited innovations, the company is applying them in a new factory for the manufacture and assembly of car engines, which was opened in January 1972. In the new plant, seven assembly groups have replaced the continuous production line; assembly work within each group is not controlled mechanically; and eventually the degree of specialization, methods of instruction, and work supervision will vary widely among the assembly groups.

In effect, the seven groups fall along a spectrum of decreasing specialization. At one end is a group of workers with little or no experience in engine assembly; at the other end is a group of workers with extensive experience in total engine assembly. It is hoped that, ultimately, each group member will have the opportunity to assemble an entire engine.[4]

In addition to the improvements that have made jobs more interesting and challenging for workers, management anticipates business gains that include: (a) a work system less sensitive to disruption than is the production line (a factor of considerable significance in the company's recent experience); and (b) the twofold ability to recruit workers and reduce absenteeism and turnover. (The company has encountered difficulty in recruiting labor and has experienced high turnover and absenteeism.)

---

[4] For a more complete description of this plant, see Jan-Peter Norstedt, *Work Organization and Job Design at Saab-Scandia in Södertälje* (Stockholm, Technical Department, Swedish Employers' Confederation, December 1970).

Another Swedish company, Volvo, also has ambitious programs for new forms of work systems and organization. Especially interesting is a new type of car assembly plant being built at Kalmar. Here are its major features:

- Instead of the traditional assembly line, work teams of 15–25 men will be assigned responsibility for particular sections of a car (e.g., the electrical system, brakes and wheels, steering and controls).
- Within teams, members will decide how work should be divided and distributed.
- Car bodies will be carried on self-propelled carriages controlled by the teams.
- Buffer stocks between work regions will allow variations in the rate of work and "stock piling" for short pauses in the work flow.
- The unique design of the building will provide more outside windows, many small workshops to reinforce the team atmosphere, and individual team entrances, changing rooms, and relaxation areas.

The plant, scheduled to open in 1974, will cost 10% more than a comparable conventional car plant, or an estimated premium of $2 million. It will employ 600 people and have a capacity to produce 30,000 cars each year. Acknowledging the additional capital investment per employee, with its implication for fixed costs, Volvo nevertheless justified this experiment as "another stage in the company's general attempt to create greater satisfaction at work."[5]

Question of Values

The designers of the Procter and Gamble and pet-food plants were able to create organizational systems that both improved productivity and enhanced the quality of work life for employees. It is hard to say, however, whether the new Saab-Scandia and Volvo plants will result in comparable improvements in both areas. (As I mentioned earlier, the assembly line presents a particularly difficult challenge.)

In any event, I am certain that managers who concern themselves with these two values will find points at which they must make trade-offs—i.e., that they can only enhance the quality of work life at the expense of productivity or vice versa. What concerns me is that it is easier to measure productivity than to measure the quality of work life, and that this fact will bias how trade-off situations are resolved.

Productivity may not be susceptible to a single definition or to precise measurement, but business managers do have ways of gauging changes in it over time and comparing it from one plant to the next. They certainly can tell whether their productivity is adequate for their competitive situation.

But we do not have equally effective means for assessing the quality of work life or measuring the associated psychological and social costs and

[5] Press release from Volvo offices, Gothenburg, Sweden, June 29, 1972.

gains for workers.[6] We need such measurements if this value is to take its appropriate place in work organizations.

CONCLUSION

The emerging obligation of employers in our society is a twin one: (1) to use effectively the capacities of a major natural resource—namely, the manpower they employ; and (2) to take steps to both minimize the social costs associated with utilizing that manpower and enhance the work environment for those they employ.

Fulfillment of this obligation requires major reform and innovation in work organizations. The initiative will eventually come from many quarters, but I urge professional managers and professional schools to take leadership roles. There are ample behavioral science findings and a number of specific experiences from which to learn and on which to build.

Furthermore, the nature of the problem and the accumulating knowledge about solutions indicate that organizational redesign should be systemic; it should embrace the division of labor, authority and status structures, control procedures, career paths, allocation of the economic fruits of work, and the nature of social contacts among workers. Obviously, the revisions in these many elements must be coordinated and must result in a new, internally consistent whole.

This call for widespread innovation does *not* mean general application of a particular work system, such as the one devised for the pet-food plant. There are important differences within work forces and between organizations. Regional variances, education, age, sex, ethnic background, attitudes developed from earlier work experiences, and the urban-rural nature of the population all will influence the salient expectations in the workplace. Moreover, there are inherent differences in the nature of primary task technologies, differences that create opportunities for and impose constraints on the way work can be redesigned.

---

[6] For the beginning of a remedy to this operational deficiency, see Louis E. Davis and Eric L. Trist, *Improving the Quality of Work Life: Experience of the Socio-Technical Approach* (Washington, D.C., Upjohn Institute, scheduled for publication in 1973).

Implementation problems in the pet-food plant

Here are four team and operator problems encountered in the design of the innovative plant:

1 The expectations of a small minority of employees did not coincide with the demands placed on them by the new plant community. These employees did not get involved in the spirit of the plant organization, participate in the spontaneous mutual-help patterns, feel comfortable in group meetings, or appear ready to accept broader responsibilities. For example, one employee refused to work in the government-regulated product-testing laboratory because of the high level of responsibility inherent in that assignment.

2 Some team leaders have had considerable difficulty *not* behaving like traditional authority figures. Similarly, some employees have tried to elicit and reinforce more traditional supervisory patterns. In brief, the actual expectations and preferences of employees in this plant fall on a spectrum running from practices idealized by the system planners to practices that are typical of traditional industrial plants. They do, however, cluster toward the idealized end of the spectrum.

3 The self-managing work teams were expected to evolve norms covering various aspects of work, including responsible patterns of behavior (such as mutual help and notification regarding absences). On a few occasions, however, there was excessive peer group pressure for an individual to conform to group norms.

Scapegoating by a powerful peer group is as devastating as scapegoating by a boss. The same is true of making arbitrary judgments. Groups, however, contain more potential for checks and balances, understanding and compassion, reason and justice. Hence it is important for team leaders to facilitate the development of these qualities in work groups.

4 Team members have been given assignments that were usually limited to supervisors, managers, or professionals: heading the plant safety committee, dealing with outside vendors, screening and selecting new employees, and traveling to learn how a production problem is handled in another plant or to trouble-shoot a shipping problem. These assignments have been heady experiences for the operators, but have also generated mixed feelings among others. For example, a vendor was at least initially disappointed to be dealing with a worker because he judged himself in part by his ability to get to higher organizational levels of the potential customer (since typically that is where decisions are made). In another case, a plant worker attended a corporationwide meeting of safety officials where all other representatives were from management. The presence and implied equal status of the articulate, knowledgeable worker was at least potentially threatening to the status and self-esteem of other representatives. Overall, however, the workers' seriousness, competence, and self-confidence usually have earned them respect.

Conditions favorable to the pet-food experiment

Listed below are eight factors which facilitated the success of the new plant.

1 The particular technology and manufacturing processes in this business provided significant room for human attitudes and motivation to affect cost; therefore, by more fully utilizing the human potential of employees, the organization was able to both enhance the quality of work life and reduce costs.

2 It was technically and economically feasible to eliminate some (but not all) of the routinized, inherently boring work and some (but not all) of the physically disagreeable tasks.

3 The system was introduced in a new plant. It is easier to change employees' deeply ingrained expectations about work and management in a new plant culture. Also, when the initial work force is

hired at one time, teams can be formed without having to worry about cliques.

4 The physical isolation of the pet-food plant from other parts of the company facilitated the development of unique organizational patterns.

5 The small size of the work force made individual recognition and identification easy.

6 The absence of a labor union at the outset gave plant management greater freedom to experiment.

7 The technology called for and permitted communication among and between members of the work teams.

8 Pet foods are socially positive products, and the company has a good image; therefore, employees were able to form a positive attitude toward the product and the company.

READING 47

INDUSTRIAL ENGINEERS AND BEHAVIORAL SCIENTISTS: A TEAM APPROACH TO IMPROVING PRODUCTIVITY

Sharon L. Lieder
John H. Zenger*

Industrial engineering has been described as being concerned with the design, improvement, and installation of integrated systems of men, materials, and machines, drawing on specialized knowledge and skill in the mathematical, physical, and social sciences. The importance of "man" and "social sciences" is recognized in this definition, but conventional industrial engineering programs have given little emphasis to this human dimension.

Although industrial engineering has accounted for much of industry's efficiency and cost saving, many industrial engineering programs have troubling aspects. First, there is considerable resistance on the part of both workers and their supervisors to having an industrial engineer look into "our" function. This resistance is often expressed through lack of cooperation or even subtle sabotage, and sometimes through grievances about standards and making these standards key issues in collective bargaining. The myth of the ruthless efficiency expert can mushroom into unreasonable proportions, with stories about layoffs and speedups that stem from the industrial engineer's meddling.

Second, the industrial engineer himself may contribute to the problem. Frequently, he is the man in the middle between labor and management and is used to effect personnel reductions and cost savings, so he has to develop a crust of defensiveness against the hostility of the workers. Rather than try to understand the resistance, he just pushes harder, with the idea that he must force industrial engineering on the workers "for their own good."

Assumptions about People

At TRW Systems, it was felt that this tug of war could be called off if the findings of behavioral science were utilized to implement industrial engineering programs more effectively. Consideration of the problems posed by conventional industrial engineering led to a look at basic assumptions about people.

At a recent conference, an attending industrial engineering group described the model of "man" as having no initiative and little judgment or imagination, as working only for money, having to be forced to work, knowing less than the industrial engineer, and being obedient and even rather stupid. In short, these concepts clearly reflected McGregor's Theory X assumptions.

Behavioral science, however, makes different assumptions. Individuals are seen as having initiative; being concerned enough about their jobs to know their work; working not for money alone, but also for self-realization; and having the ability to make and carry out decisions in their work. The career development program already in existence at TRW Systems was based on these assumptions, which create an organizational environment in which individuals can grow. Because this effort has been highly successful, it was virtually mandatory that any industrial engineering program be in harmony with it.

Early in 1964 the administrative operations group—which included such staff and service groups as purchasing, inventory control, mail, communications, moves and delivery, stores and warehouse, shipping and receiving, reproduction, maintenance, travel, and the library—decided to establish an industrial engineering department, and the career development department was asked to assist. The behavioral scientists assigned to the project started work on the premise that the concepts of industrial engineering are sound, but that difficulties crop up mainly in the implementation phase.

The Engineer as Consultant

The management group in administrative operations wanted a program in which the industrial engineers would assist supervisors and individual employees in obtaining better performance, rather than "police" operations. The intention was to provide the manager with a consultant or advisor who would, in effect, be a member of his staff, helping him set up work standards and providing him with a technique for understanding the manpower requirements for a certain volume of work.

The concept of the industrial engineer's functioning as a consultant has been described by one of the senior staff industrial engineers in this way:

> The industrial engineer must convince his client that he is there to serve and assist no one but that client. He must recognize—and make it clear to the client that he recognizes—a professional cloak of confi-

dence between him and his client, similar to that of the doctor-patient or lawyer-client relationship.

The industrial engineer must learn that he, after all, is a human being, and that he is dealing with other human beings. He should learn to sense his own feelings and emotions so he will be aware of these same feelings and emotions in others.

He must learn to say and mean, when it is called for, "I don't know," or "What do *you* think?"

He must be able to communicate his thoughts and ideas, and he must be able to listen to another's expression of his thoughts and ideas. He should recognize that the client is as intelligent as he is, and the only reason the client needs an industrial engineer is that he hasn't the time to do the work himself.

He should, whenever possible, seek the client's counsel, guidance, and participation. He should be open-minded about the particular industrial engineering technique used and leave the selection of the technique up to the client—provided, of course, that the use of one technique or another does not affect the final outcome.

Training Sessions

Most of the industrial engineering staff were experienced professionals, but some were trainees chosen from within the company. Therefore, as a first step, formal classroom sessions were held as refresher courses in measurement techniques and as a means of helping to train the staff members who had had no prior experience.

After the technical training period, behavioral science training began with a weekend meeting outside the plant. This meeting was, in part, an unstructured sensitivity training (or T-group) session designed to help individuals explore how others perceive them. The structured sessions included studies of productivity and change—exploring what happens to productivity when changes are introduced into an existing work situation—and group dynamics—understanding group pressures under change.

Reactions to the new concepts and the relatively unstructured approach of the initial weekend were mixed, but everyone agreed that one weekend was not enough. Therefore, a series of follow-up sessions was scheduled, with an outside consultant acting as the trainer. Some of these sessions were unstructured T-group meetings; some were more structured exercises pertaining to communication, motivation, and consulting skills. Still others concentrated on how the behavioral science approach could be presented to the supervisor in working with his group, and specific problems encountered by the engineers were also discussed.

A programmed human relations course designed for two persons was completed by the industrial engineers. One took the course with a line manager and reported that he found it extremely helpful in opening up communications between them.

Some Problems

The follow-up sessions in the summer and fall of 1964 presented quite a few difficulties, which did, however, provide some valuable lessons. Among the problems were the following:

- Outside consultants with conventional industrial engineering viewpoints were used for technical assistance, but they were not conversant with the behavioral scientists' approach and seemed at odds with the company's philosophy.
- The training program was started before the industrial engineers recognized the need for such training, and the result was considerable resistance on their part.
- The initial weekend was so unstructured that the participants felt threatened. Furthermore, the behavioral scientists did not give them adequate orientation beforehand.
- The follow-up T-group sessions were not notably successful, either, possibly because of the limited time allotted to them (one-and-a-half to two

Figure 1 Approaches to Improving Productivity

Conventional industrial engineering	Behavioral science approach
• Cost reduction is the objective.	• The objective is to provide better tools for the manager, especially in cost and manpower control.
• The program is imposed from above.	• The program belongs to line management. The industrial engineer is a professional consultant to each level of line management, particularly to first-line supervision.
• The industrial engineer decides on the technique of measurement and what will be counted. The manager contributes only his knowledge of operations.	• The line manager is involved in day-to-day decisions on what to measure, how to count it, the measurement technique, and the reporting system.
• Performance reports are made by the industrial engineering department concurrently to all levels of management, and industrial engineers explain to top management reasons for variance in levels of performance.	• The performance report is issued by the line supervisor to his supervisor, who is responsible for any explanation, with assistance from the industrial engineer when desired.
• Standards (and resulting performance reports) will motivate increased productivity. (Carrot and stick approach.)	• Increased productivity stems from meaningful jobs, competent supervision, and effective teamwork. Standards may be helpful guidelines if the group has helped to create them.
• Build a job requiring efficiency, and let the worker adapt to it.	• In designing a job, take into account the technical requirements, organizational goals, and human motivation.
• The industrial engineer acts as an outside expert.	• The industrial engineer acts as a consultant.

hours), insufficient guidance, or the fact that some groups comprised antagonistic individuals.
   • It was difficult to formulate a workable philosophy and action steps
in specific, concrete terms. Much of the behavioral science approach en-
tailed an attitudinal change on the part of the industrial engineer, who was
accustomed to an orderly, factual, and often numerical discipline. (See
Figure 1.)
   • The professional status of the industrial engineers was challenged
in a number of ways. The heavy emphasis on behavioral science led some
industrial engineers to feel that their skill was not respected.

Questions of Relationships

As a result of this new philosophy, the proper relationship between the
industrial engineer and the line manager was unclear and raised many
questions:

   • The strategy of giving credit to the line manager changed the industrial engineer's historical job security. No longer could the industrial engineer say, "We saved X department $10,000 by eliminating two people," or,
"Performance was at 85—now it's at 100, and the industrial engineer did
that." How could the industrial engineering department justify its existence?
   • Line managers would now participate in helping to shape the approach, the data, and the manner of reporting. To what extent should line
managers be involved?
   • The industrial engineering report would no longer go to top management and thus could no longer be used to put pressure on the lower
levels of the organization. Instead, the industrial engineer was to become a
staff consultant to the line manager. What should such a consultant do?

   Effecting these changes in the relationship between the industrial engineer and the line manager was not easy. In many ways, the changes had to
begin with the engineer, who had to alter his goals—they had to blend with
the line manager's—and his methodology—he had to involve the people
concerned.
   The engineer also had to modify the way in which he measured his
success. His supervisor had to encourage and accept this redefinition; indeed, the supervisor had to reward the engineer's efforts by these new
criteria.

Two Approaches

The contrast between the conventional industrial engineering approach
and the approach espoused by the TRW group is illustrated by one industrial engineer's experience in the reproduction department.
   This engineer had a brief conversation with the manager and then

went ahead and gathered data by himself. He observed, took notes, collected forms, talked with people, and in general behaved in the traditional fashion. The manager later said, "I was just waiting for him to come up with some standards, because I knew I could prove them to be wrong. He had not involved us in getting answers to many key questions."

The fact was that the standards that would have been set with the information available to the industrial engineer at the time would have been in error. The relationship between the industrial engineer and the manager was tense and unfriendly, and he was not getting very far in setting standards.

At a briefing session with the manager of the career development department, the industrial engineer was coached to try a new approach. He went to the manager of the reproduction facility and asked for his help, explaining that he was having trouble in getting the kind of data he needed.

This marked a turning point. The manager volunteered to help collect data and suggested that his people could also help in gathering information. The manager's interest rose to the point that he spent some of his evenings designing forms for collecting data and analyzing the information obtained.

When standards were finally established, they had excellent acceptance by all concerned. The workers in the department had helped collect the facts and knew them to be fair, and because they had worked with the industrial engineer, they felt they could trust him.

Positive Results

Other positive results of this new program are typified by those in shipping and receiving, whose manager remarked:

> Working with the industrial engineer, we pinpointed and eliminated bottlenecks and set up valid standards. We're doing work now that a year ago would have required an additional seven-and-a-half men—a 30 per cent staffing increase we didn't have to make.
> Using the standards we developed, we have a reliable means of forecasting manpower needs, based on anticipated work volume. The most important outcome is employee acceptance of these standards.

The company newspaper became interested in this new approach to industrial engineering and, after talking with some of the engineers, wrote:

> The industrial engineers are as pleased with the program as the managers and supervisors. "This is a much more effective operation than the old industrial engineering. A real gold mine for us has been our access to people, especially the employees; they're doing the work, and they can tell you ways to make improvements that no one else would know about."

"That's right," adds another industrial engineer. "I got insights from the employees themselves. I talked with all 50 people in the mailroom, for instance, and they were a tremendous source of information."

The mail services' supervisor bears him out: "We had standards before, but never as refined as the ones we've worked out. Our industrial engineer took a lot of extra time with us, making sure that his findings were accurate."

Mutual Advantages

Now, after three years, the industrial engineering effort is expanding. Other divisions in TRW Systems are requesting assistance from industrial engineers—a far cry from the usual reaction of line managers in companies with the conventional industrial engineering approach. Necessarily, the original group of six engineers has expanded to 13.

There are still some rough spots to be smoothed out, and differences and difficulties are bound to arise in the future, but it has been proved conclusively that industrial engineering and behavioral science can work together to mutual advantage.

By revising the managers' assumptions regarding the industrial engineering function, the behavioral science approach has brought about positive attitudes toward industrial engineering, which it has changed from an external weapon to an internal management tool.

On the other hand, industrial engineering has much to contribute to behavioral science. The social scientist is often seen as concerned only with people, with no commitment to efficient accomplishment of the task at hand. In his desire to find new and better ways of utilizing people through motivation, the social scientist is inclined to overlook the importance of implementing scientific management. By working with industrial engineers, he shares in the development and design of jobs, rather than simply trying to make people happy with poorly designed jobs.

A Growing Trend

TRW is not the first organization to experiment with combining industrial engineering and behavioral science; other companies that have done work in this area include Eastman Kodak, Procter & Gamble, Texas Instruments, and Maytag. Industrial engineering journals are carrying articles about behavioral science, and behavioral scientists are being invited to speak at industrial engineering conventions. This small beginning is bound to grow, both in numbers and in depth of integration between the two disciplines, as programs like that at TRW make it clear that the potential is there.

READING 48

A LAW OF DIMINISHING RETURNS IN ORGANIZATIONAL BEHAVIOR?

Keith Davis*

During the last thirty years there has been a deluge of articles, research studies, and books about behavior of people in organizations. Thousands of articles have been published and there have been hundreds of research studies and books. Some observations have been more sophisticated than others, but all have sought that elusive goal of understanding people at work. Individual managers cannot read all the materials; thus, there is a constant search for basic ideas that clarify a variety of different data. The need is to distill the essence of behavioral knowledge without losing the complex details and disclaimers.

One example of the kind mentioned is Maslow's need hierarchy which assesses information from different inputs; thus, it is of practical use to managers in actual situations. Another plan is Herzberg's motivation-maintenance model. Although some researchers question its general validity, it helps managers better understand the workplace. Because of their practical value, these ideas have been widely publicized.

Another idea seems to distill much information about organizational behavior, but it has received little publicity. That idea is the concept of *diminishing returns*. It has been well developed in economics, but has received little attention in the behavioral area. This plan distills a great deal of wisdom and applies to a wide variety of situations. Furthermore, *it is supported by extensive research*. With all these things in its favor, it deserves more publicity.

In economics the law of diminishing returns refers to the amount of extra output received when additional desirable input is added to an economic situation. It states that after a certain point the output from each unit of input added tends to become smaller. The added output eventually may reach zero and even decline when more units of input are added. For example, if a farmer has a laborer working on 20 acres of land, he could potentially double the output by adding another laborer. Similar results might occur by doubling the work force to four persons and then to eight, but soon a point would be reached where the increase in output from adding workers would be smaller and smaller. Eventually production would decline as the field became overcrowded with workers, coordination deteriorated and crops were trampled by the crowd.

Diminishing returns in organizational behavior works in a similar way. The diminishing returns model states that at some point increments of a desirable practice produce declining returns, eventually zero returns and then negative returns as more increments are added. The concept implies that for any situation there is an optimum amount of a desirable practice. When that point is exceeded, there is a decline in returns. In other words, the fact that a practice is desirable does not mean that more of it is more desirable. At some point diminishing returns and then negative returns are reached. More of a good thing is not necessarily good.

Naturally diminishing returns does not apply to every behavioral situation; there are exceptions. But the idea is so widely applicable, that it is of general use. Furthermore, the exact point that an application becomes excess will vary with the circumstances; but an excess can be reached with nearly any variable. Diminishing returns in organizational behavior is so prevalent that real managers must deal with it frequently.

Why does the diminishing returns relationship exist? Essentially, diminishing returns is a system concept. It applies because of the complex system relationships of many variables in organizational behavior. The facts state the when an excess of one variable develops, although that variable is desirable, it tends to restrict the operating benefits of other variables so substantially that net effectiveness declines. For example, too much autonomy results in too little coordination. This relationship shows that organizational effectiveness is achieved, not by maximizing one behavioral variable, but by working all variables together in a balanced way. In essence, this is the modern contingency management view. Effective managerial practice is contingent upon an appropriate combination of the relevant variables in a particular situation.

The diminishing returns model can be illustrated by applying it to selected situations. In these situations a single variable is plotted against organizational effectiveness to show how effectiveness declines when an excess of the variable is applied.

WORKER AUTONOMY

Worker autonomy is a higher-order need frequently emphasized by organizational behavior specialists. Some observers speak of autonomy as an ideal, implying that if organizational members could have complete autonomy then the ideal state would be achieved. But this kind of reasoning ignores the law of diminishing returns. As shown in Figure 1, effectiveness declines when additional increments of autonomy are added, because an excess of autonomy prevents coordination toward central goals. An inte-

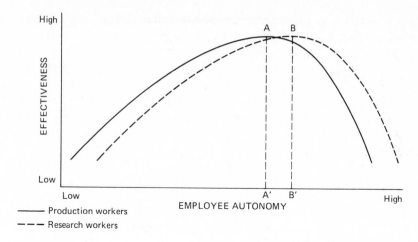

— Production workers
--- Research workers

Figure 1

gration of activities is lacking, so the organization cannot function effectively and the labor of the people is wasted.

At the other end of the continuum, the lack of autonomy is also ineffective. Although autonomy is considered a desirable practice, if its use declines below an appropriate level, the organization will become less and less effective, because it fails to develop and use the talents of employees. The result, as shown in Figure 1, is that effectiveness in a desirable behavioral practice declines with both excessive use and miserly use. Most success is achieved in the broad middle ground of use. This relationship produces a humpback curve for behavioral practices when they are charted with effectiveness.

The location of the humpback curve on the autonomy continuum may vary somewhat with different situations and the slope may vary, but the basic curve persists in organizational relationships. Figure 1 shows a curve with a solid line as it might exist for a group of production workers. Line A-A' shows the amount of autonomy that produces maximum effectiveness. The curve with the dotted line shows how diminishing returns might apply to workers in a research unit in the same organization. Line B-B' shows that much more autonomy can be provided the research workers before a point of maximum effectiveness is reached. Ten years from now the curves for both might be in different locations because of different conditions. This kind of contingent relationship, by which the most effective point of autonomy is dependent on other variables, is the essence of modern contingency management. However, whatever the situation, the humpback curve persists and a point of diminishing returns is reached.

The curve of diminishing returns serves as a warning to management that, although increased autonomy can be beneficial, an excess of it will be counterproductive. When management is aware of this kind of relationship, it can more wisely develop autonomy for employees in organizations.

EMPLOYEE SECURITY

Security is a basic human need shown at the second level of priority on the Maslow need hierarchy. Employees need it in order to free their minds from obsessive worry so that they can concentrate on teamwork and organizational goals. When there is insecurity, turnover and absenteeism increase, and employees are unable to concentrate on their work. Lack of security is clearly dysfunctional in an organization. On the other hand, as shown in Figure 2; an excess of security is also dysfunctional. Employees become complacent and unwilling to respond to necessary change. They desire to protect their status quo rather than to grow and develop. Very quickly a point of diminishing returns is reached where more security is either not worth its cost or is even dysfunctional to the organization. Managers need to be able to recognize the point of diminishing returns so that they do not waste organizational resources providing more security than is necessary. Again the relationship holds: The fact that some security is wise does not mean that more security is wiser.

EMPLOYEE SPECIALIZATION

One of the great ideas of civilization has been specialization of labor. Throughout history people have benefited from its application, and Adam Smith in 1776 made it a key principle in his economic model. Following the work of Fredrick W. Taylor around the 1900's in the United States, American management embraced specialization as a key to productivity. As so often happens with a good idea, specialization was pursued to excess,

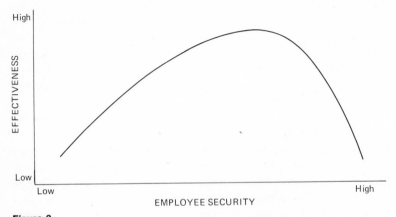

Figure 2

rendering it dysfunctional. Workers grew bored and alienated, and their work became almost meaningless as they performed smaller and smaller pieces of the whole job. A point of diminishing returns had been reached and exceeded. This relationship is shown in Figure 3. If management from the 1920's to the 1960's had better understood the law of diminishing returns as it applied to specialization, much alienation and productivity loss could have been prevented.

MANAGER'S CONCERN FOR PEOPLE

The law of diminishing returns applies throughout an organization, including management levels. An example is a manager's concern for people, also known as employee orientation. It is well established that concern for people is a significant variable for improving managerial performance. If a manager lacks concern for people, the work group is likely to be ineffective. Employees will not respond to the manager's leadership, and teamwork will not develop. Clearly, in this kind of deficient situation, more increments of employee concern are needed to improve group effectiveness.

When too many increments of employee concern are added, then a manager tends to forget other significant variables in the situation, and the law of diminishing returns applies as shown in Figure 4. A manager has only a certain amount of time available, and if he spends it relating to people, then he is unable to spend it working on production, social responsibility, long-range planning or some other important variable. He becomes what is often called a country-club manager, keeping his people happy but accomplishing little else. His concern for people, at one point highly desirable, has become dysfunctional as more increments are added. Again the relationship holds: The fact that some concern for people is wise does not mean that more concern for people is wiser.

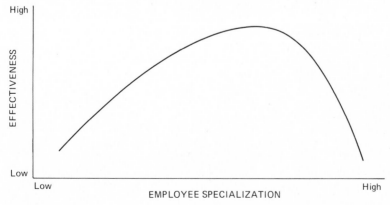

Figure 3

The law of diminishing returns applies throughout much of the organizational behavior as well as in economics. Essentially it states that moderation is required in all desirable practices. There can be too much of a good thing just as there can be too little of it. An excess of one variable disturbs system relationships so drastically that diminishing and eventually dysfunctional results occur. The middle ground before the laws of diminishing returns applies is the most effective area of operations. It is the high point of the humpback curve of effectiveness.

The message to managers is clear. They should beware of becoming so enamored with one practice that they overextend it beyond its proper relationship with other variables in the situation. Management is not a place for managers obsessed with building employee autonomy and little else, or specializing labor to the ultimate possible, or creating the most possible employee security. Moderation is required to avoid the law of diminishing returns and relate each desired variable to other variables in the complex situation. Each situation is different. In certain kinds of situations more of one variable can be used than in others. That is the essence of contingency management.

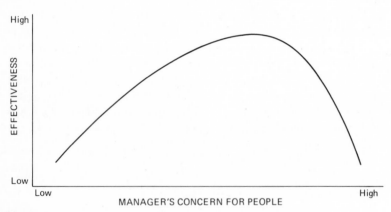

Figure 4

CHAPTER 13
ORGANIZATIONAL COMMUNICATION

READING 49

A COMMUNICATION NETWORK IN A FORMAL ORGANIZATION

Donald F. Schwartz*

- ■ Liaison role person
- ▲ Liaison set member
- ● Non-liaison person
- −− Group boundary

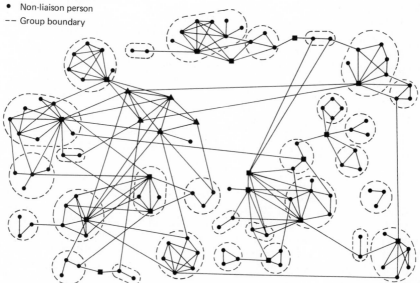

Sociogram of the communication structure of the organization. The 18 isolates are not included. Lines connecting individuals represent weekly or more often communication contacts.

*From *"Liaison Communication Roles in a Formal Organization,"* unpublished Ph.D. dissertation (East Lansing; Michigan State University, 1968), p. 103. Reprinted with permission.

READING 50

DIFFICULTIES IN COMMUNICATION

Douglas McGregor*

It is a fairly safe generalization that difficulties in communication within an organization are more often than not mere symptoms of underlying difficulties in relationship between the parties involved. When communication is ineffective, one needs to look first at the nature of these relationships rather than at ways of improving communication.

A related aspect of what is often a rather naive faith in the power of communication as a method of persuasion is closely connected with management views of "rational-emotional" man: "Tell them the reasons and they will do what we want." Management tends to assume—quite naturally but often incorrectly—that its decisions and policies are rational and objective. It further assumes that "proper communication" will transform its audience into rational recipients. Thus the primary requirement for obtaining compliance with management's desires becomes that of making sure that the reasons for a given action are understood. Of course, this is a necessary requirement, but it is by no means sufficient. Considerably more important are the characteristics of the system to which the communication input is made.

> The head of a large manufacturing unit in one company has strong feelings about the moral obligations of his employees to work hard. He expresses these by saying that they should be willing to give nine hours of work for eight hours' pay. He does not feel that these expectations are in any way emotional. They are coldly rational, and he can expand on the reasons at length. His own personality is paternalistic, but in a rather cold, patriarchal way.
>
> For years he has dominated his organization—his management as well as the workers. But recently there have been increasing signs of resistance. Despite the generous benefits that he bestows on his employees, they have become restive under his close control. The union leaders, themselves strongly antiauthoritarian, have used the situation to exploit mistrust of him and what they term his "exploitative" methods. Grievances are frequent and bitterly fought; legalistic technicalities dominate negotiations. For example, several pages in the union agreement are devoted to rules about the assignment of overtime. A series of strikes has occurred, and the situation is becoming steadily more explosive.
>
> This manager is firmly convinced that the solution to this whole

complex of problems lies in "effective communication," particularly between first-line supervision and workers. Moreover, effective communication will be achieved, he believes, if he can somehow get these supervisors to "take an interest in their subordinates." They must find out about each worker's family, his hobbies, his day-to-day problems at home. Then it will be possible for the supervisors to explain management's position, including the necessity for high productivity and high quality. When the workers are thus "informed," the problem will resolve itself. They will no longer listen to "the lies and the misinformation being peddled by the union."

This situation is extreme, but it is also classic. In my experience it is repeated constantly at varying levels of intensity, entirely outside the field of union-management relations as well as within it. The underlying set of assumptions are ubiquitous: management's reasons for its policies and actions are rational; subordinates would react rationally and accept them if they were properly informed; better communications would inform them and solve whatever difficulties exist. The same assumptions underlie the attempts of staff groups such as operations research teams, accountants, engineers, and even many personnel managers to persuade line managements to accept and utilize their proposals, their improved methods, their programs.

Human beings demonstrate over and over that they don't respond in the desired fashion to tactics based on these assumptions. The reaction then tends to be either that people are "ornery" by nature or that the communication was ineffective. The problems involved are often aggravated by the common admonition: "You have to sell them."

There is a fascinating question about all this. Management almost universally today agrees readily to the proposition that two-way communication is essential. Why, then, is there such heavy reliance on one-way communication? I have become convinced that a major reason is in the conception that many managers have of two-way communication. They believe that it consists primarily in discovering the questions or objectives generated by a management communication *and answering them.* Two-way communication is not conceived to be a transaction at all, but a means of ensuring that others understand what is being communicated. Since what is being communicated is obviously right, rational, and reasonable— if they understand, they will be persuaded.

As a behavioral scientist, my conception of two-way communication is that it is a process of *mutual* influence. If the communicator begins with the conviction that his position is right and must prevail, the process is not transactional but coercive. The process is one-way no matter how many words may be said by those receiving the communication. Even if it takes place in a face-to-face situation, it is as much one-way as mass-media advertising.

✻   ✻   ✻

READING 51

A GENERAL SEMANTICS APPROACH TO COMMUNICATION BARRIERS IN ORGANIZATION

Raymond V. Lesikar*

That communication is of major importance in the operations of a business organization is a well-established point. Over the years, businessmen have acknowledged its importance profusely. Similarly, management scholars have strongly expressed the vital role of communication in organizational operations. In the words of two of them, " . . . it is the essence of organized activity and is the basic process out of which all other functions derive."[1]

Thus it is reasonable to expect that such an important topic as communication would receive great attention by businessmen and scholars. And certainly it has. Primarily, however, both businessmen and business scholars have treated the subject in a somewhat descriptive manner. Their approach has been mainly one of identifying the causes of communication failure. More precisely, they have traced the effect of organization on communication. They have identified the barriers to communication in organization.

The "barriers" approach to organizational communication has taken a variety of directions, but all generally cover the same ground. Typically, they cover four areas which explain communication ineffectiveness within the organization. First are the communication problems of physical distance brought about by organizational growth. It is an obvious point, for separation of communicants clearly contributes to communication difficulty. Second are the equally obvious barriers caused by the hierarchy of power and status within the organization. Certainly, the bottom ranks do not communicate easily with the higher ranks; conversely the top ranks do not communicate easily with the bottom. Third are the artificial barriers workers

---

*From O. Jeff Harris (ed.), *Current Concepts in Management* (Baton Rouge: Louisiana State University, College of Business Administration, Division of Research, 1972), pp. 41–48.
[1] Alex Bavelas and Dermot Barrett, "An Experimental Approach to Organizational Communications," *Personnel*, Vol. 27, March, 1951, p. 368.

form between themselves as a result of their own job specializations. By specializing, they identify with those of like specialization; and they form antagonisms, suspicions, and general mistrust of other groups. Fourth are the effects of information ownership. Information is power and workers are inclined to seek power. Thus, they often keep information to themselves, and organizational communication suffers.

There are, of course, other classifications of barriers; but this one serves our purpose. It is sufficient to illustrate the value of such approaches; and it serves to illustrate their shortcomings as well. Quite obviously, barriers approaches do pinpoint problem areas. And with problem areas identified, an intelligent administrator can attempt to take corrective action.

As clearly as this example illustrates the advantage of a barriers approach, it also illustrates disadvantages. This approach does little to explain the phenomenon of human communication—of what goes on when two human beings attempt to communicate. Without question, the bulk of the communication that goes on in business is human communication. And organization is made up of people; and most of what takes place within the organization concerns people. Thus, no amount of pinpointing communication barriers can solve communication problems alone. There must also be present a knowledge of human communications. It is this ingredient that appears to be lacking in the efforts of businessmen and scholars to solve this problem. And it is this ingredient that I propose as a new dimension to the analysis of organizational communication.

Specifically, I propose solving the organizational problems of human communications through an application of general semantics. Probably the term *general semantics* needs defining, for the dictionary meanings of the two words do not combine to make a suitable definition. The word semantics may be especially misleading, for it is not used here in its classical sense. Classical semantics is that branch of philology devoted to word evolution. General semantics, on the other hand, is that discipline which studies man's perception of reality and of how he relates to reality through symbols. From this definition it is apparent that general semantics is broader in scope than classical semantics. General semantics encompasses the whole of man's reaction to the world about him. Only a part of these reactions are concerned with word symbols.

A relatively new discipline, general semantics was founded by Alfred Korszybski with his publication of *Science and Sanity: An Introduction to Non-Aristotelian Systems and General Semantics.* It was popularized in the late 1930s by Stuart Chase, a lucid writing accountant, in his book *The Tyranny of Words.* Professor Irving Lee's scholarly writings on the subject gave the new discipline impetus in the 1940s and 1950s. Then there were the very popular works of Professor S. I. Hayakawa, especially his classic *Language in Thought and Action.* These and others have made their impact in spreading the word about general semantics.

Because the subject has been so ably presented by disciples before me, much of what I have to say will not be new to you. Much of it already has been accepted into the subject matter of management as well as into other areas. My contribution, if any, merely is that of emphasizing application of the subject matter to an area into which I believe it fits most logically.

In making my application, I cannot cover all of the subject, for general semantics is a broad and complex discipline. I can only present selective points which in my judgment most logically apply to the subject of overcoming communication barriers. Nevertheless, I hope to present evidence sufficient to show the use of general semantics as a means of overcoming communication barriers in business.

Application of general semantics to communication barriers in business logically begins with a review of the philosophical bases of the discipline. First of these bases is the emphasis that general semantics focuses on the nature of reality. It is reality about which we communicate, and unless we know reality well, our communications about it must suffer. General semantics teaches one how to view reality; or at least it makes one conscious of the nature of reality. Specifically, it teaches one that reality is in process, unique, and infinite.

By in process, we mean that all of reality is forever changing. Nothing remains the same. The *you* of today will not be the same *you* in time to come; and certainly it is far different from the *you* of years gone by. In order to communicate precisely about reality, one must account for such time changes. Often we do not, and miscommunication is the result.

The uniqueness and infinity of reality pose another communication problem. As you know from your studies of science, no two things on earth are identical. There are infinite variations, especially at the microscopic and submicroscopic levels. Differences are the rule and similarities the exception. Yet the symbols (primarily words) we use are based on similarities. We stress these similarities; and we ignore the countless differences. For example, the word *store* applies to all retail outlets ranging from the "Mom and Pop" grocery to Macy's. A *dog* is any of a vast number of animals ranging from a Chihauhua to a Great Dane. The one word *profit* can have an almost infinite number of references in the real world. And so is it with any other reference one may need to make to reality.

General semantics does not avoid this common shortcoming. It would be impossible to do so. But it does discipline one to be aware of these problems of communication and to consider them in communicating. Thus, it works to help one overcome the barriers to communication in organization.

A second philosophical base of general semantics is its emphasis on the true nature of human perception. As we noted earlier, when we communicate we communicate about reality. Perhaps it would be more precise to say, "When we communicate, we communicate about our perceptions of reality." That is, we communicate only about that part of reality which we detect with our senses. Actually, we perceive only a small part of the reality which surrounds us. We ignore much of it. And our senses are incapable of detecting much of it.

Because of our limited perception, rarely can we communicate about the whole of an object or event, for we are not able to perceive all the details of it. When we say "John is a good worker," more than likely we are reporting on a small portion of the total of John's working experience. When we say, "Mary supported her proposal better than James," we are recounting an observation with so many happenings that even when we have given our best attention to perceiving the incident, we detect only a part of what happened. Nevertheless, we form our own viewpoint on that part which we perceive, and in our minds this part is reality. Someone else perceiving the same event might have quite different perceptions.

Certainly, such communication problems can never be eliminated— even through the study of general semantics. One trained in general semantics, however, is aware of what he is doing. He is aware of the error possibilities, and he understands why someone else may perceive differently from him. With this broader understanding of what takes place as perceptions become the bases for communication, he is better able to overcome the communication barriers that exist in the organization.

A third philosophical base on general semantics concerns the imprecise and general relationship of symbols (words) to reality. In general, language is designed to convey one's perception of reality. But as we have noted, reality is infinitely complex. To convey reality accurately would require a language as complex as reality itself. It would have to convey the billions upon billions of variations that exist in reality. No longer would we use the one word "house" to cover all houses ranging from a one-room shack to a palatial mansion. Instead, we would have as many words as we have houses. Our minds could not retain such a language, even if one were possible. So we must use a language that is far simpler than the reality it describes.

Certainly, a simpler-than-reality language is limited in its ability to communicate precisely. And a study of general semantics will not enable one to overcome this shortcoming. A knowledge of general semantics, however, will arm one with an understanding of the limitations of language. He will know that language must always serve as an inexact referent to reality. Thus, by knowing this relationship, he will be alert to the likelihood of error as he attempts to communicate.

A fourth philosophical concept of general semantics is the effect of the uniqueness of each mind on the meanings given to perception. In a very real sense, the mind serves as a filter to determining meaning; and each filter is different from all others. Each has its own storehouse of knowledge. Each has its own individual experiences. Each is affected by its own emotional makeup. Each has its own pattern of thinking, its logic, its biases, and such. Because each mind is unique, it is likely to give its own unique meaning to the perceptions that pass through it.

The fact that meanings derived in the mind are unique means, of course, that some degree of miscommunication always is present. Logically, the extent of such miscommunication can be lessened by a fuller understanding of what happens in the mental filtering process. A knowledge of general semantics gives one such an understanding.

In summarizing the preceding philosophical bases of general semantics, we can see the complexities of the communication process. First, the reality about which we communicate is extremely complex. It is infinite in nature; every item in it is unlike any other; and the items are continually changing. Certainly, it is no simple undertaking to identify precisely the reality about which we communicate. Second, human perception is limited. We can detect only a small part of the reality about which we communicate. Third, the symbols we use only loosely match the reality they refer to. Reality is much too complex for our symbols to match it in detail. Fourth, the human mind is sorely limited in its ability to give meanings to the imprecise symbols it receives. It is conditioned by bias, by emotions, by knowledge, by self-interest—in fact, by all the individual's mind has ever experienced. The total effect of all these influences on communication obviously is to bring about some degree of miscommunication.

Certainly, some degree of miscommunication always will exist. But it does appear logical to conclude that if one thoroughly understands what is happening as he communicates, he will be able to lessen the degree of miscommunication. That is, if one has a better concept of the reality about which he communicates, if he fully appreciates his own perception limitations as well as those of others; if he comprehends the limitations of symbols (words); and if he understands how each unique mind receives these symbols, he will be able to overcome at least some of the communication problems that exist between people in business. As these are the philosophical bases of general semantics, it is the logical overall conclusion that a study of general semantics would be a useful tool to use in improving communication in business.

READING 52

STRUCTURING COMMUNICATION IN A WORKING GROUP

Peter Mears*

An organization's effectiveness depends upon the performance of numerous small groups which function and interact within the overall organizational system. Because of this dependence, much emphasis has been placed on studies of subgroups, their cultures, status, and group needs, in an attempt to determine the factors which are most likely to encourage group effectiveness. Since the activity of a small group depends to a great extent upon its information flow, the communications act has been studied as a means of influencing efficiency. Thus, research on communication networks has become increasingly important and promises better understanding of the functioning of organizations.

One major criticism of past work in communication networks has been directed at its lack of applicability to a business organization; experiments have been conducted primarily in nonorganizational environments with student subjects. This kind of experimentation has resulted in a number of constraints which must be recognized in applying or "forcing" such findings to a practical application in a real business setting. The purpose of this article is to overcome these constraints by briefly presenting the major research findings regarding communication networks, and then to apply these research findings to a business situation.

A COMMUNICATION NETWORK IS THE INTERACTION REQUIRED BY A GROUP TO ACCOMPLISH A TASK

Working groups tend to be composed of four, five, or six people. Two people are not normally considered in a group; in a group of three there is a danger that two of the people will tend to "gang up" on the third person; and seven or more people in close proximity tend to split up into smaller, more manageable working units.

An organization may be composed of hundreds of such small working groups. This group idea is built into current management philosophy and is perhaps due to the notion that the managerial process involves the subdivi-

*Reprinted from "Structuring Communication in a Working Group," by Peter Mears in *The Journal of Communication*, vol. 24, no. 1, pp. 71–79. © 1975 by the Annenberg School of Communications, University of Pennsylvania. Reprinted with permission.

sion of brains as well as of labor. It is only natural for a business to try to increase the efficiency of these groups, and since the predominant activity of any group depends on the information flow, communications is one area in which the group may be made more efficient.

Three major types of small-group communication networks are shown in Figure 1. These are the circle, wheel, and the chain networks. Each circle represents an individual in a working group, and the solid line connects the individual with the other members of the group he or she normally interacts with in performing a task.

Bavelas and Barrett performed some of the initial research on the effects of different communication networks. This work is summarized in Table 1.

In the circle network an individual will normally converse with the person on his right or left, but not with any other members of the group. In the free circle group, all members converse frequently and equally with all other members of the group.

Appearances in these networks are deceptive. The wheel network on the left in Figure 1 is popularly referred to as an autocratic situation, and the wheel network on the right would be called a typical organizational

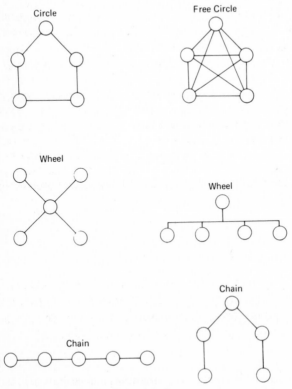

Figure 1   Communication networks.

Table 1 Performance of the Circle, Chain, and Wheel Communication Networks

	Circle	Chain	Wheel
Speed	Slow	Fast	Fast
Accuracy	Poor	Good	Good
Organization	No stable form	Slowly emerging but stable organization	Almost immediate and stable organization
Emergence of leadership	None	Marked	Very pronounced
Morale	Very good	Poor	Very poor

setup. Both networks are the same; the only difference lies in the arrangement of the circles on the paper. The distinguishing characteristic of the wheel network is that the members do not normally communicate with one another. They interact with the hub of the wheel, the leader of the group.

The chain network has all the appearances of an organizational chain-of-command: A reports to B, who reports to C, and so on. In actual practice this network may appear within a working group whose members are all at the same organizational level or rank. The two end positions might be occupied by people who tend to be introverted and prefer normally to communicate with only one person. In the three middle positions, the normal interactions may be determined primarily by friendship.

THIS CASE STUDY INVOLVES INDIVIDUALS INTERACTING TO SOLVE A COMPLEX PROBLEM

The individuals are Systems and Procedure personnel who represent specific divisions in a large aerospace firm. Each of the representatives is in charge of a small, highly skilled, semitechnical work group which develops unique systems and procedures for each of the firm's respective divisions (see Figure 2). It is the function of the division representative from "A" to coordinate the systems and procedures among divisions for consistency. To do this, A set up the working group of representatives whose communication structure is depicted in Figure 2. These division representatives communicate with each other in the interpretation and implementation of corporate directives as well as to obtain the cooperation of another representative to resolve an impending problem.

The solid lines depict both formal lines of authority and formal communication, while the dotted lines depict informal communication. This overlapping of the formal communication channel with an extensive network of informal communication channels occurs in many technical work groups. Mr. A, the formally delegated authority, may be well aware of these informal relationships as they pertain to the job, but interaction for the resolution of a common task is an accepted practice in management literature. In fact,

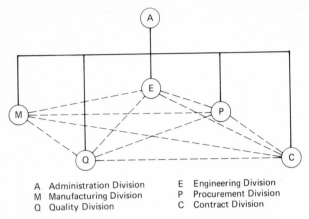

A   Administration Division   E   Engineering Division
M   Manufacturing Division   P   Procurement Division
Q   Quality Division   C   Contract Division

Figure 2   The initial organization.

the participative management approach may not only be viewed as an interaction between the subordinate and superior, but may also be viewed as encouraging subordinates to interact in the accomplishment of a task.

The communication of this systems and procedure group, as shown in Figure 2, was primarily a free circle network. Everyone in the group was free to utilize whatever channels of communication he desired, with the result that most of the group's time was spent in discussion, and very little work was accomplished. The morale of the group was very high; the only point of conflict occurred when a member felt obligated to agree with something he opposed in order that group consensus could be achieved. This result is consistent with the findings of Festinger, who states that "pressures toward uniformity may exist within a group; these pressures act toward making members of a group agree concerning some issue, or conform with respect to some behavior pattern." (8)

Each person's advice was appreciated and carefully evaluated. Because the individual group member was able to make a contribution on a complex issue, his involvement was high and there was a feeling of pride in his accomplishments. This fact is consistent with the findings of Shaw, who discovered that "morale is higher with greater independence because independence permits the gratification of the culturally supported needs for autonomy, recognition and achievement." (19)

Bales (1), Etzioni (7), and Davis (6) point out that in most groups, in addition to a formal leader, an informal leader, more commonly called the social leader, tends to emerge. The social leader, restores and maintains group unity and satisfaction. In the group I am describing, the Contract division representative filled that role. This result may not be consistent with the findings of Kahn and Katz when they say that "pride or involvement in the work group and productivity are interacting variables and that an increase in one tends to bring about an increase in the other." (12) This was only true to a very limited point: in the Systems and Procedure group, because of the lack of specific channels of communication, too much time was spent in discussion and useless debate.

AFTER SEVERAL MONTHS THE DIVISION REPRESENTATIVES ACCOMPLISHED ALMOST NOTHING. MANAGEMENT STEPPED IN AND DISBANDED THE MEETINGS

The group was reorganized by management as a wheel network. The new organization is shown in Figure 3. The change from an unrestricted network, the free circle, to a restricted network, the wheel, was essentially a change from a democratically-run group to an autocratically-run group. Under the free circle network, lengthy arguments and discussions sometimes extended well into the evening after the formal group leader had left. Under the wheel network, in order to force all information to come through the wheel hub (the Administration representative), management issued a directive stating that any communication concerning procedures outside the individual's division was to be conducted only by the Administration division. This directive was ignored until one of the representatives was severely reprimanded for reaching an agreement with the Manufacturing representative without the concurrence of the Administration representative. After the reprimand, the group again became ineffective. Every representative lived up to the absolute letter of the directive. No opinion was voiced unless asked for, and then only the exact question asked would be answered.

Since only the representatives were competent to answer detailed questions about their divisions, information had to be relayed by the Administration division to each representative. Since each representative would protect his own interest by commenting only on what affected him, the number of errors grew astronomically. The same job would be redone several times; if it did not exactly suit the divisional representative's interests, it would be vetoed. A virtual boycott of any new system developed.

FOR ALL PRACTICAL PURPOSES, THE INSTALLATION OF A WHEEL (AUTOCRATIC) NETWORK DECREASED OUTPUT

At first glance, this conclusion might seem inconsistent with the available literature. Bavelas and Barrett (2), Leavitt (15), and Guetzkow (11) quantita-

Figure 3   A wheel network.

tively show the wheel as the fastest network for problem solution. Considering that their common conclusion was based on an experiment in which the participants had only to detect a missing symbol, their conclusion was justified. The actual solution of an industrial problem, however, may be very complex and quite often is based not purely on available facts but on a mixture of the facts available plus past experience on similar problems.

Mulder (17) indicates that the important element in group interactions may be the emergence of a decision structure. The decision structure determines the pattern of suggestion acceptance from one member to another. A change in the formal structure may disrupt the decision structure of the group, thus resulting in a loss of group efficiency.

When our group operated in a free circle network, what hurt efficiency was not the morale of the group, which was excellent, but the overabundance of communication channels available to each member. Shaw (19) would have stated that the saturation level of the individual was reached, that the total requirements placed on an individual in a network were excessive.

With the wheel network, the saturation level again accounted for the decrease in efficiency. The task was complex, and the individuals refused to accept the dictates of the central person without sufficient information. This forced the central person to handle more and more messages until he could do only one of two things: either state that he could not handle the job, or try to circumvent the group entirely by pointing out to management that the group was uncooperative. He took the second course.

Changing from democratic leadership to autocratic leadership had a disruptive effect on the group. People have a natural tendency to automatically develop a system for performing a task. Not having to think about how to go about doing a job reduces the uncertainty associated with the task; when people find themselves in a condition in which they again cannot automatically perform the required tasks, they center their attention on developing a system to accomplish the task, The wheel network demands an autocratic system, because its members cannot collectively interact, and the leader (hub) represents something that has introduced uncertainty. It is only natural that this uncertainty will be met with hostility by workers who are accustomed to a more participative system.

Cohen and Bennis (5) hold the same viewpoint, and Lawson (13) points out that this knowledge holds a strong implication for training. If during a training period a group network is changed, then the individual's learning process will be disrupted; he will first concentrate on learning the new network and, after mastery, will then concentrate on the job.

After the disastrous effect of introducing a wheel network in the technical group, management recognized its error and carefully studied the interactions required by each group member. The Manufacturing division representative needed to communicate with Engineering and Quality division representatives. Analogously, since hardware under construction was ordered to Engineering specifications, problems with procured hardware should be discussed by Engineering and Procurement representatives. The addition of the Manufacturing representative would serve no useful purpose and would tend to slow the group down.

EACH GROUP MEMBER WAS REQUESTED TO COMMUNICATE ONLY WITH THE OTHER MEMBERS DIRECTLY INVOLVED IN THE PERTINENT DECISION

As a result of this new communication restriction, the "A" division was relieved of having to make all decisions (as under the wheel network), and the other divisions did not waste time when decisions did not concern them (as under the free circle network). Figure 4 shows the communication patterns in this revised group organization.

The new system, in the long run, increased productivity and morale of the affected parties. But, just after the change in structure, there was a decrease in efficiency in the short run. The Contract members and the Procurement members had the lowest work load. Under the autocratic leadership their group morale had declined, and they had centered their attention on the problems internal to their own divisions. When the new network came into existence, they had to relearn the system, and it took several months for the members to obtain the satisfaction they had previously enjoyed under the free circle network. (In fact, they never fully reached the same high level of satisfaction.) Lawson (13) experienced the same conditions of disruptiveness, then increased efficiency and higher morale, when groups were changed from the more restrictive wheel to the freer circle.

In the business world, communication networks tend to be combinations of the prototypes depicted in Figure 1. Management should avoid getting too close to one of these extremes, or it may be forced to change the networks and create disruption and inefficiency in the work group.

Communication networks are not a theoretical abstraction from reality. The formal group is aware of the existence of the networks—informal as

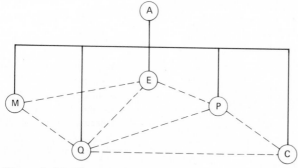

Figure 4 Modified circle network.

well as formal—and usually feels it must delegate the type of network in the interests of maximum efficiency. This may well be a desired practice, but network delegation must be done with respect to the complexity of the task, the desired morale, the desired efficiency, and the impact of the change. Omission of any of these factors from consideration will result in a network detrimental to the organization.

REFERENCES

1 Bales, Robert F. "In Conference." *Harvard Business Review,* March–April 1954, pp. 44–50.
2 Bavelas, Alex, and Dermot Barrett. "An Experimental Approach to Organizational Communication." *Personnel* 27 (March 1951), 366–71.
3 Bello, Francis. "The Information Theory." *Fortune* 48 (December 1953), 137.
4 Blair, Elenn Myers, R. Stewart Jones, and Raymond H. Simpson. *Educational Psychology,* 3rd ed. New York: The MacMillan Company, 1965.
5 Cohen, Arthur M., and Warren G. Bennis. "Continuity of Leadership in Communication Networks." *Human Relations,* 1959, pp. 359–65.
6 Davis, Keith. *Human Relations at Work: The Dynamics of Organizational Behavior,* 3rd. ed. New York: McGraw-Hill, 1967.
7 Etzioni, Amitai. "Dual Leadership in Complex Organizations." *American Sociological Review,* October 1965, pp. 688–98.
8 Festinger, Leon. "Informal Social Communication," *Psychological Review* 57 (1950), 271–82.
9 Guetzkow, Harold. "Differentiation of Roles in Task-oriented Groups." *Group Dynamics: Research and Theory,* 2nd ed., edited by Dorwin Cartwright and Alvin Zander. Evanston, Illinois: Row, Peterson & Company, 1960.
10 Guetzkow, Harold, and William R. Dill. "Factors in the Organizational Development of Task-oriented Groups." *Sociometry* 20 (1957), 175–204.
11 Guetzkow, Harold, and Herbert A. Simon. "The Impact of Certain Communication Networks upon Organization and Performance in Task-oriented Groups." *Management Science* 1 (1955), 233–50.
12 Kahn, Robert L., and Daniel Katz. "Leadership Practices in Relation to Productivity and Morale." In *Group Dynamics: Research and Theory,* 2nd ed., edited by Dorwin Cartwright and Alvin Zander. Evanston, Illinois: Row, Peterson & Company, 1960.
13 Lawson, Edwin D. "Changes in Communication Networks, Performance and Morale." *Human Relations,* May 1965, pp. 139–47.
14 Leavitt, Harold J. "Small Groups in Large Organizations." *The Journal of Business* 28–29 (January 1955), 8–17.
15 Leavitt, Harold. J. "Some Effects of Certain Communication Patterns on Group Performance." *Journal of Abnormal and Social Psychology,* 46 (1951), 38–50.
16 Lyle, Jack. "Communication, Group Atmosphere, Productivity, and Morale in Small Task-Groups." *Human Relations,* 1960, pp. 369–79.
17 Mulder, Mauk. *Group Structure, Motivation and Group Performance.* The Hague: Mouton & Co., 1963.
18 Rothschild, Gerard H., and Marvin E. Shaw. "Some Effects of Prolonged Experiences in Communication Nets." *Journal of Applied Psychology,* October 1956, 281–86.
19 Shaw, Marvin E. "Communication Networks." In *Advances in Experimental Social Psychology,* edited by Leonard Berkowitz. New York: Academic Press, 1964.
20 Shaw, Marvin E. "Some Effects of Problem Complexity upon Problem Solution Efficiency in Different Communication Nets." *Journal of Experimental Psychology* 48 (1954), 211–17.
21 Thayer, Lee O. *Administrative Communication.* Homewood, Illinois: Richard D. Irwin, 1961.
22 "The Number One Problem." *Personnel Journal* 45 (April 1965), 237–38.

READING 53

GRAPEVINE COMMUNICATION AMONG LOWER AND MIDDLE MANAGERS

Keith Davis*

The supervisor was understandably annoyed as he reported what had happened to him a day earlier. He had been at work for an hour when an employee mentioned he had heard the supervisor would be transferred to another shift the next day. This was news to the supervisor, but a few hours later a notice of the transfer reached him through official channels. He was frustrated at being the "last to know" and annoyed at management for being so slow with its communications. In reality, management was not especially slow. Rather, the grapevine was operating at its typical speed for spreading "hot news" through management networks to the employee level.

The grapevine operates fast and furiously in almost any work organization. It moves with impunity across departmental lines and easily bypasses superiors in chains of command. It flows around water coolers, down hallways, through lunch rooms, and wherever people get together in groups. It performs best in informal social contacts, but it can operate almost as effectively as a sideline to official meetings. Wherever people congregate there is no getting rid of the grapevine. No matter how management feels about it, it is here to stay.

As a regular part of the work environment, the grapevine is an influential force to be considered in all management actions. For example, a study of 100 operating employees reported that if management made an important change in the organization, more employees would expect to hear the news *first* by grapevine than by any other method. The supervisor and official memorandums ran a poor second and third respectively. As reported in that study and elsewhere, the grapevine does not always live up to its expectations. Sometimes it ranks second, third, or lower in actual results, but even in these situations it is a significant force within the work group.[1]

We have come to realize that a healthy organization has both a grapevine and official channels of communication. When both channels are

---

* Adapted from *Personnel Journal*, April 1969, pp. 269–272. Copyright April 1969, by Personnel Journal Inc. Reprinted with permission.

[1] Eugene Walton, "How Efficient Is the Grapevine?" *Personnel*, March–April, 1961, pp. 45–49.

working effectively, they are somewhat of a complement to each other. Each carries information particularly suited to its needs and capabilities, so that together the two systems build effective communication in an organization. On the other hand, the two systems can work at cross purposes. In practice, the grapevine operates somewhere along a continuum of harmony and disharmony with the formal organization, and each manager's job is to act in ways which bring the grapevine into closer harmony with total needs of the organization and work group. Action of this type requires improved management understanding of the grapevine's way of life.

Lower and middle management occupy a strategic position in communication channels because they can filter and block two-way communication between higher management and operating employees.[2] This present study investigates some of the characteristics of grapevine communication among lower and middle managers. Fifty managers attending a management development program were asked to report their *primary* channel of grapevine information about their company. The managers were mostly from the electric utility industry and came from a number of companies throughout the eastern half of the United States.

GRAPEVINES ACROSS CHAINS OF COMMAND

Table 1 shows the tendency of grapevine systems to range far and wide throughout an organization. More grapevine sources were outside the re-

Table 1   Primary Source of Grapevine Information for 50 Lower and Middle Managers in the Electric Utility Industry

Source within the company	Number in receiver's chain of command	Number outside receiver's chain of command	Total
Above the receiver:*			
One level	1	1	2
Two levels	0	1	1
Total above	1	2	
At same level as the receiver:	(not applicable)	12	12
Below the receiver:			
One level	11	8	19
Two levels	7	2	9
Three levels	0	2	2
Four levels	1	0	1
Total below	19	12	
Total within company	20	26	46
Total from outside company			4
Total surveyed			50

* In terms of organizational level.

[2] For a research report concerning how lower management filters *official* management information see Keith Davis, "Chain-of-Command Communication within a Manufacturing Management Group," *Academy of Management Journal*, December, 1968, pp. 379–387.

ceiver's chain of command (26) than within it (20). In addition, four primary grapevine sources of company grapevine information were entirely outside the company. One was a manufacturer's representative and another was a retired employee. Two managers reported that their spouses were their primary grapevine source and that the spouses said they received their information from social contacts with spouses of other employees. This indicates that spouses as a group had an influential company grapevine, and it would seem to justify the interest many companies have in keeping them informed about company activities. Spouses and other family members are often a part of a company's communication system, whether or not it encourages them to be so.

Of the twenty-six grapevine channels which were outside the chain of command, twelve (46 per cent) flowed horizontally from a manager's peers at the same level. The majority (54 per cent) flowed diagonally either upward or downward. The vast range of the grapevine is again illustrated by the fact that these sources were as far as three levels below and two levels above the managers. Most of the diagonal flow, however, was from lower levels rather than higher levels.

These data illustrate how the grapevine is able to move so quickly within an organization that it often reaches people before formal communications do. Since the majority of grapevine sources in this study were both across chains of command and from another organizational level, it is evidence that once an item gets into the grapevine, these channels can be used to reach most departments and levels quite rapidly. All that is needed are a few telephone calls, chance meetings in hallways, or comments in a group during a cafeteria coffee break. When a grapevine is started, then its receivers spread it even more widely somewhat like a chain letter works. Like the chain letter, it eventually dies because of lack of interest or because most people have already received it.

The wide reach of the grapevine reported by managers in this study confirms other reseach which I have made among managers.[3] One reason for this wide reach is extensive social networks, such as coffee groups and mutual hobby interests, which keep employees in regular contact. There also appears to be a deep psychological desire to talk about one's job, since it is a central life interest for many employees.[4] Since job events are important to people, they want to bring the news to their friends and associates. In this manner the grapevine spreads widely because their friends

[3] Keith Davis, "Management Communication and the Grapevine," *Harvard Business Review,* September–October, 1953, pp. 43–49. On the other hand, Sutton and Porter's study of mostly *employees* rather than managers reported that the majority of grapevine communications were between people within each functional department, even though some persons did spread the information to other departments. See Harold Sutton and Lyman W. Porter, "A Study of the Grapevine in a Governmental Organization," *Personnel Psychology,* Summer, 1968, pp. 223–230.

[4] Frank Friedlander, "Importance of Work versus Nonwork among Socially and Occupationally Stratified Groups," *Journal of Applied Psychology,* December, 1966, pp. 437–441.

and associates at the management level are not confined merely to the department where they work.

Another reason for grapevine spread is the vast networks of procedures and committees which bring managers from different departments together. In these meetings they are going to talk about many things other than official business, as any experienced committee member knows. For example, Shartle charted the two managers with whom each manager in a company spent the most time and found that many of these primary contacts were outside a manager's chain of command or that they bypassed some manager in the chain of command.[5] The result of these broad procedural and committee contacts is a grapevine with as many arms as an octopus.

GRAPEVINES WITHIN CHAINS OF COMMAND

The idea of grapevines *within* chains of command seems at first glance to be an unrealistic technical distinction. If any communication is between people in a chain of command, isn't it sure to be official line communication? At second glance, however, certain distinctions appear obvious. For example, an employee says to his supervisor, "Bill, did you hear that Mary Jones in Department Y was promoted to personnel supervisor last week?" In this instance, two persons in a chain of command are talking, but their subject is not an official communication. It is not required by job conditions or by company rules and procedures. It is grapevine information. A considerable portion of communication among people in chains of command is of this type.[6]

Of the fifty managers surveyed, twenty of them (40 per cent) had their primary grapevine source within their chain of command. All but one source was someone at a lower level, mostly at the first and second lower levels. In one instance, however, a receptionist four levels below a manager was the primary source of grapevine information about the company! In fact, eight of the twenty sources were from two or more levels below a manager, which indicates how handily the grapevine is able to bypass an immediate superior in a chain of command.

Suppose that a manager named August Bernstein wants to reduce this practice of others detouring around him. Then he has a responsibility to develop open channels of communication with his employees. He can require that official communications come through him, but he cannot force the grapevine to do anything. He can only influence it. For example, does he help his employees get information when they need it? If so, they will be

[5] Carroll L. Shartle, "Leadership and Executive Performance," *Personnel*, March, 1949, pp. 370–380.

[6] For a more extended discussion of the grapevine and informal organization see Keith Davis, *Human Relations at Work: The Dynamics of Organizational Behavior*, 3rd edition, New York: McGraw-Hill Book Company, 1967, pp. 212–232.

more likely to return his helpfulness by keeping him informed. Does he talk with his people only when official business requires it, or does he keep in touch with them regularly? Does he show an interest in them as persons and listen to them attentively? If so, they are likely to talk with him more openly beyond official requirements of their jobs.

Of particular interest is the fact that nine of the fifty managers reported that their primary source of grapevine information was a secretary. Six of these secretaries were in the chain of command and three were outside of it. Limited evidence suggests that secretaries were only about five per cent of the total managerial and office work force; so their representation rate (18 per cent) as grapevine sources is more than 3½ times their five per cent proportion in the work force.

Evidently secretaries play a key role in *managerial* grapevines. They are strategically located as communication centers in the work system, because they process their manager's correspondence, greet visitors, make appointments, and are otherwise involved in much that their manager does. Psychologically they are sometimes a confidante of their manager, and organizationally they often are perceived as their manager's official representative. All of these conditions establish secretaries in a significant position within management grapevines.

In summary, this study shows the remarkable versatility of grapevines to flow in all directions in organizations. They move upward, downward, and diagonally, within and without chains of command, between workers and managers, and even within and without a company. The grapevine is a normal part of a total communication system; so managers who do not wish to be bypassed by the grapevine need to learn about it, relate to it, and develop open channels of communication.

READING 54

CUT THOSE RUMORS DOWN TO SIZE

Keith Davis*

Wild rumors can sweep through an organization with the speed and destructiveness of a summer storm. Nearly every organization occasionally experiences such an onslaught. Morale at one large company hit a new low when a rumor went around that the credit authorization department was closing and 50 workers were being transferred to the equivalent of Siberia.

Another company, where variable product demand requires an occasional small layoff, suffers an 8 percent productivity decline whenever an impending layoff is rumored. The employees appear to be working as hard as ever—but the rumor affects their will to produce up to their capability. And this small decline makes the difference between an adequate profit and a marginal one.

Rumor is a natural result of human interaction. Supervisors need not be alarmed every time a breeze rustles the grapevine, since most rumors turn out to be harmless speculations that die off by themselves. Only rarely are rumors serious enough to require action; but when rumors do seem to threaten the organization, something has to be done.

There are essentially two ways to cope with rumor in an organization. The first is to try to prevent it. How can wild rumors be prevented? First, a supervisor has to recognize that rumors are not haphazard developments; they arise from definite causes. If those causes can be controlled, there is much less probability that rumors will develop.

LACK OF INFORMATION

A major cause of rumor is lack of information about things important to employees. When they do not know what is happening in their world, they are likely to speculate about the situation—and thus a rumor is born. Employees who observe an unscheduled disassembly of a machine, for example, may speculate that machines are being transferred to another plant and workers will be laid off. If they had known that the machine was being replaced by a newer model, the rumor would never have gotten started. Their supervisor unwisely left a gap in the workers' information, and they took the normal, human approach of trying to figure out what's happening—to make sense of changes in their surroundings.

* From *Supervisory Management*, June 1975, pp. 2–6. © 1975 by AMACOM, a division of American Management Associations. Reprinted with permission of the publisher.

INSECURITY

Another basic cause of rumor is insecurity and the anxiety that goes with it. Insecure, anxious employees are more likely than others to perceive events negatively, and they are better motivated to tell others about their worries. It is easy for insecure workers to imagine the worst in almost any situation. The remedy? To give employees emotional and economic security by providing stable employment and fair wages. In countless ways, day by day, over months and years, supervisors should try to build trust and keep communication open. As employees feel more secure, wild rumors are less likely to arise.

EMOTIONAL CONFLICT

Emotional conflict can also lead to rumor. Rumors thrive in such emotion-laden situations as a disagreement between a hard-driving union and an uncompromising supervisor, or cutthroat competition between two departments. Personality conflicts too can activate rumors. Sometimes, malicious lies enable one person to gain advantage over the other. In other instances, there is no maliciousness—one person is merely so biased in favor of his own viewpoint that he interprets real events in unreal or untrue ways. Strong emotions almost always influence perceptions.

An obvious remedy for the rumor that arises from conflict is cooperative teamwork among various special-interest groups in an organization. Each group should feel that it is part of a larger whole, that the goals of the whole are paramount, and that its own success depends on the success of the whole. People who feel that they are on the same team are not likely to make incorrect or malicious assumptions about each other. As the saying goes, "The people in the same boat with you are not likely to bore a hole in it."

HOW THE RUMOR MILL OPERATES

Whether a rumor starts because of job insecurity, emotional conflict, or an information gap, each person receives and transmits it in terms of his or her own biases. The general theme of the rumor is usually maintained, but not its details. Any oral communication is subject to "filtering"—a process of reducing the story to a few basic details that can be remembered conveniently and passed on to others. Generally, each person chooses the details in a rumor that fit his particular perception of reality and passes these on.

People also add new details to a rumor, frequently making it worse, in order to reflect their own strong feelings and reasoning. This is known as "elaboration." If, for example, a rumor about an employee injury arises, someone who does not like his supervisor may add the notion that the supervisor's failure to provide proper machine maintenance caused the accident. By the time a rumor has undergone both filtering and elaboration, it often bears only a faint resemblance to the original story.

In spite of all the efforts a supervisor makes to prevent rumors, some will still arise. Most rumors that flow through the work area do not cause serious harm, and in any event they soon die a natural death. It would be a waste of effort to try to stop them. Some rumors may even provide certain benefits—such as giving people a way to release pent-up emotions. They may even help maintain employee contacts and add interest to the work.

SERIOUS RUMORS

A few rumors, however, may be serious enough to require attention. It is these rumors that a supervisor will want to restrain or subdue—the second method of dealing with rumors.

If productivity is affected, or community relations suffer, or interdepartmental cooperation is hampered, a supervisor must do something. The most effective approach is to vanquish the rumor with the truth. When the true story is released, the information gap is filled and the rumor dies. Even when the truth has negative implications, it is less destructive than rumors that feed on fear of the unknown. Although the truth may sometimes sound farfetched, it is more likely to be accepted than any story a supervisor could concoct. A reputation for honesty in management will also do much to ensure employee confidence in and loyalty to the organization. The great advantage of truth is that it stands the test of time.

HOW TO REFUTE A RUMOR

In refuting a rumor, never repeat the rumor or refer to it directly. Why? Because if the rumor is repeated during the refutation, some people may hear or read only the rumor, which will thus be reinforced in their minds. Here's an example of how a rumor was refuted simply with the truth— without reference to the rumor itself. According to the rumor, which arose in a plant, an employee had lost a hand in a machine accident. To refute the rumor, the general foreman released a "weekly accident report" stating that there had been no lost-time accidents during the week.

In restraining a rumor, a supervisor should release the truth as quickly as possible; the more a rumor is repeated, the more people tend to believe it. If a rumor is not quashed quickly, people will interpret later events in light of the rumor. In the injury example just given, if employees had heard an ambulance siren outside the plant, they would have been even more convinced that the employee had been seriously injured. In the case of a rumored layoff, an employee noticing two personnel men conferring with his supervisor might see this event as reinforcement of the rumor. Then, too, rumor spreads very quickly throughout an organization—so the quicker it can be refuted, the fewer people will hear it and the less damage will be caused.

THE HORSE'S MOUTH

Communication of the truth behind a rumor is more effective if it comes from a source considered reliable by the receivers. If the rumor concerns future plans, for example, the appropriate person in higher management should be the one to respond. If it concerns an accident, the medical department might respond; if it concerns a technical problem, someone with respected technical knowledge should respond; and if it concerns a supervisor's practices, then that supervisor should respond. In many cases, the public relations department is not the best source for a response, because employees all too often consider it to be simply a mouthpiece for management's viewpoint.

Face-to-face release of the truth is a particularly effective way to deal with rumor. This method has the advantage of speed, particularly in clearing up specific misunderstandings on the part of each individual. It allows each person to be approached in terms of his own personality and outlook. The face-to-face approach can be followed up by a written statement to reinforce the facts.

Management sometimes seeks the help of the union in combating rumor. Although the union does not control the rumor mill, any more than management does, it has some influence. Since rumors can be particularly unfavorable when management and labor are in conflict, any reduction of conflict should reduce rumors. Marked improvement frequently results in a department when the supervisor gains the union steward's cooperation in combating rumor—especially when the steward is also an informal leader.

LISTENING TO FEELINGS

When a supervisor hears a rumor, he or she can profit by listening carefully, even though the rumor may be blatantly untrue. Rumors do provide important information about employee feelings and misunderstandings. They can indicate where gaps exist in employee information. And even when a story is untrue, it does show what is worrying employees. During a strike, for example, a supervisor listened carefully to what the workers said management was going to do even though he knew that their statements were rumors because management had not yet decided what to do. He listened because the rumors gave him insight into worker attitudes toward management and the kinds of issues that concerned them.

Supervisors can sometimes understand rumors better if they search for the message behind them. Some rumors are symbolic expressions of feelings that are not really offered by their communicators as fact or truth. If, for example, a worker starts a rumor that shows how unfair his supervisor is, he reasons along this line: "I think the supervisor is an unjust tyrant, and I'm going to let everybody know by telling them a story to illustrate how unjust he really is. It's okay to make it up, because he *would* do what I'm saying if he had the opportunity." The difficulty is that others along the rumor chain accept the story as fact.

Although you may never quell all the rumors in your department, you can materially reduce the causes of rumor by providing subordinates with a sense of security and with all necessary information. And you can even profit from the rumors that do go around by listening for common employee fears, misconceptions, or gripes. Rumors need not defeat you as long as you rely on the ultimate weapon—the truth.

CHAPTER 14
SOCIAL ISSUES

READING 55

GUIDELINES FOR EMPLOYMENT OF CULTURALLY DISADVANTAGED PERSONS

Sidney A. Fine*

In summary, here are the 12 guidelines for the employment of the culturally disadvantaged:

1 Make a total commitment.
2 Put the reins in high-level hands.
3 Organize a training program for company personnel.
4 Pinpoint entry jobs for the culturally disadvantaged.
5 Interview; don't test.
6 Place the applicant on the job for which he is interviewed.
7 Coach to teach and reinforce adaptive skills.
8 Distinguish between prescribed and discretionary job content.
9 Teach specific content skills on the job; teach functional skills off the job but in the job environment.
10 Keep counseling in the background.
11 Contract out; don't try to do it all yourself.
12 Advance the worker as soon as feasible.

*   *   *

* From Sidney A. Fine, *Guidelines for the Employment of the Culturally Disadvantaged,* Kalamazoo, Michigan: The W. E. Upjohn Institute for Employment Research, 1969, p. 28.

READING 56

BEHAVIOR MODIFICATION: AN ALTERNATIVE TO TRADITIONAL VOCATIONAL REHABILITATION TECHNIQUES

Karen A. Plax
Patricia B. Lacks*

For years, economists and sociologists have indicated that much of the poverty problem is the result of large and increasing numbers of unskilled and poorly trained individuals who are unable to obtain or maintain steady employment. The task of training and finding jobs for the unemployed has traditionally been assigned to the field of vocational rehabilitation. However, indications are that vocational rehabilitation techniques have been largely unsuccessful in elevating these individuals to steady employment.[1] It is true that the unemployed are a very difficult population to work with because of their multiple problems. Perhaps part of the problem, however, is also due to the unsuitability of the traditional vocational rehabilitation techniques which consist largely of verbal counseling on a one-to-one basis (usually with a middle-class, college-educated counselor) combined with immediate supervision of training by industrial staff who are generally untrained in any rehabilitation techniques.

The purpose of this paper is to suggest that behavior modification techniques offer an exciting alternative to traditional vocational rehabilitation counseling and training approaches and seem ideally suited to the field of vocational rehabilitation. Rehabilitation clients generally have low skills, particularly in the verbal area. Often there is a short period of time in which to alter clients' behavior. Also, as mentioned, clients generally re-

---

* From *Human Resource Management,* Spring 1976, pp. 28–31. Copyright 1975 by the University of Michigan. Reprinted with permission.
[1] See, for instance, P. B. Lacks, and K. A. Plax, "The Need for an Honest Look," *Journal of Rehabilitation,* Vol. 38, 1972, pp. 19–22; or R. Walker, "The Accountability Game," *Journal of Rehabilitation,* Vol. 37, 1971, pp. 34–36.

cieve their training from industrial staff who do not have particular skills in training techniques. Behavioral methods can be nonverbal, effective in short periods of time with a wide variety of problems, and are easy to teach to unsophisticated personnel such as workshop supervisors.

Despite the suitability of behavior modification to rehabilitation, there are few reports of its utilization in this field. Vocational uses have generally been to increase work productivity[2] and to eliminate specific maladaptive social behaviors of clients such as improper dress and refusal to follow directions.[3] Behavior therapy has also been combined with task analysis techniques to teach new, more complex skills such as the operation of a drill press[4] and the building of electromechanic relay panels[5] to mentally retarded clients.

The current utilization merely scratches the surface of its practical potential for clients. The following example demonstrates one potential use of behavior modification: how job skill training can be approached from a behavioral perspective.

A TRAINING PROGRAM EXPERIMENT

The setting for this project was the Training Service Center (TSC), a vocational training program operated by the St. Louis Jewish Employment and Vocational Service. TSC offers job skill training in a number of vocations to primarily poverty-level, inner-city residents. Clients in the program have a very low level of functioning and/or emotional-social difficulties which would cause them to be unsuccessful in regular industrial training programs or business schools.

At the time this project was initiated, the center was having particular difficulty placing its trainees from the 26-week clerk-typist program. Since there were many available openings for clerical workers in the local area, it was felt that some changes in training and/or placement efforts were probably needed. Consequently, the agency research staff attempted to evaluate the existing training structure in behavioral terms and make suggestions for improvement of procedures.

---

[2] See L. Brown and E. Pearce, "Increasing the Production Rates of Trainable Retarded Students in a Public School Simulated Workshop," *Education and Training of the Mentally Retarded,* Vol. 5, 1970, pp. 15–22; R. Trybus and P. B. Lacks, "Behavior Modification in Vocational Training," *Exceptional Children,* Vol. 33, 1967, pp. 405–408; J. Zimmerman, T. E. Stuckey, B. J. Garlick, and M. Miller; "Effects of Token Reinforcement on Productivity in Multiple Handicapped Clients in a Sheltered Workshop," Rehabilitation Literature, Vol. 30, 1969, pp. 34–41.

[3] M. Cushing, "When Counseling Fails, Then What?" *Journal of Rehabilitation,* Vol. 35, 1969, pp. 18–20.

[4] J. E. Crosson, "A Technique for Programming Sheltered Workshop Environments for Training Severely Retarded Workers," *American Journal of Mental Deficiency,* Vol. 73, 1969, pp. 814–818.

[5] R. G. Tate and G. S. Baroff, "Training the Mentally Retarded in the Production of a Complex Product; a Demonstration of Work Potential," *Exceptional Children,* Vol. 33, 1967, pp. 405–408.

The first step was to define the behaviors desirable for clients to achieve in order to become employable. An inventory of a variety of local employers was conducted to determine what behaviors are crucial to obtaining and maintaining employment as a clerk-typist. Based on these employer interviews, six specific behaviors desirable for clerk-typists were identified:

1 Speed and accuracy of typing
2 Optimum attendance
3 Punctuality in arriving at work and returning from coffee breaks
4 Acceptable appearance
5 Responsible social relationships
6 Spelling and math skills

The next step was to determine if these job-related behaviors were being sufficiently developed in the existing program. At that time, a typical classroom approach was being used with the primary emphasis on "learning to type." Guidance in other areas such as social relationships was offered mainly through sporadic counseling efforts. Despite the very low educational skills of the trainees, spelling and vocabulary drills were held only occasionally when time permitted. Attendance at training sessions was poor and tardiness after coffee breaks was a continual problem. The appearance of trainees was frequently inappropriate for a job (*i.e.,* hot pants, see-through blouses, informal slacks). It appeared that certain programmatic changes were necessary to maximize the attainment of all the work-related behaviors considered essential by the employers interviewed.

SYSTEMATIC REINFORCEMENT

In cooperation with the program director and the typing instructor, the research staff then designed an experimental training program structured so that *systematic* reinforcement would be given to each of the six desired work behaviors. Reinforcers were chosen with great care so that they would be truly *rewarding* for clients and would duplicate as much as possible the rewards of the natural environment, *i.e.,* a real office and employer.

Some examples of the types of reinforcement which were used include the following.

1 To insure increased speed and accuracy of typing, immediate feedback of the average words per minute on daily timings was given to trainees. In addition, each day that a trainee increased her typing speed, she was given a word of praise. Trainees who did not increase their speed received no comment. Weekly progress of typing speed was recorded on a large chart in front of the classroom.

2 Trainees receive a certain amount of maintenance money each week while they are in the program to pay for transportation and babysitting costs. To increase attendance, the reinforcement program provided that trainees were to receive this money only for the days they attended class.

3 Trainees who came to class on time received a fifteen minute coffee break as their reward. For returning from coffee break on time, trainees accumulated points exchangeable for special field trips.

4 Detailed appearance standards were developed along six different dimensions: appropriate type of dress, appropriate length of dress, clothes neat and clean, hair neat, self clean, and shoes acceptable. Daily points were given for acceptable appearance on each of these dimensions and these points were exchangeable for bi-weekly "events." The events included a visit by a hair dresser who cut and styled several of the trainees' hair, a session with a makeup specialist, and viewing of various films on grooming, care of clothes, etc.

5 Trainees were awarded points for acceptable behavior on four dimensions of social relationships: appropriateness of talking, cooperation with other trainees, cooperation with supervisors, and maturity of behavior. Points earned were exchangeable for entry into interpersonal group sessions with the staff counselors.

6 To increase arithmetic and spelling skills, daily practice sessions were instituted. Trainees who achieved proficiency in these areas received a special wallet certificate of commendation which could be shown to prospective employers.

In addition to the specific rewards given for achieving each of the six behaviors, the actual structure of the training program was organized to foster the desired behaviors. The training was divided into four levels with each section located in separate but adjoining rooms. Each level of training offered special enrichment advantages such as films and lectures related to office practice, learning of other office machines, etc. The final level of training was a simulated office in which role playing techniques were combined with actual work assignments, pressures, and demands in order to expose the trainees to a realistic work experience before placing them on a job.

Advancement to these higher levels of training with the concommitant enrichment advantages was made contingent on attainment of specified levels of typing speed and accuracy as well as maintenance of good attendance, appearance, punctuality and social relationships. Table 1 outlines the program and the requirements for entering each level of training.

The program was also altered to include an intensive job-seeking skills preparation given in the last month of training. This consisted of a series of discussions, films, and activities to prepare trainees for job interviews, and to teach them to find and get a job. Some topics were a profile of skills and

Table 1   Program Outline

ROOM 1—BEGINNING TYPING
  What is offered:
  1. Regular classroom approach to typing.
  2. Daily vocabulary, spelling and arithmetic sessions. (20 minutes)

ROOM 2—INTERMEDIATE TYPING
  Requirements to enter:
  1. 20 words per minute typing speed, adjusted for accuracy.
  2. Total points accumulated through attendance, punctuality, dress, and social behavior is at least 75 points for two weeks in a row.
  What is offered:
  1. Regular classroom approach to typing.
  2. Daily vocabulary, spelling and arithmetic sessions.
  3. Films on office practices.
  4. Introduction to adding machine and PBX.
  5. Group discussions of interpersonal office relationships.

ROOM 3—ADVANCED TYPING
  Requirements to enter:
  1. 35 words per minute typing speed, adjusted for accuracy.
  2. Two weeks in which total points accumulated is at least 110 points.

  What is offered:
  1. Regular classroom typing—advanced level work and electric typewriter.
  2. Films on basic job seeking skills.
  3. Use of mimeograph and dictaphone.
  4. Group discussions of efficient secretarial practices.

ROOM 4—SIMULATED OFFICE
  Requirements to enter:
  1. 50 wpm typing speed, adjusted for accuracy.
  2. Two weeks in which total of points accumulated is at least 110 points.
  What is offered:
  1. Individual desk and office supplies.
  2. Real work and simulated work in office atmosphere.
  3. Use of desk manual, dictionary, etc.
  4. Relative lack of supervision.
  5. Beginning work on job placement.
  6. Variations in supervisory pressure.
  7. Simulated problem situations.
  8. Answering phone, taking messages, etc.
  9. Use of mail/time stamp.
  10. Occasional opportunity to act as supervisor in office, etc.
  11. Freedom to talk informally.

interests, compilation of a personal data sheet, preparation of a resume, factors to consider in selecting a job, where to look for work, how to set-up an appointment and follow-up on a want ad, how to fill out an application, etc. Role-playing and modeling were primary techniques for these sessions. Finally, the program was also changed so that the trainees had individual bi-weekly sessions with their counselor rather than the crisis-oriented counseling which had formerly been used.

RESULTS

This behavioral approach to the training of typists proved to have many benefits. Under the reward system there was a marked improvement in clients' appearance. Most trainees dressed neatly and attractively throughout the course. The daily feedback on their appearance helped them to determine which of their outfits were apropriate for office-wear and which would not be suitable. In fact, there was such a remarkable difference in the appearance of the typing trainees under the behavior modification system that many other instructors in the center commented on the change.

Punctuality also was greatly improved over former groups. Clients nearly always arrived on time for class and returned promptly from coffee breaks. It was interesting to note that all of the former excuses given for tardiness (e.g., the line in the cafeteria was too long) were no longer resorted to. In addition, most members of the group exhibited very responsible social relationships throughout the training session.

Furthermore, educational achievement was high for this group. A comparison of a general aptitude test given during the first and repeated in the last week of training shows that the average number of errors went from 12 at entry to 1.5 at the end of training. Typing speed and accuracy were also developed under the system. Interestingly enough, although these trainees spent approximately one half the time in actual typing practice (due to their time out for films, lectures, field trips, discussions, etc.) their speed was at a level equal to or higher than graduates of the former typing training method.

The one area where improvement was not consistently attained was that of attendance. The group average of attendance did not reach an acceptable level for employment although several trainees did not miss one day during the entire six month session. One explanation for this difficulty may be that receiving the maintenance money was not a reward for attendance since it only paid for the *expenses* of attendance (*i.e.*, transportation and babysitter). Some other reward for attendance will have to be selected for future clients. Also, inner city clients have so many realistic problems (transportation, babysitting, health, etc.) that no reward may be sufficient to overcome these difficulties. Increased attendance may depend upon helping clients to solve their problems in living rather than rewarding their attendance.

OTHER POTENTIAL USES

This project demonstrated the usefulness of behavioral techniques in a clerk-typist skill training program. A similar approach could also be applied to many other rehabilitation situations. Some ideas for possible new and creative uses might include:

1   Improvement of other job skill training programs, *e.g.*, to increase the speed, accuracy, and productivity of power sewing trainees.

2   Aiding obese clients to lose weight.

3   Using assertion training to alter low self-concepts of clients. This might assist them to acquire better skills for coping with job interviews and criticism from job supervisors.

4   Teaching work-related skills such as how to use public transportation, how to relate to supervisors, etc.

Not only clients can benefit from behavioral techniques. Rehabilitation counseling supervisors might well consider using direct and immediate rewards and contingencies to improve the effectiveness of their professional staff. Counselors might receive more vacation time for each client placement which lasts for more than six months. Such a procedure might help foster a philosophy of more long-range placement. A chronic problem, late reports from counselors, might be alleviated by making attendance at conventions or workshops contingent upon speedy report writing.

In short, behavior modification offers potential for the field of rehabilitation.

READING 57

WHAT PROGRESS WOMEN AT CBS?

Judith Hennessee*

Something is clearly happening with CBS women. But in a multi-industried company with over 7,000 employees in New York alone, and some 22,000 more worldwide, ascertaining just what that something is seems to depend a great deal on just who you're talking to. Through promotions, raises or changes in their (male) bosses' attitudes, several hundred of CBS's working women seem to have already benefited directly from management's 1973 commitment to work with the company's women to find, in President Arthur Taylor's words, "solutions to the flood of problems . . . identified by the women's movement." But many more thousands of CBS women (and men) are still watchfully waiting to see if the company's 18-month-old push to change policies and attitudes toward women will, in any direct way, affect them.

This article will explore the question "What Progress Women at CBS?" And since progress is a kind of evolution, this article supplies no final answers, only signposts and directions. There are pieces of answers and a variety of perspectives—nearly 50 of which were gleaned from CBS employees high and low (and mostly in New York) to form the outlines of this status report—a report on the attempt to change attitudes, on the growing number of new policies, and on some of the criticisms that are a measure of the distance yet to go.

* This article by Judith Hennessee first appeared in *Columbine,* the CBS Inc., publication for employees, vol. 3, no. 6, February, 1975, and was adapted by *Personnel,* July–August 1975, pp. 33–44, published by AMACOM, a Division of American Management Associations. Reprinted with permission of CBS Inc., and AMACOM.

Only the most cynical would deny that a good-faith effort to revise the role of women at CBS has been in the works since a New York Women's Group first presented CBS President Arthur Taylor with a list of grievances in July of 1973. While the women of NBC and *The New York Times* have seen their attempts at a dialogue with management break down and move toward the courtroom, the CBS Women's Advisory Council (N.Y.) has, for the past 18 months, been meeting at least monthly with key vice-presidents, hammering out changes in corporate policies affecting women. The subsequent surge of corporate memos has brought some bread-and-butter results: increased promotions of women (in the third quarter of 1974, 36.2 percent of all exempt promotions were women); a general revamping of women's salaries upwards; and a new maternity and paternity benefits program designed to break the either/or deadlock of parenthood versus career that women have traditionally faced.

Management also appointed four directors of women's programs to devote full time to counseling women on career choices, to help women work out problems with supervisors, and to see that management is kept aware of the manner in which equal employment laws applying to women are being observed. Aided by a tight, no-hiring economy, personnel policies have shifted (via job posting) to an emphasis on internal promotions—notably those of women. Furthermore, some 60-plus job training programs have been developed to help women build the skills and know-how that can refute that last-ditch Catch-22 of discrimination: "Sure. We'll hire anyone who's qualified. But who's qualified?

As importantly, the CBS women's representatives have said—and top management has agreed—that long-term change for women can't really take place without substantial changes in the basic intangible of attitudes—those that men hold toward women and that women hold about themselves. This agreement has led to companywide "awareness sessions" that have, at the very least, begun to raise the corporate consciousness: "It's not fashionable around here any more to put women down," says Kathryn Pelgrift, formerly assistant to the president (Arthur Taylor) and now a newly appointed vice-president, corporate planning, in her own right. "Two years ago men did not hesitate to express the prejudices they were overtly acting out. Since then, the people I come in contact with have become very conscious of what they are saying. I've had no occasion in the past year when my blood pressure shot up."

Everyone's blood pressure is different, of course, but there are other signs that what were once just normal, workaday comments and practices are now being understood as demeaning to women. Symbolic of this new recognition is the revision of the *CBS Secretarial Manual,* subtitled "a good right arm," which has been retitled simply *CBS Office Practices Guide.* "A good right arm" was written for an underling, and one not considered very intelligent at that. "You are, when all is said and done, one of the most prominent links in the whole CBS chain of communications," the old manual began flatteringly, and then proceeded to discuss the responsibilities of this prominent link, which included getting coffee (six lines) and "playing the gracious hostess" (eight lines). The new *Office Practices Guide* is addressed to a professional person. Revised by women, it now sticks strictly to business—how the messenger service works, how to set up a letter, and how to fill out an expense account.

CHANGING DEEP-SET ATTITUDES

No one pretends that unraveling an old mind set is going to be an easy task. But it is a basic and essential one, and from the beginning of the women's program, the changing of attitudes between the sexes on the job has been tackled in a steady and programmatic way. Two management consulting firms, Boyle/Kirkman Associates and Hennig/Jardim Associates, Inc. have been conducting seminars on attitudes, the reasons underlying them, and how they affect careers.

To date [February, 1975], some 1,500 women and approximately 660 men have attended at least one of the sessions, which have been spread out geographically to reach CBS employees not only in New York, but also in Los Angeles, Washington, D.C., Boston, Philadelphia, San Francisco, Chicago and St. Louis. A few uncovered places, Terre Haute among them, are scheduled for awareness in 1975. All four CBS group presidents have attended seminars, as have most of their key division heads—invariably men. The seminars also reach down into middle management. A typical Hennig/Jardim session held in New York for men (most of the seminars are sex segregated) included two vice-presidents from Columbia House, a visiting vice-president from Terre Haute, and about 17 assorted managers and directors from various CBS Groups.

In the Hennig/Jardim seminars, one of the differences between men and women that usually surfaces is in their perception of what is important in landing a high-level job. Interestingly enough, while both men and women rank competence as most important, the men also note the need for style and the critical role of relationships with superiors; women tend to ignore these other items entirely.

Boyle/Kirkman uses a role-playing game in the men's sessions to bring out biases that most men don't even know they hold. Sharon Kirkman plays the part of an applicant for a high position who is being interviewed by the men. Time and again, the same questions come up: "How does your husband feel?" "What will you do about your children?" These questions have nothing to do with the job itself and indicate a common inability to see women foremost in terms of their work. If told they held this kind of bias, most men would deny it, and often quite genuinely. But, Kirkman notes, "Once they verbalize it, they know they've got it."

The consensus of most men who have attended the seminars is that they are a psychological eye-opener. Says one New York manager: "I went in thinking I had no prejudices and couldn't understand what all these women in the company were hollering about. Now I do." . . . There are also some mixed reviews. Typical is that of Ralph Colin, vice-president, A & R, at Columbia House: "I can't say that I agree with everything . . . But it did open my eyes to the attitudes women have toward business [that it's a tough and maybe not quite ethical human endeavor] and toward their jobs."

The seminars stress that the attitudes most women have toward their jobs grow out of the cultural training and conditions we've all been subjected to: Traditionally, women have waited to be chosen and men have done the choosing. Part of the dynamic holding women back is that they have been raised *not* to take the initiative. On the job this means the boss has to take a new approach: Supervisors whose awareness level has been raised and who want to help women will work to change the dynamic by providing extra push, inside information, and support.

For men, personally, perhaps the most significant result of the seminars is the way some begin to relate their experience to the outside world, to make new connections, to question where society and the family are headed. "A lot of men raise the point that the seminar material should be taught in the public schools," says Margaret Hennig. They tend to be men who have daughters, like Frank Datello, vice-president and controller, finance, who has a bright nine-year-old. "I saw her emulating the traditional roles," he said, "and I know she has the talent to be a doctor or a professor. That gave me some insight. What you're suddenly struck with is the realization that all people have talents and abilities they should be allowed to maximize."

Based on the flurry of activity she sees after a women's seminar, Nancy Wendt, who has been director of women's programs for CBS Corporate and Columbia Records, estimates that 20 to 25 percent of the women who attend are galvanized into making a decision about their careers. The decision may be negative or positive, because in the seminars (which, for women, include the elements of career planning) some women realize for the first time the full implications of a corporate career and the kind of competitive ladder-climbing scramble it can be. Given this insight, a few decide it is simply not their style. Following a seminar, one California woman announced, "This has changed my whole life. I'm leaving the company."

But for those who aren't put off by a clearer understanding of the art of pyramid scaling, the prime lesson that comes out of the career sessions is that God helps those who help themselves. Nancy Wendt reports that about 200 women who once waited to be chosen have come to her for career counseling in the past year and a half. Many of them are at lower grade levels—nonexempt or exempt level 4 and under—but, "In five years a significant number will make it," Wendt predicts. "Today's stars—the women who have high positions—will provide the role models for them."

NEW POLICIES WITH CLOUT

If changing deep-set attitudes is essential to any long-term progress, in the short run, only widespread policy changes carry enough clout to affect quickly the working lives of large numbers of women. Such policy changes are gradually being worked out in meetings every three to four weeks between WAC (the CBS Women's Advisory Council) and a corporate management team that includes Sheldon Wool, vice-president, development [now vice-president, administration and chief financial officer, CBS/Records Group], Drew Brinckerhoff, vice-president, personnel, and Kathryn Pelgrift, vice-president, corporate planning. The council, women's representatives elected to serve for a year, consists of six delegates and four alternates chosen from four grass-roots women's groups at CBS (NY)—the Black Rock Steering Committee; the CPG (CBS Publishing) Steering Committee; and the Broadcast Center 5:00 and 7:00 Women's Groups. These women's groups usually meet weekly, and out of the larger women's group meetings (as well as through more private individual contacts and conversations), the WAC members pick up on complaints. Patterns emerge that generally can be traced back to a failure or lack of company policy, and WAC takes up policy change in its meetings with management. Describing the meetings, one WAC member says, "We're friendly adversaries."

The meetings are not always smooth and ceremonial, but there is enough mutual sense of shared stakes for women and management to weather some eyeball-to-eyeball confrontations. Occasionally, strongly opposing views on what ought to happen have, in fact, led to some yelling out of frustration on both sides—most recently over a personnel policy of asking supervisors if women could be released for a preliminary job-hunting interview elsewhere in the company. Women employees felt they were being treated like children, and that the policy resulted in lost opportunities as well as deteriorated personal relations.

Judy Hole, associate archivist and a former council member from the Broadcast Center, felt particularly strongly that it should be up to the employee to do the notifying when ready. Sheldon Wool, on the other hand, felt that many supervisors already took too little interest in the the career development of women and that this would further diminish the supervisor's involvement. In the ensuing moments of noncommunication, both tempers and voices began to rise. And management reconsidered. There is a new policy now. Personnel is developing procedures in which an employee's supervisor is not to be notified during the first delicate stage of a job search.

One of the things that women have wanted and needed ever since they began working anywhere is the kind of maternity benefits that have come out of the policy meetings. Until last summer, as in most companies, pregnancy and related situations (including abortions and miscarriages) were not covered at CBS as paid medical sick leave. Now they are. In addition, the maternity leave-of-absence has been extended from four to six months and no longer needs to be taken immediately after the birth of the child, and six month *paternity* leaves are now available for fathers as well.

REDEFINING JOBS AND SALARIES

When it comes to the straight-line questions of on-the-job discrimination and how to right past wrongs, the company is now also committed to a sweeping reorchestration of salaries and job definitions, to opening up opportunities, to redesigning dead-end jobs, and to running a variety of training programs. Frank Welzer, director, compensation/benefits/personnel systems, is in charge of implementing many of these changes, which, he says, were under way even before the women's program began. "CBS has always been motivated by a sense of fair play," says Welzer, "but there's no question that WAC and the development of the women's program have made us more sensitive to some particulars that we weren't so sensitive to before."

To begin with the most important thing—money. Salaries in nonexempt jobs, in which women predominate, have traditionally run higher for women than men. The reverse is true in exempt jobs, with women's salaries running roughly 4 percent behind men's in exempt levels 1 to 6, where the bulk of exempt jobs are. The gap widens above level 7. In most cases, management points out, the difference is because the men have been on the job longer and have had more merit raises than the women (for whom such jobs have not been as readily open until recently). In other cases, the women were in fact hired at lower salaries to begin with, and one way of redressing the balance has been through corrective raises.

Welzer's group also has other ways of making needed adjustments. To correct one situation a women was promoted from a level 9 to a level 11, and got an extra $6,500 in base salary over a six-month period; in another, a level 1 accountant went to a level 3 and received $3,200 over five months.

Since the new focus on women's problems, a good many managers have also looked over their left shoulder to discover women in their departments who had been bypassed and sidetracked into a quiet little corner without hope of promotion. This has led to some quick and long overdue changes in duties and job grade levels—with appropriate salary raises.

Other redesigned jobs have resulted in the promotion of women from nonexempt to exempt positions, opening up a career path for those who want to advance.

TRAINING FOR CHANGE

Since WAC and management first began discussing not just if, but how women could move up in the company, the development of a set of training arrangements has been in the works to help women acquire some of the skills they will need when and if a job opening comes along. All told, in various CBS divisions, 61 training positions have been created.

Some of the traineeships are on-the-job, like one full-time post in sales development, which carries with it the assignment to provide the department with a detailed analysis of all phases of the television medium. Others offered have been internships, usually for eight to 26 weeks.

The most innovative and interesting of the training programs is "attachment," a concept borrowed from the BBC, in which a person is "attached" to a department for one day a week or month and becomes a sort of observation post, watching, doing, and learning as much as possible about the way the operation comes together.

The training programs are available, not only to women, but to minority group members as well, and as they expand, the intent is that they will also open up to men. Since the guilds of the Middle Ages, apprenticeships have been perhaps the best way for skills to pass along from one group to another—usually the next generation. But in the American corporate-management structure, they haven't for the most part existed in a widespread, formal way. The new training programs, which support the growth of skills and open the way for mobility, begin to fill this void. They are loosening the rigidity of the corporate structure, making it more responsive to the needs of people. It is this kind of change—change that is making CBS management think about people and jobs in very different ways—that Drew Brinckerhoff, vice-president of personnel, sees as a key outgrowth of the CBS women's movement: "It's causing us to make changes that ought to have existed for people all along—whether they're men or women, black or white."

MANY CHANGES; MANY SHORTCOMINGS

All told, the number of changes for women begun at CBS is fairly impressive, especially when one considers the situations in other corporations. But just ticking off a lengthy list of beginning efforts risks, in the words of one women at Holt, "giving a rosier picture than really feels accurate to most CBS women." Large numbers of women are still skeptical, partly because the pace of change is necessarily uneven in a company that embraces industries of differing sizes and traditions.

It's beyond the scope and space of this article to attempt a thorough rundown of the varied situations women find themselves in, but a few impressionistic examples are possible.

Divisions like News and Radio, which deal with the reporting of women's issues in the outside world, have tended to be fairly responsive to women in their own shops . . . Sylvia Chase, Lesley Stahl, and Connie Chung have become familiar faces [on screen] . . . However, backstage there is something of a mobility problem. The logical next step up for secretaries would be into production, a guild area—which involves a whole new set of problems yet to be worked out between the company and the unions.

Away from the competitive center of the networks, life for women gets easier—like at KMOX-TV, St. Louis, where one of the four news producers is a woman, and four of the station's other ten producers are also women. In Radio, at KMOX-AM, the station manager is a women, Virginia Dawes, and so are the sales managers for both AM and FM.

In Records, women face a far tougher situation. They feel they are up against what one woman described as the "traditional macho and 'groupie' mentality of the business," as well as the fact that the largest number of jobs are in sales and promotions to radio stations—"tough, hard-sell areas where there's always been a locker-room outlook." . . . "Great inattention is being paid," says Roselind Blanch, director, merchandising, administration and planning. "With a few exceptions, the men don't even want to talk about it."

In the publishing industry, salaries have traditionally been lower than those in many other glamour industries, and women have been at the bottom of that scale. Vassar Ph.D.s have been willing to work as secretaries for "psychic wages," for the prestige that comes from being associated with a life of the mind. Now they have a longer way to go than most to gain equal footing . . . [and] in general, there's a feeling among publishing women that while top management may be "very committed, it hasn't seeped down to the lower levels."

Throughout the company, a large number of women are also skeptical about how long it will take to work women into the power system—into high-level, decision-making spots. They point to the fact that, corporatewide, there are only three women who are vice-presidents; only two women are at level 16. Some women feel that there already are highly qualified women who could be vice-presidents tomorrow and who have been passed over for no good reasons. Others express concern that it will be a long time before a significant number of women even come on line to be considered for such appointments—before they are taken into that informal, real world of "connections" sometimes known as "the Rabbi System."

The Rabbi System (also called the Godfather System) is having someone who will adopt you and show you the ropes, take you around to budget and other decision-making meetings, and push your cause when there's a promotion to be had. It has effectively kept women out of positions of power and shunted them into staff rather than line management.

PERSUASION VS. TIMETABLE GOALS

These shortcomings of the women's program—the slow pace and unevenness of change, the dearth of women in high places—have led the strongest critics to say that an affirmative action program with goals and timetables would be a swifter, clearer course of action than trying, in Arthur Taylor's words, "to persuade others of the correctness of our beliefs," and thus prompt action.

Management has reasoned from the beginning, however, against these hard-line measures, believing that the company will be a better place without them. "As soon as targets are written on the wall," says Sheldon Wool, "you change the dynamics of what you're doing. Targets won't allow us to deal with the issue of training. When you have timetables, which are implicit in setting targets, speed becomes the important thing. The emphasis switches to quick recruiting and away from training the women you already have—away from those women who have paid their dues. And when a company has to talk numerical goals, literal compliance becomes the issue."

Presumably, one point of shying away from goals and timetables is to keep lines of communication open with management men, like one vice-president on the defensive who says, "When anyone shows initiative and ability, we encourage them. But I'm not going to have someone put a gun to my head." And there is probably something to be said for not pushing company men into a backlash. But at the same time, the lack of publicly announced numerical goals and timetables makes top management's task of proving that it is doing all it ought to do just that much more difficult. There are no easy numbers to point to, to use to quell critics with a quick "We've done our job."

The route of persuasion means just that—coming convincingly close enough (through policies, promotions, attitudinal seminars, whatever) to individual women and men way down the line in the company to affect them. Widespread persuasion will certainly take a few years, and, meantime, despite all it *is* doing, management is having to live with the fact that for every secretary or receptionist at the Broadcast Center who says "training programs are a major accomplishment," another is speaking for four when she says that the women's program has had "no impact" and "no effect on me." Many others add that it has had "no effect on anyone I know."

For these and many other women, the problem is all those layers of middle management through which changed policy must pass before it can reach and have an impact on them. Says one: "If it doesn't filter down to my boss, then it doesn't matter how good Arthur Taylor's intentions are." And even when a boss is sympathetic, *his boss* may not be. It's not comfortable to be in that position, one middle manager reports, not surprisingly. Nor is it easy for male managers on down the line to deal with the resentments of young men 25 to 35 who are vying with women for many of the same beginning-to-get-ahead jobs. The young men are liable to be heard saying, as one did, "If you're a man at CBS, forget it." With the whole mix of pressures that come into play, trying to support women, in the words of one sympathetic News producer, "can get pretty lonely."

The view from the 35th floor of CBS headquarters is more philosophical. "It takes time," says Sheldon Wool, "and it's a slow, hard change. I am constantly sobered by the thought of how far we still have to go. Many supervisors are slow to recognize that changing the role of women is company policy and that it is their responsibility to respond to it. They are also slow to recognize that this is a fundamental change that is taking place in society, and it isn't going to go away."

"Time," says Kathryn Pelgrift, "is what will do it. Attitudes instilled from birth are changing here, but they won't change overnight. It will take time not only for men in the middle to change—from division presidents on down to line supervisors—but also for women to gain the confidence to assert themselves and take advantage of newly opened opportunities."

READING 58

INSIGHT: A MANAGEMENT PROGRAM OF HELP FOR TROUBLED PEOPLE

James E. Petersen*

On July 1, 1970, the Utah Copper Division of Kennecott Copper Corporation launched a program of help for troubled employees and their dependents and named it INSIGHT. The concept is simple—it is to provide professional counseling to 8,000 Kennecott employees and their 24,000 dependents who have problems and to assist them in getting the help they need from Salt Lake County's 220 community service organizations. Program utilization is voluntary, confidential, available 7 days a week, 24 hours a day, and obtained by dialing I-N-S-I-G-H-T (467-4448) on the telephone.

OVERVIEW

Results have far exceeded expectations. Over a 20-month period, 2,407 persons have solicited help; 1,053 employees and 1,180 dependents had

*From *Proceedings of the 1972 Annual Spring Meeting,* Industrial Relations Research Association, Madison, Wis., 1972, pp. 492–495. Copyright 1972. Reprinted with permission.

been placed in programs designed to help. The volume has not yet slackened.

The impact of INSIGHT has extended beyond Kennecott. The National Institute on Alcohol Abuse and Alcoholism, in carrying out its mandate under the Hughes Act, has adopted INSIGHT's "troubled people" concept. We are informed civil service will use this approach. It is currently being effected for 120,000 civil service employees in the San Francisco Bay area and for the civil service employees in the State of Hawaii. The federal organization being established to expend $365,000,000 annually for drug addiction rehabilitation is interested in this concept—particularly as it relates to penetration and utilization of rehabilitative community facilities. The city of Phoenix, Arizona, is in the process of establishing an INSIGHT program. Pacific Telephone & Telegraph, San Francisco, has started an INSIGHT program for its 21,000 employees. Hundreds of requests for information from both the private and public sectors have been received and answered.

INSIGHT has attracted a great deal of publicity. It has been reported in the *New York Times, Business Week,* the *Time-Life* series of *Fortune Magazine,* the BNA and various other management services publications.

Experience to date convinces us that the INSIGHT program represents significant breakthroughs in mental health and employee relations. We are further convinced that the return on investment exceeds by many times the cost of the program.

Up to this point, I have tried to give you an overview of the program, its concept, its results and its overall impact. Why and how this program came about will, I believe, be of interest to you.

SCOPE OF PROBLEM

The National Council on Alcoholism estimates that in a heavy-duty, high male population industry that 5 to 10 per cent of the work force is alcoholic. The Utah Copper Division is part of such an industry. The national problem alcoholism poses is demonstrated by the following:

1 Alcoholism ranks first in the nation as a major health problem.

2 Nine million Americans are chronic alcoholics.

3 Because of problem drinking 35,000 were killed and two million injured on our highways in 1969.

4 The cost to industry approximates $7 billion a year.

5 Alcoholism is involved in 50 per cent of all arrests.

6 Alcoholism accounts for 40 per cent of all admissions to state mental hospitals.

7 Only 3 per cent of the alcoholics are skid row; 97 per cent are family-centered.

8 50 per cent of alcoholics attended or graduated from college.

9 45 per cent of alcoholics are professional or managerial people.

10 75 per cent are men.

11 In Utah, alcoholism has increased 144 per cent since 1965.

In the Utah Copper Division, using a 37-man alcoholic sample, over a 12-month period, we learned their absenteeism exceeded the average more than 5 to 1; sickness and accident costs were more than 5 to 1; HMS[1] costs were more than 3 to 1. We also learned that the absence pattern of many alcoholics does not fit the classical chronic absentee pattern, thereby allowing many alcoholics to escape detection under the division's absentee control program.

CREATION AND BASIS OF INSIGHT

We then naively set out to steal or copy an effective program from one or more organizations with experience. A comprehensive study of industry programs quickly revealed limited penetration—despite missionary zeal and dedicated effort on the part of program administrators.

We learned that industrial alcoholic rehabilitation programs are strikingly similar. The standard program has the following common primary elements:

1 A statement of policy that in effect says "drinking becomes the concern of the company only where it adversely affects job performance."

2 The front-line foreman is the key element. He is the one who initiates the action to talk to the employee about his deteriorating performance and refers him to a company-designated doctor for examination and recommendations.

3 Utilization of staff personnel (almost always a sober alcoholic) to follow up on rehabilitative efforts.

4 Threat of job loss for failure to achieve expected progress.

5 A dual standard, in that most programs are limited to blue collar or lower echelon employees.

Analysis of these five elements made obvious why penetration is severely limited. The target or goal is usually limited to the blue collar chronic alcoholic, a person approaching the end of the alcoholic continuum. Utilization of the front-line foreman for discovery and initiation of action runs counter to human nature and "on-the-job" social and peer cultures. In short, the policy determining the target coupled with the procedure for discovery *guarantees* the progress of the illness to the chronic stage. This makes rehabilitation, recovery of health, reconciliation of marital and familial schisms, and maintenance of job very difficult.

My purpose here is not to downgrade the time, money and effort of

---

[1] *Editor's note:* "HMS" is an abbreviation for "hospital-medical-surgical."

other companies or to belittle the successes achieved in the rehabilitation of alcoholics. I do, however, want to point out what I am convinced are severe shortcomings in the standard industrial alcoholic rehabilitation program.

Concluding that alcoholism is almost always a manifestation of other problems, and that employees have many other kinds of problems, we made the decision upon which our program rests. *All the problems of employees and their dependents are cause for concern and reason for help.*

Again the concept is simple. It is to make readily available, through company furnished professional counseling, on a confidential basis, the services of community organizations and other professional people to Kennecott employees and their dependents.

Successful implementation is based on the following prerequisites which, we believe, are structurally interdependent:

1 The right person in the job.
2 Voluntary and confidential.
3 Management, union, and community organization support.
4 A nonidentifying program name.
5 Service, 7 days a week, 24 hours a day.
6 A willingness to meet wherever the employee or dependent will be comfortable.
7 Every person seeking help must, in fact, be helped.

Over a 20-month period, for employees, the single greatest problem is alcohol abuse (269 cases), followed by familial, legal, marital, financial and drug abuse (74 cases).

For dependents, familial problems rank first, followed by marital, legal, financial, drug (86 cases) and alcohol (68 cases).

Penetration of the employee alcoholic problem alone is vastly superior to any other program of which we are aware.

CONCLUSION

To date, we have conducted two measurements—one relating to alcoholics and one relating to absenteeism. Twelve of the original 37-man alcoholic sample enrolled in the program for an average 12 and one-half months. Their absences decreased 50 per cent. Their sickness and accident costs decreased from $70.67 to $25.33 per month. Their HMS costs decreased from $109.04 to $59.91 per month. The performance of the balance of the sample, for the same period, worsened in all categories. The second measurement consisted of a sample of 87 chronically absent employees referred to INSIGHT through our absentee control system. 67 improved their attendance. Overall improvement was 44 per cent.

Definitions and methods of measurement have not as yet been developed for either alcoholic or drug abuse rehabilitation, nor for the other problems we deal with. Hopefully, the Department of Health, Education and Welfare, through its appropriate subsidiary institutes, will correct this situation.

We know our program has certain weaknesses, both in organization and administration, nor is our penetration and resolution of the various problem areas as good as we would like. However, we are convinced that our policy of concern and our program of help are correct and of mutual benefit.

The INSIGHT concept has applicability in any area where community organizations exist. We are convinced it can be effectively promulgated by any large organization or a consortium of smaller ones. The cost need not exceed 50 to 75 cents per month per employee. So long as the program embodies the concepts of voluntarism, confidentiality, qualified administrators and is service oriented, it should succeed and pay handsome dividends to all who participate.

Try it—you'll like it.

CHAPTER 15
INTERNATIONAL ORGANIZATIONAL BEHAVIOR

READING 59

THE MULTINATIONAL CORPORATION: MANAGEMENT MYTHS

David Sirota*

In the management of multinational corporations, it is popularly assumed that there are fundamental differences between them and purely national firms, but the success experienced by so many firms in their multinational operations has inhibited the quest for systematic, empirical validation of these assumptions. Rather, they constitute a mythology. Indisputably, there are some differences between the methods of managing a company that operates within a single nation and one that cuts across national boundaries—such as the need to take into account national variations in trade regulations, labor laws, and so forth—but many of the proclaimed contrasts between the two kinds of organizations are either nonexistent or inconsequential. Specifically, I question the severity of the "human" problems supposedly inherent in firms whose membership is multinational and suggest that these problems differ little in kind and intensity from those commonly experienced by single-nation firms.

It must be conceded at the outset that much of my evidence comes from research done in a single company—Company X—which is a large, multinational electronics firm with an advanced and rapidly changing technology. While there is some supporting evidence from studies in other companies, the use of one firm as a major source of data does make it difficult to generalize, but we have to start somewhere, and it is hoped that these findings can be treated as hypotheses for research in other organizations.

WHAT DO PEOPLE WANT FROM THEIR JOBS?

First, let's consider motivation, which, among multinational companies' "human" problems, probably comes in for more discussion than any other. There is a widespread belief that cultures differ greatly in the kinds of goals they inculcate in their members; thus, Americans are supposed to be materialistic, Germans authoritarian, Frenchmen anti-authoritarian, and Japanese security-minded. These conceptions of nationalities exert a subtle, but very telling, influence on management practices. For example, if it is assumed that nationals of a particular country have a *mañana* attitude, the

*Reprinted by permission of the publisher from *Personnel,* January–February, 1972, pp. 34–41. © 1971 by the American Management Association, Inc.

tendency is to impose rather rigorous measurements and controls on operations in that country.

There is no precise way to measure motivation. In Company X, we attempted to do it in a straightforward way, simply asking people what they wanted from their jobs and how important they considered factors such as high earnings, challenging work, advancement opportunities, fringe benefits, and so on, through a questionnaire administered to employees in 43 countries.

The results of this study have been published previously ("Understanding Your Overseas Work Force," *Harvard Business Review,* January–February 1971), so they will not be described here in detail, but basically, it was found that although there were some national and cultural differences in employee goals, there was a surprising amount of similarity around the world. By and large, the employees in all countries rated as most important to them those goals concerned with individual achievement: challenging work, high earnings, training opportunities, and advancement opportunities. The lowest-rated objectives dealt with matters such as fringe benefits, physical working conditions, and company prestige.

Certain substantial differences did, however, appear when the data were analyzed by occupation. For example, the importance of security varied significantly by employee skill level: The lower the skill level, the more importance employees gave to this goal. Job autonomy showed a similar pattern: The lower the skill level, the less the employees responded that this objective was important to them. It may therefore be that occupation and its correlates, such as position in labor market and educational level, are of greater significance in determining motivational patterns than are national or cultural variables.

These findings regarding goals are corroborated by data collected in studies in other companies. For example, Haire, Ghiselli, and Porter, in their *Managerial Thinking: An International Study,* found that goal preferences were strikingly similar in companies in 14 countries. It is to be hoped that this kind of evidence, as it is accumulated and publicized, will point management in a direction away from practices that reflect conventional, stereotyped thinking about national groupings in the workforce.

INTRA-ORGANIZATIONAL LATERAL CONFLICTS

Anyone familiar with multinational firms is aware of the frequent conflicts between personnel at headquarters and those in overseas subsidiaries. Because the headquarters is often located in the home country of the firm and is staffed largely by home country personnel, these conflicts are likely to be attributed to antagonisms between nationalities, but aren't staff-line conflicts inherent in all large organizations? Perhaps the nationality issue is another of those easy, superficial "explanations" that are actually quite irrelevant to the fundamental problem.

To explore this question, a graduate student at M.I.T.'s Sloan School, Frank Jaques, sent attitude questionnaires to both domestic and foreign managers in four international corporations, asking them about their relationships with headquarters, with primary emphasis on communications between staff and line. The results were surprising. On the whole, there were no significant differences between the domestic and foreign managers in their ratings of the quality of communications between themselves and headquarters. To quote: "The often-heard argument that communications are worse with international subsidiaries is not true. Despite less frequent personal contact, the quality of communications with international subsidiaries was as good as that with domestic subsidiaries."

What did come out was that the four companies differed among themselves. Two of the firms were superior in their communications and two were decidedly inferior, but these differences held for both domestic and foreign operations. Analysis of the data revealed that the two better-communicating companies tended to operate in a more decentralized manner; for example, they gave more autonomy to the line for day-to-day operating decisions.

The crucial variable in this study thus turns out to be not multinational-versus-national conditions, but basic management method—a finding that is bound to be unsettling to some managers, because the international-conditions argument has served so well to disguise what is simply ineffective management.

WHEN THE BOSS IS A FOREIGNER . . .

The staff-line issue is to a large extent a problem of lateral relationships; now a question of vertical relationships comes up—working for a manager of a nationality other than one's own. It is considered "enlightened" management in multinational firms as far as possible to employ within a country only the nationals of that country. This principle is based on a number of assumptions, one of the most important being that employees strongly resent management by a foreigner. Often, when there are performance or morale problems in a subsidiary being run by a foreigner, the foreign management is presumed to be a major contributor to the problems. However, in every case I have studied where a foreigner-managed subsidiary was experiencing serious difficulties, the problems stemmed not from nationality differences but rather from the administrative or technical incompetence of the manager—the same kind of inadequate performance that would produce problems no matter what the nationality of the manager.

In Company X opinion surveys, when overseas employees were asked how they would feel about working for a manager of a different nationality, the responses were amazingly "internationalist." For example, in one survey this question was asked:

Imagine the following situation: There is a promotional opportunity to a high-level position in your company and a number of employees in your country are qualified for the job. But an employee in another country is clearly better qualified. Everyone agrees (including yourself) that this other man is better qualified. Furthermore, this man speaks the language of your country and would be willing to move permanently (not just as a temporary assignment). In your opinion, who should get the job?

The response categories and the percentages of answers in each were: man from your country—18; hard to say—21; and man from the other country—61.

Another question was this:

How do you think you would feel about working for a manager who was from a country other than your own?

The answers and percentages were: prefer manager of own country—21; nationality makes no difference—79; and prefer manager of a different nationality—0.

It could be argued that these answers are peculiar to organizations like Company X, firms with an advanced and changing technology, for whom, therefore, technical competence is a very important concern. But it might just be that the assumed unwillingness of people to work for foreigners is highly exaggerated; it could be, in other words, that the problems experienced abroad are due not so much to the "ugly" American as to the incompetent American.

Incidentally, our findings and conclusions jibe well with Howard Perlmutter's description and evaluation of the internationalization process. He hypothesizes three stages in the development of multinational firms; in terms of staffing prime positions in overseas subsidiaries, these stages are: ethnocentric—positions staffed with citizens of the parent country; polycentric—positions staffed by local citizens; and geocentric—nationality makes no difference: Competence, not passport, counts.

Our data provided evidence that there is a firm attitudinal basis for progression to the geocentric stage, that, in effect; the same criterion that, ideally, is used for placement in a single country—"the best man for the job"—should be applied internationally.

ATTITUDES TOWARD OVERSEAS ASSIGNMENTS

The internationalization of a firm would, of course, involve assignments abroad for relatively large numbers of personnel, and here we come to a set of assumptions about their reactions to service overseas. The prevalent views about these assignees focus on their difficulties in adjusting to the countries of their assignment. These purported difficulties range from severe "culture shock" to a wide variety of day-to-day annoyances and frustrations, and are believed to affect profoundly both work effectiveness and psychological health. Indeed, the effects of culture shock are often described in terms reminiscent of psychiatric diagnoses.

It is undeniable that some employees do find it hard to adjust to the environment of their international assignments. However, a survey of many hundreds of Company X overseas assignees indicated very clearly a condition of considerable satisfaction with such assignments; by and large, the respondents reported that the opportunity to live, work, and travel abroad was an immensely gratifying experience. In fact, about 75 percent said that they would like another international assignment.

Of course, the respondents in this study did report day-to-day annoyances and frustrations concerning the work itself, but many of the difficulties experienced on the job were identical to those found in opinion surveys in any complex organization. For example, there were the usual complaints about bureaucratic obstacles to getting the work done and, in a number of cases, about the lack of job challenge. But since these are general problems, conditions in foreign countries can hardly be blamed. Again, as with the staff-line issue discussed earlier, those conditions may be little more than convenient excuses for problems that derive from poor management practices.

Related to the assumed discomfort and dissatisfaction of the international assignee is another set of beliefs about the reluctance of people to accept assignments overseas in the first place. For example, it is often said that Europeans are loath to leave their home countries and take assignments in, say, the United States.

In an opinion survey, Company X employees were asked this question:

From time to time, Company X offers employees international assignments—jobs in other countries for a period of time. Within the next five years or so, do you think you would like to have an international assignment?

The answers, in percentages, were: yes, definitely—43; yes, probably—35; no, probably not—17; and no, definitely not—5.

Another item in the questionnaire posed the issue in a more extreme way, testing the willingness of employees to accept an international *career*. The question was:

Agree or disagree. . . . I'm not interested in an international career. I prefer to spend my career primarily in my own country.

The answers, in percentages, were: agree—34, neither agree nor disagree—21; and disagree—45.

Given this evidence, it is instructive to explore the source of the assumption it contradicts—that people are unwilling to accept international assignments. The reason for it can probably be found in the way the place-ment process works in any firm, whether single-nation or multinational. In general, managers are reluctant to part with their competent people and erect barriers to prevent their loss, one of which is propagation of the theory that employees do not want to move from their current locations. In most organizations, it is prohibited to interview a prospective candidate for a job opening before getting clearance from the candidate's manager, so, since the employee cannot express his own preferences, the opinions of his manager prevail. Hence the widespread, often erroneous, belief that employees do not want to move.

This is a situation both unfair to employees and, in the long run, harm-ful to the organization, and it seems to call for a much more open and direct system for candidate identification and candidate acquisition. Internal ad-vertising (job posting) is one solution that has applicability in both multina-tional and single-nation organizations, where the problem is essentially the same.

INTERNATIONAL RESEARCH—NOT SO DIFFICULT AFTER ALL

The final set of myths to be discussed questions the very possibility of systematically testing all of the other assumptions. There is a view that systematic, comparative international research is extremely difficult to carry out, if not impossible, for reasons ranging from the problems in measuring subtle, but extremely important, cultural differences to more specific objec-tions, such as, "Germans will never fill out a questionnaire" (because im-mediately after World War II Germans were asked to complete question-naires about their previous political associations). It is also argued that many behavioral science techniques have been developed in an American cultural context and are received in other cultures with confusion or suspi-cion.

Nevertheless, by all methodological standards with which I am familiar, these assumptions are absolutely wrong. In Company X, we experienced no greater difficulty abroad than in the United States in getting employees to complete our questionnaires. The questionnaire administration process proceeded smoothly and efficiently, and, more important, the various tech-niques we used for testing the reliability and validity of data showed coeffi-cients in the range of what we ordinarily find for American employees.

Certainly, international research poses some special problems, such as questionnaire translation, but the research difficulties internationally are fundamentally no different than those always encountered in the United States—the limitations in applying systematic methods to a phenomenon as complex as human behavior. These basic limitations are of much greater import than are the problems posed by national and cultural differences. If one wishes to question the applicability of behavioral science methods internationally, let him begin with a critique of those methods in the United States; he will soon realize that the international difficulties are rather trivial.

The arguments presented here are purposely phrased in rather extreme terms, to help stimulate reconsideration of prevailing assumptions and to make clear the need for much more, and better, research on multinational management. In the meantime, it is my claim that the small amount of evidence available supports the general hypothesis that the differences between multinational and single-nation firms are minor compared with the fundamental similarities between the two kinds of organizations.

Perhaps this conclusion will eventually have to be modified, but modification should be based on sound, empirical research, rather than on the usual conglomeration of anecdotes and impressions so characteristic of this field. We have enough "old China hands" with their old China stories. What we need now is to put this multitude of hypotheses to the empirical test.

READING 60

THE CREATIVE ORGANIZATION: A JAPANESE EXPERIMENT

Shigeru Kobayashi*

Starting virtually from scratch, Sony Corporation had grown into a company of 5,000 employees within the short span of 15 years when the author became manager of its Atsugi plant in 1961. A company almost always reaches a turning point after its rapid early development, because the very quality of vitality that enabled it to grow has a tendency to be weakened as increasingly larger numbers of people are employed. Those who joined during the start-up period were fighters, who staked their furture on a company that might turn out to be a failure or a success, but those who come in after the company is solidly established are inclined to "ride" with it, counting on the stability it has achieved.

Moreover, as a rule when a firm grows in size, it increasingly demands a well-defined organization structure, but Sony has always been opposed

*Reprinted by permission of the publisher from *Personnel*, November–December, 1970, pp. 8–17. © 1970 by the American Management Association, Inc.

to a rigid structure, preferring to be a stage on which people, uncoerced, could display their talents for creativity and independent activity. This freedom assured Sony of its initial dynamism and flexibility; as it grew, though, it could no longer maintain control without any form of organization, and the result was the establishment of departments, sections, subsections, and what-not, all leading to smaller and smaller subdivisions and to a management hierarchy of department managers, section chiefs, subsection chiefs, and so on, with detailed rules and regulations for all jobs.

The ideals expressed in the letters of intent leading to the establishment of Sony presupposed a company in which uncoerced people saw their own well-being in the well-being of the company and in which everyone could work freely to achieve personal satisfaction and develop himself to his fullest potential. Thus, a glaring contradiction was apparent when principles of organization were adopted that took away people's planning and controlling functions.

Sony's aspirations to "do away with organization" notwithstanding, there can, of course, be no large-scale company without some form of organization; human dynamism and vitality alone cannot support such a firm. It therefore became necessary for us to organize in such a way as to permit the transformation of this human dynamism and vitality into company dynamism. A type of organization that would be conducive to this approach demanded that we base our effort on creative teamwork and excise the static and dehumanizing aspects of traditional organization patterns. Meeting these specifications called for formulating a pattern through trial and error. Above all, we had to avoid the stabilization of a structure through organization charts and rules based on the concept that organization is a vehicle for directive management, authority, and status. Teamwork is possible only in small groups, so we had to redesign our large organization as a collection of interlocking small groups.

CHANGING THE POWER STRUCTURE

Here I shall describe, first, how we set about breaking down the concept of organization as a means of ensuring authority and power.

At Sony, top management didn't have a speck of power-consciousness, but the other people, contrary to the philosophy of its top management, did subscribe to the generally accepted notion that superiors do their jobs by using their subordinates. Management based on power-consciousness became less evident as time went by, but one obstacle in the way of improvement was clear—hierarchical position as found in the traditional delineation of jobs.

Our plant organization comprises the crew (at the lowest level), which has about six members; the group, which includes several crews; the section, which includes several groups; and the department, which includes several sections. The first difficulty arose in connection with the titles given to the individuals in charge of these various units. Department superior (*ka-choh* in Japanese), section superior *(kakari-choh),* group supervisor *(kumi-choh),* and crew supervisor *(han-choh)* all reminded both managers and workers of the old superior-subordinate relationship. We therefore decided to discontinue the use of the suffix *choh,* meaning superior, head, or chief. The department superior and section superior were to be called simply manager *(shunin).* We also decided to use the English words for titles—for instance, leader, in the case of the crew, and chief, in the case of the group. In addition, we encouraged people to address a man with a managerial position not as Mr. Department Manager, for example, but simply by his last name.

A related obstacle was the fact that titles like department superior or section superior represented social status as well as company position. To move a person under any circumstances from the position of department superior to a section superior's job would have been considered a demotion in both job and social standing.

We therefore decided to change our job-assignment policies when we changed our titles. People who are not yet considered eligible for such elevated status are, nevertheless, sometimes made department managers, and people who *are* eligible for more responsibility are sometimes made section managers. In short, our practice became flexible. A man could be appointed department manager and, immediately thereafter, could be reappointed section manager, and vice versa. This new practice, once established, virtually eradicated status-consciousness due to hierarchical position.

PARTICIPATIVE DECISION MAKING

The organization climate in which people must be accorded status because they are "somebody" and are expected to exercise the authority of their position to use people was gradually eliminated. But how are managers to do their jobs if they are not to use people to get the work out? I believe they should *assist* people to carry out the necessary tasks voluntarily. When managers use people to do their jobs, orders are called for, but when managers assume a role in which they assist people, they need only explain the general situation and the relevant policies. Then all they have to do is teach people how to *act.*

Since they are not ordered to do anything, it is now the employees' responsibility to question, discuss, and even oppose any explanation or instruction they may receive from their managers. On the other hand, managers should never allow themselves to close their minds to conflicting ideas or opinions from their workers; if they do, it means that they are still harboring power-consciousness—they feel their prerogatives are being attacked. Managers who are unwilling to take any responsibility for an employee's ideas, once adopted and implemented, are not truly and seriously taking responsibility for much else, either.

The worst kind of manager is the one who blames his people in case of a fiasco, yet who wants to exercise his power and authority by taking credit for their successes. A manager who will not allow himself to dodge any responsibility has no other course but to trust his people, and when he shows this spirit, it kindles a similar spirit in those people and assures their voluntary cooperation. Here we have the real basis of leadership.

"THE RULE IS EVERYTHING"

Almost as damaging as the concept justifying managers' using their men is the one that makes manuals and rules all-important. In Japanese companies one often finds a kind of thinking that defines organizing as drawing up detailed charts, precise job descriptions, and careful statements of job authority. Employees who don't obey such rules and regulations to the letter are regarded as organization dropouts.

Nothing could be sillier. Rules and regulations are stipulated to aid efficient administration under a certain set of prevailing conditions. Even if we could arrive at perfect rules and regulations, some of them would almost immediately be made impractical by the inexorable change of circumstances.

It is a gross mistake to assume that order will suffer if rules and regulations are not enforced. For instance, we have no company-made rules and regulations in our dormitories, yet strict order prevails. People who are spellbound by normative dogmatism can hardly be blamed for believing, upon looking into our dorms, that they are managed like prisons without bars and that the workers who live in them must be suffering severe deprivation of freedom. Such is the degree of order we enjoy without rules or regulations.

DEFINING JOB DUTIES

Texas Instruments Incorporated maintains a highly commendable position on rules and regulations. On an annual basis, managers define their own duties to best serve the company's interests under the generally prevailing conditions. Therefore, their statements of job duties are not static but are reviewed, revised, and adjusted as the need arises, depending on the requirements of the company during a particular fiscal year. By coincidence, we at Sony follow exactly the same practice.

For instance, suppose that I am appointing a man to be manager of our general affairs department. I ask him to write down what he thinks the problems of the department are and how he anticipates solving them. We then discuss what he has written. I don't force my ideas upon him; I simply let him do whatever he seriously considers must be done. If, after a while, he wants to revise his plan, we hold further discussions. Moreover, when the present manager of the general affairs department is replaced, the definition of the job is bound to change as well. Even the same man may define the same job in a different way, once he has gained new experience or finds his situation altered. Not only is he perfectly free to do so; he is obligated to do so.

As was mentioned earlier, during the initial phase of management innovation in our plant, we decided that small-group organization was necessary to motivate people and ensure voluntary action on their part and to enable every member to strive for the achievement of common goals. We began by breaking down production functions on the basis of crews—teams made up of two to a maximum of 20 people. Those who work in the same process in the manufacture of transistors are grouped together, and we may have one, two, or even three crews, depending on the number of workers in a process.

SECRET OF SMALL-GROUP SUCCESS

What is the difference between such a team and the equivalent unit in the traditional organization? First, the leaders of our teams are not supervisors who get the work out by using subordinates. Most of the leaders in our plant are girls 18 to 19 years old; there is practically no age difference between leaders and operators, although we also have some old housewives in the ranks of both leaders and operators. Since our leaders are free of status-consciousness, they assume and resign leadership quite freely.

Until the crew system was established, the first-line supervisors—called group chiefs—had managed every process in the plant. Under the new setup, however, the crews were created within the old groupings and each was assigned to a single work process. Operators in each crew selected a leader from among themselves. The initial task of the crews was to record and control attendance after time clocks were taken out. With such an important control function delegated to the crews, the result was an immediate demonstration of teamwork. Autonomous checking and control over attendance led naturally to autonomy in production control at crew level.

Second, it should be kept in mind that a team is managed chiefly through meetings of its members. Herein lies the basic difference between the team and the traditional work group, in which superiors give instructions individually to their subordinates without holding any meetings.

Rensis Likert writes in his *New Patterns of Management* that management will make full use of the potential capacities of its human resources only when each person in an organization is a member of one or more effectively functioning work groups that have a high degree of group loyalty, effective skills of interaction, and high performance goals.

All our experience testifies to the truth of what he says. The large, traditional organization fails to take advantage of the aggregate power of small groups that enables them to deliver superior performance, sometimes exceeding the most optimistic hopes.

LINKING OF TEAMS

It is our goal to reach the point where the full range of our activity is based on teamwork. Each team is necessarily small in size, whereas the plant is large, but we resolved this conflict with the establishment of a cell type of organization, linking small teams with each other, as in a living organism, to make up a single larger body. This structuring did not call for any changes in the way the plant was then organized—the various groupings could remain as they were, and so could the managers at the various levels. The only things that had to be changed were management style and management attitudes.

First, the monthly meeting—in which it is intended that every manager participate—clearly brought out the management style and attitudes of the plant manager, an opponent of power-consciousness. Gradually, then, the new climate came to be understood and percolated down through the entire plant with the help of talks, the way in which those talks were handled, and a succession of new policies implemented one by one. Everybody came to welcome the feeling that grew out of working in an atmosphere of mutual trust, as exemplified by the elimination of time clocks and the introduction of a cafetria without attendants.

Then there was our practice of holding a meeting for the department managers every morning. Any matters pertaining to the plant as a whole were reported and discussed in this meeting and the resulting decisions were then implemented. The participants—the plant manager and the entire department manager group—formed a team in themselves. Thus, the top team was formed simultaneously with the teams at lower levels, and these teams at the top and bottom led to the formation of intermediary teams, like a chain reaction.

With the number of plant employees exceeding 3,000, the number of departments standing at 20-odd, and our lines of business diversified, we seemed to have reached a stage where we could no longer manage and control our affairs unless we established divisions, but I was reluctant to increase the layers of management. We solved the problem by dividing the weekly morning meeting into four sessions: general meeting, meeting for general affairs, meeting for semiconductors, and meeting for calculators.

The plant manager attends all these meetings of top management, as do the lower-level plant managers who assist him and act in his stead in the absence of the plant manager. The regular participants in the divisional meetings are, of course, the managers of various departments, but no clear line is drawn as to which meeting any one manager is to attend. It is entirely possible, depending on the nature of his business, for one man to attend two or three such meetings.

A divisional meeting is similar in its function to a meeting held within a single department, but it is more flexible than its departmental counterpart, and the plant manager participates in it personally. The general meeting also differs from a departmental meeting in that it is attended not only by department managers but by section chiefs. Thus, the plant manager establishes direct contact with both.

The general meeting, because of its very nature, draws many attendees and therefore inhibits any detailed discussion. In a divisional meeting, the discussion is likely to explore in detail information supplied by the lower organization levels, whereas in the general meeting, top management makes overall plant information available, and discussion follows on that basis.

As a result of all this, from the plant manager down no one is involved in more than three layers of meetings. Communications have thereby been reduced proportionately, but the results show that the merits of the new arrangement far outweigh its drawbacks.

THE PAIR SYSTEM

To return to organization by teams, an important role in team development is played by our pair system, a combination of two workers whose relations on the job are like those of a man and his wife in the Japanese home. The fundamental difference between team formation (including the pair system) and the authoritarian, directive type of organization lies in the fact that the latter results in human relations based on the ruler-and-ruled dichotomy, whereas the former bases human relations on partnership. In this partnership one member, it is true, is the leader and the other is a follower, but this is not the relationship between the ruler and the ruled.

A pair must necessarily be composed of two individuals with different characteristics. Man and woman, teacher and pupil, senior worker and junior worker, worker on the morning shift and worker on the afternoon shift, manager and secretary, scientist and technician, two professionals with different academic disciplines and skills, two men with different personalities—all lend themselves to pair formation. The requirements are that the two individuals be heterogeneous, that they be performing the same job to achieve an identical goal, and that they assume joint responsibility for their work.

The pair system concept is not new in Japan. Professor Jiro Kamijima, of St. Paul University in Tokyo, has mentioned, in commenting on old Japanese social organizations and their underlying mental attitudes, that a sort of pair system carried a certain significance even during ancient times. Referring to his comments, I suggested at one of our morning meetings that we should perhaps introduce the pair system as a micro-unit within the crew on the strength of the success of the chief and subchief system with which we had already experimented. Hearing of what I had said, the workers at some stations expressed interest in the idea and started to develop a pair system of their own volition.

We always try to approach organizational matters in this manner. Neither I nor any member of my staff dictates to people how they should proceed with a particular organizing job. Rather, a certain idea seems to emerge informally and workers who are interested in it begin implementing it in their own way. As a result, our pair system differs from one work station to another in both method of operation and timing of application. To this day we have work stations that are using systems that have yet to be set up on an organized basis like the one I have cited.

The prime requisite in developing basic organizational patterns and systems is never to force any particular method upon people across the board. It is only when a pattern or system is created by the individuals who will be required to function within it that we arrive at a means of motivating and stimulating people, instead of stifling them. The pair system in particular could never work smoothly if people were required to form pairs.

COMMUNICATIONS SUPPORT

Most important to organization by team is reliable information, since the employees are not individually directed or commanded to perform tasks expected of them. Each team member does his own sizing up on a given situation, makes his decision, and takes action in accordance with the facts. Obviously, unless each member understands the information that comes to him from above, below, and around him, the sum total of the action will not be properly coordinated.

Communication that supports the team type of organization depends not only on providing access to information, but also on an atmosphere of mutual respect. No one will take communication seriously if it comes from a person whom he holds in contempt, and vice versa. Nor will communication serve to establish reliable information unless both parties are free from prejudice and favoritism.

Communication cannot be accomplished simply by recording, reproducing, and transmitting messages to company levels above or below the speaker or sidewise, to other departments, as with a tape recorder. Communication has to be established among live human beings and make possible the creation of new ideas based on useful, detailed data derived from a combination of our own and others' information and judgment.

Changes in the context of information during the transmission process create no harm so long as the intermediaries try to transmit the facts in a creative way—that is, so long as the climate favors their being able to think subjectively about the information in question, grasp its true meaning, and convey this meaning on their own responsibility as if the information were their own. It is this creative interpretation that is indispensable to truly effective communication.

The establishment of a climate conducive to *creative* communication may bring astounding changes. For instance, operators' casual remarks about a certain circumstance observed on the job—remarks the operators themselves are not sure have any importance—are transmitted to staff specialists; a significant engineering discovery results, and profits are handsome. It is not too much to say that this kind of information is coming to be an important basis for technological innovation in our semiconductor industry.

At Sony we have formal reports presented at weekly meetings, monthly reports by all personnel above the level of leader, and published media, including a *Management Memo* and companywide magazines, *Sony News,* published monthly, and *Weekly Reports.* At our Atsugi plant we have *Atsugi Topics,* published every other day, and the monthly *Home News,* directed to employees' families. We also have many publications issued by dormitory residents and by members of various work stations.

However, much depends on the unrestricted flow of informal information. A case in point is the Sony "Dial 2000." Any Sony employee can dial this number directly and get or give information through the personnel who respond to his call. All are encouraged to "dial 2000" for these purposes:

- To confirm the validity of rumors being circulated or of "tips" from other employees.
- To get information on whom to approach about problems having to do with their jobs, to find out more on topics they are concerned about, or to get helpful ideas about certain problems.
- To get information as to which groups or people within Sony are trying to do or are already doing things they are planning to do in their own jobs.
- To find out who should receive information, proposals, or opinions that employees think will be helpful to Sony.

In simple terms, each person has access to a source where he can easily obtain the information he needs and discuss it with someone well informed. When it seems appropriate, he can even circumvent his immediate manager, but he has to exercise his judgment and plan a course of action on his own responsibility. And if he does act on the advice of his immediate manager, he cannot and should not be permitted to pass the buck to that manager in the event of failure.

It has become clear to us that organizations supported by free-flowing information and by responsible judgment and actions on the part of everyone of their members are lively organizations, without any confusion or chaos to disturb their order. They represent genuinely creative organizations firmly based on effective communication and identification with the company through the self-realization it affords.

CHAPTER 16
EMERGING ORGANIZATIONAL BEHAVIOR

READING 61

(A Review and Summary Article)

TRENDS IN ORGANIZATIONAL DESIGN

Keith Davis*

From time to time it is appropriate to back away from a current situation in order to examine it in broader perspective. In this manner we can get a better understanding of the significance of events around us. The following discussion has that purpose. It seeks to understand the directions in which organizational design is moving. As used in this discussion the term "organizational design" refers both to the design of the job, such as the number of work elements performed, and the design of the organizational environment itself, such as rigidity of structure, communication systems, and amount of control.

CLASSICAL ORGANIZATIONAL DESIGN

Classical organizational design dominated management thinking for the first half of the twentieth century. It had its origins in the ideas of Adam Smith, who in 1776 in the *Wealth of Nations* [18] presented a discussion of pinmakers to show how division of labor could improve productivity a hundredfold or more. However, it was not until the early 1900s that the full philosophy of classical design was presented by Frederic W. Taylor [19] and Henri Fayol [5]. As it evolved from Taylor and Fayol, classical design used full division of labor, rigid hierarchy, and standardization of labor to reach its objectives. The idea was to lower costs by using unskilled repetitive labor that could be trained easily to do a small part of a job. Job performance was tightly controlled by a large hierarchy that strictly enforced *the one best way of work.*

In spite of our tendency occasionally to think otherwise, the classical design did gain substantial improvements. There were remarkable increases in economic productivity, something which was sorely needed by an impoverished world. *The difficulty was that these gains were achieved at considerable human costs.* There was excessive division of labor and overdependence on rules, procedures, and hierarchy. The worker became iso-

* Adapted from Dennis F. Ray and Thad B. Green, editors, *Academy of Management Proceedings, 1973,* State College, Miss.: Academy of Management, 1974, pp. 1–16. © 1974 by Academy of Management. Reprinted with permission.

lated from fellow workers. The result was higher turnover and absenteeism. Quality declined, and workers became alienated. Conflict arose as workers tried to improve their lot. Management's response to this situation was to tighten the controls, to increase the supervision, and to organize more rigidly. These actions were calculated to improve the situation, but they only made it worse. Management made a common error by treating the *symptoms* rather than the causes of the problems. The job itself simply was not satisfying.

It took management—and academicians—some time to recognize the nature and severity of the problem. In 1939 Roethlisberger and Dickson published their powerful behavioral interpretation of management [17]. Then in 1949 Douglas McGregor in his insightful way warned, "Practically all the means of need-satisfaction which workers today obtain from their employment can be utilized *only after they leave their jobs*" [16, p. 117, italics in original]. He pointed out that all of the popular personnel devices of the time, such as vacations and insurance benefits, were satisfactions received off the job.

A few years later in 1957 Chris Argyris charged that poor organizational design established a basic incongruence between formal organizations and the workers' drives for self-actualization. Organizations tend to ignore the potential of people, he claimed. They fail to encourage self-development in areas that are meaningful to each individual. They do not encourage responsibility and innovation. They do not develop and employ the whole person. At lower levels the workers become alienated, frustrated, and unproductive, and they fight the company with a certain sense of social justice. The problem is also severe at management levels, because the situation lacks trust, openness, and risk-taking. The frustrated manager often abdicates his independence, becoming a servile "organization man" in the words of William H. Whyte [23].

Another straw in the wind for change was the famous need hierarchy presented by A. H. Maslow [15, pp. 370–396]. His hierarchy suggested that as society made social and economic progress, new needs of employees would arise. In turn, these new needs require new forms of job and organizational design. The problem was not so much that the work itself had changed for the worse, but rather *the employees were changing*. Design of jobs and organizations had failed to keep up with widespread changes in worker aspirations and attitudes. Employers now had two reasons for redesigning jobs and organizations.

1   Classical design originally gave inadequate attention to human factors.

2   The needs and aspirations of employees themselves were changing.

HUMANISTIC ORGANIZATIONAL DESIGN

In taking corrective action the most obvious direction for management to go was to swing the pendulum away from mechanistic classical design toward a more behavioral, participative, humanistic design, also called organic design by Burns and Stalker [4]. The new design furnished a wide variety of humanistic options, such as the following:

Classical Design	Humanistic Design
Closed system	Open system
Job specialization	Job enlargement
Centralization	Decentralization
Authority	Consensus
Tight hierarchy	Loose project organization
Technical emphasis	Human emphasis
Rigid procedures	Flexible procedures
Command	Consultation
Vertical communication	Multidirectional communication
Negative environment	Positive environment
Maintenance needs	Motivational needs
Tight control	Management by objectives
Autocratic approach	Democratic approach

The objective was to make the job environment supportive rather than threatening to employees. The job should be a place that stimulates their drives and aspirations and helps them to grow as whole persons. Work should be psychologically rewarding as well as economically rewarding. By the 1950s organizations were moving gradually in this direction.

In addition to Maslow, McGregor, Argyris, and Roethlisberger already mentioned, the following persons made significant contributions to humanistic organizational design. Rensis Likert [14] emphasized organizational development and offered four categories called Systems 1, 2, 3, and 4, to describe the move from authoritarian management (System 1) to participative management (System 4). Organizational development was used to help organizations gradually move toward System 4, which was considered the ideal system.

Blake and Mouton [3] offered organizational development in the form of a managerial grid which emphasized leadership style. It was perceived that the leader set the environmental structure and climate for the work group; consequently, the most effective way to move toward humanistic design is through the leadership structure of the organization. By using the grid various managerial styles may be identified in order to discuss both existing styles which need correction and more idealized styles.

Herzberg [10] took an unusual and controversial approach by empha-sizing a difference between maintenance and motivational factors. Herz-berg identified some job conditions that operate primarily to dissatisfy em-ployees when the conditions are absent, but their presence does not motivate employees in a strong way. These are dissatisfiers or maintenance factors, because they maintain the employee ready for effective motivation. These maintenance factors arise primarily from the "job context" or envi-ronment, such as pension, vacations, wages and interpersonal relations. Another set of conditions operates primarily to build strong motivation and high job satisfaction, but their absence rarely proves dissatisfying. These are satisfiers or motivational factors. They arise primarily from the job con-tent itself, such as achievement, growth, and responsibility. The Herzberg model provoked much controversy about its correctness, but regardless it has been an effective vehicle to convince managers of significant distinc-tions in types of rewards offered by management.

Bennis [2] presented the fundamental ideal of humanistic democracy and insisted that in the work place "democracy is inevitable." According to this line of reasoning, democracy is inevitable because it is the only form which provides the flexibility and decentralization which large, complex organizations require. In the complex organization the top executive can-not know enough about all functions of the organization to make effective decisions. The executive must depend on extensive horizontal communi-cation and functional expertise for guidance. Democratic, humanistic or-ganizational systems are the most effective for this situation. They are a decision-making necessity and also a behavioral necessity, because they provide the optimal environment for today's knowledge workers.

Without question, humanistic designs were an improvement; however, a funny thing happened on the way to this proposed utopia. Just as classi-cal design generated excesses, so did humanistic design. The model build-ers forgot that the behavioral system in an organization is part of several larger systems, such as the technological system and the economic sys-tem. If decisions are made in terms of only the behavioral system, the situ-ation becomes unbalanced and the same kinds of rigidities develop that the classicists caused.

A prime example of the descent from humanistic utopia to worldly real-ity is the experience of Non-Linear Systems, Inc., of San Diego. In the 1960s it changed its organizational design to the behavioral model, entirely elimi-nating assembly lines and time cards. As the company grew, it was hailed as the harbinger of the future. One behavioral scientist commented about his associates, "There was so much excitement it was almost seductive." The excitement died when the company met a business slump and the new system was unable to endure adversity. Sales dropped nearly fifty percent and profits disappeared. In order to restore profitability the president took a more controlling, classical role. He commented, "I may have lost sight of the purpose of business, which is not to develop new theories of management." And he added a comment about the rigidities of the humanistic model, "We didn't take into account the varied emotional and mental capacities of our employees when we changed the assembly line." [21, pp. 99-100]

CONTINGENCY ORGANIZATIONAL DESIGN

The move toward a more system-wide way of thinking about organizations is producing a swing toward contingency or situational designs in the future. This is clearly the appropriate emphasis because it escapes narrow perspectives that have restricted earlier approaches. It is still strongly humanistic, but it is more complete than that, because it includes all situational factors including the technology and economic environment. *Contingency organization design* means that different environments require different organizational relationships for optimum effectiveness [9, p. 59]. No longer is there a "one best way" whether it is classical or behavioral.

Contingency management, for example, means that job enrichment should be applied with the realization that some employees do not want their jobs enriched. Some prefer easier and more routine work. Some are troubled by a challenge. Others prefer a friendly situation and are not much concerned about job content. Each person and situation is different. Many organizations have policies and procedures that reflect a single value system based on the belief that all employees want the same work environment and fringe benefits; consequently, these firms are not able to adjust situationally to different conditions [11, pp. 8-23].

Early research evidence of contingency design was provided by Woodward in 1965 [24]. She studied 100 firms in England to determine what structural variables were related to economic success. Firms were classified according to three types of production technology: unit, mass, and continuous process production. Research disclosed that the effective form of organization varied according to the firm's technology. Mass production was more successful with classical design, while unit and process production were more successful when they used humanistic designs.

Fiedler probably provided the name for the contingency approach, with his studies of leadership published in 1967 [6]. He showed that an effective leadership pattern is dependent on the interaction of a number of variables including task structure and leadership position power. Generally a more classical approach is effective when conditions are substantially favorable or unfavorable for the leader, but a more behavioral approach is better in the intermediate zone of favorability. The intermediate conditions are the ones most commonly found in organizations.

Lawrence and Lorsch [13] popularized the contingency approach with their study of organizations in stable and changing environments in 1967. They showed that in certain stable environments the classical forms tend to be more effective. In changing environments the opposite is true. More humanistic forms are required to permit organizations to respond effectively to their unstable environment.

Since contingency design deals with a large number of variables, it is not easy to apply, but some experimental applications have produced excellent results. For example, in the Treasury Department of American Telephone and Telegraph Company, educated and intelligent employees handle correspondence with stockholders. Originally they worked in a highly structured environment under close supervision in order to assure a suitable standard of correspondence. Under these conditions, quality of work was low and turnover was high. The job design was too routine and lacking in challenge.

Using a control group and a test group, the jobs of the test group were enriched as follows: (1) the employees were permitted to sign their own names to the letters they prepared; (2) the employees were held responsible for the quality of their work; (3) they were encouraged to become experts in the kinds of problems that appealed to them; and (4) subject matter experts were provided for consultation regarding problems.

The control group remained unchanged after six months, but the test group improved by all measurements used. The measures included turnover, productivity, absences, promotions from the group, and costs. The quality measurement index climbed from the thirties to the nineties.

American Telephone and Telegraph Company also has achieved excellent results in other job enrichment efforts. In the directory-compilation function, name omissions dropped from 2 to 1 percent. In frame wiring, errors declined from 13 to 0.5 percent, and the number of frames wired increased from 700 to over 1,200 [7; 8].

Equally successful results have been achieved at Emery Air Freight using the behavioral modification ideas of B. F. Skinner. The company made design changes in the communication system in order to provide positive reinforcement for workers. In this situation the company had been using large containers to reduce handling costs for forwarding small packages. The company has a standard of 90 percent use of the containers for small packages, but research showed that actual utilization was only 45 percent.

The communication system was redesigned to give workers daily feedback on how near they came to the 90 percent goal. Furthermore, supervisors provided positive verbal reinforcement. The result was that when the new communications design was applied, *in a single day* use of large containers increased to 95 percent. As this design was applied to other facilities throughout the nation, use of large containers at these facilities also rose to 95 percent in a single day. The high performance level was maintained for three years following the new design [22, pp. 64-6].

A more complete effort was the organizational design of a new General Foods Corporation pet food plant to incorporate appropriate behavioral and system ideas. The new plant offered a completely different way of work compared with a traditional pet food plant. Work is performed by autonomous teams of 7–14 persons. Most support functions are integrated within the teams, meaning that very little staff is provided. Job design is used to enlarge jobs to increase the challenge in them. Decision making is decentralized, and group leaders encourage team members to make as many decisions as possible. Full feedback about performance is given to all members [20, pp. 70–81].

The result compared with other plants is that absenteeism and turnover are reduced and productivity has increased. Furthermore, rework of faulty quality material has been reduced 90 percent. The plant definitely shows superior results compared with conventionally designed plants, although it is too new to be sure whether these results will last indefinitely [12, p. 54].

Although experimental contingency design efforts have had remarkable success, they do not signal a quick coming of utopia at work. Classical design and strict behavioral design gave easy answers, but contingency design is difficult to apply. Much about the workplace is still unknown. We also know relatively little about people and the social systems in which they interact. The road ahead is going to be a rocky one. If predictions are appropriate at this point, my opinion is that progress in organizational design will be slower than most experts think. It is easy to theorize about how to redesign organizations and jobs, but actual practice is much more difficult. Furthermore, changes in design assume certain changes in the way managers think, and we all know that attitudes and frameworks change very slowly. Traditional ways of work and organizational design have been entrenched for centuries, and they will not change easily.

Meanwhile, workers are changing, and the resulting psychological dissonance between them and their jobs is likely to grow worse before it becomes better. There will be many conflicts as society wrestles with whether organizational design can be restructured to increase productivity and employee fulfillment. In all this turmoil, however, the important point to remember is that we are making progress. We are moving toward more contingency design with enriched jobs and open organizational systems.

REFERENCES

1 Argyris, Chris, *Personality and Organization: The Conflict between the System and the Individual* (New York: Harper & Row, Publishers, Inc., 1957).
2 Bennis, Warren G., *Changing Organizations: Essays on the Development and Evolution of Human Organization* (New York: McGraw-Hill Book Company, 1966).
3 Blake, Robert R., and Jane S. Mouton, *The Managerial Grid* (Houston: Gulf Publishing Company, 1964).
4 Burns, Tom, and G. M. Stalker, *The Management of Innovation* (London: Tavistock Publications, 1961).
5 Fayol, Henri, *General and Industrial Management* (1916) trans. by Constance Storrs (New York: Pitman Publishing Corporation, 1949).

6   Fiedler, Fred E., *A Theory of Leadership Effectiveness* (New York: McGraw-Hill Book Company, 1967).

7   Ford, Robert N., *Motivation through the Work Itself* (New York: American Management Association, 1969).

8   Gellette, Malcolm B., "Work Itself as a Motivator," speech at annual meeting, Western Division, Academy of Management, Salt Lake City, Utah (March 20, 1970).

9   Hellriegel, Don, and John W. Slocum, Jr., "Organizational Design: A Contingency Approach," *Business Horizons,* Vol. XVI, No. 2 (April, 1973), pp. 59–68.

10 Herzberg, Frederick, Bernard Mausner, and Barbara Synderman, *The Motivation to Work* (New York: John Wiley & Sons, Inc., 1959).

11 Hughes, Charles L., and Vincent S. Flowers, "Shaping Personnel Strategies to Disparate Value Systems," *Personnel,* Vol. 50, No. 2 (March-April, 1973), pp. 8–23.

12 "Latest Moves to Fight Boredom on the Job," *U.S. News & World Report* (December 25, 1972), pp. 52–54.

13 Lawrence, Paul R., and Jay W. Lorsch, *Organization and Environment: Managing Differentiation and Integration* (Boston: Harvard Graduate School of Business Administration, 1967).

14 Likert, Rensis, *The Human Organization: Its Management and Value* (New York: McGraw-Hill Book Company, 1967).

15 Maslow, A. H., "A Theory of Human Motivation," *Psychological Review,* Vol. 50 (1943), pp. 370–396.

16 McGregor, Douglas, "Toward a Theory of Organized Human Effort in Industry," in Arthur Kornhauser, editor, *Psychology of Labor-Management Relations* (Champaign, Ill.: Industrial Relations Research Association, 1949), pp. 111–122.

17 Roethlisberger, F. J., and W. J. Dickson, *Management and the Worker* (Cambridge, Mass.: Harvard University Press, 1939).

18 Smith, Adam, *An Inquiry into the Nature and Causes of the Wealth of Nations* (1776) (New York: Modern Library, Inc., 1937).

19 Taylor, Frederick W., *The Principles of Scientific Management* (New York: Harper & Brothers, 1911).

20 Walton, Richard E., "How to Counter Alienation in the Plant," *Harvard Business Review,* Vol. 50, No. 6 (November–December, 1972), pp. 70–81.

21 "Where Being Nice to Workers Didn't Work," *Business Week* (January 20, 1973), pp. 99–100.

22 "Where Skinner's Theories Work," *Business Week* (December 2, 1972), pp. 64–65.

23 Whyte, William H., Jr., *The Organization Man* (New York: Simon and Schuster, Inc., 1956).

24 Woodward, Joan, *Industrial Organization: Theory and Practice* (London: Oxford University Press, 1965).

READING   62

HUMAN RESOURCE ACCOUNTING: PERSPECTIVE AND PROSPECTS

James A. Craft

Jacob G. Birnberg*

Recent interest in Human Resource Accounting (HRA) has been stimulated primarily by a growing recognition of employees as basic organizational resources, coupled with dissatisfaction with traditional management control systems which ignore human variables. The purpose of this paper is to evaluate the HRA movement within this context. We begin by examining the movement's development and by noting the two major approaches that have been proposed to measure human assets. We then review alternate uses to which HRA can be put. Finally, we discuss the movement's progress to date and argue for a major redirection of effort away from external reporting and toward the internal use of HRA in management evaluation and decision making.

DEVELOPMENT OF THE HRA MOVEMENT

Current interest in HRA can be traced directly to the influence of Rensis Likert, former director of the Institute for Social Research at the University of Michigan.[1] Likert's scheme of organizational analysis distinguishes among *causal* variables, such as leadership, *intervening* variables, such as attitudes, morale, loyalty, and motivation, and *end-result* variables, such as profit and output. He argues that, in evaluating managerial performance, most organizations place excessive emphasis on short-run, end-result variables, and, as a consequence, managers become motivated to adopt styles of leadership and develop organizational climates which are unfavorable to the development of sound human relationships. According to Likert,

> The costs of building and maintaining an effective human organization are usually ignored in the accounting methods of most companies.

* From *Industrial Relations*, February 1976, pp. 2–12. Copyright 1976 by the Regents of the University of California. Reprinted with permission.

[1] For the foundations on which Likert's concepts are based, see his *New Patterns of Management* (New York: McGraw-Hill, 1961) and *The Human Organization: Its Management and Value* (New York: McGraw-Hill, 1967).

Similarly, spurious earnings achieved by liquidating some of the company's investment in the human organization are not charged against the operation and used in evaluating which system of management works best.[2]

He concludes that only by improving intervening variables such as employee attitudes, morale, loyalties, and motivation can long-run successful performance be obtained. Realistically, however, Likert recognizes that "so long as no quantitative surveillance is maintained over a firm's human assets . . ." managers would only have limited incentive to devote the time and resources necessary to develop these.[3] He proposes a system of accounting for human resources by estimating the value of a firm's human assets and monitoring changes in their value. Such a system would involve the rigorous measures of causal variables (e.g., leadership style, organizational climate) and intervening variables (e.g., attitudes, motivation). These measurements at regular intervals would indicate changes in human organizational characteristics, which can influence the organization's operating efficiency. This, in turn, could result in changes in the organization's end result variables, profitability, and effectiveness. The socio-psychological measurements of the causal variables could be presented in both internal and external financial reports.[4] Such information would be useful to both management and investors in their decision making. Likert avoided specifying procedures for measuring or reporting investment in human resources, leaving this task to accountants.

ALTERNATE MEASUREMENT APPROACHES

Stimulated by Likert's ideas, a few accountants began to call for extending their framework into nontraditional areas. In addition, they suggested that financial accounting reports should include "measurement of turnover, morale, absenteeism, and of other 'intervening variables'."[5] This increased interest in HRA has led to development of techniques to measure the worth of human assets in organizations. Basically, these methods can be grouped

[2] Likert, New Patterns . . ., p. 86.
[3] Likert, The Human Organization . . ., p. 103.
[4] For additional information and a suggestion that changes in the human organization should be included on financial statements to evaluate managers, see Rensis Likert and David G. Bowers, "Improving the Accuracy of P/L Reports by Estimating the Change in Dollar Value of the Human Organization," Michigan Business Review, XXV (March, 1973), 15–24; Rensis Likert and William C. Pyle, "Human Resource Accounting: A Human Organizational Measurement Approach," Financial Analysis Journal, XXVII (January/February, 1971), 75–84.
[5] Jacob G. Birnberg and Nicholas Dopuch, "A Conceptual Approach to the Framework for Disclosure," Journal of Accountancy, CXV (February, 1963), 59. Also, see Roger H. Hermanson, Accounting for Human Assets, Occasional Paper No. 14, Bureau of Business and Economic Research, Graduate School of Business Administration, Michigan State University, 1964; James L. Cullather, "The Missing Asset: Human Capital," Mississippi Valley Journal of Economics and Business, II (Spring, 1967), 70–73; R. Lee Brummet, "Accounting for Human Resources," Journal of Accounting, CXXX (December, 1970), 62–66; "An Interview with Sidney Davidson," Forbes, CV (April 1, 1970), 40–42.

into two general approaches, one "outlay-based" and the other "inflow-oriented."

Outlay-based Approach

Most of the initial work in HRA was directed toward determining organizational *investments* in people,[6] focusing on cash outlays invested in developing human assets, for example, selection and training costs. This approach appears to be generally consistent with both traditional accounting practice[7] and the concept of human capital in economic theory. The estimated investments in the firm's human assets, for example, would provide a base measure of the organization's outlays for human resources. The extent to which that outlay is consumed over time through operating activities can be approximated by monitoring the social-psychological measures of intervening variables. The latter are, of course, at best approximations.[8]

The outlay-based approach most consistent with current accounting reporting techniques involves *historical* cost. Using this approach, the out-of-pocket expenditures by the firm in securing and developing its human resources (e.g., recruiting, selection, training, etc.) are capitalized for each individual. The other major outlay-based approach involves *replacement* costs. Through this method, the worth of the organization's human resources is determined by the current cost to the firm of replacing its existing human resources with others capable of rendering equivalent services.[9] The basic unit for valuation here can be the individual, group, profit center, or the entire organization.[10]

[6] See Rensis Likert and Robert L. Woodruff, Jr., "A Brief History of the Development and Implementation of Industry's First Human Resource Accounting System at the R. G. Barry Corporation," mimeographed, n.d.; also, R. Lee Brummet, *et al.*, eds., *Human Resource Accounting: Development and Implementation in Industry* (Ann Arbor: Foundation for Research on Human Behavior, 1969).

[7] Of all the available methods to value human resources, the historical cost method is probably the most acceptable to the accounting profession given the tradition of its use, the fact that it can be documented and therefore audited, and due to the added problems that can arise in accounting when the valuation base other than historical cost is used for some of the organization's assets. See Brummet, "Accounting for Human Resources," p. 65. For criticisms of the historical cost method, see William A. Paton, "Accounting Today—A Bird's Eye View," *Michigan Business Review*, XXVI (January, 1974), 22–25.

[8] R. Lee Brummet, Eric G. Flamholtz, and William C. Pyle, "Human Resource Measurement—A Challenge for Accountants," *The Accounting Review*, XLIII (April, 1968), 223–224. Likert's procedural suggestions for converting intervening variable measurements into dollar terms are presented in Rensis Likert, "Human Resource Accounting: Building and Assessing Productive Organizations," *Personnel*, L (May/June), 8–24.

[9] For discussion of some of the advantages of using replacement costs, see William C. Pyle, "Implementation of Human Resource Accounting in Industry," in Brummet, *et al.*, eds., *op. cit.*, p. 42, and Eric Flamholtz, "A Model for Human Resource Valuation: A Stochastic Process with Service Rewards," *The Accounting Review*, XLVI (April, 1971), 264–265. For an attempt to measure positional replacement costs in an organization, see Eric Flamholtz, "Human Resource Accounting: Measuring Positional Replacement Costs," *Human Resource Management*, XII (Spring, 1973), 8–16.

[10] For some criticisms of using replacement costs, see Flamholtz, "A Model for Human Resource Valuation . . .," p. 42, and also William C. Pyle, "Monitoring Human Resources—On Line," *Michigan Business Review*, XXII (July, 1970), 30, and James S. Hekimian and Curtis H. Jones, "Put People on Your Balance Sheet," *Harvard Business Review*, XLV (January/February, 1967), 108.

Inflow-oriented Approach

The second major approach focuses on the present economic value of the organization's human resources in terms of the value of the future benefits to be derived by the organization from the services to be provided by these assets.[11] One version of this approach involves measuring value indirectly. It begins by forecasting the organization's stream of earnings over a specific period of time and then discounting this to determine the organization's present value. A portion of this value is then allocated to human resources in proportion to those resources' relative contribution to the firm's expected income.[12] Another inflow-oriented approach is more direct.[13] It assumes that an individual's wage accurately reflects his value to the organization. Under this method, future wage streams are discounted to obtain a surrogate measure of his present human resource value.[14]

ALTERNATE USES FOR HRA

How could HRA be used? At least three uses have been proposed by the literature.

In Personnel Management

HRA could help the personnel manager make better use of the resources entrusted to him. For example, it may assist him in developing measurements of costs of hiring and training new employees;[15] such data might then be employed in choosing among alternatives in selection procedures and forms of training. Costs generated in this manner, however, would probably never become part of the formal internal cost accounting system and certainly would not become part of the external financial reporting system.

---

[11] For theoretical and normative models for the valuation of individuals in organizations, see Eric Flamholtz, "Toward a Theory of Human Resource Value in Formal Organizations," *The Accounting Review*, XLVII (October, 1972), 666–678, and Flamholtz, "A Model for Human Resource Valuation. . . ." For a concept somewhat different than that elaborated on by Flamholtz, see Hekimian and Jones, *op. cit.*

[12] See Brummet, Flamholtz, and Pyle, *op. cit.*, pp. 222–223. This method has the limitation of leaving the determination of the "relative contribution" of the human resources to a totally subjective estimate.

[13] For the major exponent of this approach, see Baruch Lev and Aba Schwartz, "On the Use of the Economic Concept of Human Capital in Financial Statements," *The Accounting Review*, XLVI (January, 1971), 102–112. For another approach, see Hermanson, *op. cit.*

[14] One is left with an uneasy feeling when there is an assumption that a person's wage is similar to his value to the organization. For some criticisms of this approach, see Eric Flamholtz, "On the Use of the Economic Concept of Human Capital in Financial Statements: A Comment," *The Accounting Review*, XLVII (January, 1972), 148–152, and Eric Flamholtz, *Human Resource Accounting* (Encino, Calif.: Dickenson Publishing Company, 1974), pp. 216–229.

[15] James A. Craft, "Human Resource Accounting and Manpower Management: A Review and Assessment of Current Applicability," *Journal of Economics and Business*, XXVIII (Fall, 1975), 23–30.

In Line Management

HRA could also be used to inject additional inputs (e.g., personnel costs and perhaps social-psychological data) into the organizational internal planning and control systems. As such, it could be used both in planning for future activities (decision making) and in evaluation of past performance. This use of human resource data is broader than the personnel cost data in two respects. First, the focus of attention is on managerial activity generally, not on just the personnel department. Secondly, by including human resource data in the performance evaluation process, top management underscores its concern for developing a strong human organization. The firm benefits from this use of HRA through more efficient use of available resources, and the investor profits as a result of greater long-run efficiency.

By Investors

HRA could also be integrated into reports designed for external use.[16] The form which this external disclosure could take could vary in detail and formality. The data could appear as supplementary notes appended to the financial statements; it could take the form of a set of parallel accounts which would be included alongside more traditional reports; or HRA data would be incorporated directly into the firm's formal audited statements.

The rationale behind this form of disclosure is that these data will aid investors and potential investors in evaluating the economic condition of the firm. Specifically, it should improve their understanding of the true nature of the firm's stock of resources *of all kinds* as well as the prediction of periodic net inflows from operations. (Any argument short of concern for external parties does not require their inclusion in the formal financial statement, either as an integral part thereof or as a supplement to them. The *internal* audience could be addressed by a system of reports generated solely for internal consumption.)

HRA IN PRACTICE

R. G. Barry

The best existing examples of HRA external reporting are the annual reports of the R. G. Barry Corporation,[17] which include unaudited HRA re-

---

[16] Perhaps one of the most vocal proponents of external reporting of HRA information is Dean Marvin Weiss. See his articles, "Where 'Human Resources Accounting' Stands Today," *Administrative Management*, XXXIII (November, 1972), 43–48, and "Accounting for Human Resources," *Management Review*, LXII (March, 1973), 58. In addition, see Lev and Schwartz, *op. cit.*, and the discussion by Likert and Pyle, *op. cit.*, p. 83.

[17] See the *Annual Reports* of the R. G. Barry Corporation, Columbus, Ohio, for the years 1969, 1970, and 1971. A number of publications discuss the Barry Corporation's use of HRA. See, for example, R. L. Woodruff, "Human Resource Accounting," *Canadian Chartered Accountant* (September, 1970), 156–161; Brummet, *et al.*, eds., *op. cit.*, pp. 67–88; Robert L. Woodruff, Jr., and Robert G. Whitman, "The Behavioral Aspects of Accounting Data for Performance Evaluation at the R. G. Barry Corporation (with Special Reference to Human-Resource Accounting)," in Thomas J. Burns, ed., *The Behavioral Aspects of Accounting Data for Performance Evaluation* (Columbus, Ohio: Ohio State University, College of Administrative Science, 1970), p. 14.

ports along with reports in the traditional format. Barry's report is cost based and utilizes systematic procedures to match consumed human assets with periodic review flows. As such, it might be acceptable to a firm's auditors because it is consistent with "good" accounting procedures.

Despite the publicity given Barry's use of the human asset data in its published financial reports, the writing of some of the principals clearly demonstrates that the function of the data is to improve the quality of management, *not* the quality of investor decisions.[18] Were the latter to occur, it would be a by-product of the process.

TIPP

The prototype program developed by Touche, Ross, and Company for the Training Incentive Payments Program (TIPP) provides an example of a formal human assets accounting system, which has been integrated into the *internal* financial reporting system.[19] Here conventional and human resource accounting systems are utilized to measure "the profit improvement and cost reduction effects of employee upgrading efforts" in a manpower program. The focus in this case is on the need to communicate with operating managers in language they can understand—monetary units.[20]

AT&T

American Telephone and Telegraph has developed an outlay (cost) based HRA system which is "used entirely for management planning and control."[21] The intention here is to improve the evaluation of various personnel procedures and programs by highlighting their impact on employee values and future earnings. The system involves the capitalization of employment and development costs for operators. This "investment" is amortized with adjustments for changes in the expected tenure and increased productive capacity of the operator. A calculation is then made regarding recovery or loss on the investment for each employee. The program has apparently had some effect on management policy, since it is claimed that local offices in the organization are more "cost conscientious because the information is available."[22]

Witte

Perhaps the most sophisticated HRA system proposed to date is that of Lester Witte and Company, certified public accountants. The Witte system,

[18] William Pyle, "Accounting for Your People," *Innovation* (November 10, 1970), 46–54.
[19] Touche, Ross, and Company, *Upgrading Low Income Workers—Costs and Benefits: A Prototype Information System*, 1973 (processed).
[20] *Ibid.*, p. 30. The report states that, "a private sector manager can not be expected to undertake or maintain an extensive training program solely out of an expanded sense of social consciousness. The payoff must ultimately be expressed in measures of his own self-interest—measured or estimated in dollar terms."
[21] Thomas W. McRae, "Human Resource Accounting as a Management Tool," *Journal of Accountancy* (August, 1974), 32–38; and Florence Stone, "Investment in Human Resources at AT&T," *Management Review*, LXI (October, 1972), 23–27.
[22] McRae, *op. cit.*

as outlined by Flamholtz and Lundy, is direct, inflow-oriented,[23] as compared with the Barry, TIPP, and AT&T approaches which, despite their managerial orientations, are all cost-based, outlay-oriented systems and therefore are not completely satisfactory for management's purposes.

The Witte system attempts to value human assets by discounting back to the present the sum of future net cash flows generated by the employee. This is assumed to be his "value" to the firm. A simple example of this follows:

> Assume that a relatively recent hire to a CPA firm has just passed his CPA exam. The firm is now in the process of valuing its human resources including this staff man. Management decides that it knows with certainty what his role will be in the firm for the next four years. In years one, two, and three, he will be a senior staffman. In year four, he will be a manager. At the end of year four he will—for convenience of this example—exit the firm.
>
> The firm has estimated that the net service value (billing fees from his services less related salary and fringe benefit costs) of a senior staff accountant is $30,000 per year and a manager's salary is $50,000 per year. Thus, the potential benefit to the firm of the human resource is the present value of the net service value stream of $30,000 + $30,000 + $30,000 + $50,000. Using a discount rate of twenty percent, the result of the calculation is $87,000.

The purpose of the Witte system is to monitor the development and training of the labor force—in this case, auditors. It is argued here that the change in the value of members of the labor force ought to parallel their growth in skills and in professionalism. Thus, as the junior accountant acquires experience and is enrolled in training programs, he ought to be able to perform a wider array of tasks and/or perform them with greater expertise. This change in his skills is paralleled by changes in the auditor's rank (i.e., from "junior" to "semi-junior" to "senior," etc.) and the fee charged for his services. The underlying premise of this system is that by placing a dollar value on the development of the labor force's skills, management gains a better indication of whether it is enhancing the skills of its labor force.

The Witte system, because it is inflow oriented, comes closer than most extant systems to meeting Likert's goal of *valuing* the human resource. It is able to do so, however, because of the unique environment for which it was developed—a CPA firm. The CPA firm and a limited number of comparable organizations permit the human resource evaluator to associate a unique stream of net inflows with each employee. In the case of the auditor, this was billable hours or fees. Comparable streams are ascertainable in a number of service-oriented firms where the client's charge is the

---

[23] Eric G. Flamholtz and Todd S. Lundy, "Human Resource Accounting for CPA's," *CPA Journal* (forthcoming).

aggregate of the fees charged for the individual professionals. Unfortunately, the Witte technique has applicability to only a small but important subset of interested firms.

It is worth noting that, while the AT&T and Witte systems differ fundamentally in their approach to measurement, they are concerned with achieving the same goals, i.e., making managers more aware of the impact of their actions on their employees and ultimately on the firm's economic position. As such, they appear to be following the injunction which says that although people *are* important to managers, they assume their full significance only when they are measured in units managers understand.

Significantly, methods of measuring human assets other than historical cost which were outlined earlier have *not* been utilized by any organization for *external* reports even supplementally. There are good conceptual reasons for users preferring the more traditional cost-based presentation of these data, especially while HRA is still fighting for acceptance. Cost-based data are consistent with the other data reported in the financial statements and, as such, are "objective." However, to justify the inclusion of a cost-based representation of the value of the organization's human assets in external reports, there must be some reason to believe it will improve the quality of decision making. As yet, however, there is no clear evidence that this has been the case.

HRA's IMMEDIATE FUTURE

The current state of HRA reflects the conflict between trends in the accounting and personnel professions. While personnel is keenly interested in developing more elaborate measures of the costs and benefits of its activity, accounting is in the process of making its rules more conservative, especially in reporting intangible assets. Thus, most recently the Financial Accounting Standards Board, the primary rule-making body in accounting, has set strict guidelines as to when the costs of intangibles, such as Research and Development, may be shown on the balance sheet as assets.

The impetus for accounting's conservative position is probably twofold. First, many accountants have always been concerned about capitalizing on the balance sheet excessive amounts of outlays for intangibles. Second, many firms (e.g., Memorex) have had large amounts of these "assets" turn out to be worthless. Always wary and now burned, accountants are likely to be cautious in considering innovation which will increase the intangible assets on the corporate balance sheets. (Indeed, the proliferation of lawsuits against CPAs for purported instances of subprofessional practice has not alleviated the situation.)

The attempt by personnel managers to include HRA data in the world of external financial reports is untimely. Since accounting practitioners are currently concerned with more fundamental pressing issues, such as inflation accounting, the likelihood of HRA becoming a part of the audited external reports in the short run is slim at best. The parallel accounts mode of disclosure to external parties followed by the Barry Corporation is probably the closest that firms will be permitted to come to disclosing their human assets to external parties in an authoritative form.

It is unfortunate that so many writers are so preoccupied with the use of HRA for external reports. Aside from the aura of respectability that the acceptance of such statements would afford the HRA movement, little of value is gained by inclusion of HRA data in external reports that is not gained by their use just for internal purposes. Since managerial use of HRA seems to hold more value than investor use, any efforts to adopt HRA should be focused on internal rather than external purposes.

Significantly, accounting has a strong history of utilizing techniques for internal reports that are not accepted for audited financial statements. The most obvious and analogous of these is direct costing. In the case of direct costing the inventory method is widely used for internal purposes, such as divisional reports for evaluation of performance. However, the direct costing results of operations are then adjusted before the firm-wide reports are prepared according to generally accepted accounting procedures. Techniques such as this for internal reports are common.

Should HRA be cost-based or inflow-oriented and, if it is outlay-based, should replacement cost or historical cost be used? The preponderance of past experience would suggest that the historical cost-oriented approaches, such as the Barry or TIPP proposals, are most likely to be adopted. Even for internal reports the objectivity of the historical cost data becomes appealing. It means not only that two or more accountants will reach approximately the same answer in measuring the stock and flow of human resources, but also the system appears at least slightly less capricious to the manager involved since the accountant did not "conjure up" the number. The manager now can relate the investment in human resources to his activities and the charge for their use to his utilization of these resources.

The significant datum to the contrary is the Witte direct inflow-oriented system. This method exhibits a greater degree of objectivity than many value related methods because of the existence of an ascertainable objective revenue function for each member (or class) making up the labor force. This is not usually the case in an industrial firm.

Overall, the use of the cost-based HRA measures in the internal evaluation process is probably more dependent upon the recognition of their value by managers than by accountants. To the accounting department, special internal reports are not unusual. However, it is the manager who must recognize the value of the new information to him in allocating and utilizing the resources for which he is responsible and in measuring economic efficiency.

DISCUSSION AND CONCLUSIONS

The HRA movement has probably attempted to go too far too quickly, given the available methodologies and lack of widespread acceptance within management and the accounting profession. HRA enthusiasts have tried to get management to do four things at once: (1) pay more attention to personnel variables; (2) place dollar values on human resources and implement human asset depreciation; (3) break with the accountant's traditional reliance on historical cost data (except for outlay cost methods); (4) develop internal and external reporting procedures using HRA data. Any of these objectives alone would be difficult to achieve, but the attainment of all simultaneously is virtually impossible. The result is that in many cases managers who might be sympathetic to one or more aspects of HRA become skeptical of its value because they can't accept all aspects. And to some managers HRA appears to be a "hastily constructed discipline made up of recycled 'spare parts' from other disciplines" rather than a useful, well formulated management tool.[24]

Our review of the current HRA experience convinces us that this new form of accounting will obtain greatest acceptance as an aid in personnel management operations analysis (e.g., turnover cost analysis, training cost analysis, costing out selection procedures, and the like) and in evaluating managerial performance, especially in service-oriented industries. On the other hand, we feel it unlikely that HRA will be recognized by the accounting profession as having legitimate value in external accounting reporting.

[24] "Report of the Committee on Human Resource Accounting," American Accounting Association Committee Reports, *The Accounting Review*, supplement to XLIX (1974), 122.

READING 63

RUSHTON—AN EXPERIMENT WITH MINERS REGULATING THEIR OWN WORK ACTIVITIES*

Drawing on the experience in coal mines in the United Kingdom, where so-called autonomous groups have worked in coal face operations to improve productivity, an experiment has been under way at the Rushton Coal Mine, Philipsburg, Pennsylvania, to make professional miners competent in all the tasks in a mine section. The experiment was discussed by the president of the company and mine work force spokesmen at the Washington and Buffalo Conferences [on productivity and quality of working life].

With shared competence, the miners could arrange their work flexibly and regulate their work in relation to each other. To make such an arrangement possible, the management gave up the right to direct the work force at the coal face and agreed to pay a common rate—the top rate—to all members of the group, since all would be taking equivalent responsibility and would be equally qualified to undertake all tasks involved in the mining operation.

The main thrust of the experiment was to achieve an improvement in work quality, with productivity gains reflected in such factors as low costs, lower rates of absenteeism, and a lower accident rate. The experiment has been jointly sponsored by the Rushton Mine management and the United Mine Workers local, with technical assistance from the National Quality of Work Center. The National Commission on Productivity and Work Quality provided the initial grant for the exploratory phases of the experiment, while the Economic Development Administration of the Commerce Department has funded the continuing, operational aspects of the project.

Initially, a research team comprised of two faculty members of Pennsylvania State University and a faculty member of the University of Pennsylvania was formed to conduct action-oriented projects in work quality in the mining industry. Rushton Mining Company was chosen for the experiment.

COMMITTEE ORGANIZATION

Rushton Mine management agreed to the experiment. From the union side, Arnold Miller, president of United Mine Workers, also agreed, with the un-

* From *Recent Initiatives in Labor-Management Cooperation*, Washington, D.C.: U.S. National Center for Productivity & Quality of Working Life, 1976, pp. 51–57.

derstanding that a local labor-management committee would approve everything that was done, and that any productivity gains should be shared in ways that would be jointly determined by management and labor. Approval and support for the project was obtained from the Federal and State agencies responsible for safety enforcement.

The next step at the Rushton Mine was to set up a local labor-management committee, known as the Steering Committee. This group first convened in August 1973. Membership included on the management side, the company president and other principal management executives, and on the union side, the officers as well as the members of the Mine and Safety Committees.

The Steering Committee and the research team met regularly every two weeks in daylong sessions which were held off the mine site. The goals, structure, and procedures of the project were shaped, with particular attention to ways in which the experiment could be reconciled with the union contract.

THE PLAN TAKES SHAPE

Details of the plan were eventually agreed upon, and the text of the agreement, known as the "document," was made available to everyone at the mine. Essentially, the document provided that:

1 An experimental section in the mine, to be comprised 27 volunteers, 9 for each of three shifts, would be established.

2 Every man in the experimental section would be on top pay. (To some of the younger volunteer miners, this could mean an increase of up to five dollars a day; to others, it meant small or no increases.)

3 All members of each crew would be, or would be trained by the company to be, capable of performing any job, from shuttle car to machine operation—providing essentially full job-rotation capability. In addition, the entire crew would be given special training in State and Federal mine law to give all an understanding of what comprises a violation.

Each crew of the experimental section, therefore, would be an autonomous work team, with each man in the crew capable of performing any and all work functions involved in the underground production of coal. No craft or functional distinctions whatever, of either pay or job classification, would exist between crew members.

4 Each of the three crew foremen in the section would have responsibility solely for the safety of his crew and for planning. All former responsibility and authority for the production of coal was transferred from the foremen to the crew itself. The foremen's authority to give orders to the crew henceforth would be solely on safety-related matters. Grief* by any

* Complaints.

member of each of the three crews would be dealt with by the crews them-selves, without recourse either to foremen or the grievance committee for solution.

The union membership voted in favor of proceeding with the experi-ment at a meeting on October 7, 1973, with the understanding that either management or the union could withdraw at any time.

With the development of a work team whose members could perform all of the tasks required on a mine section, it was agreed that the foreman's responsibilities would shift from production to focus primarily on safety.

Improved safety was judged likely because a foreman responsible for both production and safety functioned in a dual role, while a foreman work-ing with an autonomous group could devote most of his time and effort to safety. His additional responsibilities would cover on-the-job training and planning more effectively for supplies and maintenance.

COLLABORATION REPLACES COMPETITION

The operating plan was to have the autonomous group members work in an entire mine section in three shifts. A shift crew would consist of a miner-operator and a helper, 2 roof bolters, 2 shuttle-car men, a mechanic, and 2 support men, making a total crew of 9 and a total section group of 27. Members of each shift would become increasingly multiskilled with time, and would interchange their tasks more frequently. Production would be tallied on a 24-hour basis so that intershift competition could be replaced by intershift collaboration.

Volunteers were requested for each job billet, and the participants were selected from among them according to seniority. Their previous jobs were held open for 60 days so they could return to their original assign-ments if they did not like working autonomously.

After 60 days, they would have to join the general work force until an opening arose in their former classification. Only one man returned to his former work slot during the initial 60-day period, and none has since that time.

Following the organization phase of the experiment, the Steering Com-mittee mapped a transitional phase of roughly three months before the designated mine section would be regarded as completely autonomous. During the first part of this period, the crews remained fully under foreman control while familiarizing themselves with the physical aspects of their tasks and the problems of working as a team. During the second half of this period, they remained partially under foreman control while continuing the familiarization process.

A six-session orientation period began in December 1973. The entire section of 27 men and 3 foremen met every Monday and Friday for all-day meetings over a period of three weeks in a classroom aboveground. Tues-days, Wednesdays, and Thursdays were regular working days on the new section underground. During the orientation meetings, the text of the experiment agreement was reviewed, autonomous work group concepts were explained, and all job tasks reviewed. The men received a job safety analysis program, and the Federal and State safety laws were reviewed. There were exercises in group problem-solving as a part of the sessions.

There followed a period of several weeks during which the men worked at the jobs they originally opted for, but they were encouraged to begin learning the other jobs on the section. As the primary focus during this period was on learning, management agreed to a moratorium on pressure for production.

JOINT COMMITTEE IS FORMED

On February 26, 1974, the section elected one man from each crew to be a representative to what was called the Joint Committee. Two representatives from the local union leadership were also named to serve as the union representatives on the committee. Management appointed five members, and the Steering Committee then declared the section autonomous and withdrew from active involvement.

During the operational phase of the experiment, from March 1974 to March 1975, the autonomous effort continued, with the research team assisting with training and development and in resolving such conflicts as arose.

At approximately six-week intervals, the entire 27 members of the section and the foremen met in an aboveground classroom where operations over the previous six weeks were reviewed and the next six-week period planned. The men were paid their regular daily rate during these meetings, with the review and planning time considered as important as time on the job.

The Joint Committee met at irregular intervals through the spring and summer to settle disputes which arose in the autonomous section. The Joint Committee began to meet regularly in September to discuss sharing of gains. Issues that were raised included how gains were to be measured and how they were to be divided. The research team considered it important that these issues be explored before it was determined whether or not there were gains.

Twice each month, the three foremen, often with other members of management, met with the research team to discuss safety, training, labor-management relations, communications, and resolution of conflicts.

Higher-level management officials met irregularly at first to consider the progress of the experiment. Toward the end of the period, these meetings were held more regularly to discuss management's new philosophy in a relationship with autonomous working groups.

The research team was invited to attend all meetings in the union hall when the project was to be discussed.

PRELIMINARY RESULTS

There were fewer violations of the Federal Coal Mine Health and Safety Act in the mine section where the experiment was conducted than in the other two sections of the mine which continued to operate conventionally. The accident and absenteeism rates were less than in one other mine section and equal to that of the second conventionally operated section.

An evaluation team interviewed all the men working in the experimental section in December 1973, and again in June and October 1974, with preliminary data revealing that:

1 The men perceive themselves as making more decisions concerning how the work is divided, what they should do, and how to do it.

2 The men recognize their interdependence, and believe that their coworkers have many good ideas to contribute to improved performance.

3 They see their supervisors as making fewer decisions affecting how they should perform their work.

Warren H. Hinks, Jr., president of Rushton Mining, reported that the experimental process has increased worker satisfaction, lowered absenteeism and reduced accident rates. Hinks expressed his appraisal of the program:

The average worker wants to make an intelligent and creative contribution. I know it may be difficult for some of you to believe, but miners like their work. They want to be involved in decision making that affects them.

In the new system, the men receive training which gives them the necessary information to make decisions. We believe that authority should go with this knowledge. Also autonomous work teams provide the worker with horizontal mobility—he can try a variety of assignments. Formerly, he had only vertical mobility—he had to wait for someone to resign or die before he could change jobs.

The report of the research team points out that members of the experimental section at the mine had a private meeting with officers of the international and district union to discuss their reactions to the project.

The men, it was reported, said they felt themselves respected by management as never before; they no longer felt tired when they got home from work. There was no longer the same stress on the job, and they did not quarrel as much or leave the workplace in a mess for the next shift.

Similar expressions of worker satisfaction were voiced by mine work force spokesmen at the Recent Initiatives Conferences.

One miner participant in the experiment, Mark Naylor, described his attitude by explaining that he had little interest in his work or the experiment, but volunteered to join the group because he was a shuttle car operator and it might have taken years in the ordinary course of events for him to get top pay. Pay was his incentive in joining, plus an interest in being a machine operator, which his participation in the experiment permitted.

Naylor points out that he didn't give a "damn" about the company and that under the old system, when a machine broke down, a shuttle car broke, supplies were late, or the foreman wasn't present, the men would sit around and wait to be told what to do next.

Under the new working conditions, Naylor said, the crew felt that machinery and the responsibility have somehow been transferred to their charge.

> Suddenly we felt we mattered to somebody. Somebody trusted us. And in a week or two we were busting our hump in a way I've never seen guys work underground before. When a machine busts down nowadays, most of the time we don't bother to call a maintenance man. We just fix it ourselves, because, like I said, we feel it's as much ours as our own car at home.

RESULTS ASSESSED

The research team reported that in order to make an autonomous working group approach operative, higher management has to invest in certain technical modifications to improve productivity and take time to learn more effective planning and interpersonal skills. On labor's side, innovation and acceptance of improved mining methods will be necessary.

In gain-sharing—or as miners term it, bonus—joint contributions from management and labor are necessary to legitimize the concept. Miners are skeptical concerning management's willingness to share gains or calculate them to their satisfaction.

All parties to the experiment seemed to believe by their earliest comments that as soon as management retreated from its immediate supervisory role, all kinds of innate abilities that had been pent up by oversupervision would blossom forth. These beliefs, the research team concludes, have proven to be naive.

A more realistic assessment, as offered by the research team, is that "intercrew communication has improved a great deal. Better planning takes place. Most men know more than one job (though actual switching remains restricted), and greater cooperation prevails throughout the mine as well as in the experimental section."

The research team stated that for any significant conclusions to be drawn, the experiment would have to be extended to the entire mine; that with only one section involved in the experiment, miners feel unsure of the project's survival and are tentative about commitment to its concepts.

The research team favors the continuance of the experiment for another year. The union feels that the experiment should be extended to the whole mine, or failing that, the mine operation should revert entirely to the traditional operating pattern. Management has indicated its willingness to put the mine into autonomous operation, but is reluctant to make the change in a single stage, suggesting a gradual approach.

The plan for extension to the entire mine that had been worked out by the Joint Labor-Management Steering Committee was turned down by the union membership by a vote of 79 to 75. At a subsequent session of the joint group, several changes were made in response to the objections of the dissenting union members. With these changes, the management and union have agreed to continue the program where it is currently operational and to extend it throughout the remaining sections of the mine.

Editor's note: This article does not give specific information on productivity gains or losses. Other sources, including company sources contacted by the editor, report that there has been no apparent increase or decrease in productivity following the changes.

READING   64

SHOULD THE QUALITY OF WORK LIFE BE LEGISLATED?

Edward E. Lawler III*

Why would we want the government to legislate a better quality of work life? I believe that unless the government acts, work life will not improve for many people. In many situations there is presently no clear motivation for organizations to provide employees with opportunities for personal growth and development, to see that employee needs are satisfied or to eliminate those working conditions that contribute to mental illness, alcoholism and drug abuse.

Little evidence exists to show that simply improving the quality of work will increase the profitability and economic soundness of most organizations. Given this situation, it is hardly surprising that many organizations are hesitant to undertake significant efforts to improve the quality of work life of their employees. Managers are held responsible for profitability; they cannot be expected to take actions which will endanger the economic soundness of their organization even though they might increase employee satisfaction. In my opinion, the only way this can be changed is by legislative

*From *The Personnel Administrator*, January 1976, pp. 17–21. Copyright 1976. Reprinted with permission.

action or by producing evidence that quality of work life improvement is good business from an economic point of view.

There are some situations in which improving the quality of work life may not, in fact, increase an organization's costs so as to put it at a competitive disadvantage. The research on job design, for example, suggests that job enrichment can, in some cases, reduce costs by bringing about higher quality products and lower turnover, while at the same time improving the quality of work life. In these situations there is economic pressure present toward improving the psychological quality of work life because it promises higher profit. These situations will probably correct themselves without government intervention, although the government could speed change by financing experimentation and information dissemination programs.

On the other hand, where the psychological quality of work life needs to be changed and increased costs are involved, the government may have to intervene to alter the economics of the situation, thus providing a strong motivation for change on the part of the organization in question. Despite the work that has gone into job enrichment, it is not clear how to enrich some assembly line jobs without increasing production costs. It is clear, however, that in many of these situations enrichment would increase the quality of many people's lives. To change the situation so that organizations can act to improve these conditions without finding themselves at a competitive disadvantage, two types of government intervention are possible.

First, the government could charge organizations for the negative social outcomes they produce. For example, if because of a poor quality of work life a company had an unusually high rate of turnover, alcoholism, drug addiction and mental illness among its employees, the government could increase its taxes proportionately. This is not dissimilar to present government practice in the area of unemployment insurance.

The second approach is to fine organizations not for the outcomes they produce (e.g., accidents, sick people) but for the practices in which they engage. In applying this approach to the area of the quality of work life, organizations could be fined or taxed on the basis of their management practices and policies and the nature of the jobs they have. For example, they might be taxed if they produce goods on an assembly line that had highly repetitive jobs. Such action could obviously serve to eliminate the economic advantages of producing goods on an assembly line.

It may seem far-fetched to envision the government taxing or fining an organization because it has a destructive human system that provides a poor quality of work life, but there are evidence and precedents available to suggest that these actions can and should happen. In the area of physical safety, for instance, there has been a long history of legislation regulating those organization practices and working conditions that can affect a person's physical health. Hours of work and equipment design are specified in considerable detail. Perhaps even more pertinent to problems of the psychological quality of work life, however, is the recent enactment of state and federal legislation controlling pollution.

A POSSIBLE PRECEDENT

Organizations that pollute the air, water and soil are now subject to fines and, in some cases, shutdown. Since it costs industry more to manufacture many products in ways that will not pollute, any organization that tries to produce a product without polluting is at a competitive disadvantage in the market because pollution control equipment is expensive and adds to the company's costs. In a real sense, when goods are produced in a way that pollutes, their actual price tends to be too low because their full production costs are not charged to the customer. They are borne by society as a whole because it is the society which bears the cost of pollution (e.g., rivers to clean up, air that increases illness, etc.)

Using this logic, legislation that fines organizations for causing pollution is very much justified; it simply involves charging organizations in the name of the public for the cost of the pollution they are causing. It is also fair if this raises the price to the customer; he or she thus bears the full cost of the product rather than sharing it with people who do not buy and benefit from the item in question.

A parallel exists between the economics of pollution and the economics of providing a poor quality of work life for employees. Providing employees with dissatisfying, meaningless work lives is a form of pollution, the cost of which is borne by the society and the individual harmed rather than by the organizations responsible. This type of pollution leads to increased costs in such areas as mental illness, alcoholism, shorter life expectancy and less involvement in the community. These are expensive outcomes and ones that are paid for by the government and private funds that support unemployment insurance, welfare payments, hospitals, mental health centers and civic programs. Because these costs are absorbed by society, some goods are underpriced relative to their real costs; and just as with environmental pollution, a case can be made for government intervention designed to correct this situation.

All this talk about government action is very heady stuff and it is indeed the kind of issue the people concerned with personnel should be debating. But before we go too far off into the stratosphere, we need to look at how well we can measure the quality of work life. Measures of it or the consequences of it are necessary if any of the legislative approaches mentioned so far are to work.

POSSIBLE MEASUREMENT APPROACHES

The behavioral science research that has been done on how people react to their work environments suggests the model shown in Figure 1. It shows that people's affective and attitudinal reactions to jobs are caused by a combination of the characteristics the person brings to the job and the characteristics of the job situation. These affective reactions in turn cause certain observable behavioral reactions which lead to organizational performance. This approach suggests three different kinds of measures: job and organizational conditions, affective reactions and employee behavior. The problem is to determine which can and should be measured.

There are three characteristics desirable for any measure. First, the measure should be valid, in that it measures accurately all the important aspects of what needs to be measured. Secondly, it should have enough face validity so that it will be seen by all involved as a legitimate measure. Finally, it should be objective. This last point is important because objective measures are verifiable, can be audited by others and are therefore less subject to distortion.

The importance of these characteristics, (and especially of the last) varies according to the purpose for which the information is to be used. It is always desirable to have objective measures, but in some instances it is less crucial. For example, it is often desirable to use self-report measures of the quality of work life and these are subjective. Despite their subjectivity, they do represent the most direct data available about the psychological state of an employee. Further, they allow us to account for individual differences better than do any of the other measures. The problem with measures of the working conditions to which individuals are exposed is that

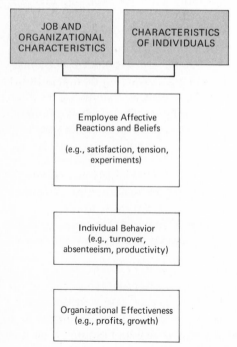

Figure 1

they cannot take into account individual differences in the way people respond to those conditions. This is not a serious problem when the issue is psychological.

Being exposed to extreme temperatures and noises of greater than 90 decibels is harmful to almost everyone; therefore, it makes sense to measure noise and temperature and to prohibit certain levels. It is not true, however, that repetitive assembly line jobs or authoritarian supervision are necessarily regarded as negative by all workers. Quite to the contrary, some see these factors as part of a high quality of work life. Others see them as very negative and as part of a low quality of work life.

Although self-reports of satisfaction do take into account individual differences, they are limited in their usefulness. They are satisfactory solutions only in those situations where there is little motivation present for the individual to report false data. In some instances the use for which the data are being gathered creates motivation for distortion as it probably would if government regulations were involved. In these cases, self-report measures would seem to be an unsatisfactory solution unless nonfakable measures are used and, at the moment, no such measures exist.

There have been some pioneering attempts in Europe to objectively define the conditions that are associated with the high quality of work life, but it is not clear that these efforts have been successful. One union in Germany, for example, has negotiated a contract that specifies the minimum repetitive cycle times for jobs. The assumption is that cycle time is a measure of job challenge and that by requiring "long" cycle times, jobs will be made more satisfying. Cycle times have the advantage of being objectively measurable, but it is not clear that they are the best thing to focus on in order to assure that workers have satisfying jobs.

The governments of several countries have tried to increase the quality of work by requiring that organizations have workers on their boards of directors (e.g., West Germany) and that they have profit sharing or joint ownership plans (e.g., Peru). Requiring administrative practices such as these makes some sense in that their presence or absence can be objectively measured. However, it remains to be established that these or similar practices will contribute to the quality of work life of most employees. Thus, as far as organizational conditions are concerned, we find ourselves in the position of being able to measure things that we are not sure contribute to a high quality of work life and not being able to specify or measure adequately what organizational conditions contribute to a high quality of work life.

One alternative to using the self-report and working condition measures mentioned earlier is to focus on the behavioral outcomes produced by working in an organization. Indicators such as turnover rates, absenteeism rates, mental illness rates, alcoholism rates and community service rates can be measured and costed in terms of their economic impact on the community. This approach has the advantage of focusing on more "ob-

jective" outcomes. However, before the costing aspects can be operation-
alized, more work will have to be done to determine the actual value of
these outcomes and the degree to which they can be linked to the work
situation. This approach also has the disadvantage that it identifies bad
conditions only after they have done their damage. Work situations that do
not fit individuals produce dissatisfaction and a psychologically poor work
environment. These, in turn, seem to produce social costs such as mental
illness and alcoholism. Where possible, it is important to identify poor work
environments before they produce serious negative outcomes.

PUBLIC REPORTING

It seems quite clear that none of the measures we have considered are
sufficiently well developed to use as a basis for fining or regulating organizations. Does this mean there is nothing the government can do to improve
the quality of work at this time? I don't think so. There are some things (in
addition to sponsoring research) that the government can do. It can, as it
has done with pollution, require organizations to prepare quality of work life
statements when they build new plants and facilities. If nothing else, this
would force organizations to think about how their way of designing and
administering a plant is going to affect their employees' lives. Presently this
is often considered only after an organization begins to have personnel
problems (e.g., turnover, absenteeism and strikes).

At the moment, companies are not required to inform stockholders
about either the kind of life they provide for their employees or the kind of
employee-organization relationship that exists. A case can be made for
requiring organizations to furnish this kind of data. The quality of life a
company affords can influence its financial success (turnover, absenteeism, etc., are expensive); thus it would seem that investors should have the
right to know what it is, so that they can make intelligent decisions. This is
the logic that underlies the government requirement that organizations report on their economic conditions. But perhaps the most important effect of
collecting and reporting these data would be to focus the attention of managers on the way the human resources in the organization are being managed. It has often been shown that managers attend to those things which
are being measured. It should also help acquaint potential employees with
the kind of work situation the organization offers; there is evidence that this
kind of information can help people make better job choices. Disclosure of
quality of work life data could result in bringing public and stockholder
pressure to bear on those organizations that engage in deleterious practices; we might even see consumers boycotting those organizations that
provide a poor quality of work life. Stockholders have recently demanded
information from companies as to whether they discriminate against blacks
and as to whether they pollute. It follows that before too long they may ask
for information about the kind of life "their" company provides for its em-

ployees. They may even demand practices that will reduce profits in order to increase the quality of the life of the people who work in the company. This has already happened to a limited extent in some companies. For example, stockholders have demanded that American companies pay equal wages to blacks in South Africa, even though such payment is not required by law and could put the company at a financial disadvantage.

What kind of quality of life data should stockholders receive? Some have suggested that Human Resource Accounting (HRA) data should be provided and this might prove to be useful. (The R. G. Barry Corporation has been doing this for several years.) However, such data indicate only the worth of each individual employee and ignore the value of the total human organization.

As a first step, organizations could provide their stockholders with data on turnover, absenteeism, tardiness, accident and grievance rates, as well as information on the rates of job-related physical and mental illness. Even though these measures may not be the kind that we would be willing to base fines and penalties on, they are sufficiently meaningful so that their release can be justified. Many of these measures can be costed so their financial impact could also be reported. They might be combined in a single "Quality of Life Index" that would provide some indication of what the consequences were of working for a particular company. If comparable data were collected from a number of companies, these could be reported in terms of the percentile standing of each company.

The difficult question to answer concerning any report to stockholders is whether it should include self-report data. This is information that investors should find very helpful since they are investing in the future of the company. However, if the employees are stockholders, they might be motivated to give invalid data. Since attitude data have never been gathered for distribution to stockholders, it is difficult to know how serious this problem would be. It is an area where some experimentation might be profitable.

The possibility of reporting to stockholders on the condition of the human aspects of organizations raises the question of who should prepare these reports. Just as with financial statements, it is not a job to be trusted to management; there simply would be too much pressure on them to give invalid data, since the reputation and value of the company are at stake. This suggests that people trained in behavioral science would be needed to audit the human system, just as accountants audit the financial system. They would have certain standard tests and procedures to use and they could eventually engage in direct observation of the management, leadership and decision-making practices that take place. As in financial accounting, they would have to develop over time a standardized set of procedures and measures so that comparable data could be obtained from different firms. Presumably they, like accountants, would have the power to certify statements. Admittedly, considerable work needs to be done before it will be practical to begin doing certified human system audits, but that time will come sooner if the government requires this kind of reporting. At present there is little incentive for organizations to develop these measures. Like accounting measures, they can only be developed by a trial and error method that allows for refinements and the development of new principles.

It appears that some sort of government action is required to improve quality of work of many individuals. However, legislative action involving standards or fines does not seem appropriate because the needed measures do not exist. There is something the government can do. It is possible for the government to focus attention on the quality of work life in organizations by legislating that organizations publicly report on the quality of work they provide. This should result in efforts to develop better measures and to improve the quality of work life. The precedents for this action exist already in the financial reporting requirements. Considerable work needs to be done on measurement development but now is the time to begin and government action is the stimulus that is needed.

AUTHOR INDEX